Sara Jeannette Duncan

A Social Departure

Sara Jeannette Duncan

A Social Departure

ISBN/EAN: 9783744726078

Printed in Europe, USA, Canada, Australia, Japan

Cover: Foto ©ninafisch / pixelio.de

More available books at **www.hansebooks.com**

A SOCIAL DEPARTURE

HOW ORTHODOCIA AND I WENT ROUND

THE WORLD BY OURSELVES

BY

SARA JEANNETTE DUNCAN

AUTHOR OF 'AN AMERICAN GIRL IN LONDON'

WITH 111 ILLUSTRATIONS BY F. H. TOWNSEND

THIRD EDITION

London
CHATTO & WINDUS, PICCADILLY
1893

This Volume

AS A SLIGHT TRIBUTE TO THE OMNIPOTENCE OF HER OPINION

AND A HUMBLE MARK OF PROFOUNDEST ESTEEM

Is Respectfully Dedicated

TO

MRS GRUNDY

'A SOCIAL DEPARTURE' appeared originally in the columns of 'The Lady's Pictorial.' The Author and the Publishers are indebted to the courtesy of Mr. ALFRED GIBBONS for the use of the Illustrations.

LIST OF ILLUSTRATIONS

	PAGE
'ORTHODOCIA STERNLY SAT DOWN ON AS MANY OF THEM AS SHE CONVENIENTLY COULD'	*Frontispiece*
INITIAL LETTER	1
'SAT DOWN REMOTELY ON THE PENINSULA OF YUCATAN'	2
'YOU SEE THERE'S NOTHING DUTIABLE IN THAT'	4
'I WAS NOT SURE OF HIM, BUT I KNEW THE SHILLING'	6
'COULD SLAY ANY MEMBER OF THE FAMILY WITH A TENNIS-BALL AT A HUNDRED YARDS'	9
'A PERFECTLY INOFFENSIVE LITTLE ENGLISH CURATE'	12
MRS. GROWTHEM'S NEAREST NEIGHBOUR	20
'WE BURIED HER UNDER A CLUMP OF TREES'	21
MR. GROWTHEM	23
'LEFT-WING-OF-A-PRAIRIE-CHICKEN'	28
'LIKE A DENUNCIATORY HOUSEHOLD GODDESS'	32
THE HON. CARYSTHWAITE	39
'YOU FEEL WITH WONDER THAT YOU ARE NOT DOING ANYTHING VERY EXTRAORDINARY AFTER ALL'	43
'A BEAR WAS A GOOD DEAL MORE PROBABLE EPISODE THAN A COW'	45
'THE RIGHTFUL OCCUPANT OF THE COW-CATCHER'	46
'LADIES AIN'T MEANT FER EXPLORIN''	50
'ANY INQUIRING SPIRIT COULD HARDLY FAIL TO FIND MOST OF THE LEADING FACTS IN HER NOTE-BOOK'	52
'ISN'T IT DELIGHTFUL TO BE SITTING ON AN AMERICAN STUMP OF ONE'S VERY OWN?'	54
OUR LUGGAGE LABEL	57
THE REPORTER'S CARD	58
'HOW OLD IS RADY?'	60
EXTRACT FROM REPORT OF INTERVIEW	61
'HE BOWED ALL THE WAY FROM THE DOOR TO THE MIDDLE OF THE APARTMENT'	63

	PAGE
'ORTHODOCIA STERNLY SAT DOWN ON AS MANY OF THEM AS SHE CONVENIENTLY COULD'	70
'TURNED HIM CAREFULLY ROUND BY HIS SLEEVE, AND POINTED OUTSIDE'	72
'EACH PULLING AFTER US A SEPARATE PIECE OF OUR HATED AGGREGATE'	74
'AS WE RODE THROUGH A SUNNY STREET IN TOKIO'	77
'I WOULD LIKE ANOTHER PICTURE SHOWING HIM IN A STATE OF CONVALESCENCE'	80
'JAPANESE MAIDEN WHO LIVES BEYOND THE CAMELLIA HEDGE'	82
AN ELDERLY PARTY	84
'TEGAMI!'	85
KIKU	86
'I DID NOT COME TO JAPAN TO PLAY LEAP-FROG'	89
'IT WAS PRINTED IN JAPANESE'	97
'THESE JAPANESE LADIES MAKE THEIR HAIRS IN CURIOUS FASHION, ISN'T IT?'	101
'I SUPPOSE THE GENTLEMAN HAD A COLD'	103
'MY DEAR LITTLE HEATHEN, IS YOUR MOTHER AT HOME?'	106
'SHE WAS A PROFESSIONAL DANCER'	115
'ONE DAY IT TOLD US OF A BAZAAR'	119
'BUT I TOOK THE MONKEY HOME'	122
'AS FOR ORTHODOCIA, SHE STOOD FASCINATED, LEANING ON HER PARASOL BEFORE HER CAPTOR'	124
'THE IMPERIAL PERSON'	127
THE MIKADO'S PALACE	129
'FOR A BETTER VIEW OF THE FEATHERS I DROPPED UPON MY KNEES'	132
'WHILE WE ARE YET AFAR OFF YANO-SAN BECOMES AWARE OF US'	141
'THE CHEAPEST THING IN DRAGONS ORTHODOCIA EVER SAW'	142
YANO-SAN	144
'IN THE SHADOW OF THE GREAT GRAY BUDDHA OF A PUBLIC PARK'	151
'LOOKED UP AT THEM WITH SHARP BEADY ANTICIPATION IN THEIR LITTLE BLACK EYES'	153
'AS WE SAT SIDEWAYS ON OUR CUSHIONS AT OUR MODEST MID-DAY MEAL'	155
BACK TO UTSONOMIYA IN THE RAIN	169
'IT WAS FAIRYLAND OVERTAKEN BY A BLIZZARD'	172
'THERE WHIRLED MADLY FROM THE GRAND HOTEL TWO BELATED JINRIKISHAS'	177

'GOOD-BYE, JAPAN! GOOD-NIGHT!'	178
'AT HOME HE IS ATROCIOUS'.	184
'WE ESCAPED WITH TWO BASKET TEA-POTS APIECE ONLY—A MERE SCRATCH'	185
'OFFERED TO LEND US HER NOTE-BOOK'	188
THE CAPTAIN	196
'THERE IS NO DOUBT THAT AS AN INNOVATION THE CATAMARAN IS A SUCCESS'	203
'AND THEN LIE SWEETLY DOWN TO SLUMBER'	208
'THE MOST AFFABLE AND AMENABLE DRESSMAKER THAT EITHER OF US HAD EVER EXPERIENCED'	215
'THE HEATHEN AND THE TEMPTATION CAME TOO CLOSE TOGETHER'.	218
INITIAL LETTER	220
'IF THE LADIES H'EAT THE PINEAPPLE AND DRINK THE MILK OF THE COCOANUT AT THE SAME TIME THEY WILL DIE'	222, 223
'ORTHODOCIA HAD HER NOTE-BOOK OUT WITH CELERITY'	225
'JOTTING IT DOWN IN HER EVERLASTING NOTE-BOOK'	233
'THE STEWARD SANG IT AMONGST THE PLATES'.	242
'OTHERS INSTANTLY SET OFF IN MAD CAREER WHILE WE WAITED'.	245
INITIAL LETTER	253
'IT WAS WITH EMOTIONS OF A VERY MINGLED ORDER THAT I HEARD ORTHODOCIA'S RESOLUTION'	255
'THEY ALL SALA'AMED SO PERSUASIVELY THAT A CHOICE WAS PAINFUL'	257
'CHEAP AT THE PRICE, EVEN TO SLEEP ON THE VERANDAH'	26?
'TO HIS EXCELLENCY THE VICEROY'S EVENING PARTY'	26?
'AND PRESENTLY THERE IS A SCRAPING SOUND OF MOVING BRICKS AND FALLING PLASTER'	27?
'THE OLD GENTLEMAN MADE ANOTHER BOW'	28?
INITIAL LETTER	28?
'MY HOUSE IS YOURS'	28?
'THE PRINCE OF RISSOLES'	2?
'BUT THE YOUNG BABOO SAT IN THE DRAWING-ROOM AND WAITED A LONG TIME FOR HIS ICE'	2
'HE HAD PERVERTED OUR INSTRUCTIONS TO THE DRIVER FOR THREE-QUARTERS OF AN HOUR'	
'CHUTTERSINGH'	
'HE, BENDING OVER THE DEAD MAN, TOUCHED FIRST THE LIPS WITH THE FIRE'	
'THAT BOY!'	

	PAGE
'THE TOWERS OF SILENCE'	316
'MERELY DEPOSITING THE OFFENSIVE OBJECT GENTLY UPON THE GROUND AND PUTTING HIS FOOT IN IT'	326
INDIAN CATTLE	329
'THE FORT'	331
'THE MORE MODERN ARTIST HAD PRODUCED BROADER EFFECTS'	333
'THE MOTI MUSJID'	336
'THE TAJ'	343
'MUMTAZ-I-MAHAL'	347
'YET ANOTHER SHIP, OUTWARD-BOUND'	350
'CONSIDER, ORTHODOCIA,' I SAID, CONSOLINGLY, 'WE ARE IN THE ARABIAN SEA!'	351
'NERVOUSLY SMOOTHING IT OUT WITH BOTH HANDS'	353
'I DON'T FEEL LIKE MOSQUES'	367
'I COULD QUITE BELIEVE HIM CAPABLE O' DOIN' IT!'	373
INITIAL LETTER	375
'WE NEVER SAW ONE THAT WAS NOT INDISPUTABLY SECOND-HAND'	378
'INTO THE BAZAARS'	379
'TO HELIOPOLIS'	388
'THE ROSE OF SHARON'	389
'I'M OFF!'	390
'AWAY INTO THE DEEPER SHADOWS OF CAIRO'	393
THE SOLEMN GLADNESS GREW IN THE FACE OF THE SPHINX'	396
'IT WAS A PROUD MOMENT FOR ORTHODOCIA'	399
THE SCENE THAT FOLLOWED'	401
WE ALL WENT UP TOGETHER'	402
HE HAD LEFT HIS WHITE TIE AND HIS DIGNITY EIGHTY FEET BELOW'	403
THE CANAL'	408
AND BORROWING SMALL WHITE PULPY BABIES'	410

A SOCIAL DEPARTURE

I

RTHODOCIA, as her name implies, is an English girl. No fond Transatlantic parent ever thought of calling any of *us* Orthodocia. It would be impossible to find a godmother to take the responsibility. She would have to be an English godmother, caught touring, and an English godmother would know better. She would focus her eye-glass with a little shudder upon the small pink bundle of undeveloped unconventionalities presented to her, and sweetly suggest Hetrodocia instead—and another sponsor. Moreover, I couldn't possibly introduce an American Orthodocia to the British public, up in its Henry James, and understanding the nature of a paradox. Nobody would look at her.

I met Orthodocia originally on a sandy point of the peninsula of Yucatan. She looked very pretty, I remember, picking up muddy conch shells all shiny and pink inside, and running to her aunty chaperon with them for admiration. I remember, too, that she did not get the admiration, but a scolding. 'Look,' said the chaperon, 'look at your front breadth!' Orthodocia was eighteen then, but she looked at her front breadth, and went away very low in her mind, and sat down remotely on the Peninsula of Yucatan and made a dreadful mess of her back one. It was this little incident, I think, that drew me to Orthodocia.

It does not in the least matter what had happened in the four years between Yucatan and the port of Montreal last September, where I met Orthodocia again. You will believe that a good deal had happened when you understand that she was quite by herself, and prepared for a trip round the world with a person her relatives had been in the habit of mentioning as 'that American young lady,' which was me. Naturally you will think of matrimony first, which casualty would have enabled Orthodocia to go to the planet Mars alone, I believe, with the full approval of all her friends and acquaintances. But matrimony had not befallen her: she was still Orthodocia May Ruth Isabel Love, of Love Lodge, near St. Eve's-in-the-Garden, Wigginton, Devon. Neither had she become an heiress, with nobody to thwart her vagrant fancies. Neither had the chaperon of Yucatan been gathered to her foremothers, leaving sad associations of grey curls and pince-nez clustering about a place which none could fill. Orthodocia had simply prevailed; but as she told me in confidence there on the Montreal wharf just how difficult she found it, and what an extraordinary amount of trouble she had with the second wife of a cousin by marriage about it, I have no intention of letting you know how she did it. I feel that a certain amount of reticence on this subject is due to Mr. and Mrs. Love.

Orthodocia was surrounded by the captain and three quarter-

'SAT DOWN REMOTELY ON THE PENINSULA OF YUCATAN.'

masters when I found her, while two stewardesses stood respectfully a little way off, but evidently also on guard. They had all received their instructions on the other side of the Atlantic, and were determined that she should not escape to the formless dangers of Mr. and Mrs. Love's imagination, unless under circumstances that would acquit them. The situation would have worried me. I should have taken a few of the quartermasters and stewardesses apart, and with silvery palms and accents entreated them to leave me. But Orthodocia stood in their midst placid and comfortable. She was evidently accustomed to it.

I have said that Orthodocia arrived in Montreal prepared for a trip round the world. This, considering her baggage, is an inadequate statement. It would have taken her comfortably through the universe with much apparel to spare, I should say, in a rough estimate. All the quartermasters who were not watching over her person were engaged in superintending the removal of her effects, relieved at intervals by the ship's officers. There were two long attenuated boxes, and two short apoplectic ones. There was a small brown hair trunk, and a large black tin case. There was a collection of portmanteaux, and a thing she called a despatch-box, that properly belonged to her papa. There were two tin cylinders containing millinery, I believe. And there was a sitz bath tub—a beautiful round, shining, symmetrical sitz bath tub. I cannot conscientiously say that Orthodocia's full name was painted on that object. In the brief instant I gave to its contemplation, I certainly saw a legend of some sort in white letters, but it may have been only the Devonshire address from which it had innocently wandered, in which case it may have been restored by this time to its native Wigginton. For there is no use in concealing the fact that in the course of my long, serious, private conversation with the drayman offering the lowest contract for removing Orthodocia's luggage, I enjoined him carefully to lose that sitz bath, and he did.

When I came back to Orthodocia, after instructing the drayman, I found her kneeling in a secluded corner before her open boxes, surrounded by a sea of fine linen, and wearing a small triumphant expression about the corners of her mouth. A man in brass buttons hovered as near as he dared, looking troubled and unhappy. 'I suppose,' she said, as I approached, 'you thought I didn't know about Customs surveillance in America. Well, you see I did. I have shown this person the inside of my handkerchief boxes, and taken out all these white skirts and dressing jackets, and collars and cuffs, and things, but he doesn't seem to want to look at them. He said a few minutes ago that I might "leave it to him!" and I told him that I would do nothing of the kind. As if one would let a *man* go through all this!' And Orthodocia waved her arm to include a quantity of the nearest embroideries. At the same moment she shook out a flannel petticoat at the man in buttons, austerely remarking, 'You see there's nothing dutiable in that!' The man fled.

'See here, Orthodocia,' I said with severity, 'you are doing something punishable over here—intimidating the officers of the Crown in the performance of their duty. That man has probably gone for assistance, perhaps for a policeman. Now, if when he returns he finds every one of these things packed up again, and you willing to deliver your keys to him, he may let you off. Otherwise'—but Orthodocia did not wait for the alternative. In three minutes there wasn't an inch of lace to be seen

'YOU SEE THERE'S NOTHING DUTIABLE IN THAT.'

anywhere, the boxes were locked tight, and my sophisticated friend, with very round eyes, was sitting on them. The officer returned with a superior, and they gently but firmly took the keys from Orthodocia's unresisting hand, opened the boxes, stared fixedly at a point in the horizon while they thrust an arm into two of the four corners of each box, locked them up again, and said solemnly and simultaneously, 'That is all, Madam.' 'Really,' said Orthodocia, sweetly; 'how nice!' Then she held out her hand to the superior officer, who took it, regarded it attentively for a minute, turned a deep terra-cotta colour, and dropped it very hastily. 'Thank you so very much!' he said, lifting his cap to her, and bowing in an angle of forty-five degrees, with his feet very close together, like an A.D.C. He was a young Customs officer and equal to the occasion. Moreover, as his salary did not, in all probability, exceed fifteen hundred dollars a year, he may have been glad of the shilling Orthodocia bestowed upon him. At all events, when he was introduced to her at Lady C. P. R. Magnum's dance an evening or two later, and begged the pleasure of the fifth waltz, it hung round and resplendent from the guard that crossed his waistcoat. 'I was not sure of *him*,' said poor Orthodocia to me afterwards, 'but I knew the shilling!'

I regret to say that the bath was the only reduction I was able to make in Orthodocia's baggage. She has been sorry for it since, but at the time it was quite impossible to convince her that æsthetic tea-gowns, and trained dinner dresses, and tulle ball dresses, and tennis costumes in variety, to say nothing of walking and visiting toilettes, with everything to match, were not indispensable to her happiness in going round the world. This was surprising, because I had always been told that English girls travelled in an assortment of old clothes, a blue veil, and a pair of copper-toed leather boots without heels, and didn't care; while American ones followed the example of their illustrious predecessor, the Queen of Sheba, and cared a great deal. Orthodocia called them all 'frocks,' declared that circumstances and climates might arise which would demand them, and would be separated from none of them, so I sadly reduced my impedimenta still further toward my ideal minimum of an umbrella and a waterproof, and felt very superior indeed. Herein I also erred, and must say seriously that nobody should start upon the circumnavigation of the planet with an ideal of this sort. If I were going again—time-honoured preface of experience!—I should avoid it, and construct a bigger one, in which necessity and convenience and a regard for the beautiful should be skilfully blended. But I should avoid Orthodocia's theory, that in a journey round the world one should be prepared for every emergency that has presented itself to the human race since the flood. Her dearest friend, for instance, fresh from a course of ambulance lectures, had given her a large quantity of bandages and splints, and one of her aunts had supplied her with several pounds of linseed for poultices; she had also a variety of 'gargles' all labelled POISON—the Wigginton apothecary and Mrs. Love only know why—several mustard plasters, and a bundle of catnip which smelled to heaven. As we never discovered any special utility in these things I wouldn't advise prospective travellers to take them, unless fired by a desire to establish medical missions among the heathen here and there as they go along. A spirit lamp and a small tin saucepan are admirable things in their way, but we didn't at all know what to do with Orthodocia's oil stove, with the gridiron and other necessaries kindly provided by Mrs. Love for our use in Japan, where she understood the people would not cook beefsteak for foreigners on account of the original cow, being Buddhists. Liebig is useful and comforting, but one can get him anywhere, and it did seem unnecessary for Orthodocia to have

'I WAS NOT SURE OF HIM, BUT I KNEW THE SHILLING.'

brought a dozen cans of British Columbia salmon for our sustenance in Japan, back again over the weary thousands of miles they had travelled to Wigginton.

While we feel deeply the responsibility resting upon everybody who writes experiences of travel, to inform people who are thinking of it as to what to take with them, Orthodocia and I have agreed to offer no advice upon this point. For we do not now believe that the best regulated wardrobe and the best informed mind would be equal to complete preparation for a trip round the world beforehand. There must be additions and subtractions, things one would have 'given anything' to have had, and things one would have given anything to have left behind. One wants old clothes and new clothes, and a little of everything in the way of garments the thermometer can possibly demand. There is the widest possible margin for the luxuries and vanities of individual requirement; for instance, there were moments in Japan when Orthodocia yearned for a piano and I for a spring bed, but we would have felt the inconvenience of them afterward.

I had almost forgotten Orthodocia's letter of introduction to an old college friend of her father's, a document the thought of which comforted and supported Mr. and Mrs. Love considerably in the hour of her departure. It was addressed to the Rev. Theophilus Thring, Sesquepediac, New Brunswick, Canada East. We found Sesquepediac on the map first—about a thousand miles out of our route. Then we discovered, by telegraphing, that the Rev. Thring had migrated, some ten years before, to the State of Illinois, which did not lie in our way either. But Mr. and Mrs. Love were so happy in the conviction that Mr. Thring would take an interest in Orthodocia's movements, and give her valuable advice about any parts of Canada that might still be infested by wandering Iroquois, that we had not the heart to disturb it.

II

ORTHODOCIA was a disappointment to my family circle. It was probably because I had always spoken of her as 'Miss Love,' maintained a guarded silence as to her age and personal appearance, and discreetly allowed the fact to escape me that she had an ambition to become a Poor Law Guardian, that she was expected to arrive a mature person somewhat over thirty, with political opinions and views upon dress reform, and the habit of wearing black alpaca and unknown horrors which she would call 'goloshes.' Instead of which, as you know, she was only twenty-two, with a pinkness and healthiness which subtracted a year or two from that; she hadn't a theory about her except that one should say one's prayers and look as well as possible under all circumstances, and her inexperience in the practical concerns of life seemed appalling. True, she could walk ten miles in her broad-toed boots, and slay any member of the family with a tennis-ball at a hundred yards, but these qualifications, original and valuable as they seemed, hardly gave my friends the sense of security they expected to derive from Orthodocia's chaperonage. It is very 'American' for young ladies to travel alone, but not such a common thing in my part of the continent that it could be acceded to without a certain amount of objection on the part of their friends and relatives. All Orthodocia's battles, therefore, in which she had the advantage of picturing me to Mr. and Mrs. Love with grey side-curls, I have no doubt, had to be fought over again for my benefit. It was Japan that gave rise to the most contumacy. Go to Japan without any man whatever—absurd! Answering which we brought down statistics relating to the surplus female population of the globe, which proved beyond doubt that to many ladies resident in Chuguibamba, Bin-Thuang-Din, and Massachusetts, the object under discussion was a luxury, and no necessity in any sense. But it was the height of impropriety. We argued that propriety was entirely relative, and that naturally impropriety in

'COULD SLAY ANY MEMBER OF THE FAMILY WITH A TENNIS BALL AT A HUNDRED YARDS.'

North America would be quite the correct thing in the antipodes. Who would look after our luggage? We suggested, with the gently disciplinary air of two who have their quarrel just, that there was only one change of cars, so to speak, between Montreal and Yokohama, and that the C.P.R. porters were reliable. It was unheard of that two young women should go wandering aimlessly off to the other side of the globe! Whereupon the intention of these present articles was disclosed with dignity, and the momentous mission involved in enlightening the home public as to the amount of truth in Gilbert and Sullivan's assertion that flirting is prohibited by the Mikado. If we penetrated into the interior we would be chopped up to give a secular flavour to missionary croquettes; if we ventured to stay in the capital it was quite likely that some fat Mandarin would take the advantage of a wife, or wives, conversant with European cookery, and entice us into his seraglio—those Japanese were known to be adopting foreign ways. People who are not going to Japan, and are unfamiliar with the encyclopædia, can't be expected to know that Mandarins grow in China and seraglios in Turkey, so we forgave this, and many other things which the Britannica would have enabled us to set at naught. We exercised forbearance, valour, and magnificent perseverance, and we prevailed.

'What,' said Orthodocia, in the days of discussion that followed, 'is the "Seepiar"?'

'The C.P.R.,' I answered her, 'is the most masterly stroke of internal economy a Government ever had the courage to carry out, and the most lunatic enterprise a Government was ever foolhardy enough to hazard. It was made for the good of Canada, it was made for the greed of contractors. It has insured our financial future, it has bankrupted us for ever. It is our boon and our bane. It is an iron bond of union between our East and our West—if you will look on the map you will discover that we are chiefly east and west—and it is an impotent strand connecting a lot of disaffected provinces. This is a coalition Liberal-Conservative definition of the C.P.R., which is the slang or household expression for Canadian Pacific Railway. In the language of the vulgar—"you pays your money and you takes your choice."'

'I'm sure it doesn't matter,' said Orthodocia, in a manner that caused me to give up her education in Canadian economics on the spot.

We were both quite aware, however, when we made our last farewells out of the car window in the noisy lamp-lit darkness of Montreal station, the September night that saw us off, that the C.P.R. would take us over the prairies and across the Rockies, and finally to a point along the shore of the Pacific Ocean, somewhere in British Columbia, we believed, where in the course of time we should find a ship. It was our intention to commit ourselves to the ship, but there speculation ceased and purpose vanished away, for who hath foreknowledge of the Pacific, or can prophesy beyond the rim of it? We had been so grievously embarrassed by kind-hearted people who wanted to know our plans in detail, with dates attached, that we refused at last to entertain a single plan or date or detail—we would send them, we said, when they had been carried out, which would be much more satisfactory. In the six days' journey across the continent we would get out occasionally and wait for the next train where the landscape looked inviting; but whenever we paused this way we would let them know. And thus we sped away.

It was Orthodocia's first experience of a Pullman sleeper, and I dare say she found it exciting. I know I did. For economy's sake we had taken a lower berth together instead of luxuriating in a whole section; and as we sat in a vacant place across the car she watched the transformation of our own seat into a bed with disfavour from the beginning. 'Extremely stuffy!' she said, 'extremely stuffy!' When the upper berth was shut down and the curtains drawn she thought it time to interfere. 'Please put the top bed up,' she said to the negro porter; 'we can't possibly sleep that way!'

'Sawry not tuh be able tuh 'commodate yuh, Miss; but dat berth's took by a gen'leman in de smokin' car at present, Miss.'

'I suppose there is some mistake,' said Orthodocia to me, whereupon I was obliged to tell her that the proceeding was perfectly regular, and that the gentleman in the smoking car would probably be a large oleomarginous person who would snore hideously, diffuse an odour of stale tobacco, and drop his boots at intervals during the night into our berth. Orthodocia then stated her intention of sitting up all night, a course from which she was dissuaded by the appearance of claimants for the only two seats that were left. Then the gentleman came in from the smoking car, and turned out to be a perfectly inoffensive little English curate, as new to the customs of the aborigines as Orthodocia, and quite as deeply distressed. 'Perhaps—perhaps you would prefer my sitting up?' he said unhappily. 'Oh no,' said Orthodocia, '*I'll* sit up.' 'But really'—protested the curate. 'It's not of the slightest consequence,' Orthodocia interrupted frigidly, and sat down on the edge of our berth, while the frightened little man scrambled up to his with the aid of a step-ladder. Orthodocia told me next morning that she sat there a long time waiting for the boots, but as nothing appeared she concluded that he must have slept in them. The curtains that screen the berths are buttoned loosely together, and the usual method of reconnoitring before making a sortie in the direction of the toilet-room is to thrust one's head out between the buttons. It was very early in the morning when Orthodocia did this: no sound was to be heard but the rattling of the train; and she did it very deliberately and very stealthily. She looked carefully in all directions, and was just about to depart, when an upward glance made her withdraw precipitately. For there above her was the anxious countenance and dishevelled

'A PERFECTLY INOFFENSIVE LITTLE ENGLISH CURATE.'

locks of the curate, also scanning the situation and looking for the step-ladder. I suppose, if I had not been willing, after performing my own toilet, to hold the top curtains together while Orthodocia made her exit, both she and the curate might have been there still.

We entered after that, the little curate and Orthodocia and I, into the most amicable relations, for it took us two days to get to Winnipeg, which was our first stopping-place, and nobody can sit within three feet of a small thin pale Ritualist, an alien in the Canadian North-West, for two days, without feeling sorry for him and wishing to mitigate his lot in every possible way. So we fed him with chicken sandwiches from our hamper and made him cups of tea with our spirit lamp, and he in return gave us each three throat lozenges and some excellent spiritual nourishment in the form of tracts. He was going, he said, to labour in Assiniboia among the Indians, and hoped it would not be long before he could expostulate with them in their own tongue. In fact, he had quite expected to have picked up something of the language by this time. Possibly I could speak a little Cree? He was disappointed, I think, to find that the aboriginal dialects did not survive more widely.

The country for the first day was very grim and barren and dreary. We rushed along through a wilderness of rocks and stunted shrubs, juniper chiefly. The great boulders thrust themselves through the scanty grasses like gaunt shoulders through a ragged gown. Now and then a spray of yellowing maple or of reddening oak broke the grey monotony, or the rocks blossomed into lichens, but this only gave an accent to the general desolation. And steadily travelling with us all along the sky-line went a fringe of blackened firs, martyred memorials of forest fires. That alliterative expression belongs properly to the curate, whose depression was frightful about this time, and whom I saw write it down in his note-book. I hope that any of the curate's English relations who may read this chapter and be able to identify the phrase by one of his letters, will charitably refrain from communicating the plagiarism to the public. It is a very little one.

But next day we hurried along the north shore of Lake Superior, and the country grew in colour and boldness and significance. We could almost touch the great wet masses of stone the railway pierced, and there were tangled forest depths to look into, and always some glimpse of the majesty of the lake. It had many moods, sometimes blue and still and tender over headlands far away, sometimes deep and darkling in great inlets that gave back the tamarack and the pine clinging to their sheer rocky sides, sometimes sending long white waves dashing among broken boulders within a few feet of the road. I think when the world grew orthodox, they exiled Pan to the north shore of Lake Superior, its beauty is so conscious, so strong, so eternal.

On the morning of the third day we began to see fences and an occasional cow, and then we rejoiced, for we knew we were nearing Winnipeg and the Manitoban approach to civilisation. At about ten o'clock we arrived. I don't think the emigration agents have left much to say seriously about Winnipeg, which they probably call the 'Prairie City,' and chromo-lithograph in other ways with their usual skill, so I will treat it from Orthodocia's point of view, which cannot be called serious. Her first surprise was a cab—a four-wheeler, with two horses. Her next was the popular style of architecture. 'Queen Anne!' she said under her breath. 'I distinctly understood that the settlers lived in log-huts!' She asked to be driven at once to the Hudson Bay trading post, to see the Indians bringing in their peltries and exchanging them for guns and knives—a scene which she said she had always imagined with pleasure. I took her to the Hudson Bay trading post because I wanted to gratify her and to buy a pair of six-button Jouvin's at the same time; and, of course, there wasn't an Indian anywhere in the vicinity of that extremely fashionable establishment, or a peltry either. Our Winnipeg hostess lived in one of the Queen Anne houses, and I could perceive Orthodocia's astonishment rising within her as she observed the ordinary interior garnishings of Turkish rugs and Japanese vases and Spode teacups. 'I rather expected,' she said to me privately, 'deers' horns and things.' And when I sarcastically suggested wampum and war hatchets, she answered with humble sincerity, 'Yes.' Orthodocia's wonder culminated at an afternoon 'At home' at Government House, where, as the local paper put it next day, 'the wealth and fashion' of Winnipeg gathered together to drink claret cup and amuse itself. There were the Governor and his A.D.C.'s, there was a Bishop, there were the matrimonial adjuncts of the Governor and the Bishop, equally impressive; there was a Canadian Knight and his dame, there were judges and barristers, and officers and visiting celebrities, and a rumour of a real lord in one end of what the local paper called the 'spacious apartments.' I was rather glad Orthodocia didn't find any Indian chiefs there, as she expected, though perhaps she would have preferred that sensation; and I was distinctly gratified when I passed her in conversation with a younger son in corduroys at the reception, looking glum, who had just come out to waste his substance in Manitoba, and heard him inform her that 'Weally, you know, for natives—it's weally wathah wum.'

The reason he found it 'wathah wum,' was because he had a shooting jacket on and people were looking at him. They all wear corduroys at first—to dances and the opera indiscriminately, by way of helping the 'natives' to feel on an equality with them. But in the course of time they commonly go back to the usages of civilisation.

III

Our next travelling acquaintance was a lady. We were speeding out from Winnipeg—out and away into the prairie world—and we stood on the rear platform of the car, watching the city sink like a fleet of many-masted ships on the rim of the horizon. She stood with us looking back too; holding up a thin, bony, much-veined hand to keep the sun out of her eyes. She did not try to keep the regret out of them, not thinking, perhaps, that anybody noticed her. We didn't notice her much either, the prairie world was so new to us. It was a wide wide world of heaving brown grasses, dotted everywhere with tiny yellow dark-centred sunflowers, and bearing as its outposts now and then, distinct against the horizon, the low-set shanties of the first comers. Miles on miles to the right, to the left, before, behind, the yellow brown country rolled away, the blue dome of the sky springing from all its outskirts, the fibrous grasses paling in the swathe of the strong wind. Here and there a reedy little pond lay on it like a pocket looking-glass, with a score or so of wild duck swimming over it; or a slight round hollow where a pond used to be with the wild duck flying high. The railway with its two lessening parallel straight lines seemed to lead from infinity to infinity. Straight into the west we went, chasing the sun, who laughed gloriously at us and mocked us with a lengthening shadow, fleet as we were. The sand and cinders that rose in the wake of the flying train began to accumulate in our eyes and to obscure the view, however, and we went in after a while. So did the other retrospective lady a little later, and came and sat opposite us. Orthodocia looked at me, and hunted for a minute in her hand-bag. Orthodocia is a little short-sighted.

'If you have a cinder in your eye, here is an eye-stone,' said

Orthodocia sweetly. 'It is quite certain to remove anything of the kind if it is inserted under the lower lid.'

The lady thanked her, and said that it wasn't a cinder, and then Orthodocia was sorry she had not looked more carefully, for there was only one other explanation of things. So she offered a railway novel by way of reparation, and subsided into one herself, but that was the beginning of their acquaintance. I looked up and observed that our companion was an Englishwoman, but evidently accustomed to the country. One knew the first from her speech, and the second from an indescribable something in the way she wore her clothes. She had lost most of her English colour, though a little of it lingered yet, darkened into lines and patches, and her face had grown tense instead of soft as it was intended to be. She did not look unhealthy, but there was something in her alert Americanised air that suggested heavy draits on her reserve fund of vitality. She was not pathetically shabby—people seldom are in America—but there was a very much 'made over' look about her, and a quarter of an inch of useless kid flapped at each finger-end of her two-button black gloves. I suppose she might have been fifty.

The first time I came out of my pirated edition of 'Robert Elsmere' they were finding out people they both knew in England. The next time the other lady had disclosed the fact that she was a niece of Orthodocia's dear bishop. The next time Orthodocia was being enlightened as to the experiences of English ladies who emigrate with their husbands to farm the Canadian North-West, and I listened.

It transpired that the lady's husband was a banker—a banker up to forty-five—but that this had never been of choice, and that the desire to go away somewhere and dig had burned within him 'for years, my dear,' before he made up his mind to throw up his Lombard Street connections and all his wife's relations and go to Canada. There were a good many reasons why he shouldn't have gone—a steady and comfortable income where he was, a cosy home in Kensington, and a picturesque little country place—the most devoted family physician 'who understood *all* our constitutions thoroughly, my dear'—the boys' education coming on, and a hundred other things, but the gentleman knew he had capital, and the emigration agent assured him he had brains, and 'of course, when he had made up his mind, *I* couldn't say anything, Miss Love.' 'No,' said Orthodocia, with singular sympathy. 'Dear me!' said I in my American mind, reflecting on the conduct-limitations of the British matron, 'Dear *me*!'

Well, there was an interval during which they were all up to their eyes in sawdust and shavings, and nothing was heard from morning till night but the sound of the hammer as the packing went on, and everything was very dismal except the children and Mr. Growthem, who were in the most aggravating spirits. They didn't know what they might need and what they might not need on the prairies—Mr. Growthem had been told that he would have a very fair chance of becoming Governor of the Territory—so they decided to take everything, and Miss Love might imagine that *was* a business! Then came the parting with the old servants and everybody, and the sailing, which made Mr. Growthem so very ill that he wanted to go back and begin life over again in Lombard Street the second day out, and the arrival in Montreal, where Mr. Growthem had written a letter to the *Times* complaining that the Canadian policemen in Her Majesty's uniform could speak nothing but bad French.

'Did you have any trouble with the Customs?' interrupted Orthodocia, anxious to sympathise. But Mrs. Growthem hadn't had any trouble with the Customs, and was desirous to get on to Assiniboia, so Orthodocia mentally reserved her adventures. The railway didn't cross the continent *then*, she said, with a reasonably aggrieved inflection, and they found themselves and their effects dumped in a tiny North-West prairie town with seventy miles to make by ox-cart between them and the 'section' Mr. Growthem had got from the Government. Here Orthodocia said 'Really!' You must understand that all through the narrative Orthodocia said 'Really!' in the proper places; occasionally, when she was very much astonished, varying it to 'D'really!' which was a Wigginton shibboleth, I suppose. I can't go on interrupting Mrs. Growthem.

Yes. Fancy that! And no regular carpenters to be had to build the house within a hundred miles. Mr. Growthem managed to get a labourer or two, however, and he and the big boys went on ahead to build something that would shelter them—fortunately it was spring time—and Mrs. Growthem and the girls and the baby stayed behind in Q'asquepekiabasis, at a little inn—Mrs. Growthem had not yet reached the American point of calling it an 'hotel'— where she always should remember getting her first tinned tomatoes, until they were sent for. She expected to be kept waiting a month, and was astonished beyond bounds when Harry arrived in two weeks with the information that the domicile was ready, and power of attorney from his papa to bring her to it, and the baby and the girls and the household goods. Then came the three sunny days on the prairie, the June prairie, covered with a myriad wild blooms, pink and red and yellow and white, when Mrs. Growthem tried to share the joy of the children, but observed the sparseness of the settlement, and thought long thoughts. But it wasn't until they arrived that Mrs. Growthem broke down, and 'then, my dear, I *did* break down.' The little lonely log house, with its fresh-cut timber ends, different so widely from the imaginary residence of the future Governor of Assiniboia! Mrs. Growthem said she simply sat down on the nearest heap of chips and cried, and the children all stood round in a circle and looked at her. It wouldn't have been so bad, Mrs. Growthem said, if Mr. Growthem hadn't raked up the chips. It was the raking up of the chips that finished her. Could Orthodocia understand that? Orthodocia thought she could, but I didn't believe her.

But Mrs. Growthem soon saw that she must dry her tears if they were ever to take up housekeeping again, and, as a matter of fact, she quite forgot them in her overwhelming anxiety about the family china, of which only three pieces were broken after all—simply wonderful! It was the busiest day the Growthems had ever known, what with building a shed over the piano till the door could be enlarged to let it in, and reducing the gilt cornice of the mirror by eighteen inches, in order to stand it straight against the wall—the unplastered, unpapered wall of the new 'drawing-room'—and. solving the problem of sleeping accommodation for themselves, six children, and the nurse, in four small rooms. Curiously enough, it appeared that what Mrs. Growthem missed most was, not the apartments of Kensington, but her linen closet, her store-room, her attic. She felt that housekeeping was almost impossible to her without the responsibility of keys, the interest of the skilful management of reserve forces. I was not at all surprised to hear her say that Mr. Growthem's very first building extension took the form of a pantry.

'And how did you get on?' asked Orthodocia with pitying interest.

'My dear, we didn't get on. It was impossible to get servants, and field labour was very scarce; so that the first year Mr. Growthem and the boys managed all the work about the place, while the girls and I did our own baking, and sweeping, and scrubbing. No, the nurse wouldn't stay, the life was too lonely she said, and she went off to Winnipeg, where she got a situation immediately, she wrote me, at two pounds ten a month. I almost envied her!

'For the life *was* lonely. Our nearest neighbour was a young Englishman, who had a half-bred squaw for a—wife, and he was four miles away. Mr. Growthem and he and the boys went shooting together sometimes, but I didn't see much of him, and the woman, poor thing, couldn't speak English. He sent her over to help with the heavy work once when I was laid up, and she was very kind and willing, poor creature—there was no harm in *her*. Our first crop was potatoes,' Mrs. Growthem went on irrelevantly. 'Nothing else came off. And we didn't understand how to take care of the potatoes in the winter, consequently they were all frozen. But misfortunes were not serious in those early days, because it was easy then to make a draft on a London bank, and supplies of all sorts were plentiful. It was harder when it began to be necessary to look after the crops seriously for the sake of returns, when the stock had to be cared for with the thermometer thirty below zero, and two or

MRS. GROWTHEM'S NEAREST NEIGHBOUR.

'WE BURIED HER UNDER A CLUMP OF TREES.'

three labourers lived in the house for weeks at a time, which made more cooking and washing.

'Indians? Oh, they never gave us any trouble. We did not dare to refuse them food or tobacco, and often when my husband and the boys were away a Blackfeet or two would come and sit stolidly down in the kitchen for hours at a time, smoke, eat, and go away, making no sign either of gratitude or discontent. It was a little alarming at first, but we got used to it. They were almost our only visitors for a couple of years, except a young Presbyterian student we used to like, from Toronto, who took us in occasionally in his " Home Mission " work, though we didn't belong to his particular fold. Yes, Mr. Growthem went on liking it; it took a great deal to discourage him. The first blow he really seemed to feel was the failure of an experiment in young trees, which cost a thousand pounds and declined to grow for reasons best known to themselves. Two years after not a twig could be seen of all the thousand pounds' worth. He took it bravely, but it told on him. He said somebody had to find out that they wouldn't grow. By this time we were in debt, and then—then the baby died.' . . . 'The Presbyterian student helped us through that,' Mrs. Growthem went on after a while.

'She was just two years old—a dear baby—the last I had. And we buried her under a clump of trees in a corner of the ten-acre wheat field—the only trees that grew in all our four hundred and eighty acres. We could see the little grave from the kitchen window—for a long time I used to leave a lamp in it, especially when the snow came. After that nothing seemed to matter.'

The soft illimitable dusk was falling outside, and the porter was lighting the lamps overhead, before anybody spoke again. Then it was Orthodocia who said some sweet gentle thing that made me look out of the window suddenly, feeling like an intruder. When I listened again I heard that all this was ten years ago, that the Growthems were picking up now, had more neighbours, and usually a servant, that crops had been good lately, and splendid this year, and that the second boy—Harry was irretrievably a farmer—had been left by his mother at college in Winnipeg, where she had made her first brief return to civilisation in ten years, 'and words cannot express, my dear, how I enjoyed it.' So I suppose the Growthems have taken root at last in the land of their adoption, though Mr. Growthem has never become Governor of Assiniboia. I know they have, for, getting out at the same station as Mrs. Growthem, we were invited to tea with her next day, and drove ten miles behind a pair of lively little 'cayuse' ponies, through the waving prairie grasses that parted for the horses' feet and curled and closed up after them like shallow beach waves, to see her again. We found the Growthems picturesque—something we hardly expected. Their original little log house had been added to, and boarded over, and painted white. A rustic fence enclosed the garden in front, where honeysuckles were climbing, still in blossom, up the verandah, and sweet william was blooming, and pansies, and mignonette. The land rolled a little about here, and over all its pleasant undulations grain was stacked in long parallels as far as one could see. We met Mr. Growthem, casually, in his shirt sleeves, driving a waggon-load of wheat into the barn-yard. He was still a pleasant-looking man, but there were lines on his face that would not have been there if he had not been a banker in London first and a farmer in Assiniboia afterwards. Mrs. Growthem looked gentler and sweeter than she had in the train. She was glad, she said, to be at home.

We took our tea in her quaint old china cups, sitting in her crowded little drawing-room, with a feeling that there must be some mistake. The soldier portraits on the wall, the inlaid tables and Chinese cabinets and old-fashioned little Parian vases, could not belong to the interior of a North-West farmhouse. Then we noticed that the gilt top of the mirror's frame was cut in two, and remembered all about it.

As we closed the gate that defined the privileges of the public, even there where there was no public, we saw a quarter of a mile away two people coming towards us. One was a girl, English, a lady, stepping vigorously along, carrying a rifle; the other a stalwart young officer of the 'P'leece,' as the tongue of the Briton hath it always, with a couple of wild ducks hanging from his hand. It was our host's daughter, and we lingered long enough to hear that she was a first-rate shot and often brought a bird down on the wing. The young fellow, a cousin of some sort, had walked over from the barracks to be her escort. So that life, we reasoned driving back, is not devoid of the interest that attaches to youth and propinquity, even in Assiniboia.

MR. CROWTHEM.

IV

WE were tarrying in Corona—which you will not find upon the map.

One has no sensation of the absolute flatness of the prairies until one reaches Corona. Before that there seems always an unrest about it, a vague undulation of line along the sky, the contour of the country never broken, but always gently changing with the point of view, like the bounds of truth as we know them. But here the country might have been ironed out; it lies without a wrinkle or a fold, flat to its utmost verge. The town strays this way and that, like a cobweb; you can see above it, around it, through it, across levels and levels beyond. The world looks very clean-washed about Corona—to keep my metaphor in the laundry. The tiny log-houses one descries at great intervals in a prairie drive are mere specks on its wide surface. And the air finds the bottom of one's lungs in such a searching tonic way, giving one such hopeful notions of things in general, that one is disposed to think that even noisome humanity, planted out here, has a chance of coming up with fewer weeds in it than are common to the crop.

I have met very few people in England who did not know of somebody in Canada. If it happened to be a relation, the knowledge was defined, and consisted of the exile's post-office address; if not he was usually 'somewhere in the Territories, I believe—Manitoba, I *think*. And now do please tell us, *is* it "Mani*to*ba," or "Mani*toba*"?' The exile was not always a Mrs. Growthem—more often, indeed, a youth who fared badly in examinations for Sandhurst or the 'Indian Civil,' and had been started, with a hundred pounds or so, to farm in Canada on that large scale and under those indefinite conditions that make farming in Canada a possible occupation for a gentleman. I dare say, now, that a good many such young Englishmen might be located, each under his own little lonely roof, in Assiniboia, that far-reaching brown region round about Corona, fulfilling the law of destiny that draws the cities to the plains and brings about the great British average.

Orthodocia knew she had a second cousin in Canada. She thought he was ranching in Winnipeg, until we got to Winnipeg and she discovered that people didn't ranch there to any extent, on account of the price of city lots for pasture. Then Orthodocia gave him up. I don't think she was very anxious to see him. She believed he had been in the country three years, and didn't know 'what connections' he might have made. And neither of us had the least idea, when a necktie-less, heavy-coated, high-booted young man, bronzed and deep-chested and muscular, came and sat opposite us at the dinner-table of Corona's pleasant little hotel, that it could be Orthodocia's second cousin in the flesh. In fact, we thought very little about him, except that he had a large quantity of mud on his boots, and nervously offered us a great many unnecessary things. At last, however, when Orthodocia had declined the Worcestershire sauce for the third time, he put down his knife and fork with an air of desperation, and said, 'I find among the new arrivals in the hotel register the name Miss Orthodocia Love, of England, and as there are no other ladies in the hotel, I think one of you must be my cousin. It is not a—a common name.'

Now, I have no doubt that you are inwardly believing this cousin to be an invention, and my dignity as a self-respecting historian will not permit me to deny this. But you would not have thought so if you could have seen the vehement manner in which those two Loves shook hands with one another, and watched the pathetic way in which the exiled Love's gravy chilled into greasiness, while he absorbed Orthodocia's English colour instead of his proper nutriment, and hung with many 'I says!' and 'By Joves!' upon the tale of our joint expedition. 'To be sure, I haven't seen any of you for years,' he marvelled, 'but how in the world you ever got round Aunt Georgina——' And being a man grown and a relation, of course he had to say that it was a 'rum go,' and to warn us against American sharpers and confidence men. Whereupon we asked him if he thought we were likely to be drawn into a casual game of poker with an insinuating stranger who wore a silk hat on the back of his head, and talked through his nose—but we did not ask this indignantly ; our indignation at such warnings had simmered down into a calm and gentle pity. He had nothing wherewith to reply—we found that they never had anything. He only laughed uneasily, and said that, well, his advice to us was to have nothing whatever to do with anybody, advice which, I might as well confess in the beginning, we scrupulously disregarded.

'If you wouldn't mind a twenty-mile drive each way,' he said, after a while, ponderingly, 'I could take you out to my place to-night and get you back to-morrow. I could borrow the aunt of a fellow about five miles off for the occasion, and I dare say he'd be glad enough to come over too. He never sees anybody besides the fellows but his aunt—nice old girl, but rather deaf and not lively. What do you think ? It would be roughing it, you know ! '

Orthodocia assented joyfully, and then added, in some trepidation, 'You are *sure* of the aunt ? '

'If she's alive,' responded Mr. Jack Love with enthusiasm. 'She was lent once before not long ago, for a dance, and she rather liked it.'

So it happened that within an hour we were breasting the vigorous North-West air as it came rolling in over the great stretches of the prairie, billow after billow of it, behind Mr. Jack Love's 'team' of little bronchos, Orthodocia, trying to hold them in, sitting up very straight as she would in her own dog-cart in the Park, and making, with her cheeks aflame and her fur collar turned up against them, as pretty a picture as you could imagine. Our vehicle was, in the language of the country, a 'democrat,' a high four-wheeled cart, painted and varnished, with double seats, one behind the other. Mr. Jack sat beside Orthodocia to supplement her very limited acquaintance with bronchos, and I shared the seat behind the two Loves with a large bundle of binding twine and certain sections of agricultural implements brought in for repairs. The road lay across the prairie like a great undulating, velvety-black snake—the original Indian trail, Mr. Love told us, curving to avoid the swampy places. We made an occasional dash away from it just for fun, through the crisp curling yellow prairie grasses and back again, but then 'Cousin Jack' took the reins himself in masterful fashion and held the ponies' heads well up to avoid a broken knee in a badger's hole. So we went speeding over a world with nobody in it but ourselves for miles at a time. In fact, we saw only three people all the way. One was a pleasant-faced German driving a pair of oxen, who suggested to Mr. Love certain hearty words of appreciation. 'That fellow,' he said, 'and his family represent more success than anybody I could show you within fifty miles. Everything they can't raise or make they do without, as far as possible, spending less money in a year than some of the rest of us, who think ourselves some on economy, do in a week. Their furniture they make of wood from the bluffs—even the nails are hardwood pins. They stuff their beds with wild dried hay, weave their blankets, spin their clothes, produce their bread, and imagine their luxuries!' Quaint, durable, poetic home-making this, we thought. No varnish, no veneer, all primitive but conscientious, good outward showing of the inward Teuton. We looked back after the man with admiration.

'Yes,' assented Mr. Jack, 'it's all true, but I can't help getting into a wax with those Deutschers sometimes in my mind. They're so—darned—contented!'

Which showed two things—first, that Mr. John Love's vocabulary had not quite escaped American contamination; second, that he had not been three years in Assiniboia without occasional fits of home-sickness.

Our next encounter was a solitary Blackfeet Indian. This Indian is memorable for having inspired Miss Love with a burning contempt for Mr. Fenimore Cooper. He rode a very small white pony of depressed appearance, by whose assistance his feet just managed to clear the ground. These members were encased in ragged leather shoes, between which and the ends of an inadequate pair of light checked trousers there glowed an expanse of red woollen stocking. He wore a dirty blanket across his shoulders in a *négligé* manner, the remains of a silk hat on his head, and a short clay pipe in his mouth. His countenance was not noble, aquiline, or red, but basely squat, with a complexion paralleled only by the copper kettles of a kitchen-maid who is not a treasure. His hawk-like eye was extremely bloodshot, and his long black locks were tightly and greasily braided into a couple of unspeakable strands that dangled behind him. I saw Orthodocia bid a silent farewell to the brave of the tomahawk as he passed, grunting 'How!' to her cousin's salutation.

'What's his name?' she asked.

'Mr. Jones—popularly.'

'But his baptismal—I mean his own name?'

'Oh, anything—"Left-Wing-of-a-Prairie-Chicken," "Old-Man-with-the-Green-Silk-Umbrella," "He-Who-Stands-Up-and-Eats-a-Raw-Dog,"' responded Mr. Love, with levity. 'They excel in imaginative efforts of that sort. Blackfeet nomenclature is one mass of embroidery.'

Just then we overtook a slim youth clad largely in buckskins, with a wide felt hat pulled well down over his eyes, stepping along beside a cart-

'LEFT-WING-OF-A-PRAIRIE-CHICKEN.'

load of lumber, whistling 'Queen of My Heart' with great vigour and precision. He turned out for us in sudden surprise, but his hat came off in a way Orthodocia thought particularly graceful in response to Mr. Jack's exuberant 'H'lo old man! Walkin' good?'

'That's Brydington,' remarked Mr. Love. 'Brydington's no end of a swell. Keeps a chest full of b'iled shirts, and shaves on Sunday. Got a toilet table! Got a tennis racquet tied with a blue ribbon hanging over it! Got a door-mat! Said to possess Early English china. Said to have pillow-shams. Said to use a hot-water bottle for cold feet. Reads Ruskin and "The Earthly Paradise."'

'Dear me!' said Orthodocia. 'How very interesting!'

'Is it?' said Mr. Love. 'We call Brydington "The Bride of the West." His shanty is about ten miles beyond mine—he won't get there before night walking. The Bride's going in for an extension, I guess, with that lumber—a conservatory, p'raps, or a music-room!'

'Dear me!' said Orthodocia, thoughtfully; 'dear me!'

Whereupon I fancied Mr. John Love whipped up the bronchos unnecessarily. Life on the prairies evidently did not tend toward concealment of the emotions.

In due course we arrived at Mr. Love's establishment. I have permitted us to arrive without describing any of the scenery *en route*, but as no scenery whatever occurred during the whole twenty miles except one little wooded rising which Mr. Love pointed out as 'The Bluffs,' and the bush-fringed borders of a stream which seemed to wander out of nowhere into anywhere, this may perhaps be forgiven. Anyway, I have observed that in reading accounts of travels people always skip the scenery.

Orthodocia's 'American cousin,' as she had begun to call him—not apparently to his great displeasure—opened his hospitable front door to us and begged us to make ourselves entirely at home while he went for the aunt. 'You may find Jim about the premises,' he said, 'but don't mind Jim. Jim's getting out the crop with me this year on shares. I say, Jim!' he shouted, driving off, as a lanky figure appeared in the distance; 'look after the ladies, will you?'

Jim came up to us with a long, astonished, and anxious counte-

nance. Jim was no importation from gilded halls beyond the seas.
Jim was of the soil. He had an honest, sun-burned face, and great
knotty red hands. He wore a grey flannel shirt, and his blue jean
trousers were hitched to his shoulders by one old white suspender
and a piece of rope. Jack Love had 'boarded' with Jim on his
Ontario farm, and probably paid him five dollars a week for a year
to be instructed in general agriculture. Then Jim had caught his
'scholar's'—by which he meant his pupil's—'shine fer the West,'
had sold out his bachelor estate in Ontario, and come thus far with
young Love to have a 'look round.' Meantime he was 'getting out
the crops on shares.' But this we discovered afterwards.

Jim's consternation did not decrease when he found that we were
actually coming in.

'I never!' he said profoundly ; then, with an awkward, doubtful
attempt at sportiveness—'Ain't ben an' got mar'd, hes he ? We
ain't fixed up fer a lady igsackly. He'd ought to have let me know !'

When we had sufficiently explained ourselves Jim showed us into
one of the three rooms the establishment boasted, to take our 'things
off.' 'That ere's Mr. Love's room,' he remarked, awkwardly, 'but I
guess you'll hev' to hev' it fer t'night, an' he'll sleep in the settin'
room or alongside me in the kitchen.' Then Jim disappeared, considering his vicarious duties done.

Orthodocia and I inspected our apartment. It was about six
feet by ten, and had one small square window wearing a demoralised
muslin flounce. A little iron bed with several blue blankets on it
filled up one end, and there was a table with a pitcher and basin, a
fragment of looking-glass, and a collection of old pipes on it, and a
chair. Two or three rifles stood in one corner. The outer walls
were roughly boarded over, and between the cracks of the partition
dividing this from the 'settin-room' we could see the pattern of the
pink and green wall-paper with which Mr. John Love had made
that apartment cheerful. A few photographs, much fly-specked and
faded, were tacked against the boards, a white-whiskered officer in
uniform, a pleasant-faced lady in early middle age and the usual
black silk, a cluster of girls in muslins—perhaps a dozen altogether.
Orthodocia went straight to the photographs and looked earnestly
at each of them.

'No,' she said irrelevantly to my remarks on the tide of immigration, 'she's not there. It's off, then! I'm very glad. She always was a flirt, and that second curate——' Then Orthodocia paused in twisting up the left coil of her hair, looked round her, and said, very softly, 'Poor Jack!'

It did not take long to explore Mr. Love's establishment very thoroughly. There were three cane-bottomed chairs in the *salon* with the pink and green wall-paper, and a table with a miscellaneous literary collection on it. A Christina Rossetti Birthday Book, from 'his loving sister on the eve of his departure for America,' Somebody on Shorthorns, a well-thumbed set of Dickens, 'The Game of Cricket,' 'Successful Men,' some old school books, and a lot of railway novels, in which a certain prominence was given to the works of Miss Amélie Rives. Decoration had stopped at the wall-paper, but a couple of polished buffalo horns made pegs for rather bad hats. The floor was covered with a rag carpet, there were some skins about, and a gorgeous nickel-plated cylindrical American coal stove upreared itself in the middle of the room, and sent at least two yards of stove-pipe straight through the roof. We followed our noses with great precision into the kitchen, where Jim was bending over a diminutive cook-stove, his countenance warmed into a deep rose madder, cooking what seemed to us a feast for the gods in a frying-pan. It was only bacon, and I dare say the smell would not have been tolerated for an instant on Olympus, even about the back premises; but we had achieved a pair of North-West appetites, and regarded Jim tenderly. He had set the table elaborately in one corner, covering it with a faded piece of flowered chintz, that fell in voluminous folds to the floor. With an eye to neatness as well as elegance, Jim had pinned it up at the corners, so that it looked very like the garment of a corpulent washerwoman. We speculated in vain, but feared to inquire what the original uses of that flowered chintz might have been. Horn-handled knives and three-tined forks of various sizes were artistically crossed for six people, and three 'individual' salt-cellars were disposed with mathematical impartiality. A large glass jar of pickles stood in the middle of the table, and a box of sardines, a plate of soda biscuit, and a tin of blackberry jam occupied three corners, the third being desperately made out with some fragments of maple sugar in a saucer. There were two white cups and saucers which matched, two tumblers, and one large moustache cup, highly ornate, with 'For James' on it in damaged gilt letters. I think that was all, except some generous slices of bread and a blue wineglass, in which were arranged with care six toothpicks. Our seats were also placed, five wooden chairs and a turned-up tub, but the tub concealed itself modestly in an inside corner under the chintz—Jim was evidently a strategist.

In the ravenous interval before we heard wheels, Orthodocia and I took feminine notes of Mr. Love's culinary establishment. A shelf behind the stove held most of the utensils that were not on the floor, and among them were several

'LIKE A DENUNCIATORY HOUSEHOLD GODDESS.'

remarkable patent contrivances which Jim scornfully refused to explain. 'He will buy 'em,' he said, 'an' they're all the same—sartin t' bust on yer hands. Ef anybody showed him a machine t' lay an egg, hatch it, an' bring it out spring chicken ready briled, you puttin' in some feed an' turnin' a crank, he'd believe it an' bring the thing home. Won't take no advice about 'em. An' I've kep' house a sight longer'n he hes!'

We came upon one invention, however, which was quite clear to us. It was a large woollen sock, half full of brown spongy stuff with an unmistakable smell. Orthodocia held it up to Jim between her finger and thumb, like a denunciatory household goddess.

'Thet!' said he, making a lunge at it, 'thet's—Canader for the Canadians!—thet's bran, strained fer a poultice!'

But Jim was a bachelor housekeeper, and the truth was not in him. It was coffee!

Meantime the tea was boiling cheerfully on the back of the stove. Jim had argued so scientifically in support of its boiling that Orthodocia withdrew her protest, and subsided into a pained melancholy—and the bacon had been succeeded by pancakes, 'self-raisin' buckwheat' Jim remarked as he mixed them; 'nothin' like it in case of compn'y onexpected.' So that when the aunt appeared, with her nephew and a pair of roast wild ducks and a pound cake of her own making, we felt that the situation was complete. The aunt was a corpulent, comfortable, uncommunicative person who was 'very happy to make your acquaintance.' She immediately produced a wonderful square of crazy patchwork, into which she subsided when the salutations were over, leaving the conversation to the rest of us.

'Weren't you very much surprised to be carried off in this way?' Orthodocia said with her usual blandishments.

The aunt looked up over her spectacles, and said with decision:

'I've been five years in this part of the country, Miss Love, and now I can't say I'm surprised at *any*thing!' which only caused Orthodocia to smile more sweetly and say that in any case it was very good of her to come.

After supper, during which the young men chaffed Jim, who sat large and absorbent on the wash tub in the corner, about his preparations, and Orthodocia nearly went into a convulsion at the discovery that as a mark of special consideration he had given the moustache-cup to the aunt, and everybody was very merry, we all wandered out under the stars to hear the crickets telling summer stories with acute bronchitis in the September wheatfields. The starlight was very clear; we could see to pick the tall brown-centred yellow daisy-like things that grew about our feet. A single Indian tent broke the long, heaving line of the prairie against the sky, and the crickets only seemed to make the great lonely stillness stiller.

'I kinder think sometimes,' said Jim, 'that th' last trump 'll sound out here—ther's so much extry room.'

Then Jim took the aunt round to see how the calf had grown, and Mr. John Love and Orthodocia wandered off to confer on cousinly matters, I suppose, and the nephew, who was a nondescript, asked me what was 'going on' in Winnipeg when we were there. And by-and-by we all gathered in the kitchen again—somehow it was a more attractive place than the front room with the pink and green wall-paper—and Jim brought out his fiddle and played upon it in the most grievous manner 'Way down upon de Swanee Ribber,' 'Home, Sweet Home,' and 'Comin' thro' the Rye,' in the order mentioned. Whereupon Orthodocia came to her own relief, and executed a brilliant little jig upon the instrument, to which Jim did a hornpipe with great glory.

The aunt was very grateful to have the whole of the small iron bed placed absolutely at her disposal, and slept therein all night long the sleep of the just—and those who keep their mouths open. Orthodocia and I on the floor talked between our blankets and buffalo robes late, and I found that she had fully satisfied herself about the conduct of the young lady who had been guilty of a 'second curate.'

V

'DID you know,' said Mr. Jack Love to Miss Orthodocia Love, as we drove past a cluster of Blackfeet tepees on a prairie road skirting Corona, 'that Carysthwaite of Tenhampton is in the P'leece?'

We were on our way to spend an afternoon with the 'P'leece,' not in any connection of durance vile, but with the peaceful prospect of tea and muffins and general information. It had been Mr. Jack Love's plan—he had thought of an officer's wife he could utilise to further it—and Orthodocia had entered into it with enthusiasm. She had heard of the Canadian Mounted Police in England, as most people have, and her ideas regarding them were wrapped in a gold-laced glory, as most people's are, and associated with prancing chargers and the subdual of the French Canadian population. It had been a disappointment to Orthodocia that no Mounted Police were to be seen in Montreal. She had supposed we should have a large force in barracks there, to patrol the country between that point and another, which she somewhat indefinitely alluded to as 'the Great Lakes.' She had found the Canadians thus far monotonously civilian, an offence which the red coats of our peaceful militia rather aggravated, in her scornful opinion. Here at last was a body of 'regulars'; here was a band and barracks and a properly-commissioned officer's wife; here were the Mounted Police; here, according to Mr. John Love, was Carysthwaite, the Honourable Carysthwaite, of Tenhampton.

'No!' said Orthodocia. 'I thought he had gone into mining in Colorado.'

'So he did—and came out again.'

'Curious,' Miss Love remarked, tentatively, 'how he managed to drift into such an out-of-the-way place as this!'

'Not so curious.'

'No? Well, we all told him that sooner or later he would be a soldier again. He looked so awfully well in uniform, and we couldn't do anything—simply—in theatricals without him. A soldier's life,' Orthodocia went on pensively, 'affords such unlimited opportunities for theatricals. I suppose the officers amuse themselves that way occasionally, even out here.'

'The officers—yes,' her cousin answered, with unaccountable amusement; 'but I haven't heard of Carrie's doing it. There are the barracks.'

'*Where?*' said Orthodocia.

Jack pointed straight in front of him, and we saw something that reminded us strongly of pioneer defence pictured in the primary readers of our schooldays—a hollow square of low, long wooden buildings growing out of the prairie, with about as much picturesqueness as a problem in Euclid. As we drew nearer the resemblance lessened. The houses were built of frame instead of logs, and had brick chimneys, luxuries which we are led to believe the early settlers largely dispensed with. There were no palisades, nor was there so much as a sapling in the neighbourhood behind which painted foes might lurk in ambush. There was a band-stand in the middle, and the officers' quarters had verandahs, and looked as if modern lares and penates, even to æsthetic antimacassars and hand-painted mandolins, might be found inside. The general aspect of the place was not warlike.

I don't think I can go into particulars about the properly-commissioned officer's wife. So far as I remember, her muffins were not surpassed by any that we came in contact with afterwards. She had a large dog and a small pony, several medium-sized children, and an apparent habit of enjoying herself. Her winter wardrobe interested Orthodocia, especially a buffalo coat for driving, in which our hostess bore a comfortable resemblance to a cinnamon bear. My friend was pleased also with a hole under the kitchen floor, which was the lady's only store-room. And with the fact that ladies living in 'the country' thought nothing of driving in fifteen or twenty miles to a ball in the barracks, with the thermometer at twenty below zero, and dressing after they arrived. The great difficulty, it seemed, was the paucity of ladies upon these festive occasions, and our hostess added illustrations of the premium upon femininity in the North-West, which made Orthodocia thoughtful.

I observed Orthodocia's education in Mounted Police matters to be taken in hand with some thoroughness by a certain stalwart and sunburned Major, who beguiled us all into his bachelor quarters for another cup of tea. He told her a great many things that she didn't know before, and though she tried to look appreciative and admiring over the photograph of Sitting Bull in full war costume, and the elaborate chart of the patrol system and the last report in the Parliamentary blue-books, I could see her opinion of Canada's military resources gradually approaching zero. It was naturally disenchanting to hear that the chief business of the Police was to visit justice upon horse-stealing Crees and to catch whisky-smugglers —that the force really exercised the functions of a magistracy among the Indians, who have never known any other authority than what is vested in these red coats and white helmets, with the rifle, the revolver, the guard-room, and the potential bit of rope behind. I could see that these were not glorious duties to Orthodocia, though she did grow sympathetic over a story or two that she coaxed out of the Major— the arresting of an Indian murderer by two young policemen alone in the face of a shanty bristling with the rifles of the culprit's friends—the untraced Indian vengeance that shot another gallant fellow in the back and left him to die alone upon the prairie—the eighteen days' ride of nine hundred and ninety odd miles after the perpetrators of a recent outrage, the men never under cover during that time, but sleeping in their blankets on the ground, and carrying their rations with them. Then we went forth in a body to see what might be seen—the men's quarters, with their long rows of narrow grey-blanketed beds, the tiny theatre which was also a chapel on occasion, the canteen where a fresh-coloured little woman dispensed sardines and biscuits and ginger ale to all the barracks, and the wooden-grated guard-room, where, for the moment, there was nobody but the guard and a foolish old Indian who lay like one dead in a lumpy heap under his blanket. Here we heard of Riel—the patriot and the traitor, you remember, the man and the mercenary, the murderer and the martyr, whom we hanged, with much agitation, a very few years ago for obstinately heading the second half-breed rebellion in the North-West. He was celled here, this conspirator whom Canada must always take account of, all the long days while our Government disputed with itself as to whether it could hang him and continue its own existence or not, and from Halifax to Vancouver everybody speculated upon his fate. They told us of him again in a narrow and enclosed court at the back of the prison, where we looked up, with a sudden chill, at a certain window above. He stepped out to the hangman, who held a grudge against him, from that window. And I remembered the sun lighting up some marigolds on a quiet grave in sleepy St. Boniface, across the river from Winnipeg, within a stone's throw of a quaint old convent where a thrifty Sister Adiposa was stooping over some cabbages in the garden. It was not yet quite time for High Mass, and a few French half-breeds, the men in mocassins, the women with the *tête couverte*, loitered about the gate and the church-door. The grave had been made for their sakes, but none of them went near it—it had lost interest for them since the sod grew. On its plain, slim, white wooden cross, in black letters, we read, LOUIS DAVID RIEL. And we thought of Death and of the Law. 'Whom none could advise thou hast persuaded.'

You must excuse these colonial trivialities; Orthodocia did. She even went so far as to write down the name of our traitor in full in her note-book, where it remains in pencil, immediately under the fact that there are thirty-four thousand Indians in the Canadian North-West to this day.

Walking back past the stables we met one of the men. He had top-boots on, with his trousers thrust into them, and a grey flannel shirt; and in each hand he carried a flowing pail of water. As we approached he put down the buckets, one on each side of him, and saluted the Major. Jack gave Orthodocia a cousinly nudge, and as she looked again the man started, turned the colour of old red sandstone, then stood very erectly as before, and saluted again. Orthodocia bowed and smiled with her sweetest self-possession. Then the two Loves looked at one another, and said with one accord, 'Carrie!'

The officer's wife came in volubly at this point, and made Jack's explanation unnecessary. 'Miss Love,' she said, 'I hope you noticed that man. By birth and education he is the superior of almost every officer in the Police. In fact, my dear,' in an awed whisper, 'he is the third son of an English lord—and we can't invite him to dinner! It's *too* trying! You see we must treat them all alike, and poor Mr. Carysthwaite has got to turn out and groom his horse at five o'clock on our bitterly cold winter mornings, and do every-

THE HON. CARYSTHWAITE.

thing else about the stables and quarters that has to be done just like the rest of them. He *can't* let his people know or they *never* would allow it!

'Of course they think he's got a commission—they all think that in England when their sons come out here, fail in farming or mining, find Civil Service positions hard to get in Ottawa, and drift into the

Police as a *dernier ressort.* Instead of which they simply join as recruits on ridiculously small pay and rough it—to—an—ex—*tent* ! We've had quite a lot of them at one time and another. Not every man of that sort can stand the life, the drill and duty is so severe, so a good many have dropped out, especially if there is any inclination to dissipation; but sometimes they stick to it in the most wonderful way.'

To Orthodocia's inquiry as to why commissions were so difficult to get, the officer's wife responded with *naïveté* that she believed a good deal of it was politics and that abominable system of promotion from the ranks in the order of seniority and on grounds of general qualification, a system which she would certainly abolish if she had anything to do with Government.

This is only a faithful chronicle of the ordinary happenings of an ordinary journey of two ordinary people, so I can't gratify you with any romantic episode later connected with Orthodocia and the Mounted Policeman so well qualified yet so ineligible to be asked to dinner, though I should dearly like to. The fact is—and I tremble to think what might become of Orthodocia if I permitted myself any departure from the facts—that we left Corona and one very melancholy John Love late that very night, and the Honourable Carysthwaite did not occur again.

We had, as we thought, but one day to spare in order to reach Vancouver in time to set our foot on the ship, and sail according to the instructions on our tickets ; and while yet the lamps were lit outside our swaying curtains, and a man from Little Rock, 'Arkansaw,' snored rhythmically in the upper berth across the aisle, we devoted half an hour to a vigorous discussion as to whether we should get off at Banff or The Glacier. When we awoke we were forty miles beyond Banff, so we concluded between the buttoning of one boot and the discovery of the other that the phenomena at The Glacier must naturally be much better worth a visit than the fashionable and frivolous life at Banff, and that there would probably be just as good a hotel there, and just as many people anyway. But these were the consolations of the crestfallen. As a matter of fact, nobody ought to pass Banff. If you do you lay yourself open to the charge from everybody who has gone before of having missed the very finest bit of scenery on the trip. You may expect it, n addening as it is, from the most amiable of your friends —not one of them will be able to refrain. The natural attitude toward this statement, and the one we persistently assumed, is of course one of flat negation, but privately I should advise you to avoid it, and see Banff.

Orthodocia and I had our first glimpse of the Rockies from the window of the 'ladies' toilet-room' between the splashes of the very imperfect ablutions one makes in such a place. It was just before sunrise, and all we could see was a dull red burning in the sky behind the wandering jagged edge of what might have been the outer wall of some Titanic prison. Orthodocia raised her hands in admiration, and began to quote something. I didn't, one of mine being full of soap, and ransacked my mind in vain for any beautiful sentiment to correspond with Orthodocia's. I found the towel though, which was of more consequence at the time; and then we both hurried forth upon the swaying rear platform of the car to join our exclamations with those of a fellow-passenger, whom we easily recognised to be the man from Little Rock, 'Arkansaw.'

As we stood there on the end of the car and looked out at the great amphitheatre, with the mountains sitting solemnly around it, regarding our impudent noisy toy of steam and wheels, we remembered that we should see mountains with towers and minarets—mountains like churches, like fortifications, like cities, like clouds. And we saw them all, picking out one and then another in the calm grandeur of their lines far up along the sky. Orthodocia cavilled a little at the impertinence of any comparison at all. She thought that a mountain—at all events, one of these great western mountains, down the side of which her dear little England might rattle in a landslip—could never really look like anything but a mountain. It might have a superficial suggestion of something else about its contour, but this, Orthodocia thought, ought to be wholly lost in the massive, towering, eternal presence of the mountain itself.

'Let us go into abstractions for our similes,' said Orthodocia; 'let us compare it to a thought, to a deed, that men have thrust high above the generations that follow and sharp against the ages that pass over, and made to stay for ever there, and not to some poor fabrication of stone and mortar that dures but for a century or so, and whose builder's proudest boast might well be that he had made something like a mountain!'

'That's so!' said the man from Little Rock, 'Arkansaw.'

Orthodocia shuddered, and consulted her muse further in silence, while the dull red along the frontier east burned higher, flinging a tinge of itself on the foam of the narrow pale-green river that went tearing past, and outlining purple bulks among the mountains that lay between. There was something theatrical about the masses of unharmonised colour, the broad effects of light and shadow, the silent pose of everything. It seemed a great drop-curtain that Nature would presently roll up to show us something else. And in a moment it did roll up or roll away, and was forgotten in one tall peak that lifted its snow-girt head in supremest joy for the first baptism of the sun. It was impossible to see anything but the flush of light creeping down and over that far solemn height, tracing its abutments and revealing its deep places. It seemed so very near to God that a wordless song came from it, set in chords we did not know. But all the air was sentient with the song. . . .

'How many feet, naow, do you suppose they give that mountin?' said the man from Little Rock, 'Arkansaw.'

Orthodocia and I stood not upon the order of our going, but went at once, vowing that it would be necessary to live to be very old in order to forgive that man.

Field is a little, new place on the line, chiefly hotel, where I remember a small boy who seemed to run from the foot of one mountain to the foot of another to unlock a shanty and sell us some apples at twenty-five cents a pound. But Field is chiefly memorable to us as being the place where the engine-driver accepted our invitation to ride with him. He was an amiable engine-driver, but he required a great deal of persuasion into the belief that the inlaid box upholstered in silk plush and provided with plate-glass windows that rolled along behind, was not indisputably the best place from which to observe the scenery. 'You see, if you was on the ingin' an' anythin' 'appened you'd come to smash certain,' he observed cheerfully but implacably. 'Besides, it's ag'inst the rules.'

Whereupon we invoked the aid of a certain Superintendent of Mechanics, who was an obliging person and interceded for us.

'YOU FEEL WITH WONDER THAT YOU ARE NOT DOING ANYTHING VERY
EXTRAORDINARY AFTER ALL.'

'Lady Macdonald did it,' he said, instancing the wife of our Premier, 'and if these young ladies can hold on '—he looked at us doubtfully, and Orthodocia immediately gave him several examples of her extraordinary nerve. We coveted a trip on the pilot—in vulgar idiom the cow-catcher—a heavy iron projection in front of the engines in America, used to persuade wandering cattle of the company's right of way. My argument was that in case of danger ahead we could obviously jump. The engineer appreciated it very reluctantly, and begged us on no account to jump, obviously or any way. And we said we wouldn't, with such private reservations as we thought the situation warranted. Finally we were provided with a cushion apiece and lifted on. To be a faithful historian I must say that it was an uncomfortable moment. We fancied we felt the angry palpitations of the monster we sat on, and we couldn't help wondering whether he might not resent the liberty. It was very like a personal experiment with the horns of a dragon, and Orthodocia and I found distinct qualms in each other's faces. But there was no time for repentance; our monster gave a terrible indignant snort, and slowly, then quickly, then with furious speed, sent us forth into space.

Now, I have no doubt you expect me to tell you what it feels like to sit on a piece of black iron, holding on by the flagstaff, with your feet hanging down in front of a train descending the Rockies on a grade that drops four and a half feet in every hundred. I haven't the vocabulary—I don't believe the English language has it. There is no terror, as you might imagine, the hideous thing that inspires it is behind you. There is no heat, no dust, no cinder. The cool, delicious mountain air flows over you in torrents. You are projected swiftly into the illimitable, stupendous space ahead, but on a steady solid basis that makes you feel with some wonder that you are not doing anything very extraordinary after all, though the Chinese navvies along the road looked at Orthodocia and me as if we were. That, however, was because Orthodocia's hair had come down and I had lost my hat, which naturally would not tend to impress the Celestial mind with the propriety of our mode of progression. We were intensely exhilarated, very comfortable and happy, and felt like singing something to the rhythmic roar of the train's accompaniment. We did sing and we couldn't hear ourselves. The great armies of the pines began their march upwards at our feet. On the other side the range of the stately Selkirks rose, each sheer and snowy against the sky. A river foamed along beside us, beneath us, beyond us. We were ahead of everything, speeding on into the heart of the mountains, on into a wide sea of shining mist with white peaks rising out of it on all sides, and black firs pointing raggedly up along the nearer slopes. A small cave in a projecting spur, dark as Erebus; the track went through it, and in an instant so did we, riding furiously into the echoing blackness with a wild thought of the possible mass of fallen-in *débris* which was not there.

Orthodocia and I wondered simultaneously, as we found out afterwards, what we should do if the rightful occupant of the cow-catcher —namely, the cow—should appear to claim it. It was impossible to guess. I concluded that it would depend upon how much room the cow insisted upon taking up. If we could come to terms with her, and she didn't mind going 'heads and tails,' she would find a few inches available between us; otherwise—but it would be unpleasant in any event to be mixed up in an affair of the sort. Cows suggested bears, not from any analogy known natural history, but because a bear on that road was a good deal more probable an episode than a cow.

'A BEAR WAS A GOOD DEAL MORE PROBABLE EPISODE THAN A COW.'

Supposing a bear suddenly hurled in to our society, would he feel fear, or amazement, or wrath? Would he connect us in displeased astonishment with the immediate cause of his disaster, or would he sympathise with us as fellow-victims trapped further back? In either case, would he make any demonstration? These considerations so

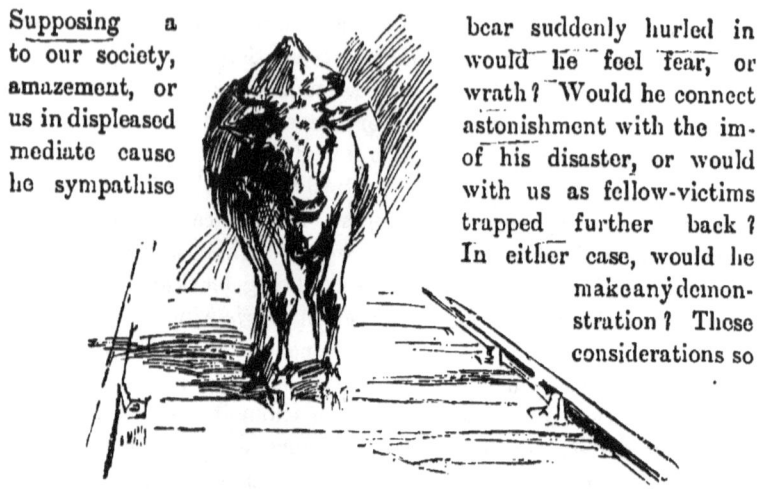

'THE RIGHTFUL OCCUPANT OF THE COW-CATCHER.'

worked upon my mind that I actually expected the bear. In imagination I saw him tramping through the undergrowth to meet the great surprise of his life and of mine, and my sympathy was divided between us. I dwelt with fascination upon certain words of an American author—'And the bear was coming on,' and I thought of the foolhardiness of travelling on a cow-catcher without a gun. With an imaginary rifle I despatched the gross receipts of the cow-catcher for a week with great glory. I wondered what would be said in our respective home circles if the bear really came on. And as we alighted at The Glacier I confided to Orthodocia my bitter regret that he did not come.

VI

It was a strange thing to find there in the silent solemn heart of the Rockies, under the great brow of one mountain and among the torrent-washed feet of its fellows, an elaborate little hostelry which pretended to be a Swiss *châlet* to match the scenery. One admires the *châlet* idea exceedingly from the outside, but with an entire and thorough appreciation of the inconsistencies of the inside, which include various attractions and conveniences unknown to the usual Swiss *châlet*—from electric bells and hot-water baths to *asperges glacées* and pretty American waitresses with small waists and high heels to bring it to one. The conception cannot be defended on artistic grounds perhaps, but one must be far gone in æstheticism not to approve it on general principles. I must be pardoned for introducing the hotel at this point, for there was really nothing else to introduce, except the 'Loop' and the Great Glacier itself, which is its own post-office address. The Loop occurs a mile or two further on, and is as wonderful a convolution in engineering as any successful candidate could make in politics immediately after an election. We walked down to inspect this railway marvel the evening we arrived, while yet the thought of the bear that we might have met on the cow-catcher dwelt in our imaginations. Twilight was coming down among the mountains that went straight and sheer up into the evening sky at our very feet, and the tall pines and shaggy juniper bushes behaved in an extraordinary manner. In consequence of these things, Orthodocia and I saw five bears apiece and ran all the way back with the ten in hot pursuit; which is one reason why I can't adorn this page with an exact description of the remarkable engineering feat we went to see. But the bears are worth something. There was one more, by-the-way, a baby-bear chained up in the hotel grounds, who would tear one's clothes in the cunningest way, in as many places as one would permit, for an apple. In Orthodocia's note-book he figures as the eleventh bear we experienced in the Rockies : but this being a sober chronicle I prefer to gives its readers what might be called the benefit of the doubt.

Next morning we sallied forth to climb the Glacier. We took a small boy as a mere formality on account of the bears, but we found him useful before long on other accounts. For, while horses and mules are promised to convey the tourist of next year to the base of the phenomenon aforesaid, the tourists of last year had to walk ; and the walk is a two-mile climb, more properly, over rocks, across (by stepping-stones) the torrent that the sun sends down from the Glacier every day, and under Douglas firs that tower seventy feet above you, with the sunlight filtering down through them upon mosses that are more vividly, vitally green than anything I ever saw out of British Columbia. The grimy small boy's grimy small hand as he skipped from rock to rock over the clear green water that swirled past them, was an invaluable member. A small dog was attached, necessarily, I suppose, to the small boy—an alarmist small dog, who persisted in making wild excursions into the forest, barking volubly in the distance, and adding potential bears to Orthodocia's note-book. This is the way she put them down :

Bear (?)

But she used a lead pencil, and I dare say the interrogation point became obliterated in the course of time.

We maintained our purpose of climbing the Glacier with the utmost steadfastness the whole way. In fact, we took it for granted that we should get to the top in the course of the morning—that everybody did—so confidently that we didn't think it necessary to mention the matter to the small boy until we were almost there. The manner in which he received our intention was not encouraging. He whistled. It was a loud long contemptuous whistle, with a great deal of boy in it : and we resented it, naturally.

'What do you mean ?' said Orthodocia. 'Don't people usually. go up ?'

'Naw !'

'Has nobody *ever* got to the top? That's just like you Americans!'—to me—'What do you think Providence gave you mountains for, if he didn't intend you to climb them? I suppose'—scornfully—'you're waiting for somebody to put up "elevators" for you?'

'Ye·p—No·p!' answered the small boy, a trifle confused. 'Three or four English blokes went up explorin' this summer, but not this way. They went round somehow'—describing an indefinite arc with his arm—'an' it took 'em ten days. Found a bed of ice up there seven mile wide, an' mountin sheep that jest stood still an' got shot, lookin' at 'em. Ladies,' continued the small boy, with mighty sarcasm, 'ginerally git s'fur's this. Then they say, "How perfeckly lovely!" an' go back to th' 'tel. Ladies ain't meant for explorin'. I ain't ben up there myself yet, though.'

Thus consoled, we decided that life might be worth living even without including the conquest of the Great Glacier of the Rockies. It looked rather a big phenomenon to take liberties with when we arrived at its base, though Orthodocia ascended it to a height of at least five feet and was brought down again in safety by the small boy. Its wavelike little hollows were slippery and ankle-breaking, and great cracks yawned through it suggestively. On close inspection it was a very dirty Glacier indeed, to look so vast and white and awful a little way off, though the torrent that rushed from its feet down through the valley to the canyon of the Fraser was clear as crystal. Being athirst, we wanted to drink the glacier water, but the small boy, for whom we were beginning to acquire a prodigious respect, would not permit this. 'Snow-water,' he said, would give us fever—we must find a spring. Then we entered, and sat down in a beautiful blue ice-cave under the Glacier, fell into the usual raptures an ice-cave inspires, and took two bad colds which lasted longer.

The windows of our special corner of the *châlet* were low and broad, and the mountains that were gathered about brought night down soon. We leaned out, and looked and listened, after the last tourist soul besides ourselves had closed his door on his dusty boots and sought repose. The moonlight gleamed broadly on the still gray sea in the gap; a shining white line chased itself, murmuring,

'LADIES AIN'T MEANT FER EXPLORIN'.'

down the dark height before us ; over the mighty head of 'Sir Donald' a single star hung luminous. We left our shutters wide for the song of the one and the benediction of the other.

There is a satisfaction that is difficult to parallel in getting as far as you can go. Orthodocia and I felt it when we had left the snow-capped mountains, in their stern, remote, inaccessible beauty, behind, and sped through the softer, kinder, cloudier heights of the Yale Canyon to Vancouver. Vancouver is the end of things generally, in so far as the C.P.R. and the Dominion of Canada are concerned, and the end of our duties and responsibilities, as indicated by our tickets. We rejoiced in the final surrender of our tickets. A through ticket is a confining nuisance. So long as one has it, one is obliged to live up to its obligations to travel ; it is always staring out of one's pocket-book in any pleasant halting-place a mute ' Come on !' It was a pleasure to survey the Pacific Ocean in the full knowledge that though we fully intended to cross it in the course of time, it had no claims on us.

For we decided not to 'catch' the ship that was to bear us fleetly Nippon-ward in the fond imaginations of our relatives next day. Vancouver was an original town to Orthodocia, whose former municipal associations had at least three centuries of blue mould on them, and we tarried in that place a fortnight, which is the space between the sailings of the ships. If Orthodocia had travelled in the Western United States she would probably not have found Vancouver so remarkable a centre of enterprise ; but she had not. Therefore our infant prodigy burst upon her gloriously, with all the advantage of sharp contrast with her native Wigginton, and she found its accomplishments quite fascinating. 'Two years old,' she murmured, 'and eight thousand people ! Extraordinary !' And it was exhilarating to be in a place whose vigorous young vitality is so strong as to get into one's own blood somehow, and give it a new thrill, especially for sober-going Canadians, whose lack of 'go' has always been the scoff of their American cousins. Vancouver's enterprise was a revelation to Orthodocia, and she took to it in a manner which was a revelation to me. I think that any inquiring spirit who wanted information about the municipal history of Vancouver from the beginning could hardly fail to find most of the leading facts in her note-book—bridges, roads, new industries, commercial blocks and all. Whene'er we took our walks abroad, Orthodocia had a new point of interest to direct them to; but what charmed her most were the unbuilt city squares, still dotted with the stumps and green with the ferns of the forest which was here two years ago. She stood and watched the blue smoke curling up out of the hearts of those trunks in a manner which, conjoined with her frequent expressions of confidence in the future of Vancouver, gave me profound misgivings. One afternoon, while we were riding in the Park— which is really a British Columbian forest with a 'seven-mile

'ANY INQUIRING SPIRIT COULD HARDLY FAIL TO FIND MOST OF THE LEADING FACTS IN HER NOTE-BOOK.'

drive round it, where they show you trees fifty and sixty feet in girth, and the pale green moss hangs its banners everywhere between you and the far blue sky, and the grouse rises and the squirrels skip, and on the broad waters beside you whole fleets of wild duck sail within gun-shot—my misgivings were justified.

'I am going,' said Orthodocia, with a little air of decision, 'to invest.'

'You are not,' I replied, with calmness. 'I do not propose to bring the gray hairs of Mr. and Mrs. Love down in poverty as well as sorrow to the grave by countenancing any such mad proceeding. You are not.'

Whereupon Orthodocia began to discuss the scenery. I don't know a more aggravating thing than to have the person to whose views on any given subject you have just expressed the most determined opposition, abruptly turn the conversation into the channel of the scenery. I returned several times to the charge. I asked Orthodocia if she didn't know that people who invested always lost their money. I spoke of taxes and repairs, and drew a feeling picture of Mr. and Mrs. Love in connection with the Wigginton workhouse. I begged her to remember the South Sea Bubble, which was the only disastrous commercial enterprise that occurred to me at the time. Responsive to which, Orthodocia believed we should have rain!

Next morning Orthodocia introduced to me in the hotel corridor a person whom I knew at a glance to be a real estate agent. He was regarding Orthodocia in an interested way, and she was putting down figures in her note-book. He had gray hair, and he looked like a gentleman, but I was certain that this was superficial and that Orthodocia was being robbed. Remonstrances were useless at that point, however, so I retired with the air of a person who washes her hands of it. Later, when I had brought myself to the point of referring to the subject again, I said to Orthodocia: 'My dear lunatic, how much has that sharper induced you to throw away in town lots?' or words to that effect.

'Oh, I haven't bought yet,' she said airily; 'I was only making inquiries.'

I think five real estate agents sent up their cards to Orthodocia in the course of the next morning, and she saw them all politely and smilingly, with constant references to her note-book, coming up after each interview with a small excited spot of colour on each

'ISN'T IT DELIGHTFUL TO BE SITTING ON AN AMERICAN STUMP OF ONE'S VERY OWN?'

cheek, and much amusement in her eyes. But it was two days before she bought. 'I'll show you my lot,' she said, in a stroll before dinner—which was the first I had heard of it—and struck off into the cleared wilderness which then represented most of both sides of Granville Street. 'As far as I can tell it's somewhere about here,' and Orthodocia sat down on one of the neater stumps and made a comprehensive curve with her parasol. 'Isn't it delightful to be sitting on an American stump of one's very own?'

'I don't know,' I answered grimly. 'But you had better arrange to spend the rest of your time in Vancouver in the enjoyment of that peculiar satisfaction, for it is probably the only one you'll ever get out of your bargain.'

'I'm afraid I can't,' regretfully. 'You see it won't be mine. I'm going to sell it.'

'ARE you?' derisively. 'When? To whom? For how much?'

'You'll see,' answered Orthodocia cheerfully, gathering a scrap of flowering weed from her own property, and pressing it between the memoranda in her note-book.

Next day my practical young English friend from St. Eve's-in-the-Garden, Wigginton, Devon, whom I was to protect from extortionate cabmen and foolish bargains in curios, made a little addition to these memoranda. Then she explained them to me, very neatly and carefully, showing a net profit in the purchase and sale of her small stumpy lot of forty pounds.

Don't inquire of me how she did it. I didn't ask her. I only know that she bought of one real estate agent and sold to another, and that she was an object of interest to the guild from that time until we sailed. For me, I retired into nothingness, only meekly remarking that I supposed she would invest again, of course.

'No,' said Orthodocia thoughtfully. 'I believe not. You see I'll want such a quantity of tea-cups in Japan.'

VII

I'M afraid I must skip the trip from Vancouver to Yokohama. In the journey to Japan a disproportionate amount of time seems to be spent upon the Pacific Ocean. It is an outlay upon which there is no return, an inroad upon one's capital of days and weeks which does not justify itself in any way except in its unavoidableness. It makes a period of tossing chaos in one's life that must always stand for an indefinite number of missed experiences, and the only thing I have to say in favour of it is that the period is a week shorter from Vancouver than from San Francisco. There are some people who like sea voyages, long sea voyages. I do not, and I decline to write pleasantly of the Pacific Ocean. What I would like to do is to nothing extenuate, and to set down a great deal in malice. That I refrain is due not to any blandishments of an occasional day of fine weather on that misnamed body of water, but to the admonitions of a conscience born and brought up several thousand miles east of it.

Moreover, there is nothing to tell of this time during which nature is revealed to you all in tossing gray and white, framed in a porthole, and you note resentfully how perfunctory is the almond-eyed sympathy of the Chinaman who comes inconsequently into your cabin and goes illogically out and remarks between times, 'Welly sea-chick welly long time! Iss ship welly lolo!' Nothing, that is, that would interest anybody. Assuredly one does not sail across the Pacific to write accounts of the diversity of the scenery. I might tell you about ourselves, meaning the passenger list, but there were so few of us that we grew to criticise one another cordially before we sighted land, and I can't trust my impressions as being unprejudiced. I might talk of the books we had with us, but they were chiefly pirated editions of 'Robert Elsmere,' and I do not propose to add anything from what I heard about it to the accumulation of critical matter that already surrounds that remarkable work. I would suggest to intending travellers, however, that it is not quite the kind of fiction for a sea-voyage. It precipitates polemics, and there grows up a coolness between you and the person whose steamer-chair you find most comfortable. For the first four or five days I remember the atmosphere was blue with dogma of one sort or another, and there was a suggestion of aggrieved Calvinism in the way our only missionary threw the volume overboard. The mere possession of the book was enough to entitle people to vehement opinions of it, and this is fortunate, since for an ocean novel it is rather stiff reading. The critic amongst us most disputative of its positions was content to leave it at the bottom of his valise.

OUR LUGGAGE LABEL.

For incidents, there was the day the steward made almond-taffy, or 'toffee,' as Orthodocia had been brought up to pronounce it—the day we hemmed the captain's handkerchiefs—the day the Chinaman died and went to Nirvana, and was embalmed and put in the hold—the last day, when we learned the delicious, palpitating excitement of being twenty-four hours from the Land of the Rising Sun—the last day and the last night, when the moon danced in the rigging, and we sat in the very point of the bows together, Orthodocia and I, and wondered how we should ever get to sleep, and watched the grayer line against the sky where slept that strange Japan.

* * * * * * *

'Perhaps,' said I, 'it is the bill!'

'This is a European hotel,' remarked Orthodocia, scornfully. She stood in an apartment of the 'Grand' of Yokohama half an hour after we had landed. 'They wouldn't send their bills in Japanese. Besides, it's a little premature, I think. We haven't been in the country twenty minutes yet. But it may possibly be a form of extortion practised by that bobbing person with a full moon on his head that pulled us from the wharf in his perambulator. So far as I am concerned'—emphatically—'he shall not have another penny. I am under the impression now that *go-jiu-sen-go-rin* was altogether too much to give him. It sounds like the price of land in Lombard Street. You can do as you like.'

Thus privileged, I turned the bit of pasteboard over and read on the other side a legend in English to the effect that the gentleman downstairs represented a certain *shimbun* in Tokio. Now *shimbun* being interpreted means newspaper.

'Orthodocia,' said I, solemnly, 'this is no overcharge. It's something much worse. It's a reporter. We are about to be interviewed —in Japanese. If he succeeds in getting anything out of us, however, it will be extortion indeed.'

Orthodocia turned pale. 'He will demand impressions,' she

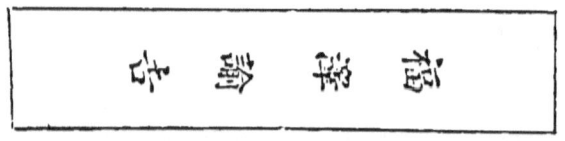

THE REPORTER'S CARD.

said. 'They always do. Have you got any convenient? Could you lend me one?'

We do not know to this day to what circumstance we owed the honour of appearing in print in Japan—whether we were mistaken for individuals of distinction, or whether we were considered remarkable on our own merits on account of being by ourselves; but we went downstairs fully believing it to be a custom of the country, a rather flattering custom, to which we were much pleased to conform; and this is a true chronicle of what happened.

It was a slender, round-faced youth who made his deprecating bow to us in the drawing-room. His shoulders sloped, his gray-blue kimona lay in narrow folds across his chest like what the old-fashioned people at home used to call a sontag. American boots were visible under the skirt of the garment, and an American stiff felt hat reposed on the sofa beside him. His thick short black hair stood crisply on end, and out of his dark eyes slanted a look of modest inquiry. He was the most unaggressive reporter I have ever seen. His boots and his hat were the only things about him that I could connect with journalism, as I had previously been acquainted with it.

'How do you do?' I said, seeing that the silence must be broken and the preliminaries gone through with by somebody.

'Yes!' he responded, with an amiability that induced Orthodocia to get up hurriedly and look out of the window. 'Did the radies arrive to the Duke of Westminster?' looking from one to the other of us.

'We believe they did!' gasped Orthodocia, and immediately looked out of the window again. I edged my chair toward the other window. Then the cloven foot appeared in the shape of a note-book. He produced it with gentle ostentation, as one would a trump card. The simile is complete when I add that he took it from his sleeve.

'How old is rady?' calmly, deliberately.

'I—I forget,' falsified this historian; 'forty-five, I believe.'

The reporter put it down.

'Other rady, your friend—not so old? Older? More old?'

'I am twenty-two years of age,' said Orthodocia, gravely, with a reproachful glance at me, 'and I weigh ten stone. Height, five feet eight inches. In shoes I am in the habit of wearing fives; in gloves, six and a half.'

The reporter scribbled convulsively.

'Radies will study Japanese porryticks—please say.'

'I beg pardon?'

'Yes.' Fills another page.

Orthodocia, suavely: 'Are they produced here to any extent?'

'We have here many porryticks—ribarer, conservative, monarchist.'

'Oh!' more recourse to the window.

'Orthodocia,' I said, severely, 'you may not be aware of it, but your conduct is throwing discredit upon a person hitherto fairly entitled to the world's good opinion—which is me. Continue to be absorbingly interested in that brick wall, and allow me to talk to the gentleman.'

'We have come,' I said, distinctly—Orthodocia bears testimony to the fact that I said it distinctly—'to see Japan as far as Japan will permit. Her politics, system of education, customs, and arts will be of—ahem—interest to us. We cannot truthfully say that we expect to penetrate more deeply into the national life than other travellers have done. In repressing this expectation we claim to be original. We confess that our impressions will naturally be super-

'HOW OLD IS LADY?'

ficial, but we hope to represent the crust so charmingly that nobody will ask for any of the—interior—of the—well, of the pie.'

'That's equivocal,' said Orthodocia, 'and ridiculous.'

'Notwithstanding the well-known reticence of the Japanese,' I continued, 'we hope to meet some of them who will show us something more of their domesticity than we can see through the windows.'

OUR JOURNEY ROUND THE WORLD

'You will acquire ranguage of Japan ?'

'Not all of it, I think. It seems a little difficult, but musical—much more musical than our ugly English,' interposed Orthodocia.

'Yes. Will you the story of your journey please say ?'

'Certainly. We came from Montreal to Vancouver by the C.P.R.—that is the best Western railroad on the continent because it is built with English capital,' bombastically. 'Some people say that you never would have heard of Canada in Japan but for the C.P.R., but I am told that they are mostly jealous Republican Americans'

The reporter bowed.

'We travelled three thousand nine hundred miles by this route across the North-West and through the Rocky Mountains.' Here Orthodocia dwelt upon the remarkable snow-sheds for protection against avalanches. She went on with vague confidence to speak of the opening up of trade between Canada and Japan by the new railway and steamship line, and I added a few remarks about the interest in Japanese art that existed in Montreal, and the advisability of the Japanese establishing firms of their own there; while the reporter flattered our eloquence by taking down notes enough to fill a quarto volume. We had never been interviewed before—we might never be again—and we were determined to make the occasion an illustrious one. We were quite pleased with ourselves as the nice little creature bowed himself out, promising to send us the fortunate *shimbun* which would publish the interview, with a translation of the same, a day or two later.

EXTRACT FROM REPORT OF INTERVIEW.

I suppose it was Orthodocia's effect upon him—the effect I had begun to find usual—but he didn't send the *shimbun*; he brought it next morning with much apology and many bows. I have before me a pencilled document in the handwriting of three persons. The document contains the interview as it was set down in the language of the translator, who sat with an expression of unruffled repose, and spake aloud from the *shimbun* which he held in his hand. Sometimes Orthodocia took it down, sometimes he took it down himself, sometimes I took it down while Orthodocia left the room. The reason for this will perhaps be self-evident. Orthodocia and I possess the document in turns, to ward off low spirits. We have only to look at it to bring on an attack of the wildest hilarity.

The reporter came entirely in Japanese costume the second time, and left his wooden sandals outside on the stairs. He left most of his English there, too, apparently, but he bowed all the way from the door to the middle of the apartment in a manner that stood for a great deal of polite conversation. Then he sat down and we sat down, and Orthodocia prepared to transcribe the interview which had introduced us to the Japanese nation from his lips. It was a proud, happy moment.

The reporter took the journal with which he was connected out of one of the long, graceful, flowing sleeves which make life worth living for masculine Japan. He told us that it was the *Hochi-Hochi-Shimbun*, and he carefully pointed out the title, date, beginning and end of the article, which we marked, intending to buy several copies of the paper and send them home. We were anxious that the people there should be kept fully enlightened as to our movements, and there seemed to be a great deal of detail in the article. Its appearance was a little sensational, Orthodocia thought, but she silently concluded, with her usual charity, not to blame the reporter for that, since he couldn't possibly be considered responsible for the exaggerations of the Chinese alphabet.

'Yesterday,' translated the reporter solemnly—I must copy the document, which does not give his indescribable pronunciation—'by Canada steamer radies arrived. The correspondent, who is me, went to Grand Hotel, which the radies is. Radies is of Canada and in-the-time-before of Engrand. They have a beautiful countenance.'

Here the reporter bowed, and Orthodocia left the room for the first time. I think she said she must go and get her pencil sharpened. She left it with me, however, and I took up the thread of the interview.

'Object of radies' rocomotion, to make beautiful their minds.' Miss Elder-Rady answered, "Our object is to observe habits, makings, and beings of the Japanese nation, and to examine how civirisation of Engrand and America prevails among the nation. And other objects is to examine the art and draw-

'HE BOWED ALL THE WAY FROM THE DOOR TO THE MIDDLE OF THE APARTMENT.'

ing and education from the exterior of the confectionery. In order to observe customs of Japan we intend to rearn a private house."'

We were getting on swimmingly when Orthodocia reappeared, having recovered in the interval, and told the reporter that he must think foreigners very abrupt and rude, and that he really spoke English extremely well. To both of which remarks he responded, with a polite suavity that induced me to turn my back upon her in an agony of suppressed feeling, 'Yes.'

'Miss Younger-Rady-measuring-ten-stone-and-wearing-six-shoes-and-a-half, continue, "The rai-road between the Montreal and Canada is passing——."'

'I beg pardon,' said the unhappy Orthodocia, with an awful galvanism about the corners of her mouth, 'I didn't quite catch what you said—I mean what I said.'

The reporter translated it over again.

'Perhaps,' said I, nervously, 'it's a misprint.'

'No,' the reporter replied gravely, 'Miss Younger-Rady.'

'Gracious!' said Orthodocia.

'And if by the rai-road we emproy the steamer, the commerce of Montreal and Japan will prevail. Correspondent asked to Miss Younger-Rady may I heard the story of your caravansery?'

Orthodocia again retired. It was a little trying for me, but when he continued, 'She answered, "From Montreal to Canada the distance is three thousand mires,"' I was glad she had gone. I am afraid I choked a little at this point, for just here he decided to wrestle with the pencil himself. When he handed the paper back again I read : 'While we are passing the distance between Mount Rocky I had a great danger, for the snow over the mountain is falling down, and the railroad shall be cut off. Therefore, by the snow-shade, which is made by the tree, its falling was defend. Speaking finish. The ladies is to took their caravansery attending among a few days. Ladies has the liability of many news.'

'That last item,' said Orthodocia, who had come in with the excuse of some tea, 'is frightfully correct.'

Having despatched the business of the hour and a half, the reporter began to enjoy himself, while Orthodocia and I tried to seat ourselves where we couldn't see each other's faces in the mirror over the mantelpiece. He drank his tea with his head on a level with the table, and if suction can express approval it was expressed. He said that there were fourteen editorial writers on his *shimbun*, and that its circulation was one million. Which shows that for the soul of a newspaper man Shintoism has no obvious advantages. He dwelt upon the weather for quarters of an hour at a time. The Japanese are such a leisurely people. He took more tea, by this time stone cold. He said he would bring a Japanese 'gentleman and rady' to see us, and in response to our inquiry as to whether the lady was the wife or the sister of the gentleman, he said with gravity, 'I do not know the rady's wife.' He asked us for our photographs, and when Orthodocia retired at this for the fifth time he thought she had gone to get them, and stayed until I was compelled to go and pray her to return. It was the ringing of the two o'clock lunch bell that suggested to him that the day was waning, and that perhaps he had better wane too.

I have told you about the reporter first, because in all the wonder of this quaint Japan, where one laughs more than anywhere else in the world, he was our earliest definite impression. We afterwards agreed that the next reporter who was to be taken in instalments should be regularly apportioned beforehand, to prevent mutual recriminations. We also decided never again to receive a native gentleman whose politeness would not permit him to go home within half a day without a Japanese phrase within easy reach which would put an end to his sufferings.

VIII

It was five o'clock of that November afternoon that found us mourning the progress of journalism in Japan, and the dusk was creeping out among the quaint-curving tiled roofs and sago palms that I was trying to sketch from the upper verandah of the Grand Hotel, Yokohama.

'Hurry!' said Orthodocia, 'or it will be pitch dark when we get there, and our Japanese is not fluent.'

We were going to Tokio. Now it does not particularly matter when one goes to Tokio from Yokohama. If it is advisable to go at one, and lunch is late, why, say two; if at two one's gloves are missing, three will do; if somebody calls at about that time there is no reason why one should not got at four. We had begun to go to Tokio, for example, when I became pencil-smitten of those clustering eaves two hours before, and our various portmanteaux were still lying restfully on the verandah beside us.

'What if it is!' I responded, indicating a chimney, 'you forget that they all speak English!'

It was our second day in Japan, and as we had been advised not to spoil the freshness of our impressions by seeing Europeanised Yokohama, we had not seen it, but had devoted our entire attention to recovering from the Pacific—and the reporter. Our acquaintance with the natives of that remarkable and interesting country had been limited, therefore, to the opportunities of the very European hostelry I have mentioned.

'I don't know,' said Orthodocia, thoughtfully, 'you can't believe everything you read. For instance, we haven't met a single Japanese carrying a fan yet, and I was under the impression that they never went out without them. I remember, however,' with a relieved expression, 'the jinrikisha man certainly swore in English with an admirable accent and idiom, and if the lower classes have acquired it so thoroughly, we may expect it as a matter of course among policemen and railway officials. A most extraordinary people!'

The manager of the hotel, the sole individual with whom we had a bowing acquaintance in the country, except our fellow passengers, who all with one accord sought opposite ends of it at once, had advised us strongly to secure immediately the services of a guide, which he said was the 'usual' thing to do. At these words I saw a peculiar expression attach itself to Orthodocia's under lip. It was a certain indrawing with which I had grown familiar, and it betokened decision.

'The "usual" thing being precisely the thing which we wish to avoid,' she said to me, 'I think we won't take the guide. Besides, we shall enter much more intimately into the national life, as *you* told the reporter we were going to do, if we come into personal contact with the people. Everybody knows, moreover, how thoroughly easy it is for English people to get on in foreign countries. "Soap" and "beefsteak" have been incorporated into every language on earth, and with soap and beefsteak you can't be *very* uncomfortable.'

So we provided ourselves on the spot with a small paper-covered book containing, we understood, a compendium of all that is useful and elegant in the Japanese language. From what we had read of the proficiency of the natives in our mother tongue, we would have expected rather to find it a 'Handbook of Popular Inaccuracies in English,' compiled by some one of them, which might have been of material use in the construction of this present history. But such as it was, we trusted it, and I sketched on.

Notwithstanding Orthodocia's professed faith in the ease and comfort of our trip to the Japanese capital, she required a great many assurances from me to the effect that the railway officials would be certain to speak English to be induced to let me finish my sketch. Finally, however, it was finished, and we rode with much joy to the station, had beautiful little Japanese labels which meant 'Tokio' put on each of Orthodocia's multitudinous boxes, and were seated in the train just as the last gleam of daylight departed, congratulating ourselves mightily upon our masterly management of our own affairs.

It was a good deal like travelling in a match-box, this first Japanese journey of ours. We were in a narrow-gauge little car, sitting on a narrow-gauge little seat running lengthwise, opposite a very small Japanese gentleman, whose native costume was crowned by a noble Oxford Street 'topper.' He held a Japanese newspaper in one hand and a cigarette in the other, and looked at us as if he had extracted quite all there was worth having in our civilisation. We wondered tremblingly if that was the paper containing the announcement that Orthodocia measured ten stone and wore six shoes and a half, and when he laid it down we tried to identify it; but that was impossible, since whichever way we looked at it it seemed to be upside down. Presently the engine gave a narrow-gauge little shriek, and we rattled off. It was dark, very dark indeed. Outside we could see only an occasional gleam of the water that covered the rice-fields, agricultural divisions about the shape and size of a schoolboy's slate. Occasionally we reached a group of bulbous yellow lanterns that swayed and danced and ran madly about at the will of shadows with flowing sleeves, and there we stopped for a moment, but never long enough to convince ourselves that this was Tokio and get out. When we did arrive at Tokio there was no mistaking it.

You will remember the individual pieces and the aggregate of Orthodocia's luggage. It is necessary that you should remember them, for I can't possibly take up my valuable space to the extent that would be necessary in order to enumerate them again. I merely wish to state that we had them all with us as the train arrived in Tokio, as well as my own modest impedimenta, to which a lady had added a small green trunk to be delivered to a missionary friend in Japan. It was a great pleasure to undertake the commission; I set down the incidents and accidents of that small green trunk in no spirit of reproach, but because they seemed at the time, and seem still, to have the importance of episodes to us. That small green trunk had been missing at the station in Montreal, had been left behind in Winnipeg, had caught up with us at Corona, been identified with difficulty at Vancouver, and had required the services of four able-bodied persons—the steward, the under-steward, the first mate, and a Chinaman—to track it to its lair in the hold when we arrived in Yokohama. As I said before, it was a pleasure to undertake that small green trunk, but by this time it had become a little wearing to the mind—anybody would have found it so. Our first anxiety, therefore, as we stepped out upon the broad, bright platform full of short gentlemen in long gowns, was as to the whereabouts of that erratic piece of luggage—whether it had finally come with us, or followed the natural bent of its vicious inclinations, and stepped off to spend the night at a tea-house somewhere on the way.

I will say of the several people whom we asked to show us the baggage-room that they all bowed, and some of them smiled, while one or two even looked concerned, but none of them appeared to have the slightest conception of what we wanted. One only regarded us unpleasantly. This was a fierce-looking little Jap, with a great many gold buttons exuberating over his person, to whom we confidently presented our luggage checks. He was an officer of the Imperial Household, and he did not take the checks. He did not even bow.

We began to find ourselves objects of increasing interest to these blue-petticoated travellers with nothing on their heads, who filled the station with the gentle, uneven, deprecating click of their multitudinous wooden sandals. Having come to see curios, not to represent them, we found the situation unaccountably reversed. It is a wise provision of nature that disposes the average young woman, by way of relieving her overstrained nerves, under circumstances particularly novel, to giggle. We giggled, and felt our circumstances less overpowering, whereupon the onlookers began to giggle too. We laughed outright—they laughed outright; and presently we stood in convulsions of mirth in the midst of a small multitude similarly convulsed. Then we remembered what we had been told of the extremely sympathetic nature of the Japanese. Just as Orthodocia was threatening hysterics and I was considering their probable effect upon the nation at large, I caught the gleam, under a lamp-post afar off, of a familiar object. It was the green trunk, and I do not over-express our activity when I say that we made for it. Of course the multitude made for it too, but we were oblivious to the multitude. It was not only the little trunk, but the big trunks and all the portmanteaux and bundles, and they were going on a succession

'ORTHODOCIA STERNLY SAT DOWN ON AS MANY OF THEM AS SHE CONVENIENTLY COULD.'

of trucks we knew not whither. We accompanied them, however, and when they were finally deposited within a certain railing Orthodocia sternly sat down on as many of them as she conveniently could, while I looked further for the English-speaking population of Japan. I took my little book, and walked into a room with a very large weighing-machine and several very small gentlemen in it. They were all in native costume, and one of them, an ancient person with many wrinkles, sat at a desk with a box of India ink and a brush before him, and a beaded frame like those the children learn the multiplication table on at home, which is the lightning calculator of Japan. They all bowed in an abject manner, and drew their breath in rapidly between their teeth—a Japanese politeness, I learned afterwards. If you try it you will see that it suggests physical distress, danger, at all events something wrong. I didn't know exactly what I had done that was incorrect, and as nobody seemed disposed to do me any bodily injury on the score of it, I selected the least decorated of the bowing uniforms this time, and presented our checks. Might we leave all our baggage there until to-morrow, but one portmanteau and a 'roll-up'?—pointing to it outside. The old gentleman got up and rustled out, inspected the pyramid, came back in perturbation of mind, made a wild demonstration on his frame and a picture of a rookery on a strip of paper with his brush, pushed his spectacles up on his forehead and looked at me. I repeated my request. Then the gentlemen all with one accord bowed, smiled, and said '*Hai!*' resuming the perpendicular and regarding me with curiosity while I looked in my little book and found '*Hai!*' to be an expression of assent. This was encouraging, so I went on. Might the small green trunk be sent immediately to the lady whose address I would give? '*Hai!*' Sweetness and light. Might I take the portmanteau in one jinrikisha, and my friend the shawl-strap in the other, to save jinrikisha fares? '*Hai!*' Beaming satisfaction at the arrangement.

'Then,' said I, with triumphant urbanity, 'will you send porters out there to bring in the luggage, and we will take what we want and leave the rest till to-morrow, when we shall have secured a permanent address?'

They all bowed and smiled again, and again they all said '*Hai!*'

but not one of them stirred. I began to lose faith in the monosyllable, picked out the smallest of the porters, turned him carefully round by his sleeve, and pointed outside. He departed instantly, and presently he reappeared with five of his brethren trundling a truck. The baggage was on the truck, and Orthodocia was on the baggage. 'I would not desert it,' she said, with pride. 'I thought they were emissaries of some hotel!'

Behold all the various pieces neatly and conclusively piled in a corner, the small green trunk and special portmanteau at the very bottom.

'You try him!' to Orthodocia.

'TURNED HIM CAREFULLY ROUND BY HIS SLEEVE, AND POINTED OUTSIDE.'

Orthodocia tries him—in Japanese, the authorised and corrected Japanese issued at Yokohama.

'These *two*'—Orthodocia, impressively—'we'll *keep*! Let me see'—with a wild excursion into the little handbook—'what's to "keep," to "want," to "possess"?—"*Arimas*"!—there now! These *two, arimas*! That small green trunk——'

'"Small" is "*skoshy*,"' I interrupt, 'and it is getting on towards midnight.'

'That *skoshy* green trunk you send by *jinrikisha*'—going to the window and pointing out several rows of these vehicles to explain to the Japanese what a *jinrikisha* is—'to Miss Robinson, Jo Gakko —savey? At once. Miss Robinson will pay jinrikisha!'

'There now!'—turning to me—'I flatter myself the matter is settled. But you see you were *quite* wrong in thinking we could approach these people in English!'

'Jo—Gak-ko!' repeats the old gentleman slowly and thoughtfully, stroking his chin; 'Jo—Gak-ko!'

Enter an intellectual-looking little Japanese in trousers, about whose English there could be, therefore, no doubt. A conference between him and his fellow-officials, who are beginning to look burdened with the cares of this world.

'Please write your speakings,' he says to me, and with a dawning hope I write my speakings, underlining the final destination of that *skoshy* green trunk, and the fact that Miss Robinson would be liable for all further charges thereupon. He looks at the speakings in an interested way, and there is a pause, during which the porters respectfully take each piece of luggage and weigh it, apparently for their own private satisfaction, for nothing else comes of it. The youth in trousers says something confidentially to the porters, and presently wishes to bow us to the platform where the jinrikishas are waiting. 'But the bag and shawl-strap!' we exclaim. 'Alright!' he answers suavely, 'I have give your informations.'

We suffer ourselves to be seated in two little hansoms leaning on their shafts at an angle of forty-five degrees with the pavement, which are the jinrikishas.

'*Sayonara!*' bows the gentleman in trousers, which means 'farewell.' '*Sayonara!*' exclaim all the rest, bowing in a last agony of amiability. '*Sayonara!*' says the old gentleman with the voluminous skirts and the spectacles, waving his calculator. And '*Sayonara!*' we politely reply.

'EACH PULLING AFTER US A SEPARATE PIECE OF OUR HATED AGGREGATE.'

In an instant we are whirling after a swift pair of brown legs into the gemmy darkness of the Japanese night, *sans* any portmanteau, *sans* any shawl-strap whatever. We look back in helpless reproach at the perfidious beings on the platform, and straightway are like to expire in inextinguishable laughter. For away behind us stretches a line of racing shadows, each pulling after us a separate piece of our hated aggregate, and bringing up the rear with a positive smile of malicious satisfaction, that unspeakable *skoshy* green trunk.

* * * * * * * *

Orthodocia was forbearing that night as she settled the jinrikisha bill, which was large. She said nothing at all at the time, but later, when, in response to her request for a towel, they brought her a nice bowl of hot rice, she could not help remarking, in a casual way, 'They all speak English—don't they ?'

IX

WE would keep house.

It arose in us suddenly and simultaneously, this feminine instinct, as we rode through a sunny street in Tokio next morning, and would not down. The experience would be valuable to us, we agreed. We might even make it valuable to other people by starting a domestic reform movement, when we went home, based on the Japanese idea. Life amounts to very little in this age if one cannot institute a reform of some sort, and we were glad of the opportunity to identify ourselves with the spirit of the times. We were thankful, too, that we had thought of a reform before they were all used up by more enterprising persons, which seems to be a contingency not very remote.

Moreover, though of course this was a secondary consideration, we could not help thinking that it would be something of a joke. Naturally not a very great joke, since it must occur in a Japanese house, but a piece of pleasantry that would not take up too much room, and be warranted to go off without annoying the neighbours. We had kept a dolls' establishment before, and it would be interesting to renew our extreme youth by doing it again, this time in the capacity of the dolls. Perhaps, too, we could get a more satisfactory idea of the national life if we sat on the floor for our point of view. And straightway we went to look at three modest domiciles from which the householders had gathered up their cushions and departed.

We rode several miles to the first, through endless wandering narrow streets of little constructions so like the one we went to see that Orthodocia declared it would be fully a year before we could avoid the most shocking intrusions by mistake. It looked in its unpainted grayish-brown wooden personality like something between a small

North American barn and a large South American bird's-nest. It was a good deal overcome by its heavy tiled roof, which it wore helplessly crowded down over its eyes like an old hat much too big. It was one of a series that climbed at intervals up the side of a diminutive mountain, and a good deal of the mountain was attached to the premises. We could go out every morning and watch the sun rise from an altitude considerably higher than our own roof by simply ascending our back yard. I use that term with a sense of its vulgarity in the Japanese connection.

The back yard in the American sense is as completely unknown to Japan as the empty lobster-can that usually decorates it.

A serious drawback to the eligibility of this house was the fact that the cook would run the risk of inundating a landscape garden, which had a beautiful lake in it as large round as a wash-tub, every time she threw out a pail of water. We could not live in constant dread of being swept into one of the neighbouring moats by such a casualty, which might occur any day. True, there was a bamboo bridge over the lake, but we could not count with any certainty on escaping that way. There was a gray and mossy stone watch-tower also where we might have hoped to take refuge, if either of us had been able to get into it. It commanded a beautiful view of all the scenery that went with the house. There

'AS WE RODE THROUGH A SUNNY STREET IN TOKIO.'

were avenues of tea plants and forests of rose bushes, while here and there a solitary camellia lifted its proud and lonely head in the midst of a rocky waste at least two feet square. We never could sit under our vine and fig-tree; we would be altogether fortunate if we avoided stepping on them. The vine was a wisteria trained gracefully over an arbour almost as large as a wood-box, and the fig-tree was an ancient pine, the topmost boughs of which waved quite three feet above their native Japan. We felt that to rent that garden would be to live out 'Alice in Wonderland' daily. Nevertheless, we did not take it. It seemed too much occupied when we were in it.

The next house had no garden but three chrysanthemums and a well curb. These, however, were so disposed as to give quite an arboreal effect to the front door and dispel the commercial air of the neighbourhood, which was redolent of many things. The red and green and blue scales of a fish-shop glinted on one side of us, on the other little yellow piles of oranges and persimmons, opposite, the limp contents of a poulterer's establishment. A yard or two of octopus, a pink-billed heron, a monkey cutlet would be within our reach for breakfast any morning we chose to put our heads out of the window and order them. The house was wedged in between two 'godowns,' fireproof storehouses, black, heavy-walled, many-shuttered, not unpicturesque, which the average newcomer to Japan takes at once to be temples. This minimised its chance of sharing the fate of the generality of Tokio houses—cremation every seven years. It maximised the rent, however, and did not induce us to take the house. As Orthodocia said, the provision would be of no benefit to us, since we had not the slightest intention of staying seven years.

I am afraid you must allow me the present tense again for our housekeeping in Japan. To live a week in Tokio is to forget entirely how one got there, and to write about it is to disbelieve that one has ever come away. The great purple stretches of the prairies are blurred like a badly-washed water-colour in my recollection now, our gallant mounted policemen are uniformed in flowing *kimonos* with hieroglyphics on their backs, the Blackfeet carry on fan flirtations, the Rockies form a dissolving chain of Fusi-Yamas, and even the Great Glacier, as I try to think about it, folds itself up and retires behind a lacquered screen in my imagination. There may be such a continent as America, where the inhabitants build for themselves hideous constructions of red brick and stone, sit down in them on four stiff legs instead of two flexible ones, and have never learned to put a flower in a vase—one may even have spent some part of a previous existence there, but one is quite willing to accept proofs to the contrary. There is a possibility of reality too in your big London with its shuffling multitudes. But there is nothing certain any more in the world except these pale half-lights that fall on the blackened tiles of the curving roofs of Tokio, creeping up to the faint yellow sky of a November evening, nothing but the swaying drops of light that begin to reel across the moats, where the dark water under the arched bridges catches and holds them undissolved for a fleet moment, nothing but a queer white castle in a gnarled tangle of fantastic pine trees, a pair of illogical liquid brown eyes, a great gray stone image seated silent in a silent grove.

Our Tokio address is Fuji-Mi-Cho, Ni-Cho-Mi, San-Jiu-Banchi, Kudan, Kojimachi, Tokio—a great deal of locality for the size of the house. When we have time and feel statistical, we intend to compute how often our address, if written out in full on strips of paper half an inch wide, would go round our residence. It is a decidedly aristocratic locality. A moat runs opposite, beyond a wide smooth street, a moat with curving bridges and walls of huge stone blocks fitted together without mortar, and green embankments where the Japanese pine trees stretch their low flat dragon-like branches in marvellous dark greens. And beyond the moat rise the heavy curved roof and dead white walls of the Mikado's new palace, all gorgeous and European within, which His Imperial Majesty cannot yet be induced to enter, doubtless preferring still the mats and fire-pots of his infancy. Plain two-storey barracks with His Majesty's gold chrysanthemum blazing on them stretch in several directions, and all day long companies of small soldiers march past, wearing their European jackets still a little slouchily, but stepping forth with the most approved martial ferocity. Now and then a Japanese officer trots by on horseback, erect, stern, sitting splendidly in a magnificent uniform, and morning and evening the oddly familiar notes of the bugle float over the dark water and across the

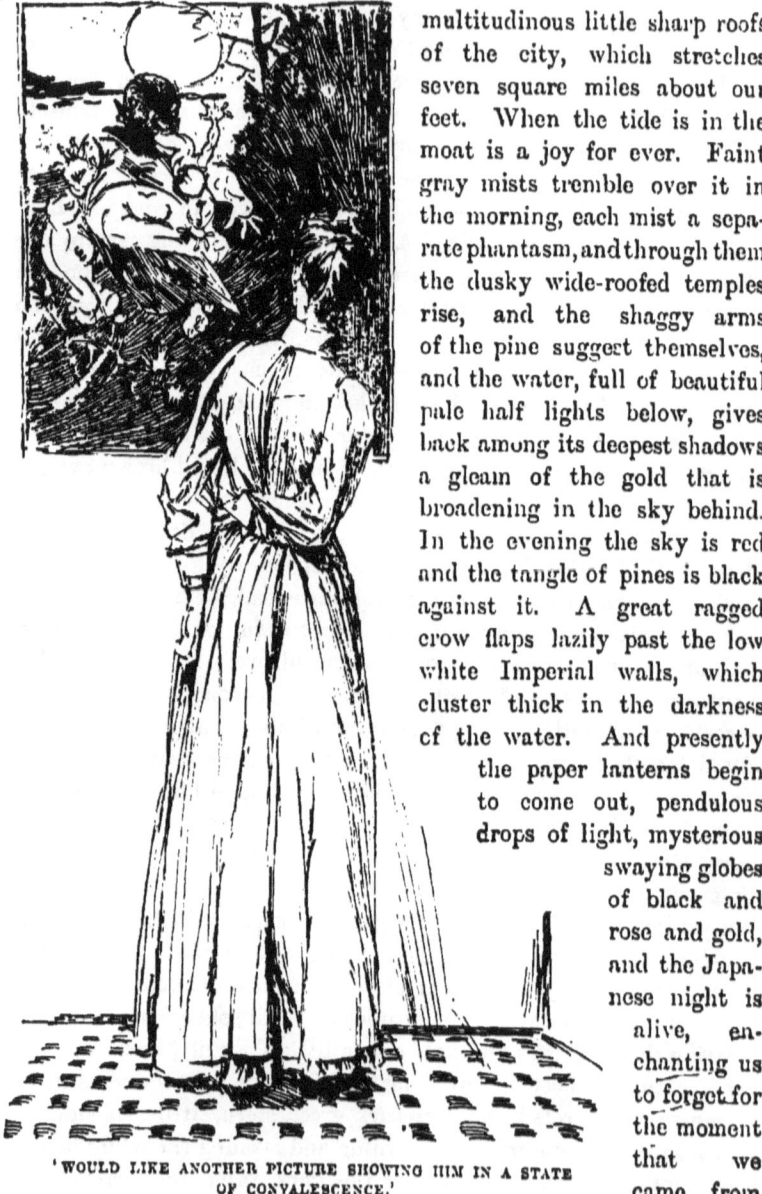

'WOULD LIKE ANOTHER PICTURE SHOWING HIM IN A STATE OF CONVALESCENCE.'

multitudinous little sharp roofs of the city, which stretches seven square miles about our feet. When the tide is in the moat is a joy for ever. Faint gray mists tremble over it in the morning, each mist a separate phantasm, and through them the dusky wide-roofed temples rise, and the shaggy arms of the pine suggest themselves, and the water, full of beautiful pale half lights below, gives back among its deepest shadows a gleam of the gold that is broadening in the sky behind. In the evening the sky is red and the tangle of pines is black against it. A great ragged crow flaps lazily past the low white Imperial walls, which cluster thick in the darkness of the water. And presently the paper lanterns begin to come out, pendulous drops of light, mysterious swaying globes of black and rose and gold, and the Japanese night is alive, enchanting us to forget for the moment that we came from a land where illumination is measured by thousand-candle power and 'turned on.'

Our house has a wooden fence around it which reaches to the second storey. There is a swinging gate in the fence, which will admit us if we take our hats off. From the outside our habitation cannot be described as attractive. It is much too retiring. Within the fence the house proper disappears again behind a sort of shuttered shell, which is closed up at night, making our domicile blankly unresponsive to the public eye. Orthodocia declares that domesticity in a house like this ought to be warranted to keep in any climate. And yet divorce is very common in Japan.

Come inside. The vestibule, you see, is about the size of a packing-box; we are careful never to turn round in it. A pair of ladder-like little stairs go straight up in front of you. The slide to the right leads to the kitchen—ah, the kitchen!—the slide to the left into the drawing-room. This apartment is neatly furnished with a picture. The picture represents a hermit in a severe spasm, blowing a little imp out of him. Orthodocia says that in the same room with that hermit you really do not feel the need of ordinary drawing-room garnishings. He is so tremendously effective. But I would like another picture showing him in a state of convalescence. Part of the walls are plastered and part of heavy paper panels. The plastered part runs two feet and a half round the room at the top and all the way down one side, and is coloured a soft dull brown. The panels reach from the plaster to the floor, and are in delicate shades of biscuit-colour, decorated in silver. One of the most graceful has rice straw waving over it in little bunches. The plastered side has two recesses divided by a bit of partition finished with the natural trunk of a quince tree polished a deep reddish brown. The recesses are the same height as the panels, and along the inside of one of them, at the top, runs a dainty cabinet with sliding doors of pale blue, also decorated in silver. On the cedar floor below it Orthodocia has placed a single vase with two or three camellias in it. This is very Japanese. The other recess we have desecrated with a small American stove—profane but comfortable. The ceiling is in strips of natural wood delicately marked, of a lighter colour; the floor is covered with thick, soft yellowish straw mats, bound with blue cloth and joined together so as to make an artistic design, and the windows are simply panels divided into little panes and covered with the thinnest, most porous white paper. A very pleasant subdued light comes through them. The window panels slide in grooves like the others, and the whole house is intercommunicative; that is to say, if Orthodocia stands in the vestibule and strikes a match, I can tell in the seclusion of our remotest apartment on the next flat whether it lights or not. If you come upstairs you must wait until I get to the top to be out of danger of my heels. The steps are smooth and polished, and very pretty to look at, no doubt, but it is a little trying to be obliged to take off one's slippers every morning and throw them to the bottom to avoid descending *à la* toboggan. Our two small bedrooms are slightly less ornate repetitions of the *salon* below, only that the sliding panels in various places disclose cupboards.

'JAPANESE MAIDEN WHO LIVES BEYOND THE CAMELLIA HEDGE.'

In one you see, neatly rolled away, the Japanese quilted *futons* of our nightly repose, in another the requisites of the toilet, in another a wardrobe, which represents Orthodocia reduced to her lowest denomination. We do not yet know our resources in cupboards, or the precise walls to take down to go into any special apartment, and are constantly discovering new ones by getting into them by mistake. Yes, we have our domestic difficulties —no household however humble is without them—but those you must hear another time. Shall I try to be polite to you in Japanese?

Be good enough to favour our poor domicile by taking a mat. Doubtless your honourable feet are tired. This tea is worthless indeed and green, yet deign to moisten your gracious lips with it, and make the cup a heirloom in the family.

Listen! That gentle melancholy twanging, ceasing, beginning, beginning, ceasing, with plaintive indetermination—that is a Japanese maiden who lives beyond the camellia hedge playing upon her *samisen*. You cannot see her, the leaves are too thick, but the timid minor notes come over two or three at a time, and bring us a fantastic sadness.

You must be going? Ah, is it not well not to speak so? There is nothing under our humble roof that could possibly please you, yet is it not well to wait a little? *So desuka!*[1] *Sayonara!* then— *sayonara!*

[1] Is it so indeed?

X

A GREAT boom through the darkness about our little house on the hill of Kudan. Soft and slow it swept around us and past us and out over the sleeping city—the muffled bell of the Buddhist temple. I heard it in the Nirvana of my dreams, and woke to the agreeable discovery that I was still human and sinful. Neither had Orthodocia, peaceful on the floor beside me, degenerated into the caterpillar which I had found so appropriate as her final state because she was always behindhand. Then I slept again, and walked with Buddha in a sacred grove and priced ricebowls under a bamboo tree. . . . And this was he who stood in dark flowing robes beside our very lowly couch, with one hand outstretched and something luminous in the other.

AN ELDERLY PARTY.

'*Tegami!*' said the figure, '*Tegami!*'

I closed my eyes and then I rubbed them, for instead of fading away after the manner of people in dreams, Buddha still stood with a halo round him saying persistently '*Tegami!*'

'It's the cook,' remarked Orthodocia, suddenly; 'and he's got a letter.'

It was four o'clock in the morning, and the first mail for the day had just been delivered by a postman running at the top of his speed. For a nation disinclined to exert itself, this seemed enterprising. We discovered afterwards that the telegraph system was one of extreme leisure.

OUR JOURNEY ROUND THE WORLD 85

'The dawn seems to be delayed,' remarked Orthodocia after several naps and further conversation; 'I wonder what has occurred!'

Hours had elapsed and the faint gray light that hung about one corner of the room still sufficed only to make darkness visible. 'Let

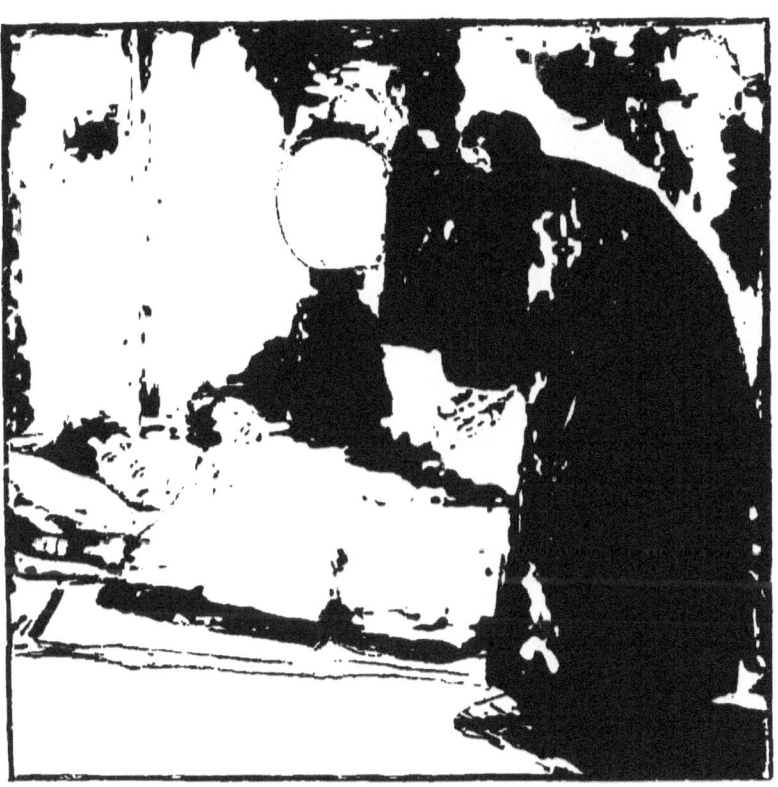

'TEGAMI.'

us inquire!' I said, and clapped my hands. It is one of the advantages of a Japanese house that your commands reverberate in every quarter of it. Presently the wall opened, and a glossy black head appeared in the light it let in. The head was arrayed in a pattern very like the trefoil conventionalised, with an admixture of pink beads and a rather warlike array of hairpins. It surmounted a shrinking little plump figure that stole across the floor, let itself out through the window wall, did a little mysterious pushing and sliding in the passage outside, and in a moment our small apartment was flooded by the yellow sunlight of ten o'clock.

We were thus introduced to the second of our domestics. We did not know how many there were. Our landlord, who was an obliging man, had engaged them for us. Her name was Kiku, which being interpreted is 'Chrysanthemum.'

We dressed, assisted profusely by Kiku, who surveyed each of our garments as she took it out of the wall with an expression of awed humility. Our toilet requisites were also very interesting to her, and she brought Orthodocia a spoon to take her tooth-powder in. We stepped out of the window for a moment to admire the view, and when we stepped in again, bed and bedclothes, pitcher and basin, everything had vanished into the all-capacious walls, and Kiku stood smiling in the middle surveying the work of her hands. We began to understand the time-hallowed emotions of Old Mother Hubbard.

KIKU.

We descended to the next floor, going downstairs backward with care, as we had fortunately been educated to do on board the steamer coming over ; and Orthodocia decided to explore the kitchen, while I took a mat where my foreign personality would best balance that of the American stove, and gave up my soul to the contemplation of the essence of things as expressed in the family porcelain. She rejoined me almost immediately with a blanched countenance.

'I can't get in,' she said. 'In fact I don't in the least see how they got it.'

Cockroaches instantly flashed upon me, and I gathered up my skirts as I went to the scene of her retreat. But cockroaches would have been uncomfortable in that apartment, it was so full of our domestics. They arranged themselves in a semicircle on their hands and knees at our appearance, each describing a respectful arc with himself by touching his forehead to the floor, and remained in that position until we thought we ought to retire for fear of giving them a rush of blood to the head. This attention was so embarrassing, after the demeanour of the *chargé d'affaires domestiques* of our previous experience, that we bowed politely in return, walked backward a little, bowed again and finally fled. But before we went we counted seven, and the jinrikisha man was outside. The landlord came in presently and explained their use and price per head. There was the cook, Buddha, of a serene countenance, at three *yen* (dollars) a month, who should prepare our modest repasts, and a sub-cook at two who would prepare his and those of our retinue generally. There was Kiku who would wait upon us in a silk dress at one *yen* ; Tomi who would sweep and dust for seventy-five *sen* (cents) ; Jokichi, her son, who would at two *sen* an errand run errands ; Yoshitane-san, who was a youth of family, culture, and education, but would be honoured to wash our dishes for us if we would supply his food and converse with him occasionally, for the sake of learning English. And there was an elderly party without any teeth, whose round brown face went into a mass of merry wrinkles when he laughed, who seemed to be of general utility, but no particular use, and who did not even stipulate for the language in return for his services, although English is the chief end of every man in Japan. All he asked was rice every day and fish once a week, and his bow was the longest and lowest of all. He had practised it all his life—it was a masterpiece of self-annihilation. He did acquire one word during the week of his sojourn with us. Listening carefully to an object lesson of mine with the cook one morning, he respectfully repeated 'spuhnn' beneath his breath.

After that he mumbled 'spuhun' at intervals every day with great satisfaction to himself, occasionally reverently picking up the subject of his remarks to look at it. I regretted very much the necessity of parting with him when we decided to reduce our staff; he was so cheerful and decorative in general effect. But somebody was always upsetting him and he had to go. As he tied up his handkerchief, made his last bow, and trotted off, he looked back at us regretfully, and murmured 'spuhnn.'

The wall of our dining-room opened on the street. We had decided to use it for this purpose on that account, although it was difficult for both of us to sit down there at the same time. To sit down in the Japanese way is to distribute one's self so largely. We did not dine there often, however, because of the inclemency of the weather. Opening as it does on the street, our dining-room had so much weather in it as a rule that we never thought of consulting the thermometer—another advantage which no Japanese house is without. We discovered it early on that experimental and memorable day, and ordered luncheon in the *salon*, where sat the American stove, and radiated heat, and hideousness, and home associations. Buddha had been engaged on the strength of his acquaintance with English and with foreign cooking. He looked acquiescent when we gave our instructions; followed us into the parlour, and sat down on his heels.

'Explain to him,' said Orthodocia, 'that we will discuss Treaty Revision after breakfast.'

I endeavoured to do this. Buddha immediately took the first position for a somersault and remained in it.

'We may as well discourage him in that practice first as last,' remarked my friend and fellow-housekeeper, hungrily. 'It is comforting to the æsthetic sensibilities, but otherwise unsatisfying. Also monotonous and a waste of time. I did not come to Japan to play leap-frog.'

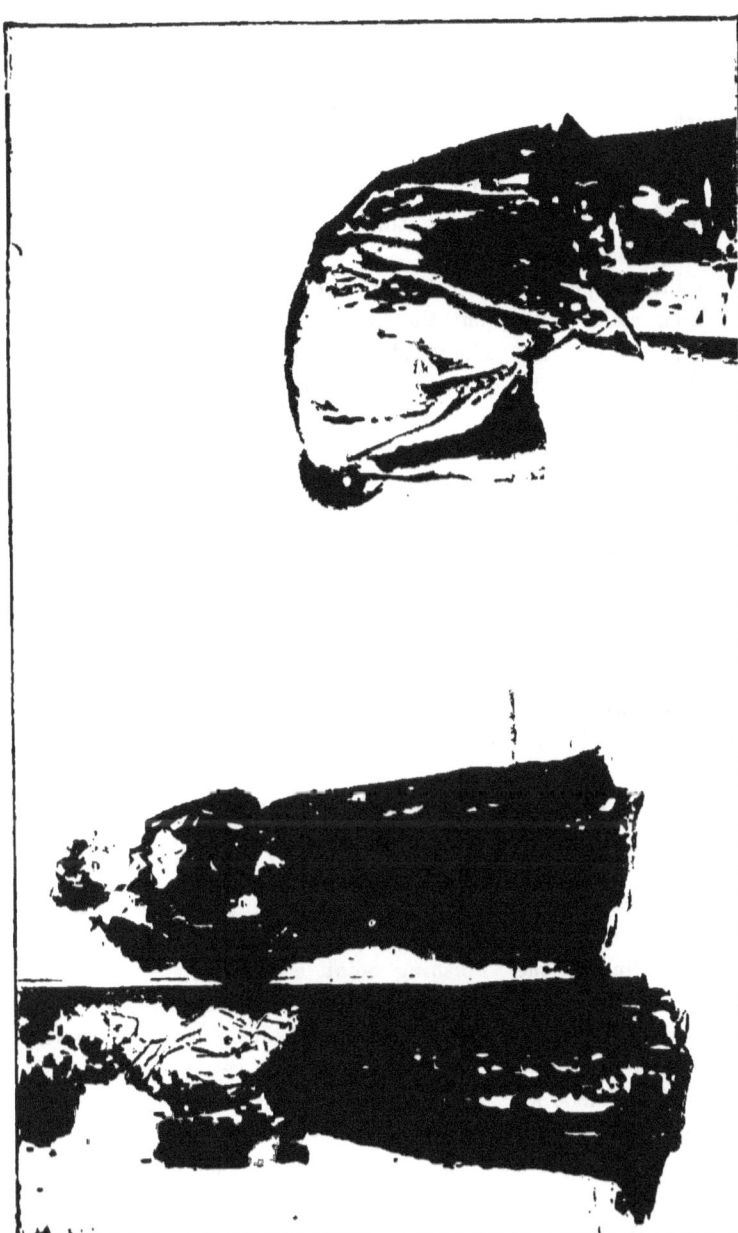

'I DID NOT COME TO JAPAN TO PLAY LEAP-FROG.'

'We want breakfast immediately,' I urged.

Buddha sucked his breath in between his teeth, and dusted the mat with his forelock in another place.

'Lunch-dinner-tiffin-food, right off!' put in Orthodocia, desperately. 'There, you see! I made him understand,' as he apologetically got up and went out. 'Nothing like being plain and forcible with the heathen intellect!'

Buddha reappeared presently with his arms full of wood and a fan. Then we observed that the fire had taken advantage of our excitement to go out. The wood was neatly arranged in bundles fifteen inches long and eight thick. You could hold five of the logs on your outstretched palm without dropping a splinter. The fan had a young moon in one corner, some clouds having been spilled on the same side. Buddha put two pieces of wood in the stove, lighted them with some kindling exactly the size and shape of visiting cards, which he took from his sleeve, sat down in front of it, and fanned it with a grace that might have been the result of a long ball-room experience. Then he turned calmly about on his heels and said, with the air of one who makes a humble suggestion, 'Chow now?'

Buddha's vocabulary, as we learned afterward, was beautiful in its simplicity and wonderful in its expressiveness. It consisted in little more than the single term, affirmatively, negatively, and interrogatively applied, 'Chow now.'

Chow then by all means we said, and while we waited for it Orthodocia recklessly piled our entire provision of fuel for the winter into the stove at once.

Our festive board appeared on a tray, borne by the faithful Buddha, and followed by Kiku, and Tomi, and Jokichi, and the others in a line to the vanishing point, each with a small black lacquered bowl covered by a saucer to correspond on another tray. Buddha went down on his knees, and so did the sub-commissioners. He presented us each with a shiny red wooden vessel and a pair of chop sticks. Removing the lid we discovered rice.

I prefer to make a hiatus here in my description, which you may fill in with the chop-sticks. I hope you will not find it as difficult in imagination as we did in fact. I do not wish to discourage beginners in Japanese housekeeping, but I am bound to say that before approaching a practical hiatus, or real life void of any kind with chop-sticks, practice is absolutely necessary. After our fruitless struggle with these implements our attention was invited to extremely minute cups of pale green tea, accompanied by red and white sugar bubbles, which melted away in our mouths leaving an impression of the family medicine chest. Bowls of soup with fish in it followed. The fish we speared very elegantly with our chop-sticks, the soup we were reluctantly compelled to drink.

Then came pieces of a fowl that never flew on sea or land, with preserved cherries and sugared beans. Sheets of pale green seaweed formed the next course. Then limp and cold and flabby, liberally dosed with pungent brown *soy*, the Japanese *pièce de résistance*. We found the rest of it in the kitchen afterward, looking very uncomfortable in a pail of water, and astonished Buddha by requesting that it should be killed and boiled for the next meal. He is probably still contemptuous of the foreign taste which prefers dead fish.

A delicate pink saucer was then presented to us, containing round slices of lilac-coloured vegetable matter with holes in it—the root of the lotus. It had a rubber consistency in the hand, and a soapy suggestion in the mouth. 'Lovely culinary conception!' said Orthodocia, 'take it away!' And we decided that we did not care for boiled poetry.

We paused at the lotus. It had seemed a lengthy and elaborate repast, and yet we were conscious of a sense of incompleteness, a vagrant and uncared for gastronomic feeling. We remembered a beautiful piece of scenery near the Seyo Ken restaurant, and went for a walk.

I think I have reached a point in the history of these untrammelled wanderings of Orthodocia's and mine where it is my obvious duty to state, for the benefit of that large and altogether worthy class of persons who expect a measure of instruction in every printed thing, that instruction was entirely a secondary object with us, and must therefore be at least a twenty-secondary object with those whom Orthodocia is pleased to call 'our readers.' Occasionally since, in certain uplifted moments—when passing the British Museum, for instance—we have been conscious of a poignant regret that this should have been the case. It would have been 'something,' as Orthodocia mourned to me one day, to be able to confront that institution with a practical, working, world-acquired knowledge of the antecedents of all the facts exposed to public ignorance in its glass cases. That struck me as ambitious. When, however, not long ago, in the course of some peaceful cups of tea, a certain impressive dame fixed me with her glassy eye, and asked me the number of cubic feet in the Pyramid of Cheops, and whether it was true that the Israelites built it, I confess that I should like to have known, just to have been able to suppress her polite inquiry as to what we went round the world *for*! I was obliged to say then, as I am obliged to say now, that we went chiefly to be amused, which probably would not have been—elaborate sarcasm—her object; an aim which you may find as unsatisfactory as she did. Perhaps, though, if we had stayed in the house and studied the Japanese classics, we might have missed a sunset from the hill of Kudan; if we had devoted more time to Shintoism we might not have gone to Mr. Takayanagi's garden party, and Mr. Takayanagi's garden party—but I anticipate.

We had been keeping house in Kudan in unalloyed felicity for two days. By shutting ourselves up in them by mistake, and taking down the wall on the other side, we had discovered most of our cupboards. We had learned to sit upon flat square velvet cushions in the middle of the floor, admire our painted hermit and our single vase, and congratulate ourselves on the convenience of the Japanese furniture idea which, leaving nothing to be possessed, leaves nothing to be desired. Dignities and classifications in the matter of our apartments were purely arbitrary. The sideboard and the diningtable and the piano being a-wanting, and the bed and toilet arrangements put securely away in the wall, we might sleep in the dining-room, dine in the *salon*, and receive in the bedroom with equal comfort and propriety. Our house did its whole duty in encouraging a taste for simplicity and keeping the rain out. It must be confessed that this palled upon us in the course of time, and I remember Orthodocia declaring one day that she took an intellectual comfort out of the bath-room which all the decorative essences of the six-foot drawing-room did not afford, on account of its distinct local peculiarity—which consisted in the bath. I must be allowed to wander still further while I describe that bath-room. You have nothing at all like it in England.

It opened off the drawing-room, to begin with, which is somewhat unusual, and 'gave' on the back yard. Considering the absence of glass and shutter, it gave immoderately on the back yard. It was protected from the winds of heaven by little wooden bars a few inches apart, and a paper pane that slid over these. One required a chair to climb into the bath, which was an imposing structure, as they say of municipal buildings in Western America, something like a wood box, with a funnel at one end for charcoal, to heat the water. We no sooner saw this remarkable contrivance than we were seized with a simultaneous yearning to get into it. But we had not read Miss Bird for nothing—how the Japanese made an elaborate ceremonial of the bath, each entering it in turn, but the most honourable first—and we had pledged ourselves, on artistic grounds, to be as Japanese as possible. We produced towels at the same moment and then looked at each other.

'You first!' said I, politely, bowing and drawing my breath in between my teeth in a manner that would have graced the Court of the Mikado.

'*Après vous!*' returned Orthodocia, with the same etiquette, indicating the bath-room with a stately wave of her towels. But I would not be constrained, and after a while Orthodocia, feeling unequal to further politeness on muscular grounds, went to order her bath. The commotion that immediately followed showed us that we had laid no light command on our household. Preparation was to be made for a function. Our retinue received the order with becoming decorum on their knees, and conversed upon the subject of it in awed tones in the kitchen. Then one by one its members filed into the bath-room with pails and pitchers and bamboo dippers, and cups and teapots full of water, which they emptied in solemn conclave into the bath. Issued forth Buddha, of serene countenance, went on all-fours to Orthodocia, and touched the floor with his forehead.

'Get up, Buddha,' said Orthodocia, amiably. 'What do you want?'

'Charcoal *arimasen*,'[1] communicated Buddha, with a depressed smile.

'Take coal, then!'

'*Hai!*' said Buddha, radiantly. 'Coal muchee smell *arimas*'[2] —doubtfully.

'Coal!' said Orthodocia, imperiously. 'Take coal.'

'You should never argue with servants about these things,' she remarked to me. And he took coal.

I suppose it was three-quarters of an hour after this command was issued that I heard my name from the bath-room in accents of the liveliest distress, alternating with high-pitched commands of '*Ikemasho!*'[3] I thought, as I sat down near the top of the stairs and descended them in my hurry in this manner, of the stories I had heard of the Japanese climate sending people mad, and I hoped that my friend's would be only a temporary aberration. The mere mention of what I saw when I got down is enough to bring on strained relations between Orthodocia and me to this day. I don't at all know what she will say when she sees it in print. Thin curls of smoke were issuing from behind the closed paper panels of the bath-room, and before them knelt our whole retinue, attracted by the voluble anguish within, each with one eye immovably glued to the small round hole which he or she had made with a wet finger for purposes of observation; and my unhappy friend told me afterwards that the jinrikisha man was at the window. As she heard me coming, Orthodocia's plaints grew louder. 'The water is nearly boiling!' she wailed. 'They won't *ikemasho*, and I can't get out till they do! And there's something the matter with the chimney of this bath—it smokes! And there's no way of turning the heat off! Ah—ow!' Convulsive splashings, and wilder cries of '*Will you ikemasho!*'

Buddha got up deferentially and helped me with the panels. 'Coal muchee smell *arimas*,' he remarked. '*Ok' san*[4] no like?'

I let myself into an atmosphere three parts smoke and one part steam, and a temperature of, I should say, 110 degrees, through which my unfortunate travelling companion's head loomed over the

---

[1] I have not. [2] Has.
[3] Go away! [4] Young lady.

side of the bath-tub like a large red moon. 'I'm only parboiled,' she gasped, 'but in three minutes more I should have been quite done.'

I wrapped her up in a dressing-gown and she escaped ; and then I choked heroically in a struggle with a funnel full of burning coal, the Japanese language, and the fire-brigade which arrived meanwhile to put out the conflagration. For an intellectual effort I commend the attempt to assure an anxious and active fire-brigade of Tokio, with the smoke pouring out of your doors and windows, that your house is not on fire—in Japanese.

Orthodocia was much hurt that I declined to conform to the best Japanese usage by going in immediately after her ; but I felt that my knowledge of statics was to be depended upon only in connection with a tap. We had the pleasure of seeing the proper etiquette observed by the whole of our household, though, who followed each other one by one, observing grave and respectful precedent, into Orthodocia's tub. Yoshitane-san first, old 'Rice-and-Saki-Only' next, and a fat little Chrysanthemum last of all. I don't think Orthodocia ever went into that bath-room again—she used to say the associations of the place were too painful—and, as I said, in order to create a coolness between myself and my friend to-day, I have only to remark, 'Coal muchee smell *arimas* ! *Ok' san no like* ?'

XI

BUT, as I was saying, we had been keeping house just two days on the hill of Kudan, when the invitation came to Mr. Takayanagi's garden party. It came with loud ceremonious rappings at our outer wall and many respectful bows and parleyings between the messengers and Buddha, who finally brought it in to us on a saucer—the only card-receiver we were ever able to persuade him to use. It was a large, square, thick white envelope, and our instincts cried 'Invitation!' before we drew out the card. It was printed in Japanese, however, address and all, with a gilt crest on top which might have been a pine-apple rampant, and our instincts were not equal to the translation. We turned eagerly to our *chargé d'affaires*. 'Dinner or dance or *what*, Buddha?' cried Orthodocia, thrusting it into his hand. Buddha contemplated it for a moment or two with awed humility. Then he said with the usual suction, 'Takayanagi-san —house.' As to who Takayanagi-san might be, or where his house was, or what was going to happen in it, not a syllable of light could Buddha afford us, though we plied him diligently. So there we were in the enviable position of being invited to a delightful Japanese something, we knew not what, we knew not when, we knew not where. Orthodocia sat down and tore her hair.

Suddenly inspiration dawned in Buddha's countenance, '*Skoshi maté!*'[1] said he, and presently we saw him whirling violently down the hill of Kudan in a jinrikisha. In a quarter of an hour he was back, riding behind two other jinrikishas, and in a moment the messengers were on their hands and knees before us awaiting our commands.

'*Darika ciyo hanasu?*' said Orthodocia, consulting her phrase-

[1] Wait a little.

book—which stood for, 'Is there a gentleman here who can speak English?' Whereupon they both said '*Hai!*' and simultaneously sat up on their heels as if she had pulled a string and made them do it. And between the English of one gentleman and the English of the other we learned that we were bidden to a 'party in the garden' of Mr. Takayanagi, who lived in a certain *cho*[1] in the district of Azabu, the next afternoon at two o'clock. Mr. Takayanagi had learned of our recent arrival from America in the newspaper, and as his garden party was given in honour of his two sons also recently arrived from college in America, he thought it appropriate to invite us thereto. Nothing could have been more beautiful than the simplicity of this, and we wrote our acceptances forthwith, joyously. After the messengers had departed

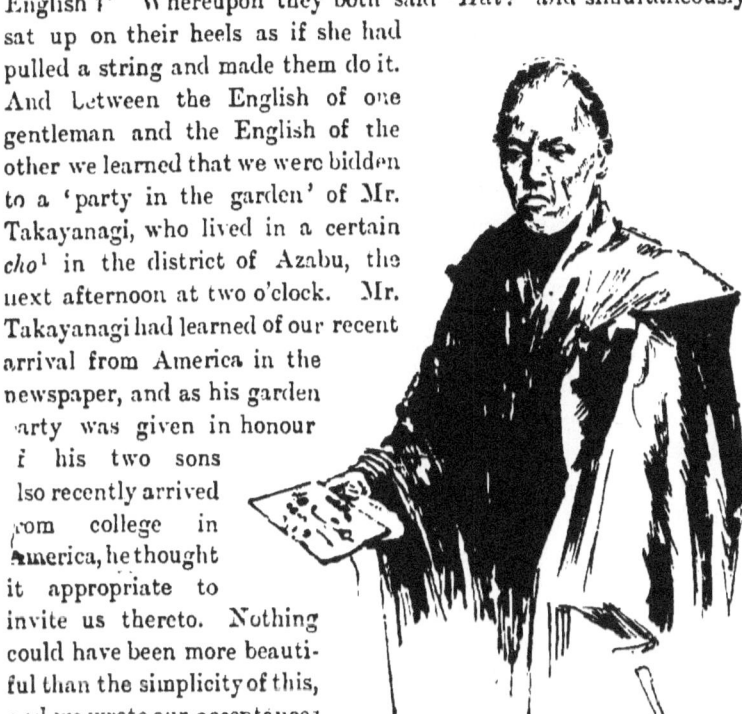

'IT WAS PRINTED IN JAPANESE.'

we wondered how Mr. Takayanagi had known our address, and then remembered that the very night we moved in a policeman had come to our residence—a smiling policeman of four-feet six—and requested to know the number of our brothers and sisters in America, and our father's and mother's first names. We had given the information cheerfully, hoping that the municipality of Tokio would profit by it, and Mr. Takayanagi had evidently been in communication with the authorities.

Orthodocia produced her most flippant and Parisian creation for that garden party, which vindicated her baggage policy, as she

[1] Street.

modestly remarked, for the whole trip. I went in a serious-minded black silk. Miles occurred between Kudan and Azabu—miles of quaint, flapping, clicking, smiling Tokio, all gay in the November sunlight and the last of the flowers; miles of gray-paved streets, many and wide, of dainty little shops heaped with yellow persimmons and queer blue platters, tiny babies exactly like Japanese dolls tottering and crowing in the midst of their entire stock-in-trade; miles of shining brown moats and arched bridges that we mounted and descended at a steady, even, easy, delightful trot. Then our willing bipeds drew up together before an imposing gate which was open, let the shafts down gently, turned round wiping their perspiring brown faces, and said: 'Takayanagi-san *arimas*!'[1]

We descended and went in, with some trepidation, and a hysterical hope that nothing would happen that would be too funny for us. The grounds were full of Japanese—ladies or gentlemen we couldn't quite determine at a glance—walking solemnly about; and several noises were proceeding from different directions. None of them knew us, and we knew none of them, so our immediate duty did not seem very clear. We concluded to go up the principal path, and see what would happen. The first thing that happened was a double file of Japanese gentlemen. 'Probably our host and his relations,' whispered Orthodocia nervously. 'Hadn't we better present our cards?' So we presented our cards, one to each of the first gentlemen in line, who took it, scrutinised it carefully, bowed very low indeed, and passed it on to the next, who did precisely the same. It was a little awkward for us, for nobody spoke, and there was hardly room enough on the path for four people, two advancing and one on each side, to bow properly in the Japanese manner, but we got through it; and Orthodocia immediately confided to me that Japan as an education for the Drawing Room was admirable. Then away on ahead of us we saw a pretty group, bright-coloured and graceful, with a centre, and when we reached it we discovered that we had made a slight mistake about the cards, and that the bowing gentlemen had been only a sort of guard of honour. This was our host, this tall, dignified old Japanese with the intellectual face, who shook

[1] I have.

hands with us in pleasant welcome, and turned to two dapper
youths in very tight-fitting broadcloth suits, to interpret it to us.

'My father says,' said Mr. Ichitaro Takayanagi, 'that he is very
glad to see you. He says that this lady, my mother, is his wife.'

At this a little old woman, all in soft brown and silver gray silk,
with her hair in wide, shiny black cushions radiating twenty wonderful
hairpins, smiled widely, showing a row of teeth blackened on her
marriage day, put her hands on her knees, drew in her breath, and
went down before us half a dozen times. As we thought it imperative to return the compliment, we felt relieved when another guest
arrived with a claim upon the old lady's politeness.

'My mother says,' said Mr. Ichitaro Takayanagi, 'that she hopes
you are well. And these are my sisters.' He indicated with that
a row of the prettiest things you could imagine, each a little shorter
than the next, every little round face daintily powdered and painted,
with narrow black eyes modestly slanting, and shiny black cushions
of hair like the mother, and a bright dab of gold beneath the full
under-lip. Their plump shoulders sloped under *kimonos* which were
pale blue and gray and rose and gold, but all with the crest on our
invitation stamped just in the middle of the back ; and the *kimonos*
were tied in at the waist with embroidered *obis*, the wide sashes which
are the pride and delight of feminine Japan, and which these maidens
probably inherited from some of their grandmammas. Their garments
were drawn much too tight round their ankles for the stage capers
of a Gilbert and Sullivan Yum Yum, and their shapely little feet
were kept off the ground by lacquered sandals three inches high. I
am afraid we stared rather, they were so new and sweet and pleasant
to look at, for after they had made their little bows they all hid their
faces, each on the shoulder of the taller one, just as you may have
seen blue-bells do in the wind.

'My sisters say,' said Mr. Ichitaro Takayanagi, 'that they hope
you are well.'

'And I also,' put in Mr. Takashi Takayanagi, who was tired of
seeing the honours usurped, 'I also hope you are well.'

We assured the entire Takayanagi family that we were perfectly
well, and inquired after their health, individually and in the aggregate, with satisfactory results. Then we permitted ourselves, under

the escort of the scions aforesaid, to be taken away and entertained It was all out of doors, Mr. Takayanagi's garden party; nobody went near the house, which retreated within itself at one end of the grounds. The grounds themselves reminded us of nothing so much as the maps of the early geographers. They were 'laid out' in mountains and valleys, lakes and rivers, islands and isthmuses. We wandered between forests as high as our knees, we stepped across roaring torrents on their way to join a *mare Japonica* situated near the front gate. Everything was on a scale of colossal imagination, and the most diminutive reality. We felt like Brobdingnagians in Lilliputia, but the idea did not occur to us in connection with the Japanese ladies and gentlemen about us, who also chatted over the tree tops and spanned streams at a stride—not because they were so much smaller than we, but because all this grotesque belittling and pretty bejuggling seemed to belong to them by nature, seemed to be a reasonable aspect of life for eyes that looked at it the way theirs did. Mr. Ichitaro pointed out with special pride certain large beds full of chrysanthemums, white and red and yellow, arranged in striking patterns. 'In America you do not so,' he said. 'It is a decoration for the occasion.' And, looking closely, I found that all the chrysanthemums were cut, and stuck separately and closely into the ground with quaint and curious effect.

Then our attendants took us to see the jugglery, which was the attraction in one corner—wonderful jugglery with umbrellas and eggs, and fans and whatnot, with the usual clown in it, too, who failed, and whose failures provoked more mirth than the successes of his companion. A band played in the middle of all—played 'Home, Sweet Home,' 'Climbing up the Golden Stair,' and 'Wait till the Clouds roll by, Jenny,' for the Takayanagis were advanced to the appreciation of foreign music. And in another corner fireworks went off with a puff and a bang, and Japanese paper ladies and gentlemen coquetted with one another high in air with fan and parasol. As we walked we met several times a man and woman, very simply dressed, wearing lugubrious faces and carrying stringed instruments, which they twanged intermittently, accompanying themselves in the most unhappy sounds possible to the human larynx. Mr. Takashi Takayanagi told me that these were the most renowned singers in

"THESE JAPANESE LADIES MAKE THEIR HAIR IN CURIOUS FASHION, ISN'T IT?"

Tokio, personating rustics and singing the latest Japanese lyrics, a popular feature of fashionable entertainments. 'The taste for music,' he went on, 'is difficult to acquire, don't you think?' I said I thought it was.

Presently we were conducted to an arboreal retreat, where sweetmeats and tea and faintly fragrant cigarettes were being served to the ladies. We sat down amongst them, a shy fluttering set, all bareheaded, cuddling close among themselves on the low wooden benches, and looking very much askance at the foreign ladies with their hats and their heels. It was pretty to see them drink tea with one another, from the same tiny handleless cup, and they smoked in a way that was simply enchanting. They did not talk much, but such low, sweet talking as it was, with such dainty deference in it, such gentle surprise, such tinkling mirth! Mr. Ichitaro and Mr. Takashi, whose conduct towards these maids of Nippon we quietly observed, took absolutely no notice of them. They had arrived at a period of evolution in which they looked at the world over high collars, indulged in 'button-holes,' and carried small canes. They were probably engaged to young American ladies of Boston, who wore spectacles and had a philosophical understanding of Shintoism. These poor little creatures were of a thousand years back; they toddled, they had never seen a dress-improver, they believed in the gods. Mr. Ichitaro and Mr. Takashi were not rude, but they brought all the pink and white rice-cakes and candy with pepper in it and tiny cups of pure green tea to us, and we felt sorry for the little maids, who probably did not feel sorry for themselves.

The afternoon wore on, and our young hosts began to present their friends, chiefly their male friends, evidently under the impression that we could not consider the young ladies far enough advanced to be interesting. They mentioned the pretty creatures in a tone of apology which we felt much disposed to resent. 'These Japanese ladies make their hairs in curious fashion, isn't it,' volunteered Mr. Ichitaro. 'You wish laugh, eh?' We did not 'wish laugh' in the very least at our dainty Japanese sisters in their very poetry of attire, and the sweet unconsciousness with which they wore it, or even at the great shiny puffs that made black halos round their modest little heads; but we did 'wish laugh' pawned su'" at some of the specimens of progress who submitted their tailors and their vocabularies to us that afternoon. I need not say anything more about the Japanese dress—everybody knows it, with its ease and dignity for men, and its special quality of dainty femininity for women—and you have only to consider the effect of that loose and flowing kind of garb upon generations of Japanese anatomies to understand that they do not readily adapt themselves to the conventional tail coat and trousers. A nation is not born in a day,

'I SUPPOSE THE GENTLEMAN HAD A COLD.'

neither is a national wardrobe. The best dressed of these little gentlemen looked narrow-chested and stooping, and very much aware of their legs; and among numbers of them the 'European costume' did not seem to be apprehended as an exact science. White cotton gloves prevailed to a funereal extent, and an assortment of hats that might have been considered fairly typical of the fashions of the present dynasty. We were sorely tried by certain hybrid costumes which were introduced to us with profound gravity. On one occasion, while Orthodocia was doing her best to converse with a young gentleman in tennis shoes, a silk hat, and a dressing-jacket, and I talked to another in tails and a 'Tam O'Shanter,' one of the young Takayanagis bore down upon us with still another, in irreproachable evening dress, lavender kids, patent-leather shoes, white tie and all —and garnished as to his neck with a large, fluffy, comfortable Manchester bath towel, best quality! I suppose the gentleman had a cold. But the gentle, unconscious, unobserving unanimity with which Orthodocia and I moved off in different directions at that moment was a beautiful sight to see. Mr. Takashi Takayanagi confided to me his regret that there were no Japanese ladies present in foreign dress, and I think he was astonished at the vigour of the sentiments I expressed upon the subject.

As the sun went down, and made a checkering of quaint shadows all among the smiling, moving, bowing little groups about us, a feast was disclosed behind the tallest of the mountains, and under the most umbrageous of the fir trees—a very wonderful feast of which I have still a souvenir in a large smooth shell of the clam variety. I ate sugared beans from this with chop-sticks, and carried the dish and the remains, for many sugared beans are a weariness to the flesh, home with me for politeness' sake.

And then, leaving the garden party of Mr. Takayanagi still elaborately complimenting itself among the chrysanthemums, we rode away out through the wide gate into the life and light and colour of Tokio's early evening. In my picture of it, which grows more like a phantasm every day, the great daintily-tinted paper globes were pulsing and glowing before the multitudinous little shops; the gay drops of light that hung from the jinrikishas were frisking up hill and down; there was still a red memory of the sun in the sky behind the dragon-like arms of the gnarled pine trees that guard the Mikado's moat; and against these three wild geese were flying, black and swift, long necks outstretched in front, short legs outstretched behind, just as they flew always across a tea-tray, that I knew long before I went to Japan. And, high over all, on its pyramid of stones, shone the great square lantern of Kudan—dusky, mysterious.

XII

'Don't you think,' said Orthodocia, coming in from the kitchen, where she had been beseeching Buddha for the sixth time that week to refrain from boiling the potatoes with sugar and flavouring the oatmeal with Worcester sauce, 'that we ought to go and call upon Mrs. Takayanagi?'

I said that I was unacquainted with the Japanese custom in the matter, but one would naturally suppose that in a country where the door-handles turned backwards, and people sat down in your presence as a sign of respect, and the horses stood with their tails in the mangers, the inhabitants would invite you to entertainments, and shortly afterwards make formal visits to thank you for giving yourself the pleasure of attending them.

'That may be,' said Orthodocia, 'but the Takayanagis haven't come to thank us yet, and I think we ought to go. Was it Miss Bird or Pierre Loti who said that the Japanese ladies received in their baths? I should like to see if they do really.'

'Yes,' I responded with levity, 'and then you will be able to conduct your next hydrostatical function on——'

I was going to say 'approved principles,' but there was a look in Orthodocia's eye which checked me.

So we went to call upon Mrs. Takayanagi, at about five o'clock on the last day of November, 1888. I have come upon this entry in Orthodocia's note-book, which she has kindly lent me to revive my impressions with. Opposite the entry I find 'Not at home.' And that simple, pregnant formula brings it all back to me.

We rode up to the same wide gate, but it was barred; through the same wonderful garden, but all its terrible dragons made of pink and white chrysanthemums had vanished, and most of the trees seemed to have been taken indoors, and it was quite empty of the bowing, shuffling groups of little people in their long drooping wings of rose and blue. Not so much as an ivory hairpin remained to tell of the shy little maids, nor a cuff-button to remind us of the quaint little men, nor a scrap of tinted paper to be a memory of all the pretty doings we had seen. The fantastic narrow walks were immaculately neat. In one of them a gardener was carefully picking up pine-needles, and I have no doubt that the bridges and shrines and embankments had every one been dusted that morning. But it all looked unreasonable and expressionless, like a Japanese drawing, and there was not anywhere a lingering smile of the charm we had found so very charming in Mr. Takayanagi's garden party.

'MY DEAR LITTLE HEATHEN, IS YOUR MOTHER AT HOME?'

We knocked at the outer door with our knuckles—and knocked and knocked again. It remained blankly unresponsive. Then we clapped our hands until the welkin rang, and just as Orthodocia's glove split explosively from her thumb to her little finger, a bobbing figure came round the corner.

'*Ok' sama arimaska?*'[1] inquired Orthodocia, who had begun to talk Japanese in her sleep.

'*Hai!*'[2] said the bobbing person, with all but a somersault, and disappeared.

Presently the door slid back gently, and before us stood the tallest, plumpest, sweetest of the little young ladies Takayanagi, not quite as gay as at her papa's garden party, but very dainty and fine in the colours of an early wild flower, with her tiny hands lost in her great sleeves and her little toes close together under her ankle draperies. There she stood and there we stood quite mute, looking at each other; and as she seemed to have no intention of letting us in, Orthodocia presented our cards. She took them bowing, smiling, blushing. '*Arigato!*'[3] she said, and put them in her sleeve.

'Why don't you say something?' said Orthodocia to me in an irritated way. 'And for goodness' sake stop laughing!'

But I couldn't help laughing, I felt so exceedingly funny, and with a malicious desire to make Orthodocia laugh too, I said, 'My dear little heathen, is your mother at home?' speaking as one who knows she will not be understood.

My dear little heathen smiled demurely. Then she said, blushing furiously, and cuddling her small person up very tight in her swathing gownlet, 'My name is Haru Takayanagi.'

'Oh!' from Orthodocia and me, with a palpable jump. 'So you speak English,' continued my friend, affably. 'How nice! We have come to make a call.'

'My father is not at home.'

'Is he not? Oh, indeed! I am sorry to hear that. But we did not come—ah—especially—ah—to see your father.' A vigorous aside to me—'If you don't say something *soon*—and stop that idiocy——'

'*Hai!*' said the little maid, forgetting herself. 'The gentlemen, my brothers, are in Yokohama. It is a great pain.'

'Dear me! How vewy extwaordinary!' remarked Orthodocia,

---

[1] Is the mistress at home?   [2] Yes.   [3] Thank you.

just as if she were standing on the steps of a house in Cavendish Square. 'She appeahs to think we have come to call upon her bwothahs!'

This sudden reversion to an earlier type in my friend entirely finished me, and I was helpless from that time forth.

'Is your mothaw at home?' I heard her demand between my gasps, very sternly and pointedly; and then the little maid gave her a frightened look. '*Wakarimasen!*'[1] she said, *Gomen nasai!*'[2] slipped the door shut again, and toddled off inside. We waited, I very humble under Orthodocia's castigations, but still decidedly 'smily round the lips and teary round the lashes,' and presently she came back again.

'My mother is in her bath,' she said.

We looked at each other. Was it or was it not an invitation? And if it *was* an invitation, had we or had we not the strength of mind to accept? In a convulsive instant we decided that it was, in another that we had not, in another that it might be insisted on; the next saw our headlong flight over the precipices and across the peninsulas of the garden, out through the wide gate, and away into the mazes of Tokio, leaving the little maid stock still in the doorway, full of consternation. Poor old lady, innocently seated at that moment in your tub, and preparing a steamy conventional welcome for us, was it ever explained to you, I wonder, that your European guests did not feel quite equal to you on that occasion?

Then on one of the long, happy days that cluster about this point in my memory, when the acutest joy was centred in the buying of a teapot, and all the dainty fantastic life about us pressed sharp upon our senses, and we wondered how the foreigners we met could look so commonplace and blind, came an invitation to dinner from Mrs. Jokichi Tomita. It was a verbal invitation by messenger, and was interpreted to us to the effect that the entertainment would be very humble indeed, and the guests few; yet the honour of our presence and the solace of our society would be so great that she could not refrain from begging us to come. It took our united efforts and three-quarters of an hour to compose a message which we considered polite enough to accept in.

[1] I do not know.   [2] Please **excuse me**.

I was sorry for Orthodocia the day of Mrs. Tempathy, or a politely
She spent it largely in the society of her various bo...ade or degree
grouped around the well curb under a tarpaulin in the ...tely with-
having been found impossible to get even the least among t...s one
the house. Her distress of mind, as she vibrated from one to the
other of them uncertainly demanding 'What shall I wear?' was
painful to witness. Secure in the unruffled composure with which
a black silk and no alternative always enables one to confront social
emergencies, I looked on and made remarks about the comfort of a
unified wardrobe. But my precepts were indignantly rejected, and
my example was of no use, for Orthodocia hadn't a black silk.

'The trouble is, one can't tell,' said my friend in her perplexity,
surveying a Bond Street tea-gown at arm's length. 'These people
are getting so frightfully civilised that we may find Mrs. Jokichi
giving the regular thing with a Russian *attaché* to take one in ; or
it may be entirely *à la Japonaise*, in which case'—thoughtfully—
'I suppose one ought to wear some thing like this. And yet it is so
early—five o'clock!' I think the potential Russian *attaché* prevailed
over both our better judgments, for five o'clock saw us arriving at
Mrs. Tomita's, Orthodocia in all the glory of full dinner costume,
and I with my robe of sobriety and general utility turned in, tucked
up and begarlanded to faintly approximate her.

Mrs. Tomita stood at an inner door of her funny little establishment to welcome us—at least it looked like an inner door then. A
few minutes later it appeared to be a wall, and the passage in which
we stood had broadened into a room, and the end of it had dissolved
into the most charming view of moats and trees and temples, with
Fusi Yama rising in the distance. Our hostess went down on her
knees to greet us, a politeness which Orthodocia found embarrassing
to return on account of the bouffant nature of her draperies. Then
she got up and bowed a great many times, with her hands on her
knees, keeping a bright eye fixed upon us sidewise, and only leaving
off when we did. Thereupon she turned to her husband, in whom
we saw the reason of our invitation. For Mr. Jokichi Tomita bent
before us in coat and trousers of the most conventional cut, and we
recognised in him the advancing European idea. He shook hands
with us gravely, and regarded Orthodocia, who looked like a large

just as if she w... ...d-gray parrot in a very small canary cage, with
Square. 'Sh... ...much resembling awe.
bwothah; ...o us a great regret that my wife does not speak the
,.. ..il,' he said, while the little brown *ok' sama* at his side smiled
.. .d shrank further into herself than ever. 'But we have here some
ladies who speak a little words.' And he marshalled us, if the word
is not too big for the occasion, into another room.

It seemed so full of softly chattering little dames in wonderful
clothes and painted faces and shiny black puffs, that must have been
lacquered over-night to be so smooth and solid, that I wondered how
Orthodocia could ever get into it. When she did, and stood in their
midst, graceful and tall and fair, with white chrysanthemums in her
bosom and a look of quiet wonder in her face, a sudden silence fell
upon all the little ladies, and they regarded her, my beautiful English
friend, with a certain pathetic perception, I thought, of the distance
that lay between her and them.

How we marvelled what they had been talking about when we
came in, these soft-voiced matrons who so suddenly found themselves
with nothing to say! Not the opera, surely, for the opera in Japan
is—well, is not a thing that is calculated to excite conversation.
Not their pet charities, for the ladies of Japan who are advanced to
committee meetings wear bonnets and boots. Could it have been
scandal, or servants, or the weather, or those curious little shaven
dolls that represented babies to them? We could not guess, and
nobody told us. But we had known their facsimiles postured gracefully upon fans and tea chests for so many childish years, during
which they never spoke at all, that their low voices seemed a strange
and unnecessary part of them.

We were introduced to those who spoke 'a little words,' but
found none of them so fluent as our host, who plied us with a great
many. I have forgotten most of his conversation, and I find Orthodocia has too. We were both so much absorbed in watching the
strange artificial little faces round us that changed so unalterably,
if you can understand what I mean, with the thought in the small
brains behind them. Their owners seemed to control a set of pretty
stereotyped expressions, and when the occasion came to pull some
hidden string, and the proper one flitted out; but always the same

quick look that said surprise, or pleasure, or sympathy, or a politely repelled compliment, and never any other, never any shade or degree of feeling. I have not seen anything in conduct so exquisitely without flaw as the 'form' these little ladies exhibited towards one another. The gentle approachings, the deferential liftings of the eyes, the deprecating bows, the distinctly well-bred laughter, and the pretty rattling syllables, all seemed part of a very old work of social art, inlaid and polished so wonderfully that one forgot to inquire its true significance. They wore no ornaments but pins and beads in their hair; not a ring, nor a bracelet, nor a necklace did we see among them. Their *kimonos* were embroidered in gold and silver, and we should hang their *obis* upon our walls for panels, so thickly they were embossed with storks and lotus flowers. Their shapely feet were dressed in socks that hooked behind, and had pockets for their great toes. In the passage outside stood all their small sandals in a row. Their little lives had been arranged for them by their parents, they might or might not have seen their *donna sans*¹ before their marriages; perhaps none of them held a matrimonial monopoly, and any one of them could be divorced if she talked too much! They had learned to read words of I don't know how many syllables, but enough to apprehend treatises upon woman's domestic sphere in Japanese, and they knew that a mother should obey her eldest son. Some of them worshipped their ancestors, others when they went to the temples to pray rang a great bell that the god might hear—and pay attention. At home they did not eat with their husbands; it was a new strange thing for them to be here on equal terms with their host, whom they could not bow before long enough or low enough. For the cares of life they had the bearing of their children, the ordering of their servants, the observance of an elaborate social etiquette. For accomplishment they played upon the *samisen*, or perhaps if their advantages had been very great upon the *koto*, and sang interminable songs, all in a minor key; or some one of them may perhaps have learned to make paper roses, as the foreigners did. No lover or husband had ever kissed them. This fashion of ours had probably been canvassed among them, and set quietly down to be another of the incomprehensible ways of the foreigners. They looked at life and bore themselves through it much

¹ Husbands.

as puppets might, and yet if its tragedy touched their curious little souls too closely they were quite capable of putting an end to it with a certain broad sharp knife, with a burlesquing bronze god on its handle.

Our host's art treasures were brought out of their hidden places for the pleasure of his guests ; not all at once with vulgar lavishness, but one or two at a time, to be handled tenderly and admiringly, and appreciated separately in dainty phrases. We wondered at the discrimination of the little ladies, and felt most clumsy and bungling and unclever when our turn came to touch and to praise the ivory carvings and the inlaid bronzes, and the tiny soft old porcelain bowls and vases. Mr. Jokichi Tomita listened with quiet pity as we stumbled on, missing always the wonderful curve or the rare colour, and bowed polite acknowledgment of our good intentions, only saying, as he replaced his joys in their sandalwood cabinets, 'The foreign taste, I think it is much different with ours. The Japanese child—small baby—is wise in these things.'

About this time dinner was announced, that is to say, a wall vanished suddenly, and showed a small empty room with about a dozen flat velvet cushions in a row upon the floor. Nothing else.

Orthodocia and I looked at one another, and I think the Russian *attaché* crossed our minds at the same moment. Mentally we commiserated, not ourselves, of course, but one another! Then came the unhappy moment when we were waved to the first cushions in the row, as the honoured guests of the occasion, and expected to sit down on them in full view of the demure little company. We stood over them as long as we could, but it became apparent that so long as we remained standing there was a hitch in the ceremony ; so we gradually subsided upon them, the most unearthly groans arising from all parts of Orthodocia's attire at once. 'I shall never get up,' she whispered to me, 'without a derrick,' and at that instant I heard the bitter sound of parting laces that proceeds only from a sylph-like form under stress of circumstances.

Then began among the little ladies an odd struggle, not for precedence, but for post-cedence. The most rigid order was observed, and they all knew that it must be, yet it would have been a horrible rudeness to take the next most honourable cushion, or the next, or the next, without a great show of deference to somebody imaginarily more worthy. Finally it was all accomplished, and we sat in a row, the silence broken only by ominous creakings from Orthodocia, and waited events.

'I think you have a custom,' said Mr. Jokichi Tomita, 'before you eat to make ceremony. I have read in books,' continued Mr. Jokichi Tomita, 'that without ceremony you do not like eat. Will you ceremony please make?'

'Orthodocia,' said I, 'I think the gentleman wishes you to say grace.'

'Grace,' said our host. 'It is the word. Quite right. Will you the grace ceremony for your pleasure please make?'...

I couldn't have done it. I don't know anybody but Orthodocia who could. But I record it to my friend's credit—immensely to her credit—that the nursery training of St. Eve's-in-the-Garden, Wigginton, Devon, failed her not in that far foreign moment, and, with perfect gravity of face and voice, she bowed her head and said, 'For what we are about to receive, the Lord make us truly thankful.' Later on I was glad she had said it. We required every available aid to gratitude.

The little ladies looked at one another comprehendingly, as much as to say, 'Yes; we have heard of this. It is a politeness to a foreign Dai Koku, who brings rice and many sons,' and the first course came in on its knees from the passage outside. I say the passage advisedly. Where it came from before that I will not commit myself by stating, but I should think from a 'Toy Emporium,' where the toys are delicately painted with much turpentine. Vulgarly speaking, it was tea and cakes, but it is difficult to bring one's self to speak vulgarly of the initial dainties of a Japanese repast. One's artistic conscience protests. For myself, I found the toy and turpentine idea more satisfying on imaginative grounds—not, however, I may add, upon any other. The tea came before the cakes, and a queer little ceremony came with the tea. It was served in trays that held five tiny handleless cups, a flat teapot, and a bowl of hot water. Mr. Jokichi Tomita drank from his cup and we from ours—a brief and bitter draught, no sugar and no milk—then, bowing before us, he begged our cups to drink from, presenting his in return. Of course we bungled our part of it stupidly, and the

I

ceremony must have been very much askew so far as we were concerned; but we watched our host exchanging compliments with those of his guests who knew how to behave in society; and, if I remember rightly, each *ok' sama* on whom he pressed the honour, shrank from it with many pretty protestations and shakings of the head, only yielding after long importunity. Then she dipped the tiny transparent thing into the bowl of water and handed it to him. He drank with grave felicity, as if he quaffed ambrosia, and washed his own. The servant filled it, and the dame-guest modestly accepted it from his hand. It was a very dainty little function, but it must have been very bad for Mr. Jokichi Tomita's inside.

Orthodocia looked at her pink spinning-top, nibbled it suspiciously, and then laid it down with a shudder.

'You *must* eat it!' I prodded her in French. 'It offends them frightfully if you don't!' and I made a determined attack upon mine. Orthodocia looked at the morsel in silent despair, then with a sudden convulsive effort of two mouthfuls she despatched it! I regret that I cannot use any term more suggestive of good manners. The little ladies who had been amusing themselves with theirs for ten minutes, absorbing them daintily crumb by crumb, stared, and one or two put their hands to their mouths. Orthodocia looked unhappy. Our host said something to a servant, and he presently came in with three trays heaped high with further confections. Orthodocia spent the next quarter of an hour in declining them.

I think—I say I *think*—for who could undertake to write accurately of the sequences of a Japanese dinner?—that it was at this point that the eels came on, split into neat little finger-lengths on tiny wooden splints and broiled, unmistakably broiled. If they had been raw Orthodocia told me afterwards that the fear of no amount of social degradation would have induced her to eat them, which made me tremble for Orthodocia, for it showed a departure from the way in which she had been brought up. The eels were not very bad, though they would have been better with a little salt, and we became more cheerful at this point. And the next thing was a wonderful fruit made chiefly of sugar and uncooked rice flour, which we gathered ourselves from the branches of the little tree it grew on

'SHE WAS A PROFESSIONAL DANCER.'

in the pot the servant handed about. We consumed the fruit, but Orthodocia grew very silent.

Then came a pause in our feasting, and the nearest wall vanished to disclose three very gay little maids postured in the middle of the floor, each with a strange stringed instrument in her arms. A tiny hand glided over its *samisen*, a low, plaintive cry came from it, and one uprose before us to dance. She was a *geisha*—a professional dancer. She represented the highest form of Japanese amusement, and she amused the foreign gentlemen, too, sometimes. And her dancing—it was not the dancing of any gnome or fairy one had ever imagined, still less of any human being one had ever seen. It was the dancing of a still little face, with a set smile of coquetry that came when it was summoned, of an undulating little body and slowly turning feet, and it all seemed responsive to the crying of the *samisen* from the flitting hand of her friend on the floor. She held a fan, too, a frail paper thing that the *samisen* opened and closed at its pleasure; and she looked like a creature of *papier maché*, that moved obedient to the laws of the Science of Decoration.

The *samisen* wailed once more and the little *geisha* sank to her first posture among her twisted draperies of blue and gold, and then the wall closed again, and our attention was diverted to a series of very beautiful fishes. They were quite dead, indeed they had been cooked in some way, but one of them was presented to each of us, and as they were at least two-pounders this was embarrassing. We had also to experiment upon them with chop-sticks, which was more embarrassing. I had just made an excavation of about half an inch square in mine when the *ok' sama* on the other side of me blushed violently, leaned toward me and said, 'It is not necessary all to eat. It is given, and will to-morrow eat be sufficient.'

Orthodocia heard with an agonised sigh of relief and dropped her chop-sticks. I looked at her reprovingly, and she made a pun which was so bad that I submit it herewith to illustrate her state of mind. 'It is only,' she said, 'the groaning of the festive bored!'

More dainties, and then three *geishas* again, one of whom sang a *koto* song, which was a mournful melody in three notes. Orthodocia grew very restive under the next set of dishes, which included a roasted bird of some sort, stuffed with preserved cherries, with all its feathers on. The little ladies removed the feathers very daintily before helping themselves, but they got hopelessly mixed with the cherries in the little Owari bowls in the laps of Orthodocia and me. By this time I did not dare to be restive, the lightest movement brought on a series of the wildest tortures. And after we had disposed of the feathered cherries or the cherried feathers, the third and last *geisha* performed her little performance, which was a story—a haggard tale of woe, I believe, but it made all the *ok' samas* laugh consumedly. . . .

At last, just as Orthodocia had implored me to 'make a move' and I had assured her that it was physically impossible, we were politely made aware that the feast was over. The process of farewell was a long one, and cost us elaborate agonies; but we were finally straightened out and stood on our more or less incapable legs, and sent home feeling much like very valuable pieces of furniture of the reign of Queen Anne. In our jinrikishas, when we arrived at *ichi banchi, ni chome, Fugi-mi-cho Kudan*, each of us found a daintily-made square box, with a carved twig for the handle of the lid. In each box was the *tai* fish as our feeble chop-sticks had left it, a large pink rose with green leaves in rice-flour confectionery, and Orthodocia had the head and I the tail of the cherried fowl I have told you about. It was the last of Mrs. Jokichi Tomita's dinner party.

XIII

Now, Orthodocia and I kept ourselves reminded of our foreign origin, there among the flapping blue gowns and clattering wooden sandals that resounded so endlessly round the *bon-bon* box we lived in on the hill of Kudan, by taking in an English newspaper of Yokohama. We did not care much about the newspaper, because it insisted upon treating the droll, wonderful, many-tinted fairy tale that Japan was to us, quite seriously, and disposing of its affairs in paragraphs that might have been written in Fleet Street or Broadway—paragraphs upon the navy and the universities, and the import duties and treaty revision, that alternated with news notes about the electric light system of Yokohama, or the extension of railway lines into the interior, or the 'political banquet,' at which Count Kuroda was 'in the chair.' What business, we thought resentfully, had Count Kuroda 'in the chair' when, according to every tradition of his delightful country, he should have been on the floor? After an evening ride through Tokio, dreaming among her thousand dainty lanterns, or wakeful under her thousand flitting shadows that jested and coquetted and passed on, it was like a disagreeable waking up to open next morning's paper, damp with disillusionment and bristling with these things—to say nothing of news 'by cable' that told us of the other world from which we had come and to which, alas! we must soon return. But occasionally we found compensation in the *Herald*. It informed us of the coming and the going of the mails, for instance; and one day it told us of a bazaar to be given in aid of a hospital charity by 'the ladies of Tokio.'

Orthodocia read this aloud in a displeased manner; then, in spite of the lingering Japanese idea in the garments of Mr. Takayanagi's garden party and the indisputably Japanese flavour of the *entremets* at Mrs. Jokichi Tomita's dinner, she made the following statements:

'We are too late for Japan!' she said, bitterly. 'The island that once existed on this side of Asia has invented a new process of lacquer, with European designs, and disappeared under it. The "ladies of Tokio"—who ought to be

'ONE DAY IT TOLD US OF A BAZAAR.'

playing their dear little *samisens*, and sitting on their dear little heels—where are they? Molesting unprotected young Japanese gentlemen with entreaties to buy a lottery ticket for a hand-painted pincushion!'

I begged my friend, for her consolation, to remember the feathered cherries of Mrs. Tomita and the soaring compliments of Mr. Ichitaro Takayanagi; also the visit which she had premeditated, and then basely fled from, to Mr. Takayanagi's mamma; but privately I agreed with her complaint, and publicly I advise you, if you want to see the Land of the Rising Sun in anything like pristine simplicity, to travel eastward soon, for already she is girt about with a petticoat, and presently she will want to vote.

We went to the bazaar, however, and found that we were not altogether too late for Japan. It was conducted upon European principles, but its conductors were not Europeans, and the principles seemed to work erratically, as if they did not feel at home.

The bazaar was held in a building put up by the paternal Japanese Government to foster social intercourse among the official classes on the European plan—to be a club-house in short. It was the advanced idea of a certain foreign minister, who returned from special plenipoing somewhere in Europe with the opinion that his countrymen sat down too much in the evenings. The Government, therefore, built, upon foreign plans, a place of resort for them, in which they could be induced, among other things, to stand up; and put billiard-tables in it for muscular development, and a bar, doubtless to stimulate circulation. I regret that I cannot give you the figures of the mental, moral, and physical improvement that immediately followed. Orthodocia tried to get them, but they had not yet been tabulated.

I cannot say positively that the Mikado and his advisers had anything further to do with the affair than granting the use of the premises, but that bazaar certainly seemed directly under the supervision and control of the State Department. We passed through a double file of solemn-faced little policemen to the door, and there met an official who took our tickets as if he would have preferred a certificate of character attached. One gets in the way, in Japan, of trembling before the least of uniforms, they take their gold lace so seriously and wear the little shining chrysanthemum of their emperor with such a redoubtable air of authority. The atmosphere inside was full of officialism and severe-looking monkeys in braid and buttons, whom we could not possibly connect with any triviality in Kensington stitch that might be displayed upstairs. They stood helplessly about in the lobby, these prim and dapper representatives of the bureaucracy of Japan, eyeing the ladies as they tripped in and up, but filled with a reasonable fear of following them. The reputation of our charity shop had evidently preceded it, and a civil service income is a civil service income all the world over.

But upstairs there were no trivialities in Kensington stitch, or any other stitch. There was no gruesome vegetation hand-painted by amateurs. There were no baby-jackets knitted to imitate the warmth and durability of an April cloud, no perfumed handkerchief sachets, or embroidered tobacco-pouches, or beaded chairbacks, that give the sitter cold agonies—but let me not grow maledictory under a possible feminine eye that acknowledges and loves these things! All I want to say is that this bazaar wasn't really related to the family of that name that we are acquainted with at all. It had simply been bought up, every article of it, at bazaars outside that were not charitable, and it looked more like a little narrow street of Tokio wholly devoted to the elegant requirements of society than anything else. Why was the antimacassar absent and the mantel-drape a-lacking? Because the 'ladies of Tokio,' laudably ambitious of the correct thing in charities as they are, are not yet quite equal to it from a manufacturing standpoint. The pleasant embroideries of Japan are the employment of people who make them a business, and the foreign needle is not conquered yet. It is even so that certain of the bolder ladies of Japanese fashion have shaken their little heads disapprovingly over the crewel-work perpetrations of their Western sisters, and confided to one another that they might be very wonderful and difficult to achieve, but they were hideous— very hideous indeed. And why should one devote one's life to the production of ugliness at infinite pains? And for the little *ok' samas* who had not the foolish audacity of this opinion, their lives had other idylls probably—the fingering of the melancholy *koto*, the arrangement of the household vase—or domestic cares supervened the charge of many cupboards and innumerable mats.

In other respects, however, we found that these gentle almond eyes had slanted across the Pacific at our commercial charity to some purpose. Their faithfulness to our tariff left nothing to be desired, and they had improved upon our method of enforcing it.

Beside the main attacking body behind the stalls, there were flying squadrons, and outposts and scouts. The solid work was done by the dowagers; recurring charges were made by bevies of young married ladies, and these were reinforced by numbers of native gentlemen who went about single-handed with most insinuating and destructive effect. Entering, Orthodocia and I were blandly captured by one of these. He approached us with the modest, ingenious air of the man who has been introduced last season, and is afraid he is forgotten, yet has every intention of obtaining the next dance. He had a charming manner, the manner of a diplomatist; his smile, and his bow, and the wave of his hand toward the most seductive of the stalls seemed to melt and run together into one gracious complex curve. When his small brown member was not indicating a stork in gold lacquer, it was caressing, with the little finger outstretched, as an old maid holds a teacup, the thin black line on his upper lip which is the Japanese imitation of a moustache. He wore his European clothes not awkwardly at all, but a little like a very elegant dummy in a tailor's shop. A tiny gold star shone in the lappel of his coat. His English was careful, select, syllabic. He belonged to New Japan, and had probably danced with the daughters of princes at foreign courts. He was equally polite and persuasive, whether we admired a fifty-yen enamelled screen or a five-sen lacquered sugar spoon. He made an agreeable effort to step back, as it were, to our British point of view in considering purchases, and amiably speculated with us. I vacillated between a really clever little carved wooden monkey at twenty sen, and a trashy paper workbasket at one yen fifty. He

'BUT I TOOK THE MONKEY HOME.'

looked at one and at the other, and then, picking up the painted humbug with the air of a connoisseur, 'com-*par*-a-tive-ly cheap,' he said, 'com-*par*-a-tive-ly cheap.' But I remembered the antipodal character of Japanese views generally, and took the monkey.

Orthodocia fell a victim to an old lady in native costume, a countess, I believe, as countesses go in Japan. She was of a past generation; she spoke no English. Doubtless she regarded her children proudly in their imported garments, and made flattering obeisance before her elder son; but they had departed from the ways of their mother and of ancient Nippon, and she understood nothing of their strange new ambitions. Her face was round, and brown, and sweet, and her gold comb shone above it as other coronets do. Her shoulders drooped womanly beneath her silk *kimono*, and her toddle was worth many strides of the female suffragist. She did not quite plead, or quite coax, or quite command Orthodocia into that bronze goddess; but her soft, low Japanese phrases, with their ever-recurring '*So desuka?*'[1] her beguiling bowing attitudes, with her head now on this side, now on that, in gently persistent inquiry, suggested all three. As for Orthodocia, she stood fascinated, leaning on her parasol before her captor, wonder and amusement lurking behind her eyes. She was finally startled into paying for the bronze goddess, which still charms her now and then into an absent smile.

They told us that there were a few countesses among the young married ladies also, but apparently this was a distinction which nobody thought it worth while to advertise; and we did not hear of any aristocratic enhancement of values. The young married ladies, moreover, were homogeneous in their foreign clothes, and the uninitiated could not tell them apart. So far as we could observe, some of the clothes came from Paris, some from Oxford Street, some from the Bowery, and some from a Tokio dressmaker inspired by vague European ideals. These latter rather made us think of the Japanese lion, popularly decorative in wood, stone, bronze, and porcelain, and commonly taken for a dragon. The artist who introduced him had never seen a lion, and the innocently fat and ferocious

---

[1] Is it not so?

looking creature he originated pily conscious of a wish that seems unhappily he might have been anything else had circumstances permitted, over which he had no control.

It seemed to us quite wonderful that these little dames of Tokio, after the freedom of their antecedent wardrobes for so many generations, could adapt themselves so easily to our cramped bodice and multitudinous skirts. No suffering whatever was visible upon their countenances, countenances which Orthodocia suggested were

'AS FOR ORTHODOCIA, SHE STOOD FASCINATED, LEANING ON HER PARASOL BEFORE HER CAPTOR.'

not pretty, but neat perhaps. They looked snugly and complacently out from behind the bonnet-strings tied in bows under their unaccustomed little chins; and yet Orthodocia declared that the size of their waists was entirely incompatible with dining on the floor without the most appalling tortures, and she spoke with conviction. We learned, though, that they have not yet fully entered the bonds of servitude, that the comfortable *kimono* is still in a convenient cupboard for private wear, and the gorgeously-embroidered *obis* are not yet all sold to the curio dealers. They are still experimenting, still amused; and nobody seems to have told them that they are trying to do what we have concluded to try to undo. They have not put on our manners with our clothes; they cling to their dear little bows of extreme humility, hands on knees; and it was interesting to watch the rear elevation of the stiff, short, puffed skirts and the fashionable *tournure* when countess met countess in a shock of politeness. And it was very funny to find, even in Japan, that nervous lady who never knows exactly what society requires of her. She was quite sure of her clothes; from a jet pin to a glove-button she was entirely and properly European. Her bonnet-bows were the tallest, and her heels the highest in all the quaint little company. She climbed the broad staircase with great self-respect. At the door she paused, looked about her in anguished uncertainty, made up her mind with a pang of resolution, remained faithful to the way she was brought up, stooped down, and took off her shoes!

'*Mata kimasu!*' ('I will come again') was our only weapon of defence against these alluring shopmen and shopwomen of the Mikado's aristocracy, who might have sat on the pavements and sold curios all their lives, so had they mastered the wiles of persuasion. That little phrase left them with nothing but a bow of assent and a smile of hope, though never one of them believed for an instant in our sincerity. '*Mata kimasu!*' we said to the sellers of ivories brown with age, of gods and goddesses, fans and paper-knives, Satsuma vases, and *cloisonné* plaques, and boxes, and teapots, and trays. '*Mata kimasu!*' and so fled.

But would we not go downstairs and have tea and cakes—very cheap? We would, and did. Ah! there were the daughters of the nation clustering about in little shy knots in the middle of the room, all in narrow pale blue draperies drawn tight round their ankles, with a glint of gold round their short little waists, and a great plump cushion behind, and faintly-tinted long silk undersleeves, and their own wonderful shiny black *coques* of hair, that gave their delicately cut faces the relief of ivory. Here had no impertinent Western fashion interfered ; here were grace, simplicity, and sweetness ; here were the originals of all the dear little teacup ladies we used to know. Perhaps even now they are toppling about like their mammas in high heels, imploring Nanki Poo to buy chrysanthemums for his buttonhole at twenty-five sen apiece ; but last December they were still unobtrusive, still Japanese, still brought to bazaars for decorative purposes only ; and we rejoice to have seen them then.

'*Mata kimasu !*' we said again, taking smiling and unwilling departure. And I hope you will be as polite and agreeable about it as were the 'ladies of Tokio' when you find from Orthodocia at the end of this finished chapter '*Mata kimasu !*'

XIV

It had come from the Secretary of the American Legation, with a polite note which translated it to be an invitation from His Imperial Majesty the Mikado, to visit and inspect the new palace that has been years in preparation for him, on one of three Last Days before the Au- gust Presence moved in. There was no 'R. S. V. P.' on the invitation so far as we could discover, so we did not answer it, and Orthodocia hoped that our American friends would make our acknowledgments properly to the Mikado the next time they saw him. 'These Americans are such unceremonious people though,' she said. 'I dare say it will never occur to them.'

'THE IMPERIAL PERSON.'

On the way:

'*Huydah!*' . . . '*Houdah!*' '*Huydah!*' . . . '*Houdah!*'

It was such a patient cry, with such submissive gentle cheer in it, and so musical withal! Not glad or light-hearted, nor with anything of reckless strong courage; for how indeed could that be, when it panted forth from the straining lungs of men who labour as horses do, with all their might of arm and strength of will and power of purpose, harnessed between two shafts! Up the long paved hill streets of the great cities all over Japan they toil, these man animals, heads bent, eyes suffused, wet brown skin shining over tightened muscles; one pulling before, the other pushing behind, sending great loads of rice and timber through miles of narrow roads from sunrise to sunset, and calling the one to the other for the nameless sympathy and encouragement of the human voice, '*Huydah!*'... *Houdah!*'

It filled in the gaps between all the sounds we heard as we rode to the Emperor's palace.

And it was a long ride to the Emperor's palace from the hill of Kudan, though the moat that guarded it curved through the city within a stone's throw of our sliding door. If it had not been for the sentry we might have crossed one of the arched wooden bridges, and entered privily the seat of the Imperial representative of the gods of Japan. But the sentry was there, and the moat was deep, and the walls were high; and only one gate of all the many entrances to the palace was opened by mandate that day. So we had to follow the brown shining water and the quaint granite defences for quite two miles before we found ourselves admitted within the outer wall of the grounds of the sacred habitation.

I am not at all sure that I am warranted in saying that this was a veritable Last Day before the moving in of the Imperial Person. For aught I know he may still be inaugurating Last Days and inviting confiding foreigners to believe that he is just on the verge of changing his ways for theirs. It was difficult to get him to begin to inaugurate them, I believe, on account of the conservative nature of his tastes, but now that he had begun there was no reason why he might not conciliate his advisers by going on indefinitely. His habit had been, up to that time, to appoint a date with vague amiability some distance off, settle down on his *tatami* to the solid comforts of life till the date came round, and then obligingly reappoint it. The reason I understood to lie in the fact that His Majesty is not keen on all he's seen that's European, and the fundamental ideas of the new palace are distinctly European. Being a Mikado he feels himself superior to the fashions. He has an enormous respect for his ancestors, of such proportions that he finds it difficult at times to carry about with him; and the fact that they sat on the floor weighs with him. Then he was opposed to the actual change from the old palace on superstitious grounds. The abode he was accustomed to came to him ready hallowed, the new one he will have to hallow by his own unaided exertions; and people who are well acquainted with him say that he will find this difficult.

But the embarrassment of the situation for the Imperial advisers carried us straight back to the plaintive difficulties of Koko. There seems to be no easy or obvious or reliable way of disciplining a Mikado.

'What is your business?' inquired the first small gold-laced person who took our cards of admission.

'To see the palace!' answered Orthodocia with promptitude.

The little official looked up at her fiercely from under his eyebrows, but as his glance dwelt upon her the fierceness faded out of it, and we passed on, leaving him gazing ecstatic with uplifted chin at the spot in the firmament above him where the radiant vision had appeared.

THE MIKADO'S PALACE.

'What is your dignity?' said the next obstruction, who received our visiting cards and scrutinised us very closely. It seemed that this also should be self-evident, but I regret to say that we obscured it still further by levity, which

K

the solemn functionary with the gold chrysanthemum in his cap resented, so far as a severe Japanese expression of countenance can resent.

'We have rather lost sight of it since coming to Japan,' said Orthodocia, again rising to the occasion; 'I have not seen mine since we left the Grand Hotel in Yokohama. But I have no doubt,' she went on politely, 'that if I have left it there it will be forwarded in the course of a few days.'

This seemed to be satisfactory, and they let us in.

I don't believe there is anything in the world that a Japanese palace is like from the outside except itself, and perhaps the temple wherein the lord of the palace worships his unknown god. A great, low, in-going curve of a blackened tiled roof with wide eaves that seem to be quite two-thirds of the whole, and low white walls; and this repeated in varying sizes that cluster together, the whole set in such gardens, ingeniously pinched and tortured, as I have told you of, or perhaps half-hidden behind a score of grotesquely gnarled pine trees—that is the abode of blood-royal in Japan, and the most imposing architectural idea one finds there. It is repeated in the temples, with a dusky riot of coloured beasts all round where the frescoes ought to be, and a succession of many steps leading to the squalid mystery of the interior. And we saw very little more than that as we walked up the broad drive within the walls of the palace of the Mikado himself.

We found ourselves presently in a wide corridor. The ceiling was high, and squared off with partitions like frames, and from each frame a vari-coloured design shone down on us. Some of the designs were painted on silk, some were lacquered on wood, some were made in tapestry, and looked like antimacassars transfixed in their flight to a better world. The walls were done in cream silk, covered with a beautiful sweeping design in gold, the floor was of cedar and inlaid, and the plate-glass doors, through which one saw the magnificence of the reception-rooms, stood in great, massive, lacquered red-brown frames that gave back one's face like mirrors. Let into the lower parts of them were marvels in ivory relief, ferns and flowers, buds and berries, fruit and fishes, standing forth in perfect imitative beauty, as they might have grown out of the wood.

It was late in the day, and we found ourselves almost alone in these strange surroundings, which expressed an odd mixture of Japanese art and foreign ideals. One little *ok' sama* toddled on in front of us, her small black head bent curiously forward like a bird's, full of nervous alarm, and bowing low to the official who passed her. It was a very great episode in her life, this glimpse of the halls of the Mikado, though she must have been the wife of an officer of rank to be admitted, and she knew it beseemed her to walk reverently.

At the door of the corridor I felt a curious sensation in my fingers, which led me to draw forth my note-book and try to put on one of its pages what I saw before me—the wide, smooth courtyard; the queer dark walls with their concave outlines, the stone bouquet of electric lights, the gaunt pines beyond. There was nobody about but a little policeman, who looked at me with serious alarm. He stood on one foot with perturbation, he stood on the other with vacillation; he brought up on both of them with dignity, approached, discovered my presumption, and scurried off. Orthodocia was convinced that he had gone to bring the Mikado, and implored me so that by the time he had returned with seven others greater than himself I had finished, and was simply standing with my friend in an affectionate attitude and rapt admiration of the view. There seemed no reason to interfere with that, so they circled round us once or twice and then retired to confer. But in any case it would have been impossible to be afraid of guardians of the peace—even seven of them—who wore carpet slippers. Orthodocia said that any enterprising foreigner would simply have used them for implements of chastisement.

Except that the colour schemes differed, the great reception-rooms were very much alike, Japanese as to the ceilings and the walls, and European in every other place. One had a floor of inlaid squares in pale brown woods, and a cornice embossed in metal on a pale blue ground. The furniture was of blue plush, figured in yellow, and the walls were luminous with gold. Two great imported bronzes, German equestrian things, stood in the middle of the room, and about these were arranged those circular seats that give people such admirable opportunities for conversing with the backs of their necks. It was all very ambitious and very huge—the big

K 2

dining-room where His Majesty can do the Imperial honours for eighty-two guests at once, the waiting-rooms for people who are to receive an audience, and the throne-room itself. We paused at the throne-room, which was done wholly in crimson, with stunning barbarism. The walls were crimson flocked with gold, the floor was black and crimson, the furniture was crimson and gorgeously tasselled, and the tall canopy under which the Mikado and the Empress sit as the throng passes by, was crimson too. The curtain at the back of this was silk and cream-coloured, and covered with tiny gold chrysanthemums, while a big one blazed in the middle. Two tall golden rods, each topped by three white plumes, supported the affair, and a heavily-lacquered slab at each side bore marvellous cha- racters in gold on it. I suppose it was poetry—whenever we saw any- thing particularly intri- cate in Ja- panese hieroglyphics we were gene- rally told it was poetry. The curious sensation returned to my fingers, and my note-book came out again. So did a wiry little official in European clothes who had been watching us ever since I had had the audacity to commit a bit of the Mikado's courtyard to memory. I drew the daïs, and he peeped furtively over my shoulder. Orthodocia made a remark to him to divert his attention, but he took no notice of her, which convinced me that he was bordering upon temporary aberration. I went on with the side hangings; he began to wring his hands. The policemen were all there. They discussed the matter volubly among themselves. They made a ring round me and danced, and very

'FOR A BETTER VIEW OF THE FEATHERS I DROPPED UPON MY KNEES.'

nearly took to fisticuffing with one another in their hysteria. They came closer, and I didn't know whether to expect death by asphyxia or decapitation. For a better view of the feathers I dropped upon my knees. They took the posture to be one of adoration, but still failed to understand the pencil. They began to talk to me, and one ventured to twitch my sleeve. '*Ok' sama!*' he implored, '*Ok' sama!*' But it is reasonable to be deaf to Japanese, and '*Ok' sama!*' was oblivious, and sacrilegiously sketched on. A messenger was despatched, and went with trembling speed. He returned with an official who spoke English, but his English was at such a white heat that it was practically useless to him. The fact bubbled forth, however, that I was doing a thing unlawful and punishable, so I stopped. I didn't want to risk anything lingering.

We can never, never tell by what means we got a glimpse that afternoon, not only of the State part of the palace, but of the domestic Japanese part—the part sacred to the use of their Imperial Majesties themselves. If we did, somebody might get boiling oil. Orthodocia says she knows now exactly what it must feel like to be a Freemason, and go about longing to tell what nobody wants to know, and she wishes we hadn't seen it. But this is what it was like.

It is under a separate roof, is twenty-five feet higher up, and is connected with the rest of the palace only by corridors. In its heart there is a little chapel, very plain, perhaps eighteen feet square, with bamboo blinds on the windows, and simple *tatami* [1] on the floor. Very little else, except the inevitable Shinto looking-glass—to remind the prayer-maker who looks therein that his sins are seen as he sees his face. There the Mikado would retire every morning when he took possession, and muse upon the ancestors without whose aid he would have no palace, and no chapel to muse in. There is a popular statement to the effect that the Mikado inspects his own face carefully in the looking-glass every morning, and then prays diligently for all the shortcomings of the people. It may be true, and again it may be only another of the little Imperial scandals the stranger hears.

For one does not gather much that is reliable about Imperial domesticity in Japan; and this is not surprising in a country that can still look over its shoulder at a time when the person of the

[1] Matting.

Mikado was so sacred that he could not take it out of the palace himself. The air is full of stories, told by Europeans; but they bear their own stamp of unveracity; and the Japanese themselves protect their sensitiveness about their Mikado's moral and intellectual stature by a lacquer of polite ignorance. To queries as to his interests, his aims, his occupations, they have only one answer, usually accompanied by a shrug, which is not quite discreet—'*Makarimasen!*'—'I have not the slightest idea!' So between the prejudice of its guests and the pride of its subjects, the gold chrysanthemum is very well protected from any trial by fire, and glitters before the world with all the virtues of true Imperial metal taken for granted. Orthodocia has a photograph of the gentleman in question, however, and I mean to borrow it for Mr. Townsend to make a picture of. Then you will see for yourself that he looks more like the subtraction of the graces than the sum of the virtues.

As you have perhaps gathered from these pages aforetime, the Japanese idea of household decoration does not admit of much variety, and it is not surprising to find the only difference between the rooms of the Emperor and Empress and those of their well-to-do subjects to be an added fineness of texture and richness of lustre and grace of line. The same paper panels for walls, the same dainty alcoves, the same polished tree trunks for division, the same suggestion of colour and curve for beauty, in these rooms of the twelve ladies-in-waiting, as in the house of a servant of the Government at fifteen hundred a year. Of course the glittering birds flashing in and out of dark storm-clouds on the wall are pure gold, and designed by an artist who is much more than the William Morris of Japan, but there the distinction ends. Art is art all over this quaint little island; art is almost air, for everybody breathes it; and the person of the Mikado himself is not more sacred from travesty on the walls of any of his subjects. When the furniture, or the Japanese substitute for it, goes in, however, majesty may assert itself in some upholstered way. I did not see the furniture.

There is one place more sacred than the chapel, more sacred than any spot in the whole island of Nippon—a certain small room in the very centre of the Imperial quarters, used exclusively by the Mikado, which does not know the profanation of the foot of man—for the

Mikado himself is not a man but an Emperor. There he is served by pages and women, and the noblest of his ministers dare not enter. Orthodocia could not understand this objection of His Majesty to his own sex. To her, she said, its members and adherents had always seemed harmless enough; but we concluded that it was for some obscure reason connected with his ancestors.

He has an Empress, and a son, this Mikado. The son is being educated at a school for nobles—we often met him being driven to and from his lessons—and they told us that he had absorbed the idea of his own consequence to such an extent that he would not play with other little boys unless they took their caps off. The Empress is occasionally to be seen—rather a pretty little woman, and much in sympathy with the progressive movements of the country. I don't know how far an Empress of Japan is permitted to rule the affairs of her own household, but there is no doubt that the Court —at all events, the Court *en évidence*—is conforming more and more to the customs of the West. Ten years ago Her Majesty stared impassive into the space immediately surrounding the prostrate figure of the person enjoying the honour of presentation, like a Japanese doll on exhibition for its ability to wink. Now she smiles and bows, and to certain privileged people gives her hand. A year or two ago the Court went so far as to forbid the appearance, anywhere in its sacred vicinity, of anything but full dress according to European standards. The edict has been lately withdrawn, but very few of her subjects have gone back to the Japanese Court costume in consequence, as she has not. Two chamberlains and the Court physician still sit at the door of the State dining-room to taste the dishes and expire first, in polite indication to their Majesties that the cook has not been irritating enough to put strychnine into them; but this is a survival, and otherwise the official banquets might be given by the Lord Mayor in most respects. And though these gastronomic *attachés* of the Middle Ages invariably accompany them, their Majesties go out to dine upon occasion now. They even receive the bureaucracy of Tokio, and such foreigners as are introduced by the Legations at two garden parties a year—poetical garden parties that celebrate the flush of spring on the blossoming cherry trees, and the glory of autumn in the coming of the tattered yellow chrysanthemums.

But we must come back to Orthodocia in the wide corridors of the palace, who observed dotted here and there about the grounds other white temple-like habitations, and was given to understand that they were sub-matrimonial.

We stood for a moment upon the lacquered threshold of this descendant of the gods who rules Japan, looking away across his capital city with its thousands of tiny roofs, its curving moats, and the dark wandering lines of pine trees that mark its greater highways. It was not yet time for darkness and rest, and we heard the labour and the weariness and the failing heart of the long day's end in the call and the answer that throbbed up to us there at the door of the Emperor's palace, '*Huydah!*' . . . '*Houdah!*'

XV

I WONDER, as I regard all that I have already told you about the doings of Orthodocia and me in Japan, how I have kept away from them so long—I mean the shops; the marvellous, whimsical, quaint little shops. I have some qualms of conscience about it, too, for I have been submitting what purports to be a full and faithful chronicle of the way we spent our time there; and the undeniable fact is that we spent a great deal more of it in the shops than anywhere else. It was not intentional. We often walked out for exercise, opportunities for it being limited indoors; but the exercise was invariably taken in sittings of three hours each upon the floor of some small wonder-market that we particularly affected. Or we sallied forth in our jinrikishas, guide-book in hand, determined to do our duty by the stock sights of Tokio. The jinrikisha men are not allowed to run side by side for fear of blocking up the thoroughfare; but as soon as Orthodocia in advance missed me in the rear, she simply cried 'Halt!' in Japanese to her biped; descended and shopped until I turned up, which was usually too late for the guide-book. You have heard of the eruption at Bandai-san? On one occasion we were going to the scene of it, about twenty-four hours' journey from Tokio, having made an appointment with the Japanese railway system for ten A.M. On the way to the station Orthodocia fell among porcelain vendors, and that is one reason why we were obliged to leave Japan without any practical working knowledge of earthquakes whatever.

And it is not reasonable, in pages of a volume published primarily and particularly for the sex that loves to shop, to postpone an account of the Japanese method further. Will you go a day's bargain hunting then, in the Land of the Rising Sun, with Orthodocia and me?

This you must learn first—that a '*yen*' is a dollar, a '*sen*' is a cent, a '*ri*' is the tenth of a cent. More than one '*ri*' are so many '*rin*.' '*Ichi*,' '*ni*,' '*san*,' '*shi*,' '*go*' express one, two, three, four, five to the native mind. '*Jiu*' is ten, and in the multiplication of '*jiu*' you prefix the lesser numbers, as '*ni-jiu*,' for twenty. In adding to '*jiu*' you affix them, as '*jiu-ni*' for twelve. The proper understanding of this point is indispensable. The difference looks unimportant in print, but after you have paid '*san-jiu yen*' a few times for a thing you thought you offered thirteen dollars for, you begin to realise it. '*Yasui*' is cheap, '*takai*' is dear, and '*takusan*' is 'plenty,' used for 'very' by the hob-nailed tourist who does not object to ungrammatical bargains—'*Takusan takai!*' And the indispensable 'How much?' is '*Ikura?*' When a person dies who has once visited Japan, '*Ikura?*' will be found indelibly stamped across his acquisitive faculties. It becomes the interrogative of value to him for all time. Whatever his tongue may say, his soul will never ask a price again in any other terms.

This may seem a little inadequate as a Japanese vocabulary, but I am not coaching you for an examination in Oriental tongues; and when you go to Japan you will find it a compendium of all that is useful and elegant in the language. I present it with some gratification as the net result of philological researches that covered an area of six weeks, and beg that you will use it just as if it were your own whenever you require it, on this present or any subsequent occasion.

I don't know that I ought to say that we are going 'shopping.' The term is improper and impertinent in the Mikado's empire, but no appreciative person with a sense of commercial niceties has yet invented a better one. You don't 'shop' in the accepted sense in Japan. Shopping implies premeditation, and premeditation is in vain there. If you know what you want, your knowledge is set aside in a moment, in the twinkling of an eye, and your purchases gratify anticipations that you never had—to be entirely paradoxical. The taint of vulgarity which great and noisy 'emporiums' have cast upon the word is also absent there. So is the immorality of competing prices. To shop in Japan is to perform an elaborate function which operates directly on the soul; its effect upon the pocket is an ulterior consideration which does not appear at all until three days later, when one's first ecstasy is overpast. Then, perhaps, psychical luxuries strike one as being a little expensive.

And you never fully know the joy of buying until you buy in Japan. Life condenses itself into one long desire, keener and more intense than any want you have ever had before—the desire of paying and possessing. The loftiest aims are swallowed up in this; the sternest scientist, or political economist, or social theorist that was ever set ashore at Yokohama straightway loses life's chief end among the curio shops, and it is at least six weeks before he finds it again. And as to the ordinary individual, like you and Orthodocia and me, without the guidance of superior aims, time is no more for her, nor things temporal; she is lost in contemplation of the ancient and the eternal in the art of Nippon; and she longs to be a man that she might go to the unspeakable length of pawning her grand-aunt's watch, or selling her own boots in order to carry it off with her to the extent of the uttermost farthing within her power. At least, that is the way Orthodocia said she felt. Don't imagine you ever experienced anything like it in a Japanese shop in London, where the prices give you actual chills, and the demeanour of the ladies-in-waiting lowers the temperature further. Japan can't be exported with her *bric-à-brac*, and, after all, it is Japan you succumb to first, and her bronzes and porcelains afterwards.

Our European friends, who live in the district of Tsukigi, in the only houses in Tokio that have chimneys, have the temerity to advise us to go to the foreign shops of Yokohama to make our purchases. 'There,' they say, 'you will see a much greater assortment, and you won't be cheated.'

'Go to a *foreign* shop!' Orthodocia exclaims. 'Traffic with an ordinary, *business-like*'—with loathing—'Englishman or American, when one may be charmed into a transaction by these charmers of Japan!' while I say something indignantly about not having lived a month in the country without knowing the Japanese scale of prices. All of which they receive in smiling silence, telling us later that they did not expect for a moment that we would listen, that nobody ever did at first.

He sits there, doth Yano-san, all in the midst of his temptations, with his *hibachi*[1] beside him, his wife behind him, and his various offspring round about him. Yano-san smokes thoughtfully. His pipe is a bamboo stem with metal ends, and the bowl thereof would not make a baby's thimble. He fills it at intervals, lights it at the *hibachi*, takes two long whiffs, taps out the ash, and relapses into meditation, his blue *kimono* falling over his stooping shoulders, his face the face of one who takes life with serious philosophy. While we are yet afar off Yano-san becomes aware of us, with an intuition that makes us wonder. His face changes, he no longer ponders the problem of life and the future state; he is up and doing, smiling, bowing, dusting off his best curios with a lively hope. And we? We stand fascinated, giving over our hearts to greed. It never occurs to us that curio shops in Japan are as thick as the leaves on a mulberry tree. This is the only one the land has for us; this pleased and flattered person with a world of calculation behind the politeness in his eyes, the single vendor of Tokio with whom we have the slightest desire to do business. Four bareheaded women with babies on their backs, five small boys, and a couple of young students in felt hats are presently regarding three pairs of buttoned boots on the threshold with attentive interest. Their owners are inside getting great bargains.

I fancy I see you.

'That Satsuma incense burner—*ikura*?'

Yano-san picks it up musingly, turns it round, and steps back a pace for a point of view as if he had never seen the article in his life before.

'*Sono*[2]—*takusan* numb' one—very many old—*sono!*—*san yen, go-jiu sen!*' with a mighty effort at decision.

'Three dollars and a half!' I ejaculate at your elbow. 'It would be at least six in America! Better take it, hadn't you?—quick—before he raises the price. Lovely thing! But they always cheat foreigners—offer three twenty-five for it.'

'*San yen, ni-jiu-go sen!*' You enunciate distinctly, but with trepidation lest your bargain be lost.

A gentle shade passes over the countenance of Yano-san, con-

[1] Fire-pot.   [2] That.

'WHILE WE ARE YET AFAR OFF YANG-SAN BECOMES AWARE OF US.'

cealing his triumph. He shakes his head doubtfully and looks sadly at the incense-burner. Suddenly he looks up. '*Yuroshi!*'[1] he says, with cheerful resignation, and compunction steals into your soul. Perhaps, after all, you have been overreaching—you have so many *sen*, and he such a small stock-in-trade. You look at his little family, at his placid brown wife preparing his poor meal of rice and pickled turnip, and you are covered with bitter reproaches. And for your next fancy, which is a *kakemono* with a didactic Buddha sitting on a lotus blossom in the middle, surrounded by his disciples, you pay the full price ungrudgingly.

'THE CHEAPEST THING IN DRAGONS ORTHODOCIA EVER SAW.'

[1] All right.

Orthodocia is sitting rapturous before a particular variety of Japanese dragon in wood, a most delightful and original and impossible of beasts, who vaults playfully into your affections on the spot, with a smile on his broadly impertinent face and his tail flourished high in air. He is amazingly cheap—the cheapest thing in dragons Orthodocia ever saw ; she buys him at about a *ri* a pound. Unguardedly she says so. ' *Yasui !*' she remarks, pleasantly, ' *Yasui !*' And the price of everything in the shop goes up fifty per cent. higher than it was before. Then we fall victims collectively and individually to an ivory monkey smoking a pipe, and a bronze stork holding a lotus blossom in his beak, and sets of saki cups and rice bowls, and old steel mirrors that reflected Japanese beauty in the days before foreigners introduced it to the modern article called so appropriately by the North American Indians a 'she-lookem.' The crowd about the door swells visibly, and begins to enjoy our purchases almost as much as we do, quietly laughing at every fresh negotiation. We grow more excited and more enthusiastic, the glamour of Japan is over all we see ; and we congratulate ourselves on our knowingness in making Yano san 'come down' a certain amount on almost every article. We grow bold and cunning in our negotiations, and Yanosan plies us with innumerable cups of green tea in the intervals between them, to stimulate the spirit of investment. It is somewhat in this wise. Picking up a *cloisonné* vase from the floor beside you, you ask the price.

'*Shi yen shi-jiu sen*,' says Yano-san, grown prompt with practice.

'*Takai—takai !*' smiling ingratiatingly.

'*Takai-na ! Yasui !—takusan yasui !*' still firm but polite.

'*Takusan takai !*' keenly feeling your impoverishment of speech. '*San yen go jiu sen !*'

Yano-sen shakes his head and puts the piece back in its place. '*Dekimasen !*'—'I am not able '—he answers.

'*Shi yen !*' you offer, conceding the half-dollar. Then it appears that Yano-san can make concessions also. He will not meet you half-way, but he will do something.

'*Shi yen, san-jiu-go-sen-gorry !*' he says, with the air of one who makes a final statement. He has taken off four cents and a half.

YANO-SAN.

This beating-down is demoralising to one's self-respect; but it must be done, and you accept the reduction. Farewells occur — happy farewells. Our jinrikisha man lifts up the seat of his vehicle, and bestows our purchases under it, after some conversation with Yano-san. Then we ride home, jubilant with the joy of her who has got a great deal for very little to our foreign friends resident in Tokio.

They regard the lot with a trifle of superciliousness, we think, but set it down privately to be the jealous criticism of people who have missed a good bargain.

'And how much for that thing?' indicating the Satsuma *koro*.

'Three twenty-five only!' with pride, defiance, and resentment.

'Three twenty-five *only*! Do you mean to say—well, of course, if you like it so much as that—and how much for the *kakemono*?'

The price of the *kakemono* is received in silence. So is that of the rampant dragon and the ivory monkey, and the stork and the mirror, and the other objects of interest. This lack of criticism begins to become oppressive, and vague alarms prey upon our minds.

'Well,' one of us says; 'cheap, weren't they?'

'If you had paid one-third of the price you did pay,' replies our candid friend, 'you would have got them at their market value; but even then they would not have been cheap, for they are worthless at any price.' This is unpleasant, but salutary. It is followed by a disquisition on each of our purchases, by which we learn that your *koro* is a base imitation of Satsuma; that your *kakemono* is gilt meretriciously, and likely to peel; that my stork is copper, and not bronze; that Orthodocia's monkey is vulgar, and her china coarse.

And we are reduced to a state of mind more nearly bordering upon desolation than anything we have yet known.

But there are joys to come. After all, we have not left our whole fortune with Yano-san; and we turn our footsteps with humility towards the despised and rejected foreign usurpers of Yokohama. I remember one place which became a perfect resort for Orthodocia and me after we had acquired our education. It was the only art gallery we saw in Japan. We affected it to an extent out of all proportion to our incomes, as most people do, and we may as well take you there on this—reminiscent—occasion.

It is a distinctly agreeable thing to see the proprietor come forward to greet us as a fellow-being. We feel that we would like to shake hands with him for doing it. We didn't realise how deeply we yearned for the business methods of the Philistines, for assortment and choice, and room to walk about in, and unmercurial prices, and the English language, and information To buy a curio in a Japanese curio-shop is like investing in a piece of the Dark Ages, unlabelled. It might be almost anything, and it is not at all likely that your curio-dealer could enlighten you much about it if he could talk, which he can't. Neither does our art-collector profess to

L

understand his treasures fully. But it is one of his objectionable enterprising foreign innovations—I have a distinctly American memory of him—to introduce a Japanese connoisseur or two in his establishment, who undertake the education of the tourist of average intelligence in Japanese art, with alacrity and enthusiasm. I don't mind telling you that one of the things Orthodocia and I pledged one another to do with great fervour, was to look deeply and carefully into Japanese art, inquiring of the Japanese themselves. This vow is made by everybody who goes to Japan; but I do not mind asserting that most of the information the average tourist acquires he owes, as we do, to one or two of the foreign dealers of Yokohama.

One sees nothing, anywhere else in the world, like the wonders that tempt us to ruin in this other sort of shopping in Japan. As a nation, she measures us, and manufactures to suit what she believes to be our taste; and these things she sends us and no other. For the best Japanese art we must go to Japan. It does not leave the country as merchandise.

Just inside the door, as we enter, a Japanese artist stands in the loose, graceful, native costume. He has been at work, and is holding, with admirable pose, his bit of ivory carving at arm's length to note the effect. His face is the patient, brooding, unconscious face of the Japanese who makes beautiful things with his hands. His expression of absorbed appreciation is perfect. His face is pale, and his black hair falls loosely back from his forehead. His lips are set with gentleness, and there is great pleasure in his narrow dark eyes. The figure is a model, and the artist made it like himself. It is marvellous in our eyes.

Ivory wonders—*takusan*! The loveliest is a maiden, Japanese, slightly idealised, as the heroine of a romance might be. She holds a bird-cage in her hand, empty; and her head is turned in the direction of the truant tenant's flight. The soft dull white of the ivory is not vexed by any colours, but fine lines and patterns of the most unobtrusive blacks and browns, that shade away into it delicately. The folds of her dress are exquisitely long and thin and graceful—she stands there an ephemeral thing caught imperishably, and her price is five hundred and fifty dollars—height ten inches. At your elbow is a tiny teapot, value five cents. Orthodocia buys the teapot and longs for the maiden. As she cannot possibly have the maiden she buys another teapot.

Perhaps the most remarkable ivories there, for ingenuity and workmanship, are two dragons, one four feet long, the other about two, made of innumerable scale-like pieces, each piece a separate work of art. Their claws are fantastically realistic, their pink tongues loll and dart, their eyes have curious lights in them. There is no spring in their long, sinuous bodies, yet their mechanism is so perfect that when you place them on the floor their long necks erect themselves, and their diabolical heads look forth, tense and alert.

As to Satsuma, our eyes are opened. We had thought 'old Satsuma' abounded in porcelain shops at least as freely as it does in the drawing-rooms of modern novels. But we learn that 'old' Satsuma hardly exists at all now, and that 'gorgeous' old Satsuma never did exist. When the Coreans began their wonderful work for the use of the Court and the nobles they understood and used only the simplest designs, and even the imitations, of which we can buy —and alas ! have bought—many, are decorated in the scantiest way. Our Japanese lecturer explains that in a search of two years, undertaken by his employers, only one bit of real antiquity turned up—a *koro* two and a half inches high, for which they paid fifty dollars.

We ask humbly if there is any good modern Satsuma, and are shown a few pieces, which convince us, if by the price alone, that we have never seen any before. He brings tenderly forth—the lecturer —a five-inch vase. It habitually nestles in an embroidered silk bag. Groups of children appear in the decoration, each tiny face perfect under the glass, though not one is more than three-tenths of an inch in size. The gold is pure, the colours are delicate, the arabesques drawn with dainty truth. And we conclude simultaneously, you and Orthodocia and I, that many rhapsodies over 'old Satsuma,' indulged before we came to Japan, were inspired by enormities in Awata ware, which were much too vulgar to stay in their native land.

On the farther side of a great black door, arranged like the gate of a temple, is the inner sanctuary, where the inquiring tourist may penetrate and be instructed in many other things by this high priest of porcelains. And the next thing we learn is that we have never seen *cloisonné* before. An object lesson of six common plaques, in the six different stages of the process, convinces us that we have been previously familiar only with unlimited editions of the sixth common plaque all these past years, when we fondly imagined we had profited by a whole cult of *cloisonné*. We knew the process theoretically before—the first plate hammered into symmetry out of copper, with the design drawn on it with ink, the second having the design outlined with a flat, upright wire, fastened down with cement, the third covered with the first filling, the burning having fastened the wires to the body, the fourth the second layer of filling and second burning. One more burning, when the plaque is ready to be polished, and we see it after being rubbed down with pumice and water. Then it is a round, blue, commonplace thing, with a pink chrysanthemum or two on it, perhaps, and a conventionalised bird in flight towards them, possibly worth a silver dollar. I should have thought it beautiful in America, but here it suffers by contrast with *cloisonné* that does not go to America or to England either, except in the boxes of tourists of the skilled kind. Here is a piece captured on its way to the Paris Exposition, a ball-shaped vase, about five inches in diameter. Its polish is so perfect that it seems to gleam through from the inside, and innumerable specks of pure gold glint in it. All the tints imaginable contribute to its colour harmony, yet it leaves in the main a soft rich brown impression. Each separate leaf and flower and bird of its marvellously intricate design gives one a special little thrill of pleasure, not by its fidelity, but by its exquisite ideality. Only one man can work like this, and he is not a man who knows anything about 'realism' or pre-Raphaelism; not a man who votes or reads the magazines, or takes an interest in sanitary science or foreign politics—but a man whose life lies in the doing of this one thing, and who knows its value only by the joy it gives him.

It grows dusky and late in here behind the great black temple gate among the screens, and the kotos, and the tall bronze vases, and the daimios' swords. Across the harbour the junk lights are beginning to shine out in clusters and long lines. The artist at the door, as we glance back and close it, still looks—an artist always—through the gathering shadows at the ivory in his outstretched hand.

XVI

IT was New Year's Day in the morning.

'*Omedette!*' said I to Orthodocia, bowing in the manner which represented my sole Japanese accomplishment. I had acquired both the expression and the bow with great care, wishing to felicitate her in an original way upon New Year's Day, and to impress her with my progress in the language at the same time. I found it difficult to impress Orthodocia with my progress in the language as a general thing. She is a linguist herself, and linguists are intolerant, contemptuous people.

Just to be aggravating, Orthodocia bowed still lower.

'*Omedette de gozarimas!*' she remarked triumphantly, with perfect self-possession, and without at all acknowledging my politeness; and then we looked at one another in a manner which I might almost describe as ruffled. A little explanation and translation made everything clear, however, and our appreciation of ourselves immediately rose to par again. We had merely wished one another a Happy New Year out of different phrase-books—a circumstance insignificant in itself, but which threatened at the time to cast the gloom and shadow of a doubt over our respective attainments in Japanese, and therefore to mar the peace of a habitation not constructed to withstand dissensions. Harmonious living must be the rule in Japan. A genuine family jar would bring the house down.

The New Year had come to all Japan, and all Japan was brimful of rejoicing. We had looked about us for festivities at Christmas, but they told us then to wait for New Year's Day; so we solemnly presented each other with little bronze pins in the morning and a 'Merry Christmas!' that was rather choking, and rode through the twinkling streets in the evening to a little restaurant that dispensed 'foreign foods' in the shadow of the great gray Buddha of a public park. There we pledged one another in the wine of the land, and wondered what Japanese turkeys were fed on to make them so different from the turkeys of other Christmases, and Orthodocia talked Wigginton, Devon, with such exile in her voice that I very nearly shed tears into the pudding-sauce. But the occasion of our foreign feasting was passed, and the day of the year for Japan had come. We went downstairs to see what it was like.

There in the kitchen our little idolaters one and all were making merry. They were accustomed to make merry; in fact, they were obliged to do it to while away the time, their responsibilities being light. If their mirth became too uproarious at any time, we had only to put our heads through the wall and say with severity '*Yakamashi!*' and a blighting silence fell at once, accompanied by awe and despondency. We had not the slightest idea of the moral force of '*Yakamashi!*' and its effect was so dismal that we used it as seldom as possible, and only as extreme discipline. On New Year's morning, when there was a special note of hilarity among our domestics, we did not use it. It was pleasant to have the holiday in the house.

They were sitting round the *hibachi* in a smiling circle when we descended, and Chrysanthemum was very gay in a blue *kimono* and an *obi* that could vie with Joseph's coat. Yoshitane-san made a profound obeisance, and expressed their collective congratulation, to which Orthodocia responded in feeling terms. Then, while Buddha elaborately arranged five bits of charcoal under the oatmeal with a pair of iron chop-sticks, and Chrysanthemum blew through a long piece of bamboo upon three discouraged embers that were trying to boil the eggs, we despatched old 'Rice and Saki Only' with fifty sen to buy the wherewithal for kitchen festivities. One and ninepence was not a large sum to grow riotous upon, but our ancient servitor came back laden with good cheer for more than one reckless repast —his round brown face all twisted into merry wrinkles, his decrepid legs two crooks of grateful deprecation. A salted salmon, three feet long; a great basket of sweet potatoes, split in halves and roasted brown; two square yards of half-baked *mochi*,[1] white and viscid and three inches thick; a special New Year's delicacy, of which the

---

[1] Bean-cake.

chief ingredient seemed to be mucilage; half a dozen neat little fish rolls; several parcels of seaweed that looked like smooth-mottled dark-

'IN THE SHADOW OF THE GREAT GRAY BUDDHA OF A PUBLIC PARK.'

green paper, and vegetable accessories. The fish rolls were particularly appetising, half a small raw fish wrapped round a ball of rice—somebody may like the recipe. It was a feast for the gods of Japan; and jolly Dai-koku himself could not have wished for better spirits than it brought.

After breakfast we walked out of our inhospitable little front gates to find an extraordinary growth on each side of it not bargained for with our landlord. It shot straight and stiffly up out of the ground about four feet, and consisted of a bushy bunch of pine branches and three sections of green bamboo. We had stopped giving way to astonishment in Japan, finding that it made too much of a demand upon our time; so we simply contemplated this addition to the scenery about our residence, and asked Buddha if it had come to stay. As we expected, Buddha was responsible for it. Buddha was responsible for everything, from the Japanese cat without a tail, that made night hideous for a week, and took no notice whatever of her proper name, but answered to a chirrup and made incomprehensible remarks, and was an idolater, to the hanging of a large soap advertisement in our small *salon* under the impression that it was a masterpiece of foreign art. We looked to him, therefore, for the general explanation of our domestic matters. And Buddha gave us to understand, with the assistance of an old American almanack, that it devolved upon us as temporary citizens of Tokio to decorate for the New Year as the custom was. He had bought and planted the decorations, trusting to our sense of our responsibilities for justification, and it was not withheld.

We sped away through the city in our jinrikishas with that comfortable sense of duty done that predisposes one to the scrutiny of other people's behaviour. But we found Tokio ready for it. Nobody had quite forgotten to welcome the New Year, however tiny the bird-cage dwelling over which it would dawn for him. His tiled roof might be sunken and his paper panes ragged and black, but over the door surely waved a few palmetto fronds with a bit of white paper fluttering among them, if nothing else; and his ivory-lidded babies, crowing and tottering in the street exactly as you might expect a Japanese doll to crow and totter, looked up at them with sharp beady anticipation in their little black eyes. Our own decorations were extremely popular, and a common gate-post ornament was a bit of twisted rice-straw rope, fern leaves, and a fruit that looked like a half-ripe bitter orange. The more ambitious had arches of the glossy camellia twigs with strings of yellow mandarins twined in them; and flags, a red sun on a white ground; and that quaint crustacean which is not quite lobster and not quite crab, red from the pot, bent and sprawled before every door of pretension. The rice straw means prosperity; the craw-fish, because he has always looked decrepid, a good old age; the universal tag of white paper, a request to the gods, long honoured in Shintoism, for general favours. It was all so *naïf*, so touching, that I should

'LOOKED UP AT THEM WITH SHARP BEADY ANTICIPATION IN THEIR LITTLE BLACK EYES.'

think even the woodenest, stoniest god, moved by the discovery that he is not yet quite forgotten, would exert himself a little on behalf of the decorators.

People were flying about in jinrikishas with all sorts of purchases in their laps, and the eastern approximation to a Christmas look on their faces. A small wooden bird-cage, with two dainty little inmates all in white with pink bills; a long willowy branch, with a gay little conception in candy on every dancing twig; a plum tree in a pot in full blossom, eighteen inches high; a close-shut wooden box, in which we had learned to expect something specially sacred in curios. Even the Japanese customers in the shops seemed inspired by an unusual excitement, and made their investments in lacquer and porcelain almost at the rate of one investment per hour, putting on their sandals and clicking off again with comparative recklessness. The buying enthusiasm became infectious, and one result is that if anybody wants a black silk gentleman's *kimono*, embroidered in purple dragons and green storks, warranted worn steadily by at least three generations, I think Orthodocia would dispose of it for almost anything.

The wide, pale gray streets were all flung open to the sun, and the great blue arch overhead seemed inconceivably far above the gay little wooden habitations that bubbled up on each side of them. Many of the shops were shut; few sat at the receipt of custom but the sellers of yellow *mikan*[1] and sweet potatoes, and the whole city seemed to be making holiday, clattering up hill and down in its very best clothes. The ladies of position who have borrowed our skirts were at home receiving in them, but plenty of hybrid costumes were abroad among the men, the favourite article of masculine attire being comfortable woollen under-continuations which should not, of course, be so much as mentioned among us. O-Haru-San, who tottered past us on her high black-lacquered *getas*, was not a lady of position. Very dainty and very fine was O-Haru-San on New Year's Day, with the ivory hair-pins, the beads, and the flowers in the wide black puffs of her hair, with her face all artlessly whitened and reddened, with the never-failing tiny dab of gold on her full under lip. The soft folds of her inner *kimonos* were white and gray and delicate about her plump neck; and the outer one was of the tenderest blue, with a dash of scarlet where the wide sleeves parted. Her sash was a marvel to behold, and from top to toe she was all in silk, this daughter of the Mikado. Nobody at all was O-Haru-San; only a singer or a dancer, perhaps, or she would not be abroad in a

---

[1] Oranges.

crowd like a dog or a foreigner; but she made the Japanese picture of New Year's Day that we shall longest remember, I think.

Even the children were tricked out in quaint imitation of their elders—girl babies of five and six painted and powdered like the veriest coquettes. They were all playing in the streets, and their fathers and mothers with them, flying kites—wonderful kites, with dragons and gods on them, that hovered thick in air like charmed birds. Not a soul was sad, indifferent, contemptuous, and nobody laughed except at the glorious sport of it.

That day, as we sat sideways at our modest mid-day meal, on our cushions Buddha approached with an air of importance and a tray, which he presented, kneeling with the usual ceremony. On the tray lay a paper package, sealed with a diamond shaped piece of black paper, and tied with red and white twisted string. A paper trifle, also red and white, and folded like a

'AS WE SAT SIDEWAYS ON OUR CUSHIONS AT OUR MODEST MID-DAY MEAL.'

kite, was stuck under the string. That and the string and the black diamond all betokened a gift. We opened eagerly one wrapper and another, and found our first Japanese New Year's present to consist of half a pound of moist brown sugar. Orthodocia ascertained that it came from the grocer from whom we had bought our preliminaries. The preliminaries were indubitably fraudulent; but we were so affected by this kind attention to two alien young women, six thousand miles from home, that we immediately sent for a large additional supply. This at once threatened to become a precedent, and, if it had, we should have gone into insolvency by six o'clock. For the fruiterer, who had a large establishment round the corner with nothing but ground rent to pay, sent us a dainty bamboo basket of mandarins, with green strips laced across the top; the rival grocer, to whom we had temporarily encumbered, enticed us further with a string of peppers; a city confectioner, whose foreign nougat and pistachios we had greatly appreciated, touched our hearts with a real plum cake and a pink rose on it. And, as we were comparing conclusions about the plum cake, the House having gone into Supply, there came a box. The box was delicately wooden, with four feet, and a bamboo twig for the handle of the cover. The card of a Japanese friend came with it, and the gift token. We lifted the cover rapturously, and it disclosed two dozen of as neat little brown eggs, each reposing on its sawdust cushion, as ever entered a larder of civilisation. Eggs are the most popular of New Year's gifts in Japan, we had always heard; but to know this theoretically, and to practise it practically, are very different matters. Each smooth little oval had a separate charm for us; it appealed directly to our housekeeping susceptibilities; it seemed to fill a long-felt want as nothing in the way of a presentation ever had before. We had been told that it was the custom of people who received several thousand eggs annually to send them forth again on their errand of congratulation and potential omelets; and we had heard of a gentleman who marked one of his eggs for future reference, and had the selfsame egg returned to him after many days—tradition says the next New Year. Orthodocia said that she did not believe this egg story; but we thought we would not be graceless about our eggs and redistribute them, but grateful and scramble them.

Re-entered Buddha with another mystery. It reposed on a lacquered tray, and was covered with a blue silk square. On the square was embroidered in gold a peacock *flamboyant*. Under the square a piece of white paper, under the paper a bowl of red lacquer, in the bowl a large green rose with yellow leaves of Japanese confectionery, a bunch of celery in candy, a woodcock with his bill under his wing, and a dough-cake of pounded rice flour, pink and pernicious. This gift was purely Japanese, the other had a flavour of cosmopolitanism. Purely Japanese also was the card that came with it, which made the situation embarrassing. We summoned Buddha, but the card was beyond Buddha. He studied it long and earnestly, and finally gave us to understand that it was not English —if it had been he might have told us more about it. But he made a demonstration when Orthodocia folded up the embroidered square and I attempted to put the bowl and tray carefully away in the wall. His demonstration was one of such extreme anxiety that we let him carry it out. He took the bowl and washed it, put it on the tray as before, and threw the silk gracefully over it. Then he went to our foreign hearth and picked up one of the neat little oblong bits of kindling which lay there, and put it in the bowl. We argued and entreated to no avail. 'Japan way,' he said with quiet obstinacy, and we were obliged to see him return the whole with many bows to the person who brought it. We discovered afterwards that Buddha's acquaintance with the latest thing in Japanese etiquette was to be relied upon, perhaps because the latest thing is usually also the earliest thing by several centuries. The antiquity of this custom of sending a small quantity of comparatively inexpensive nourishing matter in a gold embroidered ceremony and taking back the ceremony, for example, is incalculable, and the chip dates back to the days of the real dragons, I have no doubt. It was a great comfort to us afterwards, when we found out that the rose and celery had been intended for somebody else to whom it would have brought no indigestion, to know that Buddha had attended to that matter of the chip. At least the sender could not reproach us with ingratitude.

'Visiting on New Year's Day is a Japanese custom,' a native gentleman translated to us from the *Jiji-Shimbun*[1] of the day after, 'but foreigners are becoming so Japanised that we met many blue eyes and red moustaches making calls yesterday.' This was delightfully cool of the *Jiji-Shimbun*, and we said so, but the native gentleman only lifted his eyebrows a little and smiled. The smile said: 'We have got our sciences from you, and our educational system, and certain ideas for our new Constitution, but in matters of etiquette we copy nobody—we lead the world.'

[1] Daily newspaper.

Orthodocia and I had no blue-eyed or red-moustached visitors on that memorable '*jour de l'an*,' but were very happy to receive one or two whose eyes and moustaches properly belonged to the custom. We had rehearsed the ceremony of their reception with care, solemnly agreeing that it should be carried out strictly in the Japanese manner. 'When they come to our country,' Orthodocia said very properly, 'they adopt our customs, our chairs, our knives and forks. It is only polite that we should return the compliment.' So we had our bows in our pocket as it were, and our raw fish, our boiled *daigon*, our seaweed, and our sugared beans all ready in the lacquered compartment box of ceremony. The hot *saki* steamed in the quaint long-nosed bronze *saki* pot, used only on New Year's Day ; and the tiny, thin, handleless *saki* cups, in sets of three, suggested a prescription rather than wine and wassail. The square flat velvet cushions were ready too, on which we were to drop gracefully, kneeling with palms outspread upon the floor, and bowing as low in that position as circumstances would permit. We surveyed our arrangements with nervous anticipation, and every time a jinrikisha passed outside Orthodocia flopped down on her cushion to be entirely ready when the visitor entered.

Our first caller, whose name was Mr. Shiro Hashimoto, by his card, came early, very early indeed, following the mandates of their Imperial Majesties across the moat, who take their congratulations before they take anything else, I believe. We did not see Mr. Shiro Hashimoto, the New Year not having dawned for us at the time of his arrival. This was a source of bitter regret to Orthodocia. 'If we had only been up!' she said. 'To have received a Japanese visit of congratulation in the dimness of the early morning—so nice and characteristic!' She was still mourning Mr. Shiro Hashimoto when Buddha appeared in the wall solemnly ushering in another.

Orthodocia dropped, according to agreement, with dramatic effect. In the midst of her third bow she cast upon me a look of agonised reproach, which I felt all too keenly that I deserved ; for, covered with ignominy, I was shaking hands with the native gentleman—Japan had required too much of me. And he, in horrible uncertainty, was making a superhuman gymnastic effort to pay his respects to both of us at once, which must have resulted in dislocation somewhere.

I should be glad to record this reception the distinguished success Orthodocia and I intended it to be, but I can't with rectitude. We wanted to pay our guest the compliment of conversing in Japanese, he wanted to pay us the compliment of conversing in English ; and the compliments got confused. We were very generous with our Japanese, we kept none of it in reserve. All we had we brought out freely for his benefit, and his English was submitted to us in the same candid way. When he fell back upon Japanese, therefore, or we upon English, the situation became even more complicated, and the simplest phrases of an infant's primer in either language assumed a subtlety that demanded two grammars and a dictionary. Our refreshments were also a source of mortification to us. The *saki* was fairly appreciated ; but our Japanese 'solids' were ignored in a way that cut deep into Orthodocia's housekeeping sensibilities. In vain did she press our pearly rice in a red rice-bowl ; in vain did I offer one tier after another of our storied box of delicacies. Our visitor received one and all with a bow and a grave smile, laid it carefully on the floor beside him, and drank more *saki* to console our wounded feelings. After he had departed, little Chrysanthemum, coming in to remove the *débris*, appeared to go into a suppressed convulsion. In the kitchen the convulsion became a series ; and when we sternly demanded its cause, that dear little heathen, her small fat body doubled up with mirth, pointed to a corner where stood in a desolate row six pairs of the forgotten chop-sticks !

It is difficult to acquire the domestic economy of Japan thoroughly in a month. The chop-stick might be called one of its chief features, and yet it had utterly escaped us.

Mr. Ichitaro Takayanagi and Mr. Takashi Takayanagi sent in their cards a few minutes later, and Orthodocia kept them waiting a disgracefully long time in the vestibule while Chrysanthemum whisked away every vestige of our Japanese preparations. Then she sat up very straight and stiff on her cushion, and talked to Mr. Ichitaro and Mr. Takashi in five o'clock tea English that neither of them understood, for they only knew American. They both apologised very profoundly for having been away from home the day we called—and the more Orthodocia assured them that the call was made upon their mamma, the more deeply they regretted not having been there to receive the honour of our visit—it was 'so very kind' of us to come !

* * * * * * *

And after a time we went forth into the merry street, and with a feathered nut and a painted wooden bat, we played battledore and shuttlecock, and all our household with us, till the sun went down behind the roof of the temple, and the wind came in from the sea.

* * * * * * *

That night Tokio went tipsy. It was a gentle glowing tipsiness, that shook and swayed and trembled under innumerable low roofs, over the bare heads of clattering multitudes, aimlessly happy, smiling, bowing, because one always smiles and bows at this especial season ; content to bridge all the problems of life as they bridged the mud with their wooden sandals. Down the long streets miles on miles the paper lanterns shone, bulbous, serene, rows on rows, clusters on clusters, lines of tiny red balls curving far up in air to the top of some ambitious pole, great faint yellow orbs, glowering close to earth, globules of light, palpitating, swinging, quivering, in rings and wheels and arches, dainty and wonderful. Don't think of any metropolis you know, blazing with the vulgar vari-coloured lanterns that live their short hour on the night of a strawberry garden party. Think of a low, broad, far-stretching city, covered with a tiny heavy-eaved growth of houses that gnomes might have built in the night, softly illumined from one end to the other with hundreds of thousands of the palest, most exquisite and artistic lantern ideas that ever night brought forth. Every tiny interior opened wide to the wonders of New Year's Eve, the moats shining up at the stars, the young moon sailing high. And the Ginza fair that night ! Where, in all the gentle lustre of the myriad soft lights, the sellers sat on the pavement in the great street of Tokio with their wares set forth around them, and tempted and chaffered and laughed ! The sellers of tiny carved ivories—a skeleton, a toad—of bamboo flutes, of blue and white rice-boxes, of long-necked *saki* bottles and lacquered *saki* cups, of tall twisted bronze candlesticks, of marvellous hair-pins, of cookeries manifold ! Up and down we wandered fascinated, wondering what any of our friends from the European settlement would say if they should meet us under the spell which made us buy two quaint yellow lantern balls to swing as we walked. Presently they did meet us — rather, perhaps, we met them—two stalwart Englishmen dressed up in flowing kimonos, high clacking getas, bare heads, and extremely foolish facial expressions. Then we went home rejoicing in the conviction that we had succumbed only where none could escape, not even a man and a Briton.

That night as we sat in our tiny house the streets were full of a cry that falls on the ears of the Yedites only on that night of all the year. '*Tarafuni!*' '*Tarafuni!*' with a sharp accent on the second syllable, it went flying up and down through the broad gemmy spaces of darkness about Kudan. We sent forth Chrysanthemum, and she brought us two *tarafuni* for half a *sen*, two slips of paper with a picture on them. The picture was of a ship full of gods, comfortable old Dai-koku laughing in front ; and a line or two of poetry connecting the ship with the dreams of the sleeper ran down the side. All true citizens of Tokio put Dai-koku and his luck ship under their pillows for twelve months' good fortune, and we did it too.

Then the candle burned low in the square white paper lantern in the corner of the room, and a space in the wall let in a panel of the sky, with the silver new moon hanging low among the pine branches. The darkness grew silent, only now and then, sudden and shrill like the cry of a night bird, we heard '*Tarafuni!*' '*Tarafuni!*' In a last fantastic moment we, too, slipped away to join all Tokio in its golden dreams. . . . And in the morning Dai-koku was still laughing at us.

XVII

ORTHODOCIA and I did not travel much in Japan. Tokio was so entirely delightful that we dreaded the discovery that others of the Mikado's cities failed of its consummate charm. Of course they might have possessed it in the superlative degree, but again they might not. There was always the risk. And we agreed upon Orthodocia's theory, that once you get an Impression you ought to keep it inviolate. But we made a few journeys into the interior for fear of reproaches when we got home, and once we went to Nikko.

To depart anywhere in Japan out of the five treaty ports one must have a passport, obtained through one of the Legations. Ours came to hand the day before we started—a solemn and portentous-looking document, with a large black seal—and we gathered from it that the British Government would be temporarily responsible for our behaviour, and that the Mikado covenanted to see that we were politely treated. The next time Orthodocia and I go to Japan we shall have to apply for our passport through some other Legation, for the British Plenipo told us inside ours that if we did not return them we should have no more, and we both thought they would be interesting as souvenirs.

Now, it is only once in a lifetime that one can go to Nikko. One can't do anything twice in Japan—one only approximates it the second time. Most of all Nikko.

Nikko is the temple city of Japan. It lies away to the north, where the mountains begin to rise and dip, and it is a very sacred place, for the great Iyeasu himself is buried there. Iyeasu was a Shogun, and the Shoguns were not dragons, but military gentlemen of distinction, who have achieved tombs. I was sorry for Orthodocia and her note-book in connection with the Shoguns' tombs—but that is another story. Unless you go to Nikko, or read volumes upon ancient Japan, I dare say your information about Iyeasu is quite likely to be as limited as ours was. If you go to Nikko, as we did, you will add to it, as we did, the fact that he lived and fought and died about three hundred years ago, and that his bones are deposited at the top of an incredible number of steps. This is not exhaustive regarding Iyeasu, but you will find it satisfying at the time. As we did.

Politeness is the soul and essence of all things truly Japanese, and as most of the railways are directly in the hands of the nation, we were not surprised to be presented with a cup of tea at the outset of our journey from the authorities of the road. Otherwise, the precise reason why the Japanese Government should insist upon tampering with the nervous system of every foreigner who buys a ticket from it does not appear. It must be pure, though mistaken, amiability. But in our tiny first-class carriage there was a tiny first-class table with holes in it for the safe reception of teapot and teacups, which the guard brought in with a bow. The tea was green as usual, without either sugar or milk to mitigate the bitterness of it, and the cups were the handleless cups of Japan, but Orthodocia drank the decoction with all the fortitude of Socrates to show her appreciation. Appreciation, she declared, that required sugar and milk, wasn't worth showing.

I wish I could put windows in this letter through which you might see the country we travelled that day, stretching away as it did, in all its careful little parallelograms of fields, to the feet of the blue mountains along the horizon. Nature never allowed herself to be arranged on a smaller scale. The tiny rice paddies, green with the coming of the second crop, the small square plots of vegetables, the camellia hedges, the baby hay-ricks, the domicilettes dotted amongst it all, the odd little cone-shaped mountains that seemed to have dropped here and there for decorative purposes purely. It was by all odds the neatest thing in landscapes we had ever seen. I had to remonstrate with Orthodocia for throwing mandarin peel out of the car window. It is very trying to travel with a person who can't be relied upon to pass through a rural district without upsetting it.

Now and then we saw a stable with a horse standing in it, looking meditatively out of the door and switching his tail where the manger would be in our country. Trees were bolstered up in rice straw—not to protect them from the frost, but to dry the straw. A husbandman picked his way nimbly among his fresh furrows, a white kerchief about his head, in blue 'tights' and loose blue coat, with bags on his shoulders. Ripe yellow persimmons as large as apples hung among the leafless twigs. The little windowless houses, with their heavy overhanging thatched roofs, looked blind and unintelligent; they did not understand themselves to be homes, we considered. The colour that morning was dainty and cool, in clear delicate washes of grays and blues, as it might have come from a brush in a firm hand for detail. And away off, describing a long arc through the fieldlets, and making apparently for a funny little mountain that stood all alone in the midst of a wide flatness, shrieked another tiny locomotive, leaving an erratic smoke track along the sky. Many stations, each with its European railway building and its gentle, clattering, staring Japanese crowd, half bareheaded, in kimono and geta, half in ill-fitting coat and trousers topped by last year's 'Derby' hats; and finally Utsonomiya, where we should abandon this foreign innovation of steam and wheels, and take to man-power for the rest of the way. We got out with our various bundles, and watched the foreign innovation out of sight with a strong conviction of its value to the country and the vaguest idea what to do next. If there is one comfort in travelling in Japan, however, it is the mind-reading capacity of the Japanese. They anticipate your ideas even when you haven't any. Orthodocia drew my attention to this, which I considered unkind—I don't know whether any other observing person has noted it or not. On this occasion they gathered up our effects and led us politely into a small room in the station-house, where they indicated that we might with propriety sit down. A youth brought us a fire-pot with the usual five embers arranged in it in a pattern, and it appeared to be our duty to warm our fingers. Then we obediently followed our bundles again to a low, rambling, open sort of a structure, which was a hotel. We sat down on the threshold, a foot and a half above the ground, and our friends looked at our boots consideringly. We shook our heads; we had forgotten the buttonhook again, and we hadn't a hair-pin between us that could do its whole duty. So then a little maiden toddled out to us with tea and cakes—the eternal green tea and pink cakes. Do you remember how, when you were very small and blew soap-bubbles out of a halfpenny clay pipe, you sometimes made a mistake and drew the soap-bubbles in? The pink cakes of Japan revive many such gustatory memories. By the time we had finished toying with them, we were surrounded by jinrikisha men, who also had divinations of our plans. 'Nikko?' they said; 'Nikko? dekimas, oka san!'—'I am entirely able to take you there, young lady!' We tried to make a choice, but I think the jinrikisha men settled it among themselves, for the pair of bipeds apiece that we started with would have been the last to recommend themselves to us on the score of either personal beauty or accomplishment.

We went through the long, straggling streets of Utsonomiya at a steady trot. The little, open, neutral-tinted shops were full of the pottery and vegetables and wooden buckets that had for some time ceased to excite in us the lively joy they give to new-comers. We could ride past them without so much as a comma in our course. The people came out to stare at us; it was quite two weeks since their last foreign entertainment; the frost nipped off the tourists, as it did the mandarin buds. From every group came a cheerful word for our runners, and the answer went gaily back.

It is a long way from Utsonomiya to Nikko, quite twenty-three miles. And all those miles climb slowly up between two solemn lines of tall pine trees, the dark erratic pine trees of Japan, whose twisted arms must have made the people first think of dragons, we were sure. They are the only very tall trees in all the region near, and they are so uplifted about this that they have quite lost their heads, and lean this way and that in a manner which suggests a sort of dignified inebriation. Overhead they meet sometimes, and the sunlight glorifies the dusky greenness of the topmost branches, and always they march on in endless mysterious toppling columns, shadowed aslant, up the long arrowy Pilgrims' Road to Nikko, and always one rides between.

The long silent stretches of the gradual ascent were very empty.

Now and then a pilgrim, now and then a pack-horse, occasionally a group of men urging along a cart full of trailing bamboo trunks. The sincere pilgrims to Nikko went in the spring time, and sent up their prayers with the incense of the wisteria vine. We were very, very late. It was doubtful whether Iyeasu would even take the trouble to feel complimented by our coming; and as to our petitions it was practically useless to offer them at all at this time of the year. We had to seek what consolation we could in long glimpses of the country, that slipped away to the right of us, glimpses framed between the slanting trunks of the pines, full of tender autumn colour-thoughts, and stretching far to the beautiful blue masses and strange white curves of the snow-tipped mountains that held in trust the veneration of all Japan and the bones of Iyeasu.

It is quite true that our men ran half the way to Nikko in two hours and a half without once stopping. Then as the evening sky reddened behind the lowest branches of the pine trees, we came to a tea-house hidden away under them. The walls of the tea-house were open, and through them we saw the fire curling up from the middle of the earthen floor, and all the household gathered round it. Our runners refreshed themselves mightily here, and we ate rice and eggs, with one battered tin fork between us, and drank hot *saki*, and were greatly comforted. Orthodocia confided to me as we started off again that she didn't know how her runners must feel, but, judging from her own sensations, her jinrikisha was getting very, very tired.

Then, as we rode on apace, the shadows clustered and grew between the eaves of the pines, and fell silently at our feet, though all about the country still lay fair and visible in the twilight. Presently they deepened into night, and as we toiled further up, strange dark shapes began to appear between the trees and to lean forward, peering at us—the outer guard of gods about the bones of Iyeasu.

That evening, as we sat on the floor of the Japanese inn and constructed sentences to ask for a bed in, and soap, and other essentials, our host entered, bowed on his hands and knees with supreme humility, and made a remark.

'*Nanto hanashimashita ka?*' said Orthodocia.

'*What* did you say ?' I asked her, jealous of a surreptitiously acquired sentence, for Orthodocia had the phrase-book.

'That's what I said,' she returned.

'What?'

'What did you say?'

'*I* asked *you*'—with some irritation—'what you said.'

'Well, what you said was what I said—what did you say?'

'*I* asked *you*'—and I don't in the least know how the matter might have terminated if our host, who had seated himself, had not repeated his statement, which was apparently a request, and I, turning to the phrase-book for relief, found '*Nanto hanashimashita ka ?*' —'What did you say?'

He said it again.

'He said "*iru*,"' put in Orthodocia astutely. 'Evidently he *wants* something—"*iru*," "I want." What do you *iru* ?' encouragingly, to the man.

He smiled painfully and drew his breath in between his teeth. There was a pause, and then he said it again.

'Really,' said Orthodocia, 'this is an unexpected contingency. I didn't undertake to supply the interesting native of Nippon with anything he might take a fancy to.'

'It's the bill,' said I sagely, and produced a yen or two.

But our host shook his head—it was not the bill. Orthodocia then offered him a few soda biscuits, an orange, a tin of sardines from our private provisions, but he politely declined them all. She even opened a bottle of lemonade with a pop that frightened him horribly, but he would none of it. Then she began with her personal effects, and brought him a handkerchief, a collar, an assortment of hair-pins, and a pair of Wigginton goloshes. None of them, though he regarded them with pleased and curious interest, seemed exactly calculated to fill his long-felt want.

Finally, for most of the inhabitants of Nikko were by this time, alas! sitting on the floor of our apartment watching the progress of events, Orthodocia brought him her satchel, and opened it under his eyes. He looked over its contents very daintily and carefully, seized something at the very bottom with great joy, and drew forth her passport!

I have never before or since participated in such a scene of mutual felicitation as followed.

We slept that night between two *futons* on the floor in a room with absolutely nothing else in it, trusting Providence and the phrase-book for morning supplies. They warmed our bed for us by putting a fire-box between the upper and the nether *futon*, which is a heating apparatus calculated to excite the liveliest emotions if you do not know of its presence until after you get in, which was our experience. We removed it then; but we could not remove the charcoal fumes, and we dreamed asphyxia all night long. In the morning we clapped our hands, and a fat little maiden brought us water in a lacquered bowl, which might have held a quart, and tiny blue towels, rather less closely woven than cheese cloth, which one rub only reduced to the consistency of a damp cobweb. She implored us not to splash the matting or the poetry on the walls, and then sat down on the floor in an interested way, and watched our ablutions.

After breakfast, at which our host proudly presented us each with a poached egg—his own poaching—we went to see the temples.

They stood far up the mountain side, the great temples, all clustered together under their curving roofs of red and gold, within the outer courts of the trees and the sky. Broad, damp, mossy stone steps led to them, and we heard a ceaseless sound of trickling water from the overflowing stone vessels for the purification of the pilgrims that stood inside the gates. The ubiquitous Japanese lion, foolishly amiable as usual, kicked up his heels in stone on either side of every approach.

One temple was to me very like another temple in glory, except that those now devoted to Shintoism were simpler than the Buddhist ones, and had only empty spaces and meaningless screens, where formerly Siddharta sat in bronze. The interiors of the Shinto temples, erected to the mighty dead, signified nothing to me. Perhaps if one could see behind the great tasselled curtains that hung in vague secrecy from the further walls, some distinct religious idea might reveal itself, if it were nothing but a relic or a bit of writing. But one does not see behind them; their mysterious folds are never disturbed. The souls of the Shoguns come and go with easy ceremony. And the wonderful cocks and cats and dragons, in all colours and all circumstances, that are carved in high relief round the top of the walls, the lacquered pillars, the gold poetry l the portraits of many Japanese poets, all taken in the ins͵ ·. act, failed to tell us of anything of faith or law. But Buddha, imaged

'BACK TO UTSONOMIYA IN THE RAIN.'

great and tall, had speech for us there in his temple. He told us of the endurance of great apostleship; the words trembled about the shapen lip with its ineffable smile, the lip that taught a divine ideal, and smiled ever after. His great bronze hand, stretched forth among the temple shadows, above the fumes of the incense and the tinkling of the bells, and the prostration of the single shaven priest, caught a gleam of light as the heavy door opened to let us out. It is our one vivid memory of the faith of Japan.

We climbed to the tomb of Iyeasu, with its bronze lotus and guarding stork, and we looked upon that warrior's helmet, and sword, and chair of state with all the reverence we could muster for heroic annals in Japan. We saw a pale, weird woman, all in waving white draperies with scarlet under them, make strange passes with a fan and a bell-rattle, strange posturings, strange measured steps in a semicircle, within the cell-like little temple where she sat all day to do her religion this service. And when that pale weird woman sat down again among her draperies, and cast one level look upon us from beneath her lowered lids—a mechanical, incurious look—we felt that no sum of years, or of miles, or of human difference could avail to express the shivering distance that lay between her and us.

We went back to Utsonomiya in the rain. The long green vista of the leaning pines was darkened and blurred as it stretched out before us in the late afternoon. Orthodocia rode ahead, her jinrikisha, with its hood up, looking like a corpulent beetle in full scud. By-and-by we sped through utter night, hearing only the dripping from the branches and the steady splashing of our coolies' bare feet. Then sometimes there would come a faint cool irradiation, and beyond the fringe of shining white drops on the edge of my jinrikisha hood would be set, solitarily, daintily glowing through the darkness and the rain before some tiny portal, the familiar spirit of a great golden paper lantern. . . . For statistics about the temples, their heights, and breadths, and dates, and the types of their individual pretensions, as well as for much valuable information about the earthquake-resisting construction of one of them, I believe a thoroughly reliable volume has been written by one Dr. Dresser, and have much pleasure in referring you to it. I can do this with cheerful conviction that you will find all you want to know in it. The book was recommended to Orthodocia and me by a professorial friend of Tokio, and we carried it all the way to Nikko and back again.

XVIII

THE air had a familiar feeling that January night; a familiar feeling paradoxically strange in this country I tell you of, where even the winds and the clouds are unfamiliar. The streets of Tokio, as we rode through them from Kanda to Kudan, were very quiet. The paper doors were all shut, the gentle lights that shone delicately through the tiny white panes, and the wide eaves that hung over the little habitations protectingly low, expressed a thought of home, the first I had found in Japan. The sky was flat and gray and furry, and it was softly cold. I carried a budding camellia branch, with one conscious red flower open-eyed. I mused upon it, thinking how curious it was that a flower could grow and blow to be just the decorative essence that it seemed, and nothing more—without soul or fragrance, or anything to give it kinship with the sweet companies of other countries. Suddenly I saw my camellia through the darkness red and white. I looked up—the snow had come.

I called to Orthodocia, riding behind me, in the wonder of it; but she did not answer. She was much too intent upon trying to bring this new phantasm into place among the rest.

It fell silently, lightly, with a sigh; the streets were soon white with it, and the foolish little roofs by the wayside, and the shoulders of my jinrikisha man trotting hardily between his shafts. It whispered among the twisted branches of the tall pine trees as we rode into the deeper shadows of a sacred grove, and made a soft crown about the head of Dai-Butz—the great gray stone Dai-Butz that sits there on a little eminence all day under the sun, all night under the stars, and preaches to the people with folded hands. As we rode over the moat into the Ginza the flakes began to fall more thickly, became unfriendly, drove into our faces. The long wide avenue of

'IT WAS FAIRYLAND OVERTAKEN BY A BLIZZARD.'

tiny shops, each with its dainty swinging lantern, stretched out behind the storm in dazzled bewilderment; the bareheaded little folk we met bent and shivered, and clattered along on their high wooden *getas* under great flat paper umbrellas, with all their graceful garments drawn tight about them. It was fairyland overtaken by a blizzard, in a state of uncomprehending collapse. Presently, as we turned into our own deserted *cho*, through which our runners' footfalls sounded with soft dull pads and thuds, we saw the square lantern of Kudan, on its pyramid of stones, glowing high among the swirling flakes with a new eccentricity. Next morning a strange white blight lay over our toy garden, and thick upon the camellia hedge, from behind which no sound of our little neighbour's samisen came at all that day; and it seemed to us that the heart of our beautiful Japan was chilled and silent, and that it was time to go.

Yet it seemed to walk suddenly into the seat of our affections and make a riot there, this idea of going, of riding for any last time beside a dancing paper globe through the *grotesquerie* of Tokio's dusky evening, over the moats, and past the white palace walls — of saying to this strange little world, new with a thousand years of old, '*Sayonara!*' and of going forth into the one we knew before, not to return. For one does not reach Japan often in the course of the ordinary lifetime, and the farewells of youth are always for ever. The riot lasted three days and three nights, and left us with the conviction, which I consider it my duty to make public, that no weak-minded person should go to Japan unless he is able to bring his days to an imbecile close there, or is prepared to make shipwreck of his gentle affections and his feeble brains on the rock of departure.

In view of the foregoing statement it is with some compunction that I dwell upon Orthodocia's sustained hostility to the idea of leaving, long after I had succumbed and begun to take farewell glances at Fusi-Yama. But, as a truthful narrator, I must not know compunction, and I am compelled to say that Orthodocia's conduct was indefensible.

'*Skoshi maté!*'[1] she murmured in the morning, looking regretfully into the glowing depths of the three charcoal embers of the family *hibachi*. '*Skoshi maté!*' she suggested at noon, joyful in the acquisition of nineteen tea-pots and a new verb. '*Skoshi maté!*' she entreated at night, diluting with one small impotent tear the *saki* in the *saki* bowl. And when I would not *skoshi maté*—no, not for the return of the wild geese or the cherry-blossom garden party in the spring—then was I attacked on the score of all we had jointly promised to the small domestic public of St. Eve's-in-the-Garden, Wigginton, Devon, if Orthodocia were allowed to go—the long letters full of valuable, nutritive, and interesting information, which the oldest could profit by and the youngest understand, to be

[1] Wait a little.

read aloud in the rapt communion of the Wigginton Dorcas Society. Had we come to Japan with serious and honourable intentions of carrying out that vow or not ? I protested that our intentions were all that could be desired. And thus far—with a great deal too much indignation for the person who was chiefly responsible—how, she asked me, how had that vow been fulfilled thus far ? 'My own darling mamma,' sarcastically, ' Japan is the most charming, delicious, enchanting spot on this terrestrial globe. I bought you this morning the sweetest five o'clock you could imagine—you could *dream*—and for papa such a curious original pair of monkey slippers, which never will stay on his dear old feet, but which he must *always* wear for the sake of his very far away, but more loving than ever, Orthodocia. The quaint little postman will be round in two minutes for this, and it is the very *last* minute for the mail, so, with tenderest love to all, I remain your own, O. P.S.—This country gets funnier and funnier !' Orthodocia blushed to compare this imaginary but fairly faithful epistle with the instructive volumes that were to have been.

Did I or did I not remember our drawing, together, on the tossing Pacific, bright pictures of dear mamma and all the home circle— tears—supplementing what the encyclopædias had taught them from 'the graphic pages' of their daughter in Japan—and what had been the proud result ? To what extent had the thirst for knowledge inspired in the deserving family at Love Lodge been gratified thus far ? I ventured the suggestion that really very little of the information Orthodocia had sent home about Japan could be found in the Britannicum, and received a glance which made me feel the brutality of my remark.

The discussion left us with a largely increased sense of the responsibilities of the situation, and very vague ideas as to how they should be met. We took our note-books from the respective walls into which they had retired, and scanned them anxiously for facts— civil, religious, social, military—any kind of facts available for transhipment in the haste of departure. My note-book appeared to my inspection, then and since, to be chiefly filled up with Japanese poetry, with an occasional dash or exclamation point which might be recognisable in these pages, but which seem to be hardly significant enough to make the reproduction worth while. From Orthodocia's note-book, however, I shall take a few extracts. It was a large, black, shiny, respectable note-book, and it went impressively with her everywhere in Japan. Neatly written at the top of one page we found

'EDUCATIONAL.

'December 14. Visited university with S. J. D., Mrs. Gallicus, and Professor B.

'No. of students in university . . . . . ⎫
'No. of professors . . . . . . ⎬ To find
'No. of departments. . . . . . ⎪ out.
'No. of graduates and matriculants last year . ⎭

'Met President. Short and stout. Coat and trousers. No kimonos permitted on teaching staff (?). Inquire and note hardship. Youth up in flowing kimonos, suddenly thrust into collars and seams, &c. English professors gradually being ousted by Japanese ditto. English professors, mostly bachelors, living in pretty little houses about university grounds. Great shame. All tiffined with Professor B. Charming tiffin. Blue china. Secured reports.'

Some distance under this, to leave room for other instructive matters, appears the sententious statement, 'Lost reports.'

'EARTHQUAKES.

'Tiffined with Professor M., General Manager, Earthquake Department, Japanese Government. (Joke of S. J. D.'s, but I do not consider it particularly funny.) Earthquake machine invented by Professor M., called by him seismometer. Professor M. explained working of seismometer, but I cannot see practical utility, as seismom. is not warranted to stop even slightest earthquake. Magnetic needle traces movements on revolving cylinder covered with blackened wax. Very interesting. See pamphlet. Another invention of Professor M.'s—Drawing-room or baby seismometer. Sweet thing. Stands on mantel. Can always tell by looking in morning how many earthquakes have occurred during night, and whether chimneys down or not. Professor M. says thing no family subject to seisms should be without. Burglars known to escape B.—alarms—

seismom. in every case fatal to seisms. Wished to buy one for mamma, but felt delicacy about asking price.

'Saw model, Chinese idea, earthquake machine. Globe on stand —six dragons' heads sticking out round globe, loose ball in mouth— six frogs sitting round at corresponding intervals, mouths open, looking up. Shock occurs. Balls fly in direction of shock—mouth of north-east frog, south-west frog, as case may be.

'NOTE.—Chinese idea much simpler to unseismic mind. Professor M.'s pamphlet inadvertently packed up with Nikko curios.

'SOCIAL.

'December 26.—Heard to-day of another Japanese Cabinet Minister married to *geisha*, or professional dancer, which makes four. Extraordinary state of things. Example of extent to which Japanese are adopting Western civilisation—called on Government official and wife just returned from Amer.; was shown room of new house expressly designed to hold the lady's band-boxes! Heard dreadful story of newly-emancipated Jap. young married lady dancing three times at ball, each time with different man. Japanese propriety would prefer same man.

'NATIVE INTERCOURSE WITH FOREIGNERS.

'December 29.—Japanese still vicious. Saw whole silver service belonging to foreigner (Englishman) destroyed by Japanese cook. Articles thrown at cook's head and severely dinted; loss irreparable.'

I don't know whether Mr. and Mrs. Love and the Dorcas Society have been made familiar with the foregoing valuable facts by any other agency than this, but if not they are herewith submitted to all Wigginton with the greatest goodwill, and many apologies for their tardy appearance. As to the note-book, I have Orthodocia's permission to keep that as a monument to certain noble intentions untimely perished. . . .

And so it befell that one day there whirled madly from the Grand Hotel to the jetty along the sunny sands by the wide blue harbour of Yokohama two belated jinrikishas. In one Orthodocia, with twenty-four packages, the gayest of paper parasols, and the saddest of countenances; in the other this present chronicler, with twenty-four more, a Japanese cat without a tail—warranted tailless from earliest infancy, and not cut off untimely — and emotions that shall go unwritten. The little tug was screaming itself hoarse at us. Orthodocia had dallied too long over her last tea-pot. And thus it was that as an unrelenting quartermaster bundled us into it we had only time to single out of the kindly

'THERE WHIRLED MADLY FROM THE GRAND HOTEL TWO BELATED JINRIKISHAS.'

group of friends that had gathered to see us off two or three quaint little sad-faced figures bowing and bowing at the jetty's verge, and to cry to these with a very genuine pang, '*Sayonara, Buddha!*' '*Sayonara, Chrysanthemum!*'

We sped away through the dancing blue waves to the great P. and O. steamer lying with her prow turned toward China. It was a desolate moment. Orthodocia, between her emotions and other impedimenta, required the assistance of three quartermasters and the fourth officer to mount the ship's ladder. I struggled blindly up behind through the mist with which the sun, acting upon her feelings, had considerately enveloped her. Which reads a little like a sentence from a very old-fashioned romance, but which is my best approximation to the verity of the situation.

We stopped at Nagasaki, with its old Dutch memories and its dainty investment of the romance of 'Madame Chrysanthème'; at Kobe, with its mountains behind ragged and blue, its mandarin sellers, and its softer air. And then the ever-marvellous Inland Sea. . . .

That is to say, a voyage through the scenery of a dream; for here abides that most shy and exquisite Spirit of Japan—the Spirit that whispers in all her winds and sings in all her streams, and smiles in all her cities. Here, among these dainty water reaches,

GOOD-BYE, JAPAN!
GOOD-NIGHT!'

opening and reopening, alluring and realluring, always within the charmed boundaries of tinted mountains that might guard fairyland. A spell is over it all and over us as we move slowly into the liquid silence and marvel at the gentle phantasm which is the soul of Japan, though neither the missionaries nor the geographies may acknowledge this. It rains a little—a playful sprinkled tenderness that nobody could take seriously—and through the rain the quaint curves of the mountains near and far rest upon the water in the upper and under colours of a dove's wing. All at once, far and away down a clear narrow space between two strangely-tortured purple peaks, there comes a burnished bar in the sky. It glows and melts, and spreads into another sea; it drops to a weird red burning; it leaps up and wavers and pales, and all these goblins of mountains in gray and white, and purple, and rose, and gold seem to let their garments slip into the dreaming water and troop toward the dying light. . . . 'And so good-bye, Japan,' said I, leaning back to it, as we slipped away into the wide grayness that lay between us and China. 'Good-bye, Japan! Good-night! The gods you love and ridicule keep your palms soft, your thoughts sweet, your manners gentle!' And Orthodocia, my friend, looking her last at it over my shoulder, echoed me softly, 'Good-bye, Japan! Good-night!'

XIX

It was a strange thing to see China that third day after the witchery of the Inland Sea. We did not come upon it at all in the usual way, sailing in between the open arms of a great harbour city to the sights and sounds of wharves and warehouses; but suddenly at four bells of a gray morning somebody on deck said, 'There is China!' and there it was. China, rising out of the sea away off on our lee in a single line of little irregular round mountains, just as it used to rise in the small square woodcuts in the big pages of the school atlases, beside paragraphs which related to the Chief Rivers, Principal Mountain Ranges, Population, Religion, Exports. It was distinctly the country of the geographies, the country of one's early and feeble association with tea-chests and missionaries, although I am quite sure that I can't enter into any analysis of this impression that you would find satisfactory. I only know it is quite true, as Orthodocia said, that if we had sailed to this lumpy, lonely land through unknown seas, with all the joy of the early navigators we should have named it China—and sailed away again as fast as possible. For it was even then, I think, at that remote and inexperienced moment that Orthodocia and I made up our minds that we didn't like China, and wouldn't stay there. 'It is a painful conclusion,' said Orthodocia as we stood together looking at it, 'for I had vowed a private vow to Miss Gordon Cummings that I would wave my parasol in triumph on the top of the Chinese Wall at Pekin; but that there is anything picturesque or interesting enough behind those ugly little hummocks to make it worth while I am not disposed to believe.'

The shore began to trend into stronger, bolder headlands, and behind one of them we presently found Hong Kong. We regarded it from a great mountain-locked cannon-guarded water-basin, with night settling down over it. The mighty semicircle of the hills seemed very near the sky, and, as the stars came dropping through the silence up there in the surprised way that stars have all over the world, the city, climbing its peak, began to hold vain torches up in emulation. And they all fell together into the peace of the harbour, between the French frigate that lay white and ghostly, remembering the graves at Tonquin, and the Russian corvette with strange gold characters glittering at her prow, and the sharply-defined long black bulk of Her Majesty's ship *Impérieuse*, darkly portentous among the rest.

So we had come to China, and as we slept that night on the ship at anchor between the upper and the lower firmament I dreamed that Orthodocia and Confucius sat on the bottom of a turned-up teacup and disputed the doctrine of the survival of the fittest, Orthodocia closing the argument by pushing the father of Chinese philosophy, so that he slipped with precipitancy down the side of the teacup, and fell with a large splash into the Yellow Sea.

Next morning, while we yet hesitated whether we should come all the way to China and depart the day after because of a prejudice against its geographical outlines, we were introduced to its domestic and social conditions as they exist on a sampan. The sampan was one of many that swung about the ship's ladder tempting us to slip down and be taken ashore. A large family in two or three generations floated through life on our sampan; and the members of it, round-headed, narrow-eyed, flat-faced, wide-mouthed, seemed to have brought the simplicity of living to the nth degree. They pounded rice in an iron pot, and nourished themselves therewith. They slept on some scraps of matting in a roofed-over space in the middle of the boat. Family dissensions went on in the stern, social amenities in the prow, probably, where the matting was cleanest. Over our heads swung two large rats, split and dried—sight of ineffable gastronomic suggestion. I caught a glimpse of Orthodocia's expression as she regarded them, and I thought on Miss Gordon Cummings and sighed, for I knew that this hint of the national diet would prove final and fatal.

'The "woman question" appears to have made progress in China,' remarked my friend, who is not a suffragist, disapprovingly; and I observed that our sampan was manned by the grandmother, daughter, aunt, and female cousin of the establishment, who rowed us lustily with much perspiration. We were disabused of this idea, however, when we noticed that the small moon-faced object that stood in the stern and gave orders which the women obeyed with promptness and unanimity, was a boy. He was a full-blown tyrant, at the age of seven.

The prow of our sampan was liberally frescoed in blue and red, and adorned on each side with a large expressive eye. Observing that all the sampans were thus decorated, Orthodocia fixed hers upon the grandmother, and said, inquiringly, 'Why eye?' She answered with the brevity, precision, and condescension of a personage talking to a newspaper reporter, 'No got eye, no can see—no can see, no can savey—no can savey, no can go!' And we felt that the decorative ideas of China had a basis of unfaltering logic.

Going round the world the wrong way, as we did, one gets one's first impression of British consequence in it from a Sikh policeman of Hong Kong. He stands sadly about in the shade of the trees on Queen's Road, or under the wide, cool, many arched stone verandahs that run before the shops, tall, erect, dignified, looking as if the whole history of Asia since the Flood passed in revision daily before him. When I said that, Orthodocia contradicted me, and stated that in her opinion the man probably didn't even know British history. This illustrates a solemn peculiarity of my friend's which I found trying at times. In case the peculiarity should be shared by any of her fellow Englishwomen, I hasten to state that I don't believe it really does pass. If you were to ask one of those policemen the family name of either Noah or the present Governor of Hong Kong, in all probability he couldn't tell you. But when I explained this to Orthodocia, she said she didn't see why I kept saying things if I couldn't substantiate them.

We were much impressed by these tall guardians of the peace of Hong Kong from the hills of India, though, and stood looking at one of them so long that he became uncomfortable and went away. The fidelity that shone in the liquid brown depths of his eyes was obvious, but not as obvious, perhaps, as his turban and his feet. There were eight red yards of his turban, wound round his head in majestic curves unknown to the millinery of other continents. I don't know that any true estimate of the length of his feet has yet been arrived at; they remind one of the course of human events. He disposed of them sectionally in boots for which we believed with ready confidence that the Government makes a special contract, and they precede him everywhere.

'Why,' said Orthodocia to me as the special object of our admiration disappeared, 'is that policeman like a stopped pendulum?'

I said I didn't know.

'I didn't think you would!' returned Orthodocia triumphantly. 'Because he's gone off his beat!'

It may seem disagreeable, but I feel that I must instance this as another of my friend's little peculiarities.

It is a strange sad thing how as one grows older the objects one venerates in youth become fewer and fewer. Orthodocia and I, before we left China, had entirely lost respect for the almanack, even Whitaker, whom Orthodocia at least had venerated up to that time as she did the equator. We will henceforth speak of the torrid rays of the January sun and the Arctic rigours of the storms of July just as casually as we had been in the habit of doing before we went round the world, with the months attached, as we thought, appropriately. It is provincial, not to say local and bigoted, to believe in the Seasons or very much in the Sun; and almanacks are inventions to excite certain narrow bucolic expectations and sell patent medicines. This is written in Latin across the diploma of every graduated 'globe trotter,' and is a fact that survives all of Baedeker's. You will observe that I have quoted the expression 'globe trotter' to give it an alien look. Orthodocia objects to it in any personal connection with our trip. She has invented 'planet pilgrim' instead, and insists upon it, as more dignified; and I let her have her way.

For our day with the Celestials was an extremely hot one. And as all Japan's seductive confectionery was iced when we left, we resented Hong Kong's perspiring vegetation and rampant thermometer as entirely unjustifiable. For who, all these unreckoning days since she left school and ceased to have it required of her, would think of making climatic differences between China and Japan! The experience of more intelligent people may differ; but we found this heightened temperature of China as unreasonable as the fact that it took us a week to get there, instead of being, as one vaguely imagines, perhaps a day's sail!

And when we left the streets of tall, white European buildings, with just a hint of the Orient in their arches and casements, and turned our exploring feet into China's Hong Kong, we found the thermometer ably supported by a large and in- fluential family of Odours —a combination which easily accounts for the in- vincible Celestial resistance to the advance of the Modern Idea. Not even an abstraction could travel far through those unsweet mazes. It would resolve itself into a single palpitating olfactory nerve and perish.

We stood at the top of the crowded stairs leading down into them, and looked over upon lanes and lanes, narrow, winding, crossing, creeping, full of hideousness. I can't tell you how to realise this hideousness. It might possibly be approximated by placing the three- primary colours and the six books of Euclid in the hands of a North American Indian, and giving him a contract to build a Dakota railway centre; though Orthodocia says

'AT HOME HE IS ATROCIOUS.'

she doesn't see how it could be done that way. Long signs, in staring red and blue and purple and yellow, projected a foot or two from the walls on each side and hung down covered with black cross-bones playing cricket. The vendors squatted under these, and sold sham jade bracelets, and joss-sticks, and split fish and unimaginable greasinesses to eat; and a busy shuffling stolid-faced crowd in queues, caps, and petticoats elbowed itself continually past. That doesn't sound half so ugly as the scene was, but I can't put a Chinaman bodily into this chapter and let him radiate hideousness as he

'WE ESCAPED WITH TWO BASKET TEAPOTS APIECE ONLY— A MERE SCRATCH.'

does at home. It all diverges from the tan-coloured expanse, with incidental variations, that serves him for a countenance, through which his smug, self-satisfied, uncompromising identity looks forth upon a world with which it has no relation of trivial æsthetics. The Celestial abroad, where he is properly subdued, is unprepossessing; at home, where he permits himself an opinion of you, he is atrocious. We went from force of habit into some of the shops notwithstanding this, where we saw such a large number of uninteresting things that Orthodocia, discovering a small Satsuma dragon in exile in a corner, was moved to tears. After the land of the Mikado, one may encounter the commercial temptations of China without fear; and I write down with considerable and reasonable pride the fact that we escaped with two basket tea-pots apiece only—a mere scratch.

One buys basket tea-pots in China because there is never any room for them in one's trunk, and they have to be carried separately; because the spouts invariably come off on an unattached journey round the world; because they are not nearly so pretty as the exported ones; and because they cost about sixpence apiece less than they do at home. The present historian was peculiarly fortunate, her spouts having come off among the vicissitudes of the first five hundred miles; but the experience of Orthodocia, who preserved one and two-thirds of hers as far as the Suez Canal, and was never happy unless they pointed to the East, ought to be a warning to curio collectors.

We had no Baedeker or any such thing—Orthodocia wouldn't hear of buying one, for fear it might beguile us into staying the necessary week before there would be another P. and O. ship to take us away—but somebody had told us that the proper and usual thing for strangers with a couple of hours in Hong Kong to do was to go up the Peak. Although Orthodocia reminded me that we had not come to China in search of hackneyed commonplaces, we also went up the Peak. It was one of the things that we did which convinced us that the travelling public quite understands what it is about, and that the hackneyed commonplace exists only in the minds of people who stay at home.

One goes up the Peak in a cable car. Two cable cars, in fact, travel constantly up and down the elevation behind Hong Kong, for a considerable distance at an angle of forty-five degrees. I can state this fact confidently, for it is down in Orthodocia's note-book. I remember it very well, moreover, because Orthodocia and I embraced one another fervently several times during the angle of forty-five degrees. She sat opposite me, and it was a matter of necessity.

When we got out we found that a magnificent distance still lay between us and the top. Whereupon four or five Chinamen strolled forward and signified, in a desultory way, their connection with the cable car as a means of transit. They had a sort of legless armchair on two poles, into which we got amidst much garrulity. One Chinaman arranged himself between the shafts before, and the other behind. They raised it to their shoulders with several solemn grunts, and presently we started. Orthodocia was distinctly nervous in the cable car, but when angles of forty-five degrees occurred to her arm-chair, she spoke of the strides of mechanics in the most feeling and intelligent way.

We looked away from our feet, there at the top of the Peak of Hong Kong, and our eyes wandered, wavered, lost themselves, and returned helplessly to the familiar grasses beside us. China rolled before us, grim, grotesque, dreary, and silent. Strange hills threw shadows into strange valleys, where no flower grew and no bird sang. The sea, gray on the horizon, thrust dead-white arms in between solitary misshapen mountains, whose gauntness a ragged mist tried vainly to soften. Hong Kong, far below, looked like a penal settlement from the planet we knew before, and its war-ships in the harbour like the foolish toys of the convicts made in the hope of escape. One's eyes dwelt pleasurably on their tennis-courts, their race-grounds, their green gardens and churches, and other contrivances to amuse and comfort themselves, for nowhere else in all the hem of this strange land's garment could one find a touch of tenderness, a breath of ideality. It was not yielding enough to be melancholy, or conscious enough to be grand; it seemed to be the long-forgotten work of the gods of China, as stony, as stolid, as ferocious as they.

Orthodocia made complaint in the cable car going down of the art and of the people, and the lady next us, who had just returned from Canton, where she had spent a day in minute observation of the tortures, detailed them at length. But it seemed to me that from the top of the Peak we had seen the reason of it all— the blue and green china, and the Mandarins' faces, and the spiked

'OFFERED TO LEND US HER NOTE-BOOK.'

collar for criminals—and that no-ness could be born of hideousness thing but hideous-for ever and ever.

The tortures lasted all the way to the bottom, and heightened Orthodocia's determination to take ship at the earliest instant and fly to the uttermost parts of the earth. The lady thought we should at least go to Canton, and offered to lend us her note-book that we might find the most delectable tortures without unnecessary trouble, but we assured her that her description left nothing to be desired. It was a dainty little gilt-edged note-book, and she was a dainty little gilt-edged lady, who would have felt herself a monster in sticking a pin through a butterfly, yet both she and the note-book were quite full of the tortures, to be applied to every victim allured into conversation with her between Hong Kong and London.

'Do you know,' she said, 'they actually put people's heads through holes in the doors, and starve them to death that way'— but at that moment we saw a chance of escape, and took it.

And in this chapter you have the whole, absolutely the whole, of 'What we Did in China!'

XX

I SUPPOSE you will hardly believe me when you read this chronicle, you to whose house in town or place in the country the Indian mail comes every week, and to whom the initials of the great steamship company that brings it are as familiar as 'H.R.H.' or 'G.W.R.,' when I tell you that in the part of the world I come from you might ask three-quarters of the people you met what 'P. and O.' stands for, and get the answer, 'Dear me ! That sounds like a thing one ought to know, and yet—P.—and—O.—P.—and—O. ! Really, I'm afraid I can't inform you ! '

For an Eastern voyage on a Peninsular and Oriental ship is a vague dream that haunts the gay, hard little parlour where what we call 'sewing circles' meet to hear books of travel read aloud, in our substitute for villages in the New World—chiefly that and little more. People who do not belong to the sewing circles, and are not fond of improving their minds with the printed abstract of other people's fun, don't think about it. Living several thousand miles from either end of this popular medium for sending English brides to India and Australian letters to China, and the nomads of the earth all over, they are not really so very much to blame—there is no particular reason why they should know—unless, indeed, some kindly magician like Mr. Black takes them as far as Egypt with a 'Yolande,' which was the case with me. The reflected pleasure lasted, I remember, only while the novel did ; but the unfamiliar letters gathered and held a fascinating halo that will endure in my mind as long as the alphabet ; and from that day in school girlhood until that other in Yokohama, I longed to set my foot on a ship of the 'P. and O.'

Orthodocia and I both found it something altogether new and strange in travelling, quite apart from the various queernesses of the countries it took us to. You may have crossed the Atlantic in an upholstered palace, at all sorts of shifting angles, with three hundred other people, once or twice, and think, as we thought, that you know all there is to know about lay navigation, but you don't. You may even add to your experience, as we did, the great gray skies and tossing monotony of two weeks on the Pacific, during which your affections learn to cluster about a ministering angel in a queue, and yet leave the true philosophy of voyaging unimagined. But Orthodocia and I, from Yokohama to London, sailed with intense joy and satisfaction upon seven of the ships of the P. and O., so I know whereof I speak.

In Orthodocia's note-book the items round the corner of the page labelled 'P. and O.' begin, I observe, at Hong Kong; for though we took the voyage from Japan to China under the same paternal guidance, the conditions were so different from those of our—perhaps theatrical—expectations that we declined to recognise them as Peninsular and Oriental. We took it in January for one thing, and in January there are no punkahs, but a coal stove in the saloon instead. Also, I remember, when we partook of afternoon tea and plum cake and reminiscences in Captain Webber's cosy little cabin, there was a fire there, which didn't help us to realise the tropics. Orthodocia was obliged, moreover, to spend most of the five days in contending with her emotions about leaving the Mikado, for whose dominions she had found Hong Kong so slight a compensation. I know it was not until we were on board the stately *Sutlej*, with her prow turned towards the Straits of Malacca, that the prospect of Ceylon began to revive the drooping interest she took in the rest of the planet.

The first thing that happens when you embark on a P. and O. ship on the other side of the world is the discovery of somebody you had no special reason to believe you would ever see again in it— somebody connected in your mind with another hemisphere, perhaps, from which you had sailed together in the time B. J. (that is the focal point in Orthodocia's chronology, and means, 'Before Japan'). And it is one of the pleasantest things that can possibly happen, this sudden recognition, on a deck full of strangers, of the familiar head and shoulders of some planet pilgrim gone before. It is quite probable that I did not tell you, in my hurry to get to Japan, about a certain gentleman from New York—a certain portly, and jovial, and ripely-bald gentleman from New York, whom Orthodocia and I found on the deck of the *Duke of Westminster*, watch in hand, calculating in an incensed manner the precise number of minutes we had delayed his arrival in Yokohama by keeping the ship waiting for us. I should have mentioned him because he was the one bit of colour, the one exhilarating fact in all that grievous time. And there we fell upon him, there on the *Sutlej* aft of the smoking cabin, round, and rubicund, and funny, and New-Yorky as ever, rejoicing above everything in six extraordinary Chinese petticoats which some Celestial dame had so forgotten herself as to sell him in Canton.

Well, of all things ! The very *last* people he would have expected ! And *did* we remember the 'grilled bones' on the *Duke of Westminster* ? Didn't we ? It was like the Pacific Ocean giving up Charles Lamb. And had we observed the peculiarities of pidgin English ? 'John ! run topside—catchee me one piecee gentleman—savey, John ? Quick !'

John savied, and shortly returned with the special piecee gentleman required, who turned out to be a great American author we had met at Lady C. P. R. Magnum's the evening before leaving Montreal.

'You know each other, I believe,' remarked Rubicundo, genially ; 'and you're certain to have read this chap in any case. He simply infests the bookstalls—there's no getting away from him.' 'What *did* you say he'd written ?' said my friend to me in a terrified whisper, and in the confusion of the moment I confounded the gentleman to be complimented with Mr. Howells, and answered, 'A Foregone Conclusion.' 'No getting away from him,' went on Rubicundo, cheerfully ; 'we'll count a dozen of his last edition on this ship.'

'Yes,' fibbed Orthodocia, gracefully. 'Your "Foregone Delusion" is delightfully familiar to everybody, that is to say '—as he looked aghast—' I mean *by reputation*. How very warm it is !'

Rubicundo choked suddenly, and went away ; but the great American author was very amiable, and only gave the situation the slight emphasis of asking Orthodocia which part of England she came from. Later my friend took occasion to say to me privately that she had always been told that there was no such thing as American literature, and she didn't believe there was ; and anyway, the careless manner in which I pronounced my words was getting to be really——

* * * * * *

'So they sailed away for a year and a day
To the Land where the Bong Tree grows,'

quoted Orthodocia one day dreamily, when the time-spaces began to melt into one another, and nobody knew and nobody cared, as we pulsed southward over rippling seas and under soft skies, how many knots they put up in the companion-way at eight bells as the ship's run, or how far we were from Singapore. It was a charmed voyage, a voyage to evoke imagination in the brains of a Philistine or a Member of Parliament. The very hold of the *Sutlej* was full of poetry in its more marketable shape of tea, and silk, and silver, and elephants' tusks, and preserved pineapples ; and all the romance of the Orient was in the spicy smell that floated up from it. The *Sutlej*, moreover, was returning to England after discharging a Viceroy at Bombay on the way out, and her atmosphere was still full of the calm and conscious glory of it.

Your days of tropical voyaging begin in a great white marble bath. Then, if you want to indulge in the humbug and pretence of 'exercise' before breakfast, you pace up and down in the shade, awnings overhead and at the sides, over the broad white quarter-deck—holystoned hours before—and look away across the bulwarks to where morning in the sky melts into morning in the sea, and a wandering gull catches the light of both on its broad white wings. But it is easier to lie in a steamer chair and fall into a state of reflection. There is just enough ozone in the air to keep your lungs gently in action, and make the languorous energy of your pulses a virtue, and philosophy is easy. You fancy yourself very close to the infinities, and you find the delusive contact pleasant. Rubicundo, in garments of pongee silk and a pith helmet, leaning over the taffrail in the middle distance, becomes invested with the tenderness and profundity of your own emotions ; and you wonder if he too is dreamily playing ninepins with the eternal verities. Presently he takes out his watch and regards it absorbedly, giving you a shock which suggests certain sarcasms, and leaves you better pleased with yourself than ever. It was only breakfast after all.

We pass the punkah-wallahs as we follow him at the clangour of the bell to the companion-way—four or five handsome little Bengalis with the Indian sun in their liquid brown eyes, barefooted, dressed in a single straight white garment reaching half-way down their small mahogany legs; red cotton sashes, and turbans. There are punkah-wallahs and punkah-wallahs, we discover later; and punkah-wallahs may be as unappetising as those of the *Sutlej* are stimulating, in a gentle, æsthetic way, to one's idea of breakfast. It is a peculiarity of Rubicundo's that he never can pass them without a facetious poke or two, from which the punkah-wallah poked squirms delightedly away, and of Orthodocia's that she must needs chirrup to them and cast her new-gotten Indian wealth in annas among them. It takes four of them to keep the punkah waving below, and a quartermaster is told off to see that they do it. Systematically, when the quartermaster is unaware, they attach the rope to their great toes, and agonise on one foot while they pull with the other, which goes to prove that the Aryan small boy is quite as ingenious in self-torture as any other.

It is wide, and cool, and spacious below where the long white table is laid, and the stewards are standing about looking weighed down, as stewards always do, by the solemnity of the approaching function. The walls are tiled in cool blue and white; outside the big square ports the sea sparkles and splashes in the sun—the sweet-voiced laughing southern sea, that bears us so merrily, as if she loved it. Quaint dwarfed cherry trees in full blossom, and orange trees laden with twinkling fruit the size of a marble, and tall waxy camellias from Orthodocia's dear Japan win her affections at first sight. Over head a large railed oval opening gives into the music-room, and across this run bridges of palms and ferns, cool and graceful. Orthodocia told the captain once that it was a little like breakfasting in the suburbs of Paradise, whereat he made as if he were shocked, but as he claimed the palm canopy as his own idea, I don't think he found her simile very objectionable.

At the breakfast-table one's first interest is naturally in the ship's officers, and there is always somebody who has already ingratiated himself with them and will point them out—the captain, the 'First,' the 'Second,' the 'Third,' the doctor, and the rest. 'P. and O.' officers ought to have a chapter to themselves—and I am convinced that I could find enough material for one, duly initialled, in Orthodocia's note-book—for they become a distinct species after one has experienced a few shipfuls of them. But we will never get round the world at this rate, and I must put the theme aside; only telling you that there is always, for instance, the engaged officer, with an absent look and a disposition to take his food indiscriminately; the musical officer, who sings 'White Wings' or 'Queen of My Heart' to the accompaniment of the young married lady at the captain's right; the flirting officer, who has a very pretty cabin to show, full of the trophies, hand-painted or worked in crewels, of other trips; the tall dark oldish officer, and the short fair boyish officer, and others whose accomplishments would take up altogether too much space, but who help, I fancy, to make a great many voyages pleasantly memorable. Captain Worcester, I remember, was rather particular about the niceties of uniform, so that the galaxy of the *Sutlej* were always apparelled exactly alike. The 'First' never appeared in cloth if his 'chief' wore ducks, nor did the 'Second' wear white raiment if black lustre monkey jackets were the order of the day. To the ancient mariner, if such a one happen to read this chronicle, these things will doubtless be trivialities, but to the feminine and æsthetic eye I know their importance will be manifest.

After breakfast one finds the breeziest spot on deck, and reposes oneself on the long Chinese steamer-chair of the person whose card of possession is most obscurely tacked on. Perhaps there is a fire muster to enliven the morning, and one languidly watches the Lascars taking prompt orders with splashing buckets, the officers getting the boats out, and the stewards trooping up with provision for the same. Captain Worcester made this a very serious function indeed, and the nutriment his pantrymen sent up was of the most solid and uninspiring character; but on another ship I took note of the provisions one morning, and found that the head steward intended us to live luxuriously to the last. They included two tins of preserved ginger—most inspiring diet for castaways—a box of

macaroons, and a quantity of marmalade. Orthodocia, I remember, immediately conjured up a picture of
the consumption of that marmalade, each unfortunate
putting in a finger in turn, and began to
select her fellow-
passengers.

Or perhaps there
is 'stations,' and all
the ship's crew, the
officer in buttons, the
quartermasters in
blue, the stewards
in their smug
black coats,

THE CAPTAIN.

the Lascar sailors
in such finery as
they have, and the
African firemen
in long, clean and
white garments,
round the quarter-
ing as the captain

primitive
make a line
deck, salut-
and first officer pass on a round of inspection;
then, at the quartermaster's whistle, disappearing to
the depths from whence they came. The popular
Nubian robe deserves another word : it is cut
with great economy straight from the shoulders

down to the calf of the leg, and there is an aperture at the neck, by which it is got into. It is almost ugly enough to be adopted by a dress reform society, and when the African who owns it is particularly big and black and solemn-visaged, it is usually made of spotted muslin. One or two patterns were quite sweet, and gave a special interest to 'stations.'

Then 'tiffin'—lunch is a solecism on the P. and O.—and fruits and ices in paper boats, and other tropical alleviations, while the long canvas flounce of the punkah swings lazily to and fro over the table, and Captain Worcester tells a second best story, for the best are not to be had from him till dinner-time. And then the afternoon wears goldenly away with ship cricket perhaps, at which Orthodocia once distinguished herself by sending the ball so vigorously high in the air that it carried Rubicundo's pipe into the yeasty deep, and gave him a sympathy, he said, for men who had seen active service, which he never had before. Or the five o'clock tea of the lady who always carries her own tea set, and has a private plum cake, which is quite the prevailing idea in fashionable Oriental travelling. One afternoon we pass within half a mile of a steam yacht which the 'First' declares to be sailed by the Sultan of Jahore. We descry a stout person in white in her stern, waving his handkerchief vigorously, and immediately invest him with spotless robes, ropes of jewels, and great condescension. The Sultan of Jahore! The one touch of romantic magic needful to make the East tangible to us, to give a world of realism to all that fantasy of opal sky and sea. It was altogether sublime, and we can't help regretting the later experience that would make us more or less contemptuous of sailing Sultans—suspicious of the propriety of their linen, and the intervals between their pocket-handkerchiefs. One is fortunate, Orthodocia has since concluded, in seeing one's first Sultan with a half-mile perspective.

Early missionary associations came back upon one forcibly in a trip through the Indian Archipelago, and there is one especial association that comes back to everybody, and comes to stay. I mean everybody on the saloon list. I have seldom heard it expressed by any of the ship's officers, though I have seen numbers of them move off almost in a terrified way on hearing something about it from the lips of a passenger. In fact, I have reason to believe that a violent and distressing end was put to a most promising affair between a certain First and a charming young person from Australia once, when it became apparent that she was hopelessly addicted to the association that I refer to.

There is a high broken line on the horizon one morning, which we are given to understand indicates Sumatra, a mass of darker blue against the sky—only this and nothing more. Yet it is enough to make every individual on deck exclaim with one emotion, 'India's coral strand!' It's not India, and there's nothing even remotely suggestive of a coral strand about it, but 'our imaginations,' as the old lady who is aunt to a bishop piously remarks, 'were not given to us for nothing'; and the association is well started. She begins by looking thoughtfully for a long time at the geographical suggestion on our lee, and repeating slowly just as the bishop might have done:

> 'From many an ancient river,
> From many a palmy plain,
> They call us to deliver
> Their land from error's chain.'

Then she proposes that we should sing the entire hymn, but somebody—the 'Second,' I think—hurriedly interposes. He declares it would be madness to let the association take such complete hold on us so early in the trip. 'Wait,' he says, '"until the spicy breezes blow soft o'er Ceylon's isle."' And then he goes away, I think, and has himself put in irons. But we don't sing it; we content ourselves with saying it over from beginning to end, internally, seven times. By that time it has grown tolerably familiar, and we begin to resent the slightest inaccuracies in anybody's quotations from it. It takes entire possession of us; we hum it at intervals all day. I have seen two elderly gentlemen on terms of intimacy suddenly pause in the midst of an exciting political discussion and chant solemnly and simultaneously:

> 'The heathen, in his blindness,
> Bows down to wood and stone.'

Then glare angrily at one another for an instant, and take chairs at remote and dissociated ends of the ship.

We fly to literature for surcease from affliction, and find that every author of 'Round the World' travels on board has quoted the hymn in full on the page we open—doubtless to ease his mind.

The conjunction of Rubicundo and a certain unfortunate bachelor named Viall brings our sufferings to a climax. Rubicundo begins to twit Mr. Viall on his state of single blessedness—to twit him ominously. We wait in nervous anticipation—presently there is a chance for it and it comes :

> 'Though every prospect pleases,
> Yet "only *man* is Viall!"'

I am pleased to state that Rubicundo goes away looking thoroughly ashamed of himself. The joke is given to the public simply to show the malign influence of an essentially innocent hymn upon a person who, under other circumstances, had won a reputation for humour.

One can't expect Captain Worcester's stories to 'print' half so funnily as he told them. The story, for instance, of the first two Chinese Mandarins the P. and O. brought to England, and the special instructions the captain got from headquarters to look after them when they came aboard. How the captain turned in after a while, leaving the instructions with the 'First'; how the 'First' delegated them to the 'Second,' and the 'Second' in the course of time to the first available quartermaster. And how the quartermaster, with unshaken rectitude, came to the captain in a stilly hour of night with the terrifying message, 'Please, surr, they kings is come aboord, an' one of em's fell down the coal-hole!' Or of the terrible encounter of his chief once, while he was yet only a 'First,' which demanded all the nerve of a commander of a man-of-war, with two enraged and horror-stricken members of the Bombay Civil Service, who confronted that stern person in port with tumultuous inquiries for their beauteous brides that were to be—and had to be told, with what fortitude the captain could summon, that the young ladies, lingering too long among the ever-fascinating bazaars, had been left behind at Gibraltar!

Or of the occasional contumacious maiden he has had consigned to his fatherly care for Indian ports. Of one especial young woman who refused to 'turn in' at ten o'clock as beseemed her, but rather preferred the society of a callow subaltern and the seclusion of the hurricane deck. How he remonstrated in vain, and finally hit upon a luminous idea to preserve discipline, and set a quartermaster to place four lanterns round the young woman wherever she might betake herself. This was conspicuous and embarrassing, and as the quartermaster, acting under orders, pursued her from Dan in the prow to Beersheba in the stern, her haughty spirit was finally humbled, I believe. We heard much, too, of the whole bevies of extremely young persons who are often entrusted to a P. and O. captain, and succeed in making his life a burden to him. A favourite message from one lot of Captain Worcester's was that 'Amy'—actat. nine —'won't go to bed; please come down and slap her!'

And I must not forget the time-honoured P. and O. story, at the expense of a short-sighted young officer who longed to be a Nimrod, and whom some humourist sent to shoot scavenger crows near Yokohama, under the impression that they were a species of Japanese wild fowl. He brought down two brace of birds, and sent them with lively joy to the wife of the agent at Yokohama with a polite note, stating that they were the first-fruits of his gun. Meantime the joke was explained to him, and he sent in severe spasms of mind to recover the crows, instructing his coolie to buy two brace of ducks in the market to fulfil the promise of the note. The lady, who had been out, was delighted to receive the note on her return, and ordered the first-fruits to be brought to her in the drawing-room. There was some delay in executing the order, and apparently some confusion in the back premises. Presently the first-fruits, lustily pursued and in a state of great excitement, flapped into the room. The coolie had only made the interesting improvement of buying live ones to represent his master's sport, and probably does not understand the reason of his chastisement unto this day. I believe the officer is still in the service. He must recognise his own ducks very often in the course of a year.

Singapore and Penang occurred during the course of this voyage, but as I am devoting my chapter to a faint picture of the joys of the voyage itself, I think I will not impart the more or less valuable impressions we were able to gather during the two or three hours we spent at each port. Orthodocia took her note-book each time to pick up any stray statistics that might come in our way, but the only note I see under 'Singapore' is 'Three yards Indian mull for hat, 2s. 6d.,' and Penang has something about fan-palms and pongee silk.

And the voyage of every day was like the voyage of the day before, always ending in the cool soft darkness that fell suddenly, and brought with it a myriad of strange stars. The watching great Venus slip down into the sea, and the waiting for the Southern Cross to lift its beauty up from the dark verge of the sky, and the listening to the meeting and the parting of the waters, as this majestic black creature of a ship pulsed onward into the infinity about us—that was all we did at night, yet each night seems to have a separate chronicle as one reads backwards, a chronicle that vanishes in the writing and is dumb in the telling.

XXI

On the wide quarter-deck of the *Sutlej*, in port at Colombo, Ceylon.

'*Iké!*' said Orthodocia. '*Ikəmasho!*'[1] My friend clung tenderly to the vocabulary of her lost Japan. 'It is all,' she was wont to say pathetically, 'that I have left.' Which, considering the amount of room taken up in the ship's hold by packing-boxes labelled 'Miss O. Love, Wigginton, Devon, Eng. Curios. With Care,' seemed a preposterous statement.

'*Iké!*' she said.

The man looked at her wonderingly. He was a short, brown heathen, of the Cingalese variety, with a round, shining countenance, radiating much guile. He stood before her in his white draperies in the manner of one who will not be discouraged, and he held in his hands a tray full of precious stones. He was a 'tambie,' a pedlar-pest of these waters, and we had foreknowledge of him.

'Eekay!' he repeated slowly and thoughtfully. 'I doan' know dat "go away!" De French, dey says "*vatton!*" de German, dey says "*s'eer dich aus!*" de In'lis, dey says "be off!" de Mer'can, dey says "clear out!" I doan' know wat lan'widge dat "Eekay."'

'De Cingalese,' he added, politely, 'dey says, "*pallayan!*"'

Who could say it after that *naïf* confession of familiarity with the brutality of all Christendom? Not Orthodocia, at any rate. I saw her hesitate and fall. I left her fingering silver stars of 'moonstones'—little round valueless things like drops of watered milk, which one gets only in Ceylon; and when I came back from engaging what I believed to be 'catamarans,' to take us ashore, I found that she had 'remembered' every inhabitant of Wigginton with one of them, and was telling the tambie how inexpensive they were.

[1] Go away.

We arranged to go shoreward in this manner, because it was an innovation, and we were opposed on general principles to the ordinary and the commonplace; but I cannot conscientiously urge the claims of the catamaran as a convenient and comfortable method of public transport. As we wanted all the innovations we could get we took three, one for Orthodocia, one for me, and one for her Chinese tea-pots. I considered the third a measure of over-caution, and urged my friend to take the tea-pots in her lap; but she declined, in the opinion that they would swamp her catamaran.

'THERE IS NO DOUBT THAT AS AN INNOVATION THE CATAMARAN IS A SUCCESS.'

There is no doubt that as an innovation the catamaran is a success, but one should have an extreme taste in innovations to appreciate it thoroughly. There is no awning, for one thing—a drawback in the tropics. There is no seat. There is only a small wet wooden half egg which protrudes an arm across the waves on one side in a wild effort to keep its balance. It was extremely wavy in the harbour of Colombo the day we essayed upon it in catamarans, and it was only occasionally that I could assure myself that Orthodocia and her tea-pots were still extant. And I suppose that two more water-logged passengers never disembarked at Colombo. We advised each other warmly, as we wrung each other out, to travel in future with our luggage in the steam launch.

It was pleasant enough, driving about and drying ourselves, and choosing a hotel, a quaint old castellated-looking affair in a clump of cocoanuts by the sea, about half a mile from the town, which was all we did that day. One's first tropical hotel is always amusing enough to keep one in it for a while. It took half an hour to appreciate the points of our bedroom, with its great windows, opening like shutters on hinges, through which floated the rainy, pattering sound of the wind-stirred cocoanut palms, and the splash of the waves on the beach, and the multitudinous cawings of the big black scavenger crows, that flap heavily in themselves occasionally with an eye to booty. We became well acquainted with our crows, and discovered variations in their sage impudence that gave a personality to each of them. The beds are invisible behind their mosquito-nets—not casual draperies such as protect one's slumbers in America, but securely tucked in and guiltless of the smallest hole whatever. The partitions stop within three feet of the ceiling— the terms of rebuke our neighbour had for his wife on the score of her extravagance were quite embarrassing for Orthodocia and me; and several times it was a question of debate with us whether we should rap resonantly upon the wall and say distinctly, 'We're here!' The bath is a huge tub that looks as if it might have been hollowed out of solid wood, and our ablutions were frequently shared by a small green lizard or so. Beautiful and interesting objects— when one is able to bestow one's entire attention upon them. The first lizard that occurs in one's bath tub is invariably a scorpion— in fact, with Orthodocia the terms were interchangeable—and this accounts, I dare say, for the number of scorpions we found in what books on the tropics we had with us.

At tiffin one has a chance of observing the transplanted European variety of tropical humanity as it takes its accustomed place, speaks commandingly to a waiter in bad Cingalese, and subsides behind a newspaper to await the fulfilment of things. There is the bronzed young officer in mufti and the bronzed old officer in mufti, the mufti in both cases being white ducks, and differences and distinctions lying chiefly in the fact that the old officer has the redder nose and the young one the more deeply bored expression of the two. There is the up-country planter in town on business for a day or two ; a jovial fellow he, brown as a nut under his broad double soft felt hat, keen-eyed, loose-garmented, with an independence of manner and speech acquired a long way from Mayfair, and a suggestion in all he says and does of the lavish, hospitable, happy-go-lucky life he leads under his vanilla vines and his mango trees. And there is the old resident who came 'out' as a boy, thinking to make his fortune in ten years and go back, but who has meanwhile stratified into the permanent social body of Ceylon, and forgotten that he ever intended to do more than earn a respectable living. Then there are the ladies, all in cool English muslins, a little pale, perhaps, but otherwise just like 'the ladies' wherever femininity is gathered together under the sun ; and the 'planet pilgrims,' of which happy band are Orthodocia and I, looking very new and hot, and proud of their tropical attire.

Among all these the Cingalese waiters move, tall and sinuous and silent, each in his white jacket and flowing nether draperies, each with his long, sleek, black hair drawn back by a large tortoise-shell comb. We thought at first that the comb might be an idiosyncrasy of the hotel — a compulsory measure adopted for the sake of the soup ; but we soon discovered it to be a Cingalese masculine vanity of the low country. The Kandyans do not wear combs, and you will remember that the British had more difficulty in subduing them than their low country brethren who were given over to the pomps and vanities. Trincomalee, of the south, was probably taken while the garrison was making its toilet. However that may be, it takes time for the tourist to become accustomed to this Cingalese originality — to acquire a taste for it must take eternity. A heathen with his hair neatly drawn back under the halo of a tortoiseshell comb is a disturbing object in nature, and one that the Sunday-school papers neglect to prepare you for.

Then there are the tropical fruits to make acquaintance with, and by the ineradicable legacy of Paradise the fruits of a country are the first interest and the soul's solace of everybody. The mango, the 'custard apple,' the 'bullock's heart.' The mango looks like a large corpulent green pocket-book, about eight inches long and four wide, and tastes like nothing else in the world, with a dash of turpentine which is sometimes strong enough to spoil the pink ambrosia inside and sometimes is not. It is extremely juicy, leathery of cover, and has a large stone inside. It is not, therefore, an easy article of consumption to the novice from over seas. I shall always remember Orthodocia and her first mango with emotions that time cannot mitigate. It was a very ripe fat mango, and looked as if it ought to be peeled. Orthodocia thought to peel it round and round with precision as if it were an apple. At the second round she began to hold it carefully over her plate ; at the third she tucked her sleeve well up from the wrist ; at the fourth she laid it down blushingly, looked round carefully to see if anyone observed her, made several brilliant maps upon her napkin, and tackled it again. This was too much for the mango, and it bounded with precipitancy into the lap of an elderly person across the table, who restored it with frigid indignation in a table-spoon. Orthodocia then harpooned it with her fork, and took the rest of the skin off in transverse sections, which left her in possession of a very large amount of stone with a very superficial amount of fruit irregularly distributed over it. This she did not consume, having acquired enough mango, as she said, externally. We learned the proper way afterwards, which is to slice the fruit longitudinally into three, leaving a bit of skin at each end of the stone piece, to take the pulp out of the side slices with a spoon, and to attack the middle slice with an end in each hand, much in the American manner of consuming green corn. This makes the mango unpopular as a dessert fruit for æsthetic reasons, and confines its consumption, in fact, with many people who are particular, to the only place which seems to give room enough for it and the opportunity of properly repairing its ravages—the matutinal tub.

The custard apple and bullock's heart are related and equally objectionable, the chief difference being that one is nasty in a sweet way, and the other is nasty in a sour way. The prevailing flavour is that of French kid, the consistency that of very thick porridge. As I have hinted in Orthodocia's experience, the proper mode of consumption of tropical fruits is in itself a liberal education. A 'bullock's heart,' for instance, is almost the size of a small melon. Two were set before us when Orthodocia and I first made their acquaintance; and we, with the careless joy of tyros in the tropics, possessed ourselves each of one. It was not until our spoons were deep in their pasty insides that we discovered, by the various expressions of our neighbours' countenances, that those two 'bullock's hearts' were intended to be divided sectionally among at least five people. It was a matter of the more painful regret to us in that the defrauded would have liked them so much better than we did.

We spent our first evening in Ceylon as nineteen travellers in twenty spend it, enraptured on the hotel verandah. As we strolled up and down there, looking at the evening light on the pale green sea, and listening to the wind among the cocoanut fronds, there was nothing and nobody else apparently but half a dozen knotted bundles and two or three dark, expectant figures, sitting cross-legged behind them. But we had only to take lounging chairs, and look absently into space, to work a transformation. Instantly the knots were untied, and a wealth of colour rolled out of the dingy wrappings. Silks of India and of China, 'puggeries,' 'kummerbunds'—scarfs for belts—woven in all sorts of brilliant combinations, native cottons, soft and loosely made, strings of pearls, heaps of uncut rubies and sapphires, real green beetles set in gold and silver, old swords and daggers curiously carved, round metal boxes for carrying betel paste, curious Cingalese vases in alternate bronze and silver, tiny hammered silver coffee spoons, with Buddha sitting on the handle—but I am beginning to read like an auction list. And the embroideries—before their splendid barbarism my pen fails. Most of them, wonderfully worked in colours that can only be called internecine, would profane a modern drawing-room; but others were in exquisite patterns of gold thread upon cream silk, and were altogether ravishing. The Oriental scale of prices we began to understand, falling back on our expensive Japanese experience, and in our chaffering and bickering we got a valuable Kindergarten lesson in the current specie of Ceylon. A rupee, for instance—who, not an Anglo-Indian, or any connection of his, has not had dazzling visions of the value of a rupee? To my untutored American imagination a rupee had always been a large and luminous coin of pure gold, with strange characters cut upon it by dusky Indian fingers. I knew that viceroys were paid in rupees—in lakhs of rupees—and a lakh had always represented a pile about as high as the table. I had had visions of Their Excellencies encanopied by the British flag, receiving tribute of this sort. It was a little trying to find that at current rates of exchange it took about three of them to be worth a single small gold dollar. There were also annas to be struggled with—copper annas and silver annas — and pies and pice, with plentiful illustrations in bargains. And we took to it all with great en-thusiasm, especially the illustrations, and speculated

'AND THEN LIE SWEETLY DOWN TO SLUMBER.'

so late upon the verandah that my first night's rest in Ceylon was disturbed by dreams of barter, and Orthodocia went back in her sleep to the tables in the primary arithmetic. I heard her myself, sitting up in bed, solemnly say—

> 'Twenty pies one scruple,
> Three scruples one pice,
> Eight rupees one furlong,
> Seventeen hundred and six'y annas one mile.'

And then lie sweetly down again to slumber.

XXII

BELONGING as we do to the sex that adorns itself, the first thing that Orthodocia and I coveted in the Asian tropics was naturally clothes. Not the vulgar garnishings we had bought all our lives by the yard, and had made up according to the dictum—'at the cannon's mouth,' Orthodocia said—of a tyrant 'Madame' This or That, but these soft, loosely-woven fabrics of silk or cotton, with their fantastic borders, that had never been classified under the head of 'Imports,' but came to us straight from Indian looms as cheaply as we had the cleverness to take them. It was for some time a source of wonder to us that the European lady resident did not buy these native things for her personal adornment, instead of driving about as she did dressed very much as she would be on a hot day at home. How much more graceful than that stiff 'sailor,' thought we, would be the loose end of one of these soft *saris* drawn over the head and shoulders as the brown women draw them; how much more artistic than that pink cambric the Oriental design and colour of the native drapery! And Orthodocia almost meditated, being a seriously artistic person, appearing in the costume of the native ladies, with certain amendments, to introduce the idea. But we happily stayed long enough to find out that this wealth of colour was chiefly in combinations of red and yellow and green, not wholly to be approved of on artistic grounds after the glamour had worn off; that cheap native silk is apt on the second time of wearing to produce a fungus of fuzz all over it; that the better 'Indian' fabrics are chiefly made in Manchester for this particular trade; and that a great mass of barbarism becomes so revolting by daily contact that even its decorative ideas are objectionable by association. By that time Orthodocia had dropped the idea of adopting the native costume, and consigned her *saris* to the bottom of her trunk, to be made into window curtains or twisted over the backs of Wigginton sofas in the manner that Wigginton approves of.

It was before our initiation that we bought native silks on the verandah, and listened to the Australian lady who sat beside us at tiffin, and had 'been told' that the Cingalese men made very fair dressmakers. They looked so much like women, with their delicate features, long hair and flowing garments, that we were not surprised to hear it. Gathering up our bargains, therefore, we sallied forth to find the Worths of Ceylon and see Colombo at the same time.

I am instructed by the guide-book to say that Colombo is divided into the 'Fort,' the 'Pettah,' and the 'Bungalow District'—the Fort being the business and barracks part of the town, the Pettah the native and nasty part, and the Bungalow District the outskirts chiefly, where the British resident keeps house under tropical conditions and a very big fig-tree. All of which I suppose we examined according to the precepts of the guide-book at the time, but I should doubt the reliability of anything topographical about Colombo that survives either in my memory or Orthodocia's note-book, beyond the fact that our particular man lived in the Pettah, whither we betook ourselves first.

After the clothed barbarism of Japan and China, one's first drive among one's Aryan brothers is apt to be interjectional, unless one is a person of extreme stolidity. The women are too much clad, if anything, to attend one of Her Majesty's Drawing Rooms, but the men present a broad glistening acreage of mahogany epidermis that is startling, while the costume of the small boy consists of a chain and amulet of some sort which he wears round his fat little waist. Like other small boys, he outgrows his clothes, and until his mother lets them out looks much like a plump brown pillow tied in with a string.

The children, lovely little imps, with eyes like pairs of liquid lamps in the darkness of their hair and faces, clustered all along the road, ready to besiege everything on wheels that came that way. They ran after us with tiny bunches of flowers, a curious jumping, gliding inflection in their soft voices, as they pleaded, 'Nice rose flower, laidy ! Please buy this, laidy ! You give me sixpence, laidy !'

There was a world of persuasion in it, and I cannot testify to any resistance on our part. Orthodocia even stopped the carriage and got a couple of two-year-old brown Cupids into it, who wept so lustily, however, that she abandoned her idea of taking them home to hold lamps in the hall, and returned them to the bosom of their families with despatch. They were perfect little beings, exquisite in mould and colour, and could have been got, I suppose, for about three-and-sixpence apiece—tropical curios of unmistakable genuineness and great artistic merit. But they slipped through our hands, as we held them over the side of the carriage, like many another bargain I dare say. The mothers, who regarded us curiously out of their secretive dark eyes, half hiding their faces in their cotton *saris* as we looked, carried their babies astride over their hips, awkwardly enough. Frequent family tubbings were in process in front of the small domiciles built of mud and sticks and thatched with cocoanut leaves or roofed with coarse tiles, that huddled together by the roadside, the little wet, naked figures positively flashing in the sun. Round the street pumps, which seemed to stand at every corner, there was always a picturesque group—a woman with a pail on her head, graceful as Rebekah, a coolie splashing the cool water over his dusty black legs, and the fascinating brown infant everywhere. I remember one special glimpse -- a little beauty of a girl with long, tangled, shiny black hair and eyes like stars, a bit of red handkerchief draped round her limbs, and a half-cocoanut in her hand for a cup. She splashed the water at us saucily as we passed, and one doesn't often see anything prettier than she was as she did it.

Europeans were driving as Europeans drive everywhere, but the popular native conveyance was a two-wheeled wooden cart, attached to a pair of small buffaloes. When I first heard of the extent to which buffaloes are made use of in the East, I thought at once of our prairie buffalo, with his large frontal development and unsociable ways, and reflected on the power of man. You who do not belong to our continent, and naturally know more about it than its inhabitants do, would have been able to tell me that ours are not buffaloes at all, but bison, and that the term properly belongs to the funny little animals and their kin that we saw going at full trot through the streets of Colombo. The ox of one's early primer is such a meditative animal, and takes such heed to his ways, that it is a sensation as remarkable of its sort as any Barnum gave you to see the pace their drivers get out of these small creatures, and the sense of direction they have. There is a look of having been surprised into a novel occupation, mingled with an intention to make the best of it, in their honest little faces, that is very funny indeed. Many of them are not more than ten hands high; they have no horns, and are harnessed to their poor little humps and driven by a rope through their poor little noses. I have authority for saying that they will go nine and ten miles an hour, but no experience, as I declined Orthodocia's proposition to try them tandem. One may be a very fair whip and yet not an adept at tail-twisting, which is the native Jehu's art of persuasion.

Our vehicle, that once, had a back seat. Afterward, we chose vehicles without back seats.

Turning into the Pettah we passed a group of natives in the first position of hotel loafers. Two of them ran as fast as possible after our carriage, and one of them vaulted lightly into the back seat aforesaid. He was a good-looking fellow with an impertinent fat face; he might have been an imitation 'end man' of an American minstrel show.

'What do you want?' said Orthodocia, whose nerves were shaken.

'I'm a puhson puffeckly qualified to act as guide and interpolater, Miss. I'm fluent in de lan'widge, ye know! You see dese fellahs dey cannot speak youh lan'widge, ye know! You address dem and dey cannot address back. Dis circumvents trouble fo' you, laidy. Now, I'm fluent in de lan'widge, ye know. Ah you from America? Oh, indeed? Oh, indeed? Well, I'll tell you w'at I'll do fo' you. If you take me to Kandy, I'll go fo' five rupees a day an' fin' my own food—an' you save ten per cent.!'

'Get down!' said Orthodocia.

'I'm a puhson puffeckly qualified——'

'Get down!' said Orthodocia.

'Oh, very well, laidy! I simply wished a lift down 'cre—dat was my objeck in coming with you, laidy! An' now I'll say good-bye to you, laidy! You won't forget my numbah—a puhson puff-eckly qualified an' fluent in you' lan'widge, laidy!'

And long before the policeman I had beckoned to had reached us he was out of sight. He was a Portuguese mixture, and he made the atmosphere alcoholic. We wondered where he had got his English—his accent was so affably cockney. His 'numbah'. was ninety-nine; but if you are thinking of going to Ceylon, I am afraid you would find him quite too 'fluent in you' lan'widge.' We did.

The dirty little shops that line the narrow, crooked, crowded little street were full of the commonplaces of European trade. This we observed with sorrow, expecting to find in the Pettah endless repetition of the wonders of the hotel verandah. But where we looked for Oriental head-dresses there we found bonnet-shapes; where we desired jewelled daggers, linen cuffs. Plenty of Europeans were chaffering in the shops, which we did not understand until we were told that these native merchants having no high rents and no wages to pay, compete everywhere for British rupees against the British. The soft-voiced, soft-mannered Cingalese with whom we were presently talking, for instance, would make a silk dress for six, while a fashionable dressmaker in the Fort would have asked at least twenty-five. He was squatting on the floor of a room behind when we went into his dark little shop, with two or three fellow seamsters, all industriously chewing betel and sewing, one end of the seam neatly held between their large brown toes.

'Sala'am!' he said, coming forward with dignity, and then we went into matters which you find discussed every week in the ladies' newspapers. He was probably the most affable and amenable dressmaker that either of us had ever experienced. He was entirely open to suggestion, and took up ideas with a smiling appreciation that was to us as the balm of Gilead after the frowning autocrats we had known. He fitted us with gentle consideration and politeness in another dark little room before a mirror, which was his accomplice, and under a swinging punkah which distracted our attention from the theory of dressmaking. And he said 'Sala'am!' again as we went out, entirely pleased with ourselves. It was some time after, about the time the dresses came home, I think, that we remembered that he hadn't shown us any fashion plates and that we had left a good deal to his imagination. He, in turn, had left a good deal to ours wherever he could in both fit and fashion, and especially in a volume of skirt material. If he had only abstracted a few more yards we could have attended a fancy dress ball anywhere in those gowns, and been recognised as representing poorly-draped clothes-pins. Moreover, he had changed the silks for cheaper ones of the same colour. I believe they will always oblige a stranger that way. And then we began to understand how it was that the European merchants were not entirely starved out of existence, and to consider our 'Sala'ams!' dulcet as they were, a little dear.

The Pettah, I remember, was full of memorials of the rigorous old Dutch days of the 'Reformed Presbyterians,' two hundred years ago, and we drove past the curious old yellow Dutch belfry, a long way from the church where the Reformed Presbyterians used to gather when the rusty bell that still hangs in it told them it was time. The same old bell rang every night to warn the taverns and the roystering sailors in them that it was the hour to shut up, in those quaint times when nobody could misunderstand the law and a Board of Works was still iniquitously unimagined. And we saw the church itself, built on the site of its Portuguese predecessor, 'Aqua de Lupo,' named after it too, in the burly Dutch tongue. 'Wolfendahl'—a fine, stern old building in the shape of a Greek cross. Inside, the guide-book said there were 'many interesting souvenirs of Dutch rule,' including the coat-of-arms and memorial-stones of the old Vans and Vons that governed the island in the gospel according to Martin Luther; but the doors were locked, being still Reformed Presbyterian, and we couldn't get in.

About this time, the weather being extremely Cingalese, we concluded that the inner tourist required refreshment rather than retrospection, and drove to the chief restaurant in sight. There was a little Scotchman inside—Scotchmen flourish like thistles in Ceylon—and we made request for ices.

'I'm sorry to say 't, miss,' he said sincerely, 'but we've got none in stock.'

'Do you usually *keep* them?' asked Orthodocia with disappointed sarcasm.

'Not usually, miss. But we generally hae some aboot the time the Australian mail comes in.'

It seemed invidious to all the other mails, and Orthodocia thought

'THE MOST AFFABLE AND AMENABLE DRESSMAKER THAT EITHER OF US HAD EVER EXPERIENCED.'

we ought to write to the papers about it, but we contented ourselves for the time by enviously congratulating the Australians, and went dejectedly away. We told our 'muttoo' to take us to the cinnamon gardens, having been told that the cinnamon gardens were something to see.

We drove apparently for miles and miles. Every now and then the muttoo drew up and pointed at a public building. We had grown to hate public buildings, but we didn't know Cingalese and couldn't say so. Happily, the muttoo didn't know English either, and was unable to tell us whether it was an hospital or a museum, a college or a gaol, and by whom it was erected and when. This was merciful and fortunate, and made the muttoo's society infinitely preferable to that of the public-spirited citizen whom we had learned to dread. But he didn't seem to understand 'Cinnamon Gardens,' either, and at each of our vain repetitions of it he stopped and pointed out another public building. The situation seemed impossible, for there wasn't a white person in sight. We drove on, staring hopelessly at public buildings. At last something occurred to me. Prodding the muttoo diligently, I leaned forward, looked at him intelligently and repeated slowly and sonorously—

> 'What though the spicy breezes
> Blow soft o'er Ceylon's isle.'

The effect was instantaneous. A look of relief overspread the man's countenance, and he whipped up his horse, nodding violently, and making some remark in his native tongue which Orthodocia interpreted to mean 'Why didn't you say that before?' and we sped on with hope and exhilaration. I suppose he had driven several hundred planet pilgrims to the source of the spicy breezes yearly, and not one of them had ever failed to make the quotation. When we arrived at the cinnamon gardens, however, we should not have known it, had it not been for the spicy breezes aforesaid. There were no gates or enclosures, nothing but a road winding through a tract of white sand, in which low bushes with pointed, glossy, dark green leaves were growing in rows, some of them half covered with ant-hills. But the smell was unmistakable and heavenly. Little brown urchins, moreover, were lying in wait in all directions with long green sticks of it to sell, which they bit with their sharp white teeth to make a freshly odorous place. To be quite sure, we asked a tall, dark, strong-featured man in semi-European dress, whom we met sauntering along in meditation, whether we were right. His complexion was much lighter than the native type, and his features were markedly different. When he answered us politely in French, we wondered still more who he might be. Our driver waited till we were well past, and then pointing his whip back he grinned, and said, 'Arab' Pasha'! Presently we passed a wooden house, the upper part closely shut up, not by any means a palatial residence for an exiled rebel chief. 'Arab' Pasha house,' remarked the muttoo, grinning again; and we found out afterwards that he was right. We heard that Arabi grumbles a good deal, naturally, when he is not drawing up beautiful assurances of love and loyalty to the Queen, and declares that the climate is too moist for him. This we could quite believe, for the moisture of the climate impressed even Orthodocia, who came from England, and we were able to account three or four casual showers a day as nothing before we left. Arabi ought however to know enough English to borrow an umbrella, though he may not have the vocabulary to return it. He was a source of the bitterest regret to Orthodocia after we discovered his identity. 'If only the carriage had been upset,' she said, mournfully, 'and you had dislocated your collar-bone, what a lot of information I might have got from him about his Egyptian Past!'

We finished up with the 'Bungalow District,' a wide road with open pillared tropical white houses on either side, each set far back in a luxuriant glossy tangle of flowering shrubs, each overshadowed by its group of waving cocoanut palms or broadly-branching breadfruit trees, each with its idle group of dusky servants, waiting commands from the cool and shadowy interior. They had identities, these bungalows, each painted on its gate-post, which showed an extraordinary sense of humour in the British householder. One was 'Monsoon Villa,' another 'Icicle Hall.' Why not 'Blizzard Bank,' or 'The Refrigerator'? But one always wants to improve upon things.

Going back, we passed a wonderful place—a great, shining, green-brown lake, in the midst of the town, with grassy banks, and mangoes, and palms, and tulip trees reflected in it, half covered with the broad green leaves and the marvellous blossoms of the lotus. It was afternoon, and the shadows were long and grateful, and the native

'THE HEATHEN AND THE TEMPTATION CAME TOO CLOSE TOGETHER.'

groups, clad in white and yellow, together and fell apart in them, that clustered together were full of slow indolence. We looked at the lotus-flowers—our first lotus-flowers, if that is any extenuation—and grew covetous. I beckoned to the native whose garments I thought would suffer least, showed him a four anna bit and pointed to the lake. His heathen mind assimilated my sinful idea instantly: in he went up to his neck. In a breathless moment, during which our guilty consciences suggested policemen and a felon's dock to each of us, we had a lotus apiece, and were off. I suppose this is the sort of thing that counteracts missionary enterprise. But as Orthodocia said, for a lotus—a great, creamy, waxen water-lily thrice glorified, with a separate phial of perfume at the end of every stamen—well, the heathen and the temptation came too close together.

We sent our muttoo off, and walked back along the curving pink shore, which is the loveliest in the world. The opal sea, light and delicate in all its lines, sent in a single long sweeping white wave to break upon the sand. The marvel was that nothing more beautiful than pearls should come out of that colour and light. The sky was a strange pale green, with trailing glories of amber and gold. Halfway between us and the cloudy group of palms beyond, an Afghan knelt on his praying carpet and swayed and bowed to the west. The sun had gone to England, but there were divine memories of him where the Afghan looked. We could not think it wonderful that he prayed.

XXIII

'DESIRE pardon,' said a respectful voice behind us; 'but if the ladies h'eat the pineapple and drink the milk of the cocoanut at the same time they will die.'

We turned hastily and discovered the owner of the voice. We were in a second-class compartment of an afternoon train going north through Ceylon. We had just passed the third little station beyond Colombo, and the low-country air of February had excited us to thirst. The little station had swarmed with natives selling bananas, and pineapples, and cocoanuts, and unknown green spheres that only other natives, gibbering and peering in the third-class compartments, bought. Observing this, and remembering the unutterable mushiness of the 'bullock's heart' and the inexpressible flavour of the 'custard apple,' we had confined ourselves strictly to the tropical fruits we had grown tolerant of in youth; and were consuming pineapple with a penknife, and drinking fresh cocoanut milk through a neatly-plugged hole in the top of the cocoanut—our outlay three pence—with greedy joy. When we heard that if we did this thing we would die, Orthodocia and I paused suddenly, looked at one another, and made a rapid mental calculation of how long we had been doing it already.

The person who gave us this pleasant bit of information smiled as he gave it, showing two rows of beautiful teeth. His clothes fitted him—light tweed trousers and black coat. He wore, besides, a look of decided intelligence, and he had been reading the *Ceylon Observer*. When I add that his linen was anything but immaculate you will guess that he was black; and he was, black as the ace of spades, singularly black—what Orthodocia called a lovely tone of black. He was the first native who illustrated to us in his speech and attire the progress of Western civilisation in the Orient, and on this ground he interested us largely. We had not realised before that natives spoke polite cockney English and read the daily newspapers, at least natives who were not of royal blood and went about in second-class carriages; and this one was a surprise to us. But that was afterwards. Our first thought was naturally of the pineapple-cocoanut-milk combination, and the probable length of our further stay in this world.

'My mouth,' said Orthodocia, in sudden alarm, 'feels prickly inside all over. Is that the first sign of dissolution?'

'That is because you 'ave h'eaten a little of the h'outside of the pineapple, I think,' said the native, smiling again.

'When will I die?' demanded Orthodocia, with lively interest.

'I 'ope—never!' returned the native, in a climax of politeness.

Then it dawned upon us that we had merely been informed in the Oriental manner that pineapples and cocoanut milk in conjunction were unwholesome for globe-trotters; whereupon Orthodocia threw our entire refreshment out of the window with despatch.

'It would be extremely awkward,' she said, thoughtfully. 'You see, neither of us would be there to receive the last words of either of us. We are very much obliged to you'—(to the native)—'*very* much obliged.'

'IF THE LADIES H'EAT THE PINEAPPLE AND DRINK THE MILK OF THE

The native bowed and relapsed into the folds of his collar.

'Don't you think,' said Orthodocia to me, under cover of the train's rattle, 'that we might get him to talk a little? He might give us some information.'

'Are you sure,' said I, 'that you want information? Look at the landscape.'

Orthodocia said that she was *quite* sure she wanted information. She said she had ears as well as eyes, and did not believe in going round the world with either shut. Moreover, she said it was all very well for *me*, who had no Wigginton expectant at the other end——

And Orthodocia resumed the native.

He seemed pleased and grateful to be resumed, and he gave her to understand that he was quite full of information, and ready to supply it by the pint, pound, or peck, according to her desires. ' If it is not h'ettymology,' he said, ' I 'ave not learned perfectly the science of h'ettymology—nor the h'art of h'orthography '—modestly.

Orthodocia assured him that she had no curiosity in the directions he specified, and

COCOANUT AT THE SAME TIME THEY WILL DIE.'

then—it was so like Orthodocia!—turned and inquired intelligently what it was that I would like to know. Not that she deserved it, but to help her out, I suggested the vegetation we could see from the car windows; and the native started out jubilantly.

We asked about a wandering tangled growth, with a pretty yellow-red cluster of blossoms that covered the banks of the railway track, and heard that it was *Latana*. An English lady had introduced it as an experiment a few years ago, and it had thriven and spread until it had become a pest to the planters. He himself was a planter—a coffee-planter—and he regarded it with despair. Although he was sure the English lady meant no harm, and he hoped neither of us would take offence from his mentioning the matter. Those fields we would recognise to be rice paddies. The Cingalese still cultivated rice more than anything else; they were so very radical in their views!

Orthodocia inquired the connection between rice and Radicalism.

'I wish to express by radical,' said the native, with modest pride, 'that my poor and still benighted countrymen like to cling to the customs of their h'ancestral grandfathers who 'ave cultivated rice since the days of Shem, 'Am, and Japhet, as it were. Oh, they are very radical, not to say h'agnostic, I am sorry to h'inform you. But westward the tide of Empire makes its way, as the poet beautifully says, and every cloud has a silver lining.'

Orthodocia and I looked at one another in some alarm, but were reassured when the native went on to say that we would probably recognise the cocoanut palm growing everywhere, the *Cocos nucifera*, with gentle ostentation. He believed we had a saying that bread was the 'staff of life.' Well, to the people of Ceylon the cocoanut palm was the staff of life. They thatched their houses with the leaves, and made mats, and fences, and baskets of them; they ate the meat of the nut, made dishes of the shell, and drank the sap after it had fermented and become arrack. Here the native shook his head, and said that, in spite of the regulation and protection of the arrack traffic by the British, the foolish Cingalese spent several millions of rupees annually upon the flowing bowl. He gave us the figures as if he liked it; but it was not until he followed them up by the fact that in 1886 the sale of arrack licenses brought the Government one million three hundred and seven thousand and twenty-nine rupees that I began to suspect that we were shut up in a railway carriage going at the rate of at least twenty miles an hour with a coloured statistician. 'There are one thousand and ninety-two arrack taverns in the h'island,' he went on, with the fated air of a person who has just started to run down-hill, 'or one to every two thousand five 'undred and twenty-seven of the population. It is very sad.'

Orthodocia had her note-book out with cele- rity. 'Just the thing,' she whispered to me, raptly, 'for the Wig- ginton Tempe- rance Union. They'll be *so* interested!' And she made him roll the numerical periods forth once more. The na- tive looked pleased and flattered, and rolled up his eyes so that he could see into the back of his head for more figures. In a fatuous moment Orthodocia said to me, 'Do you know, it's cu- rious, but I don't be- lieve we have any idea of the popula- tion of Ceylon. Perhaps this gentleman can tell us.'

This gentleman could, and would, and did, licking his lips anticipatively, in a manuer which

'ORTHODOCIA HAD HER NOTE-BOOK OUT WITH CELERITY.'

must be purely Cingalese. 'Persons,' he said, 'two millions seven 'undred and fifty-nine thousan' seven hundred and thirty-*hate*. Europeans, four thousan' eight 'undred and thirty-six; Cingalese, one million eight 'undred and forty-six thousand six 'undred and fourteen. Tamils——'

'Oh!' said Orthodocia, panting a little, 'that will do, thank you! I only wanted the—the round numbers!'

He looked disappointed, but subsided.

'I can give you h'all the nationalities if you wish,' he said; 'h'also the males and females.'

I thought him safer in arboriculture, and led him back to the cocoanut tree by asking, in an uninterested way, if Europeans planted it to any extent. He said they did fifty years ago, when a great many people lost money by it, from refusing to believe the popular saying that the cocoanut palm will not grow beyond the sound of the sea waves or the human voice. There were still a few European cocoanut estates, but out of six hundred and——

'Yes!' said I, 'quite so! Is it always so warm as this in Ceylon?'

'Not always, Miss—six thousand one 'undred and thirty-four acres planted, only thirty thousan' belong to Europeans. We 'ave an average rainfall of'—but Orthodocia was scratching away so beamingly at the cocoanuts that he returned to them.

'Average number of trees per acre, eighty; average number of nuts per acre, one thousan' five 'undred and twenty-five; total h'export for 1886, nine 'undred and twenty-four million two 'undred and seventy-five thousan' one 'undred and sixty-nine.'

'Yes,' said Orthodocia; 'now to get the number of nuts per tree.' She put the end of her pencil to her lips and went into mathematical epilepsy.

I saw that a diversion must be made, so I asked desperately whether the milk of the cocoanut was considered wholesome for very young children, and if it were really true that the monkeys climbed the trees and threw the nuts on the ground to crack them. I could tell by the inflection of the negatives I got that I was irretrievably lowered in the native's opinion. He turned to Orthodocia and asked, with an invidious distinction in his manner, if there was anything further that *she* would like to know about the cocoanut.

'Let me see,' said Orthodocia, briefly scanning her notes. 'Staff of life—mats—dishes—arrack—sea waves—human voice—acreage—average—a little more, please, about the uses of the tree.'

I looked desperately about for means of stopping the train, but there were none.

The native leaned back and prepared to enjoy himself. We did not know then how sweet a morsel was the topic of the cocoanut tree under the tongue of the dweller in Taprobane. It was not long before we would as soon have made a quotation from *The Mikado* as have mentioned the *Cocos nucifera*, but this is what he said :

'The following are h'only a few of the uses of this invaluable tree. The leaves for roofing, mats, baskets, torches, fuel, brooms, fodder for cattle, manure. The stem of the leaf for fences, yokes for carrying burdens on the shoulders, fishing-rods, and innumerable domestic utensils. The cabbage, or cluster of h'unexpanded leaves, for pickles and preserves. The sap for arrack, toddy, vinegar, and sugar. The h'unformed nut for medicine and sweetmeats. The young nut and its milk for drinking for dessert, and the green 'usk for preserves. The nut for eating, for curry, for milk, for cooking. The oil for rheumatism, for h'anointing the 'air, for soap, for candles, for light. The refuse of the nut, after h'expressing the oil, for cattle and poultry. The shell of the nut for drinking-cups, charcoal, tooth-powder, spoons, medicines, 'ookahs, beads, bottles, and knife-'andles. The fibre which h'envelopes the shell within the h'outer 'usk for mattresses, cushions, ropes, cables, cordage, canvas, fishing-nets, fuel, brushes, oakum, and floor-mats. The trunks for rafters, laths, sailing-boats, troughs, furniture, firewood, and when very young, the first shoots as a vegetable for the table.'

The native paused and closed his eyes, exhausted, and Orthodocia's pencil dropped from her nerveless fingers. I thought her thirst for information had been quenched for ever, but it wasn't. She feebly inquired if the native could tell her the exact value in gold of an average-sized cocoanut to the possessor of it ; and while he searched the pigeon-holes of his mind for the answer, she begged to know if I remembered whether it was table-cloths or tomato catsup that was manufactured from the fibre which envelopes the shell within its first shoots. I said that to the best of my recollection it was infants' wardrobes, but I could not be sure; whereupon she upbraided me, and asked the native if distinctions of caste existed in Ceylon. We had stopped at another of the interminable little stations, with their unpronounceable names and their tidy flower gardens; and a man in native dress came out of the indolent crowd to our window and addressed the native with vast respect as *Muhandiram!*

'That man,' said the native, 'is much richer than I, but 'e is of the Karraba caste; his grandfather was a fisherman, and he calls me *Muhandiram!* because I am of the Vellala caste, or h'agricultural. I will speak with him, but I will not h'eat with him, and none of my daughters can marry his sons. There are many castes with us, according to the occupations of our ancestral grandfathers. Our greatest family is that of the Mahamudaliya, the interpreter to 'is Excellency the Governor. He is h'extremely elated—yet he is as a beast of the field, which to-day is and to-morrow is cast into the h'oven. Myself, I am not in favour of caste; h'it is against progress; and h'it is not philosophy that one caste should command another not to dress above the waist, and not to wear the crooked comb or the 'igh comb, or belts or swords, but it is the custom. Buddhism is as much against caste as the Christian religion. We 'ave a Buddhist poem which relates—

> A man does not become low caste by birth,
> Nor by birth does one become high caste.
> High caste is the result of high actions,
> And by actions does a man degrade himself to a caste that is low.'

'Yes,' said Orthodocia, 'that is curious. We have a poet who has said almost the same thing—

> Howe'er it be it seems to me
> 'Tis only noble to be good.

Tennyson. I suppose you have heard of Tennyson?'

'Yes,' said the native, and, unconsciously, 'he is now a lord, I think?'

Which showed the native about as much in earnest as most people are in their objection to caste distinctions.

The country began to grow very beautiful by this time. We were climbing up into the heart of it, and coolness had come with the higher levels and the lengthening shadows. Here and there a little lake lay in the jungle, giving back strange blooms of yellow and scarlet; Indian cattle standing in it up to their shoulders. Long lines of palms wandered hither and thither, and in the planted land not given over to rice, coffee, and tea, and cocoa were growing. Far away to the right of us a jagged blue line of mountains ran along the sky. A whole panorama of the tropics stretched between them and us, full of wavering light and soft shadow, of boldness and of gentleness, full everywhere of that throbbing, sensuous life that sends young leaves forth in great curves and dips, that puts a flame into the hearts of the flowers and a flash on the wings of the birds. Orthodocia and I confided to one another our opinion that the Sunday School books and the chromos had not overdone it. The native showed us Adam's Peak against the sky, which had a miraculous shadow and bore the footprints of Buddha, left when he visited the island, and was the point of many pilgrimages.

'We 'ave in Ceylon many reminiscences of Adam, our first parent,' remarked the native instructively, 'this being, we believe, the spot on which the well-known "garden scene" occurred. But that was a long time ago. *Tempus fugit!*' And the native sighed.

I did my best to keep him in Paradise, where he promised to be entertaining, but Orthodocia disapproved of what she called my American irreverence, and brought him from the contemplative mood to the consideration of practical matters. And I had to sit and listen to the formation and functions of the Governor's council, and what reforms were necessary; to lists of facts about municipal self-government; to things about rice-taxes and land-taxes, and the codification of the laws—at which point I think slumber came and blessed me, for I forget what came next.

We were drawing near to Kandy when I awoke. Orthodocia's face had a tense expression, and her pencil was sharpened down to half an inch. The native looked ready to go on for three hours longer. He said he supposed we were familiar with the history of the taking of Kandy. I affected a silence with reams of history in it, but Orthodocia, always unnecessarily candid, declared that neither of us knew anything about it, which was entirely true. And the native filled up the rest of the journey with the monstrous deeds of the tyrant, Rajah Singh, dilating on them with much graphic fervour, wherein his nativism showed like the cloven foot. You shall be spared them.

I have never yet got Orthodocia to acknowledge that the native was not an unmixed blessing; but I observed a singular intensity of manner in her farewell to him. For my part, it seemed to me that the paternal Government which provided the native with culture of the statistical sort ought also to get him a special railway carriage to transport it. But that is a matter of opinion.

XXIV

KANDY was once Muragrammum. I don't know that this makes any particular difference, since it was probably one of the Ptolemies who called it Muragrammum, and all the Ptolemies are, you may say, beyond the reach of criticism ; but in considering what I shall write about Kandy it is the first thing that occurs to me. Moreover, the guide-book also begins with this fact, which gives it a certain *cachet* of respectability, for the writer of the guide-book is an Oxford man.

I don't know what Muragrammum was like, but it couldn't possibly have been as well worth while looking at as Kandy is now. It had no lake in the heart of it, for the wicked Rajah Singh made the lake, and the hotel accommodation was probably much inferior. These two points are worth noting, for the tourist's Kandy is the hotel and this exquisite little lake. As Orthodocia remarked, Rajah Singh is entitled not only to our respectful consideration as a monster, but to our admiring gratitude as an æsthete.

There is only one hotel, a quaint little concern with a wide verandah running round it, where all the tourist family assembles after dinner to compare purchases, and drink demi-tasses of coffee, and use bad language to the pedlars of unknown gods, who are then more pertinacious than ever. The men smoke, the knowledgeable German, the dapper Frenchman, the loquacious American, the worried-looking little English lord. The ladies mostly amuse themselves in palm-shaded corners, in a candid and unabashed manner that can be observed to perfection only in the tropics. There is a dark glimpse of the lake to the left, and out of the shadows of the road into the shadows of the banyan trees strange figures pass singing strange words to a familiar air. They sway to and fro as they go, and the lights fall upon their bare heads and waving arms and long robes of white and yellow with startling effect. 'What *is* it?' whispers Orthodocia to me in our remote and unacquainted corner. 'Way down upon de Swance River?' 'By Jove!' says a smoker loudly, 'are those nautch-dancers?' Everybody subsiding when the word goes that they are members of the Salvation Army in the costume of the country, singing the songs of Zion in a strange land.

'Another fine day!' said Orthodocia on the first of our sojourn in Kandy, thereby running the risk of bodily assault. The days were so monotonously fine, so opulent in sunlight which the frequent showers only burnished and exhilarated, that we sometimes longed for a little genuine bad weather—a dear disconsolate drizzle, a lovable leaden sky, a delightful depressing east wind. We had to do without it with such philosophy as we could muster, assuming a pronounced hostility, however, to the expression quoted above.

Since there was no getting over the fact that it was another fine day, we decided to support the infliction in the society of the guide-book, which informed us primarily that it is situated in lat. 7° 18' north and long. 80° 40' east of Greenwich, at an elevation of 1,680 feet above sea level, 'enjoying' a mean annual temperature of 75·5° Fahr., which I submit to the public generally chiefly because Orthodocia claimed a finder's right to it, and put it in her note-book as a *bonne bouche* for the Dorcas Society of Wigginton, Devon. Orthodocia had a bad habit, which I can look back upon forgivingly now, but which was very trying at the time, of exclaiming whenever she found anything particularly delectable, 'That's mine!' and jotting it down in her everlasting note-book. In the case of a mere sentiment or impression, one didn't mind, but when it came to an entire assortment of choice geographical facts, I leave it to the general public whether the proceeding was regular or not.

Naturally our feet turned in the direction of the native quarter, though if we had followed our noses they would have led us contrariwise. It is a drawback to travelling in the Orient that one's æsthetic sensibilities are always attracted one way, and one's olfactory nerves the other.

A long, unpaved, pale brown, dusty street stretched out in front of us, lined with low dark shops for trinkets and clothes and European crockery, and full of a leisurely throng of dark-skinned, bareheaded, half-naked men, with a sprinkling of women, who went about their business while the coolness of the morning was still in the air. The languor of the East was over them all, whether they loitered along with trays of sweetmeats on their heads, or gathered together in knots to talk and laugh, or slept in their doorways, all their supple length uncoiled among the shadows. The men wore white chiefly, yards of muslin wrapped round them in some mysterious way, that left an end to drape about their heads; the women, who were fat and unctuous, affected largely the colours of one's great-great-grandfather's bandanna pocket-handkerchief, gathered up toga-wise, with their hair in what we used to call a 'Langtry' knot behind. A few tall turbaned Afghans mingled with the crowd, blacker and more muscular than the rest, and now and then a shaven priest of Buddha passed, all in flowing yellow. We wandered into the market, where the corpulent tropical fruits that are beginning to bore you, I am afraid, lay piled in heaps about

'JOTTING IT DOWN IN HER EVERLASTING NOTE-BOOK.'

each dark-eyed impudent vendor. 'Very good cat,' they said, with much mirth, recognising fresh victims for imposition, and offering us the great green spheres of the jack-fruit, the delicacy of which we imagined when we saw it growing straight out of the tree's trunk, without any assistance of branch or twig. I picked up an elephant of brown 'jaggery' sugar, got from the jaggery palm, and the trunk came off in my hand. The owner, in great wrath, immediately demanded eight annas and the restitution of the animal. I paid him two and carried it off, whereupon he rejoiced as one who has made a bargain, and all his fellows showered derision upon us. Jaggery, at all events in its elephantine form, is very like our American maple sugar, which the gods love, and is extremely good; for in spite of Orthodocia's protestations that it would give me leprosy and divers kinds of death, I devoured a large section of that elephant and found him wholesome.

I find '*atrurium regale*' down in my own note-book immediately under the sugar elephant incident, so I conclude it was at this juncture that we went to the Botanical Gardens of Kandy, which are very marvellous indeed. Botanical gardens occur in great numbers in the tropics, which is natural enough, seeing that you can make a very fair botanical garden out of your own backyard by tacking a few Latin labels on its rampant vegetation, and making the monkeys feel at home in it. Tropical nature beguiles the authorities into showing her off in botanical gardens wherever there are any authorities to beguile. But I take Orthodocia to witness that I have hitherto refrained from the expression of any emotion whatever on the score of them. This may be largely because the sole outburst of feeling regarding them which my note-book contains is written large in Latin with a stubby pencil—'*atrurium regale.*' I have no doubt it was very significant when it was set down, but it has become a label now, suggesting nothing but reproaches. If I had more valuable memoranda like it, it might be worth while to invent a few vegetable marvels to go with them, but who would risk his literary reputation for the classic glitter of a single '*atrurium regale*'? When once it is printed, moreover, as Orthodocia suggests, I dare say it will look quite as well without the plant.

I remember a marvellous soft plumy group of palms that met us at the gate with great graciousness, bending and waving and rustling under the luminous blue of the sky in every curve of gentle majesty that has ever been thought of; palms of many sorts, from the tall talipot, that lives for sixty years to bear one splendid creamy crown of blossom, and then dies, to the palmetto of the home conservatories, arching in its beautiful youth straight from the soil. Creepers, purple and blue and yellow and white, made living pillars of dead trees, and hung, a twisted mass of colour, from every withered limb. Broad paths led in all directions past glowing beds and under masses of foliage we did not know. A great rubber tree spread its branches over us, its roots winding about over fully twenty square feet, and standing so far out of the ground as to make actual corridors between. We stuck a penknife into one of them, and the rubber oozed out, milky and viscid. The gardener gathered spices for us from the waving boughs they grew on. Nutmegs, looking like walnuts, black inside and wrapped ever so neatly in their red mace waistcoats; cloves in blossom, funny little green clusters of four or five in each spray, and a tiny fuzzy yellow flower where the ball is; 'allspice' in long, narrow, dark green, glossy leaves. It was a revitalisation of a certain large round tin box associated with the home store-room, a box one had forgotten the existence of, and carried one back to days of juvenile pilferings, and the awful results of being found out. Orthodocia wondered, very reasonably, who the first carnal spirit could have been who thought of putting such exquisite odours inside him.

Strange insects hummed about us. Marvellous butterflies floated sensuously from flower to flower. A lizard like a streak of pale green fire darted from the shadow of one great plant to the shadow of another. Far in the theatrical distance a gigantic emu stalked and pondered. We found ourselves in the glass houses covered with matting where the orchids were, which I shall not ask you to try to imagine. There is nothing in the world, I think, with which they have any relation. The most exquisite poem, or picture, or fairy-tale would be a coarse setting for them. I can only say that one was a pale purple white, deepening to royal purple at the tips, and carrying a faint yellow flame in its heart, and that another, the 'dove plant,' was precisely the shape and colour of a tiny dove with wings half furled sitting upon her nest; but these things you have heard before many times, and from them you cannot gather at all the texture and the poise of those strange flowers, that are surely here by a mistaken flight from Paradise.

We wandered along by the river which skirts the gardens, the Mahaveliganga, the greatest in Ceylon, under trees whose leaves were pale pink flowers. The river was all light greens and golden browns, and flowed in deeps and shallows over its white sands, softly and slowly, as it learned to flow in Eden. Great clusters of filmy bamboo grew along its edges, and groups of tall cocoanuts, bending always as cocoanuts do, to hear what the river had to say. The air was heavy with the perfume and the passionate life of everything. It was very silent, except for this palpable, audible throb and for a single note, like the clashing of steel, as a bird like a blue flash went from one clump of bamboo to another.

We concluded that it would be possible to stay long enough in the Botanical Gardens of Kandy to be totally unfitted for the ordinary scenes of earth. So we went back to the hotel, and to persuade ourselves that we had not really died and gone to heaven, took a most unangelic tiffin.

Civilised Kandy grows all about the lake, which I have mentioned as the most popular tradition of Rajah Singh. Cool little bungalows look out upon it on every side, and tennis-courts border it, and skiffs sail upon it, and all Kandy turns out and drives round it in the evenings when the sun goes down. The late respected Rajah made it very picturesque with an ornamental stone embankment into which he put the idea of the endless curve; and on the palm-feathered little island in the middle there are architectural remains of him, probably representing the quarters of his harem. It seems to have been a particularly advantageous place for a harem, being entirely secluded and supplied with plenty of water for drowning purposes, besides natural attractions quite enough to reconcile any harem to the doctrine of the survival of the fittest. But we were not interested in civilised Kandy, Orthodocia making the eminently characteristic British remark that one got all the civilisation one wanted in England. We were much more desirous to see Buddha's tooth, which both the guide-book and Rubicundo had solemnly assured us was on exhibition at Kandy—although we were somewhat discouraged in this by the scornful incredulity of a lady tourist at tiffin, who said that people would believe in anything nowadays—even the tooth of an idol.

So we walked round the lake to the temple that held all that was osseous of Gautama Buddha—an irregular white octagonal little building, with numerous quadrangles and verandahs about it, jutting out into the water, and curiously reflected in its evening calm. Two handsome brass lamps at the entrance struck me forcibly, not as handsome brass lamps, but as 'the gift of a former Governor, Sir William Gregory.' Sir William must have been singularly liberal in his views about heathenism, and singularly indifferent to those of the Ceylon missionaries, to have actually thrown a light upon what is popularly known as the broad road that leadeth to destruction. Beyond these we went through several pairs of pillars, carved with elephants and various demons, climbed a set of steep stone steps and found ourselves in a verandah, round which ran a remarkable chromo, chiefly in red and yellow, of the lower regions. The artist's specialty had been the appropriateness of the punishments enjoyed by the various classes of sinners he depicted. He had no further sense of the fitness of things, however, for he made the population of his nether world almost exclusively feminine! This led us into an inner verandah, where the dusk was lighted by sulky wicks floating in the oil of many glass lamps that hung from the roof. It fell on the lustrous, passive dark faces of a few native stragglers, and the strenuous perspiring ones of the temple orchestra, who beat upon drums and blew into conches and flageolets with awful din and fury. Besides these and ourselves there were only the sellers of champak flowers for altar offerings, who sat on either side, and besought the worshippers to buy. Wonderful, sacred, starry champak flowers, trumpet-shaped and creamy, yellow inside, and streaked with pink outside, fragrant as a distillery of Paradise. Their incense was overpowering that night in the temple, rising almost like something palpable from the laden trays, filling the weird dusky place, and weighing upon one's spirit like a strange Eastern spell.

Presently, as the braying and the banging culminated, a priest came through the gathering crowd, tall and silent and dignified.

carrying a great iron key. We followed him, closely pressed by the crowd, up more narrow steps, along a gloomy landing, and paused before a massive door, carved in metals so dark with age that one could hardly tell the silver from the ivory, or either from the gold. He opened this with great ceremony, and let us into a tiny, black, air-tight chamber, choking with the perfume of a silver table full of champak offerings which stood before a shrine. The shrine was only just visible through the wide iron bars which guarded it.

'Tooth,' said Orthodocia to the bonze. He nodded and pointed to the shrine.

'Open!' said Orthodocia, imperiously.

The bonze shook his head violently, and set the heads of all the barbarian crowd behind us wagging as if they never would stop.

'Open!' said I engagingly, showing a silver rupee.

The bonze shook his head again, this time sadly, but firmly.

'Nobody see?' asked Orthodocia.

He nodded. 'Great Queen's Big Boy!' he said. 'Sala'am!'

From which we gathered that, unless you happen to be the Prince of Wales or a near connection of his, the relic is invisible to you. Something glimmered behind the bars, but we had to take the guide-book's word for it that the shrine was silver-gilt and bell-shaped, and enclosed 'six lessening shrines of the same shape, all of pure gold, ornamented with splendid cat's-eyes, rubies, pearls and emeralds.' The tooth rests in the smallest of these, 'supported by a loop of gold wire over a gold lotus,' which fact, of course, made Orthodocia muse wonderingly as to whether Buddha could have been a lotus-eater!

Our fellow-worshippers cast champak flowers upon the silver table, but we had none to offer, and were turning away out of the hot, dark, reeking, little place, looking and feeling like large ripe tomatoes, when the priest touched us and pointed significantly at a single round rupee which shone on a plate in the midst of the flowers. That rupee was the most suggestive coin I ever saw—it pointed an actual finger at the duty of the foreigner. We reduced the duty of the foreigner to its lowest denomination, however, and left a four-anna bit apiece to keep the rupee company, whereupon much dissatisfaction overspread the priestly countenance, 'and yet,' as Orthodocia very properly remarked as we went out, 'it was quite as much as one would usually put in the collection plate at home.'

On our way out of the tortuous passages and many-sided chambers where they show you Buddha seated on his lotus, cut out of a single emerald, a single crystal, and what not more beside, we stepped for a moment into the clear sweet air that streamed about a little pillared balcony. The pillars were quaintly carved and so close together as to make a frame for the picture behind them, fringed by the quivering cocoanut trees with a young moon peering over them, the shadowy distance pulsating with mysterious torches, and the broad silent water broadening and widening at our feet.

We had come from a Buddhistic 'service,' from the manifest form of all that was left of the whole Asiatic revelation that once glowed and surged from the waters of the Ganges to the walls of Pekin. The perfume of the champak flowers stole out to us there, and a broken note or two of the flageolet came up from below. It was a moment to wonder, in a fascinated way, about the possibility of spiritual permanences in this carnal, beautiful, drunken world

XXV

STOPPED!

The champagne glasses tinkled lightly against the frosted water-bottles with the subsiding vibration, and in the shock of that sudden stillness that seems for the moment the very end of all things, everybody paused without knowing it, in the midst of his mango or his pink-frilled ice, and looked at the captain. But the captain did not rise in his place, as we half expected he would, and proclaim to the forty or fifty people who sat in evening dress under the punkah at their dessert, on board the fair ship *Coromandel*, midway up the Hooghly river on her passage to Calcutta, the precise reason of our surprise. I have observed that captains have not, as a rule, this considerate and amiable habit, even those of the P. and O., who permit themselves to occupy a plane of ordinary human intercourse with passengers more nearly perhaps than any other captains in the world. This one, though a gentleman of most agreeable address in general, merely settled down into his white waistcoat rather more comfortably than before, and cracked a walnut explosively, as much as to say, 'If any lady or gentleman desires to know the reason of our present stoppage, let him or her dare to ask.' Then he ate the walnut in a manner which was terrifyingly conclusive. Such is the power of moral suasion, accompanied by a walnut, that nobody asked. Whereupon Orthodocia declared that she saw him confide the whole thing to the lady who sat on his right, which may or may not have been the case. It is as characteristic of captains, however, as of other members of the human family, that if they have any reason to suspect you of inquisitiveness, upon that matter they maintain a silence deep as death; whereas, if you adopt a calm and indifferent exterior, careless as to when the ship arrives, or whether it ever

Arrives, incurious as to what sort of weather 'we are going to have' or whether we are going to have weather of any sort, a date or a prophecy usually escapes them, just by way of stirring up your dormant imagination.

But later, we knew all about it, for word went round in the cool of the evening on deck, among the reposeful ghosts on steamer-chairs and the flitting shades that kept little glowing spots of fire alight aft of the smoking-cabin, that we would lie there in the broad brown reaches of the Hooghly till the favour of the tide came with the morning. So we lay and listened to the soft gurgling of the river round the ship—the great sacred river that was bearing at that very moment, out there in the darkness beyond the electric light, some dead Hindoo out to sea; and once again heard the pretty little married lady of Calcutta sing, 'White Wings, they never grow weary,' to the picturesque group that gathered about the deck piano. Many songs had the pretty little married lady of Calcutta, but this one she sang oftenest of all, for the 'white wings' of the *Coromandel*, when they happened to be spread, were taking her home to her dear lord, who was a dignitary of the Court, and she sang to encourage them. It was a catching and a pleasing song, that 'White Wings,' for it had not reached the inside of the hand-organs then. Orthodocia trilled it at her toilet in the morning; a baritone among the stewards voiced it in the clatter of the matutinal plates; the officers hummed it, the Jack tars whistled it, even the Lascars were reported to have been heard emitting sounds akin to it. That last night on the Hooghly everybody took up the chorus, and it swept tenderly and far out upon the still wide river from every nook and corner of the quarter-deck—'I'll spread out my white wings, and fly home to thee.'

By-and-by Orthodocia and I entrapped a wandering quartermaster, who told us strange stories of the 'James and Mary' quicksands, over which we should sail steadily enough with the tide in the morning, but which had dragged more than one good ship down to death before, and might do the same with this one for all her great tonnage. There in the darkness, with the heavy tropical wind blowing softly off the low-lying sunderbunds, where the tigers and alligators crept through the jungle to the river's edge, the nearness of the famous quicksand seemed a vague horror—a nightmare that

R

one knows to be a nightmare, and yet cannot put away. Orthodocia was sure, as we walked up and down the deck together and wondered what India would be like, that James and Mary were frightful genii of the place, who sat within their quicksands like spiders in a web, and lived upon the unlucky mariners who ventured too near them.

'THE STEWARD SANG IT AMONGST THE PLATES.'

Next morning we sailed over them as gaily as possible and never knew it; for the sun lay broad and bright upon the river, and upon the thatched huts and green rice-fields that began to appear along the banks, and everybody was making ready for India. And presently we were all on deck looking at the long low water front of the

Palace of the King of Oude as we moved slowly past it, where that eccentric monarch lived with his menagerie, you remember—a cruel slight to Calcutta society. Then we saw Calcutta itself, lying green-girt and pale-pillared and imposing as roof and spire and shaft could make her behind her forest of masts in the river. The flutter of arrival was interesting to look at—in the pretty little married lady whose husband was waving a frantic umbrella on the wharf—in the young lady missionary who had fallen in love on the way out and didn't at all know what to do about it—in the boy of sixteen coming back from ten years in England and wondering if his father would recognise him—in our dear Rubicundo, the joy of the quarter-deck, with his *topee* all tilted on one side and his eyes twinkling with an inward pun—in the just married little pair from Berkshire, to whom life in India was to be a new rare joke, and who had sat apart most of the voyage and cooed in happy anticipation; and to other people I suppose, in us, Orthodocia Love and I, who turned our boxes so that the Japanese labels showed to all the world, and sat amongst them with prodigious airs. Orthodocia and I were in no special haste to depart, for reasons which she would never let me own to if she could see this chapter before you do, for she felt them much more deeply than I did, being British—reasons, let me tell you privately, of Tips. Orthodocia found Tips, Tips in liberal multitude, whenever occasion seemed to require it, necessary to her present happiness, and, I verily believe, to her future salvation. Up to this time my friend had been in the habit of bestowing gratuities upon the head steward, and the steward who looked after her individually, the cabin steward and the stewardess, to say nothing of odd functionaries whom she impressed to hoist her steamer-chair to the hurricane-deck, or heat her curling-tongs in some fiery furnace below the haunts of passengers. I didn't. I tipped when I felt generous, but never because it lay in the path of duty; and my impulses occurred much more seldom than Orthodocia's ethical promptings did, which she said was the fault of my bringing up. However that may be, my emotions were much less poignant than Orthodocia's when the hour of retrenchment came. For a P. and O. tip, as instituted by English lords and American millionaires, in spite of the discouragement of the company, would read like a Budget deficit were I to set it down, especially in rupees, and the hour of retrenchment must come to all who, like Orthodocia, indulge in a riotous course of them. It is bound to be a painful one. 'Blessed are they from whom nothing is expected,' I often found occasion to remark to Orthodocia, observing that functionaries dallied much longer at her elbow than at mine. It was out of deference to her feelings that we resorted to the strategy of staying behind rather, and allowing the more portentous of the stewards to occupy themselves with other people's luggage and the prospect of other people's 'remembrances.' For when a steward fixed his cold blue eye upon Orthodocia, in all its awful forth-compelling power, and said, 'Is that h'all right, Miss?' she found resistance impossible. I considered it invertebrate in her; but what really troubled her was the steward's opinion, which I found difficult to understand.

And so, standing a little back, we got our first glimpse of India from the deck of the *Coromandel*—of its gorgeousness, as the little lady of the Court dignitary drove away in her carriage, with two gold-braided Mahommedan servants in Government scarlet en the box, and two more standing behind—of its pitifulness in the eager, yet half-constrained meeting of the son with his father, who did not recognise him—and of its great, seething, problematic masses of human life in the dark-skinned throngs that gathered en various businesses along the wharf.

We had arrived at the dignity of *memsahibs*. We felt this dignity the moment we walked across the gangway and stepped upon India—an odd slight conscious uplifting of the head and decision of the foot—the first touch of Anglo-Indianism.

One's primary business in Calcutta is to seek a boarding-house, Calcutta being the one place in the world where the boarding-house has justified its existence and become an institution. To seek a boarding-house one must first find an equipage, so we walked across the broad dock to look for one, and through the gate which marks the authority of the customs. Its guardians regarded us suspiciously, as if we were wandering pieces of somebody's luggage that had escaped examination, but concluded, on the whole, that we were not dutiable, and let us through. We did not wait long for the conveyance of Calcutta. It espied us from afar, and bore down upon us with mighty gallopings and crackings of the whip, a bundle of rags with two brown legs sticking out of them on the box, an attenuated creature distantly related to a horse in the harness. The conveyance itself looked like a once painted and varnished packing-box. The

'OTHERS INSTANTLY SET OFF IN MAD CAREER WHILE WE WAITED.'

driver sat on a bunch of straw, which, though decorative in general effect, did not impart what Orthodocia calls 'form' to the turn-out.

'*Ticca-gharri*,'[1] memsahib? Ver' good *ticca-gharri*!'

[1] Hired carriage, lady?

We looked up the street and down, but nothing else in the way of a vehicle was to be seen except two or three somewhat less desirable than the first, that instantly set in mad career towards us while we hesitated. And it was exceeding hot. So we scrambled into it, thinking on the Anglo-Indian luxury we had heard of aforetime and deeply marvelling. Orthodocia was not of opinion that any respectable establishment could be induced to take us in out of a trap like that; but she gave the driver the addresses we had, and in the devious ways through which that guileful Hindoo took us to find them, we had our first look at Calcutta. It was an intensely interesting look, and we took it with open eyes and mouths and necks craned far out through the side shutters of the rat-trap we rode in. The great solid British warehouses and railway offices and Government buildings were tremendously impressive, planted there in the midst of the shifting tide of Aryan humanity that beat through the wide streets and filled them with wonderful colour and poetry and grace. They were so enduring, it was so ephemeral; there was the pang in it that always comes in the contrast of conscious strength with conscious weakness. And suddenly there shone out among some dull stone walls a brass plate inscribed, 'Office of the Secretary to the Viceroy,' which deepened the curious exultant half-painful conquering feeling, and seemed to throw a flash upon what it must be like to be Viceroy to these sinuous brown-skinned multitudes. I think it was that brass plate that gave rise to a contentious spirit between Orthodocia and myself as to the ethics of a British India. Orthodocia was very sorry for the brown Bengali, with his pathetic eyes and delicate features. 'He has no country,' she said. 'We have robbed him of his holiest emotion—patriotism. He cannot know any joy in living—with our foot upon his neck.' Whereupon I responded disdainfully of the brown Bengali's holiest emotion, and there came to be strained relations between Orthodocia and me, so that we craned our necks out of the opposite sides of the *ticca-ghari* further than ever.

I almost forget what we saw, which is the penalty attached to craning one's neck round the whole of the world at once; but there remains with me the picture of a great, fair city lying under a dusky yellow glory where the sun sloped to the west—lying low and

level under it, piercing it with masts that seemed to rise round half
her boundary, cleaving it with a shaft in the midst of a green
maidan, reflecting it in a wide water-space darkling in her heart,
breaking it softly with the broad, heavy clusters of the gold-mohur
tree. A British city, for the British coat-of-arms shone here and
the Union Jack floated there, but a British city with few Britons
abroad in it—the throngs in the streets were nearly all Mahommedans, bearded and wearing little white embroidered caps on the
sides of their heads, or smooth-faced Hindoos in turbans; all flapping
nether draperies, all sleek of countenance and soft of eye. *Chup-
rassis* [1] in long red coats that reached to the knee, and from that to
their toes in their own brown skins, hurried hither and thither
solemnly with leather bags slung across their shoulders, much burdened by their own importance. *Baboos* [2] in flowing white went
ceaselessly in and out of the swinging doors and up and down the
broad stone steps of the great shipping and merchants' offices; and
the streets swarmed with lower creatures. *Beestis* [3] who watered
them from black distended dripping goatskins, sellers of fruit,
women hod-bearers, little naked children, half-clad groups under the
trees by the wayside, drinking water from round shining brass *lotas*,[4]
or prone in sleep. In the road itself we met scores of *ticca-gharris*,
almost all, we noted painfully, more respectable than ours, and some
private ones quite smartly painted, and equipped with servants who
looked as neat as the lean-chested and leggy Hindoo can be made to
look, I fancy. The pale faces of young Englishmen appeared inside
most of these; and we learned afterwards that they were 'office-
gharris,' that took the *sahibs* to the daily tasks of the Civil Service,
the office, or the bank. Now and then among the carriages of
fashionable Calcutta there rolled by one in which we eagerly noted
a slim languid young figure in purple and gold—'Rajah,' we named
it deliriously—'Maharajah'—or a portly Parsee, unctuous-faced
under his tall red cap. And we stared, fascinated, at the closed
carriages we met, that sometimes rewarded us with a glimpse of the
tinselled finery within, and the soft eyes of the 'purdah-nashin'—
'the curtain hidden.'

[1] Government messengers.
[2] Clerks.
[3] Water-carriers.
[4] Water-bottles.

We found ourselves among the shops, and then even to my untutored perception from over seas, it became absolutely clear that we were in British territory. For, from the saddler to the draper, from the confectioner to the great diamond-merchant who has set his seal on three-quarters of the engagements in India, they were all blazoned high 'Under the distinguished patronage' of somebody or other—the Viceroy if they could get him, and failing His Excellency, the next luminary in line. We stopped before two or three of them for trifles we wanted, and found them spacious and tempting, but all governed by that 'slack,' happy-go lucky kind of spirit that seems to prevail all over the European East. English goods and English prices ruled—low compared to the conscienceless tariff I had known, though Orthodocia pretended to be shocked at some of them, and I looked pathetically for a pair of American boots in vain. Temptation stalked on every counter in the shape of delicately embroidered 'Indian' fabrics made in Manchester, but purchaseable only here, they told us; and we discovered, in paying one bill, the temptation made easy.

'Will you pay for it now?' said the shopman, ' or sign a chit?'

We asked to have the alternative explained, and were informed that 'the more popular way' in Indian shopping was to sign for the amount of the bill a *chit*, which means a note, a memorandum, anything—and to have the chits added up and sent in at the end of one month or six in the shape of a bill. A certain discount was allowed for cash, but it was the same, quite the same—politely—to them whether we paid or signed. And would we look at their new assortment of parasols?

It was alluring, very; and helped us to understand a proportion of the after stories we heard about how shockingly people often lived beyond their incomes in India. No rupees available till the first of next month, and the memsahib without 'a thing to wear' to the next *tamasho*?[1] But a simple chit solves the difficulty at once, and if the chits and the salary grow somewhat disproportionate in course of time, it is always possible to increase the chits and live in trustful expectation that a beneficent 'Raj' will see the emergency and meet it by a promotion—without counting at all upon that good

[1] Great affair.

time coming for the earners of rupees—the bi-metallic age. The extent to which poor little real memsahibs must encounter this temptation may be imagined from the fact that it was offered to us, who were perfect strangers. As Orthodocia very properly remarked, however, on re-entering it, 'They didn't see our brougham,' or they might not have been so confiding.

A strange persecution attended us wherever we paused in our dislocated career through the streets of Calcutta that day. It took a domestic shape, the shape of long soda-water tumblers, such as the sahib useth for what is called in Anglo-Indian 'the peg,' and earthenware pots highly glazed, blue outside and white inside—a common useful hardware article which no well-regulated kitchen range is without. These two commodities, only these two, were thrust into our *gharri* by lean brown hands the instant it drew up at any point whatever; and we had to take them out of our laps and hand them back before alighting, first with mirth, then with wrath, then with threatening. They came upon us from above, from below, from either side. The heavens seemed to rain preserving kettles, and the earth to give forth tumblers. We speculated deeply as to why these special sorts of *bric-à-brac* should be expected to attract the tourist's eye; whether it was his love of the beautiful or his appreciation of the useful that was reckoned upon, but arrived at no result. We were not equal to repelling the vendors properly, so at times we had a sort of flying column of them on both sides of our equipage, which must have given us an imposing look to the residents we met. And once Orthodocia, getting into the *gharri* backwards to avoid the tumblers on the one side, put both feet into the preserving pot that had been inserted on the other. That, to the unprejudiced beholder, was very funny, though Orthodocia didn't seem to find it humorous at the time. In fact, she resorted to extreme measures. Holding the article firmly over the side of the *gharri*, she said, with the plain enunciation she always kept for the heathen, 'Savey?—It drops!' and let go. The heathen caught it in a wild acrobatic feat, and withdrew, discouraged.

Through devious ways of the bazaars our driver took us that day, in long-drawn-out misunderstandings--where the houses were low and whitewashed, and the walls high and thick, and the windows narrow and the streets odorous, and only occasionally, from some fastness of an inner court, a spray of scarlet hibiscus or purple bougainvillias smiled out into a world that had nothing in it but brown-faced men and merchandise. He made suggestive pauses now and then before small interiors, gay with Indian silks or Japanese screens, but it takes a great deal of persuasion to get one unnecessarily out of a *ticca-gharri*, and we succumbed only once. '*Choke!*' said the driver, reining up and pointing at a little dark door that bore in crooked English letters a Hindoo's name—it might have been Ram Dass—'Seler of Precis stones and Mutiny Curiositys.' I think I must tell you now about the shop of Ram Dass, for fear of passing it by another time. It seemed to us to be by far the most wonderful shop we had ever seen, or ever should see. For no matter how gorgeous or how strange the rest of the marts of the world may be, one never experiences again the charm and marvel of one's first Indian 'choke,' where, like Sinbad, one might drop a leg of mutton and pick it up again sticking with precious stones.

Ram Dass would not have called it a 'choke'—that was the contemptuous Anglo-Indian name for it—and would probably have been offended somewhere in his calm, quiet, sly Hindoo mind if he had heard you do it. We walked in, and he met us, sala'aming and showing his glistening white teeth in a smile. The four walls of the little room were hung with Rungpore chuddars—those soft, light, loosely-woven Indian shawls that you can draw through a finger-ring—and gold embroideries and carpets from Mirzapore, chased brass vases from Benares, and marbles from Agra, inlaid with jasper and chalcedony; and silver discs and slender perfume bottles, long-necked and scorpion-handled, stood on shelves behind glass doors; and shields embossed and murderous Ghurka knives flashed over the door. Orthodocia asked to see Indian jewellery, and Ram Dass begged us to honour him by taking the chairs, which he placed beside a white cloth, spread upon the floor. Then he disappeared, and presently brought from some unknown region a big black box. He put the box on the cloth, sat down beside it, unlocked and opened it. Inside lay a glittering heap of gems, flashing every colour known to flame or flower, from which Ram Dass slowly and lovingly disentangled a necklace, a bracelet, and held it up to us. Jewels had never meant before what they meant in those dusky hands. It was fitting that Ram Dass, with his shining eyes and eager brown face, should handle these things, and not we. What had our pale faces and bloodless lips to do with these burning Eastern treasures that the barbaric skill of the Delhi craftsmen had revealed in such radiant fashion and then pierced and hung upon a wire? Strings of pearls and turquoises, bands of gold with the gems set as if they had been dropped in while it bubbled over the fire, in curious devices; beaten gold, gold enamelled in blue and green and red, in long pendants, such as the Ranees wear; manifold strings of pearls, with a pierced topaz hanging by a little gold hook between every two or three; and other strings that might belong to fairyland, of which the dangling jewels all differed in glory; and here hung an amethyst, here an emerald, here a ruby. Orthodocia paid for her purchases in I.O.U.'s. Ram Dass, while he probably cheated the memsahib, believed in her.

But it has taken you nearly as long to get to our Calcutta boarding-house as it took us. It was late in the evening when we finally fixed upon one, because we so frequently forgot in the course of the afternoon just what we were looking for, which was eminently characteristic of the researches of Orthodocia and me. It was a spacious mansion, with wide balconies on all sides of it, and many servants congregated in the 'compound.' 'Compound' is Anglo-Indian for the enclosure round about. The compound was decorated with branching tropical plants set about in pots, which gave us the impression of private theatricals and made us wonder what the play would be. The room we took together was a generous Anglo-Indian room, large and lofty windowed, with the luxury of a dressing-room apiece, and swinging doors upon the balcony. Sitting there in the short Indian half light when the sun was gone we could see the people of the next house taking an evening walk upon their own roof, which was also liberally adorned with those theatrical pots; while the white-clad, swinging masses in the street below grew indistinguishable, and the carriages rolled duskily between us and the cool green Maidan.

Downstairs at the long dining-table, lined with pale Anglo-

Indian faces, we learned the reason of the popularity of the boarding-house way of living in Calcutta. It is not because of its freedom from housekeeping bothers, which is so largely the reason in America; for housekeeping in India is a sort of viceregal function for the memsahib, and she usually finds it entirely enjoyable; but because of the rent-rolls of the Parsee landlords, which make a local habitation all to one's-self a very expensive luxury indeed. Some people get over the difficulty by sharing houses, dining and receiving in the same apartments, but this does not lead to consummate domestic bliss. On one of our home-going steamers were said to be five families not on speaking terms: and the explanation seemed to satisfy all the Anglo-Indian passengers—they had lived with one another.

XXVI

It is one of my friend's characteristics, if she is minded to do a thing, to do it thoroughly. You may have observed her very enthusiastic temperament, in so far as the casual incidents of a trip like ours could show it. This enthusiasm, so long as it lasted, was of an eminently practical, working order—exhaustive, remorseless. Very early in the course of our travels I developed a submissive fear of Orthodocia's mind, when it was made up.

It was with emotions of a very 'mingled' order, therefore, that I heard Orthodocia's resolution, on the second morning of our stay in Calcutta, to the effect that severe measures of economy should immediately be resorted to. Economy, in the hands of Orthodocia, might mean so much. She said that she had not arrived at this conclusion without giving the subject careful consideration. She had put the resolution to herself during the night, but had not carried it until morning, when she was able to consult her note-book, which held financial statements as well as other kinds. I ventured to inquire if a full quorum of the executive committee was present, and Orthodocia said it undoubtedly was. Whereupon she produced the note-book, at the mere sight of which I succumbed, and begged to know how we intended to proceed.

Then it transpired that Orthodocia thought the tariff of our boarding-house exceedingly high, and that we should materially reduce our expenses by taking a room only. 'You see,' she said, 'we must in any case provide our own servants—oh, that *dear* Buddha! So it will be comparatively easy to arrange about the food. I'll see the landlady directly after breakfast. I'm sure you think this the best plan, don't you, dear?' And Orthodocia kissed me affectionately. She came up from her interview with the landlady a little later, with beaming satisfaction. 'Madame was a little obdurate at first,' she said. 'I had to talk her into it. It seems that it is not the custom. But as it is towards the close of the season she consents, temporarily, of course, on condition that we pay in full for this week upon which we have entered. She said she would really like to oblige us, as we are travelling alone, and hoped if we wanted salt or pepper, or any little thing like that, at least for *this* week, we should let her know. *Such* a nice woman! And you will come down and look at the servants, please, dear? She has an assortment connected with the house, and they are all below in the compound.'

'I had often heard,' said Orthodocia, as we descended the stairs, 'of the number of servants people needed in India, but never realised it before. Now according to my calculation, the least we can get on with is a *beesti* to carry water, a *mater* to sweep, a *dhurzie* to sew, a *dhoby* to wash, and a bearer apiece for general utility. Properly, I believe we ought to have a *khansamah*, or head butler, a *kitmutgar*, or second ditto, a *baburchi* to cook, and a *müssalchi* to wash dishes, and at least one ayah between us; but if we are going to exercise economy, we must really not consider appearances.'

Fortunately for our powers of discernment, which were sorely enough tried as it was, Madame's assortment consisted entirely in the 'bearer' variety of Aryan. Our bearers, she assured us, would be responsible for the rest of the staff. There were some six or

'IT WAS WITH EMOTIONS OF A VERY MINGLED ORDER THAT I HEARD ORTHODOCIA'S RESOLUTION.'

eight, Hindoo and Mahommedan, all in spotless tinted white turbans, or embroidered caps, white jackets and nether draperies, and some with a foppish dash of colour in a sash—a kummerbund—of scarlet or blue. They all sala'amed so persuasively that a choice was painful, but my affections gradually centred upon a jolly little fat Hindoo whose hypocrisy was deliciously artistic, and Orthodocia's upon a tall, sad-faced Mahommedan whose sala'am 'appealed' to her. The name of my choice was Lucky Beg, there was no uncertain sound about that; but Orthodocia never could be absolutely sure of her Mahommedan's. It sounded like Ram Chan, and he answered to that, so Ram Chan we called him from first to last. Lucky Beg and Ram Chan at six annas apiece per diem were to wait upon us at table, to purchase our supplies, go upon our errands, and be withal Grand Viziers of our affairs.

Then we entered upon a period of unruffled domestic happiness which lasted until the following day. We had presented our Japanese landlord with Mrs. Love's coal oil stove and kitchen necessaries, a donation which convinced us as we had never been convinced before how much better it is to give than to receive; but we had clung to our spirit-lamp, and we made it the fundamental fact in all our domestic operations. Orthodocia bought a tin saucepan with a lid to fit the spirit-lamp, placed both in the middle of a table in a little ante-chamber of our apartment, and declared that our entire nourishment while we remained in Calcutta must come forth from it. Whereupon I anxiously consulted our list of engagements for those that seemed to offer solid attractions. It was not yet time for punkahs, but Orthodocia said that one didn't realise India without them, and as we had been so moderate in the matter of servants, we might conscientiously afford a punkah-wallah—so she engaged one. We were dining with friends that evening, too, and lunched, in the midst of our purchases of bazaar cups and saucers, in the city; all of which tended to make the first twelve hours of our experiment serenely satisfactory. And as we came and went Ram Chan and Lucky Beg, asquat outside the door of our apartment, rose ever and sala'amed.

Ram Chan and Lucky Beg were gone to their own habitations when we returned that night; but a small dark inert bunch had

'THEY ALL SALA'AMED SO PERSUASIVELY THAT A CHOICE WAS PAINFUL.'

collected itself in their place, which seemed to be attached to a string. We looked at it uncomprehendingly for a moment; then Orthodocia touched it gently on the shoulder, and said 'Punkah-wallah?' The bunch started into a boy, and went galvanically to work on the string; and we, with an exhilarated sense of having made one of the institutions of the land our own, sought retirement within.

The punkah-wallah was the institution; but it was only the wallah part that sat outside the door—the punkah swung from one side to the other of the mosquito-house over our bed. This was not really intended for the accommodation of the mosquitos; but the term is admissible, for the mosquitos were, and we found always a great many more inside than outside. On the particular February night of which I write, however, the punkah was in active exercise and there were none.

'Delightful! isn't it?' said Orthodocia, as we settled down to slumber, and the breeze passed to and fro over our faces.

'Heavenly!' I responded, drawing the counterpane a little more snugly under my chin, 'Good-night!'

Perhaps half an hour later I awoke with torpid fingers, a frost-bitten feeling about the end of my nose, and a strong conviction that it was time to interfere with the punkah-wallah. I touched Orthodocia, and as she opened her eyes she said dreamily, 'Do you know, I thought we were still at the Great Glacier—in that beautiful blue ice-cave—don't you remember?' And then she would have lapsed again; but I, remembering the awful effects of slipping into unconsciousness in a temperature like that, shook her severely. Moreover, I had no mind to remonstrate with the punkah-wallah myself; he was Orthodocia's luxury. Meantime the Arctic gale continued—and the beds of Anglo-India are furnished almost entirely with the counterpane aforesaid.

'Orthodocia!' I remarked firmly, 'if we had buffalo robes or sealskins, or even blankets—anything with which to withstand the rigour of this tropical climate—I wouldn't say anything; but you see how it is, and I conceive it to be your immediate duty to put on your dressing-gown and stop that wallah. Send him home!'

'He hasn't stopped!' I informed Orthodocia when she came back. 'He has misunderstood you. Tell him again.'

Orthodocia told him again, and this time I told him also, to cease from his too fruitful labours. The punkah-wallah nodded intelligently, and pulled harder than ever. He appeared to be a very low order of punkah-wallah and we did not like to lay hands on him. We had not then bought our 'Manual of Hindustani,' and were without the dimmest, remotest, most protoplasmic idea of any species of Aryan 'talk' whatever. The house was silent as the grave, and we did not feel on terms of sufficient intimacy with the rest of the boarders, whom we had not yet learned to tell apart, to apply for assistance in the matter of an insane, unseasonable punkah-wallah, whom we had, in a manner, brought upon ourselves. And the more forcibly we remonstrated the harder he pulled. The whole trouble lay in his being out of season, for no memsahib had ever addressed him except in terms of obloquy for laziness, and he had never, in the whole course of his punkah-wallahing, been told to stop before. Naturally, he did not understand it. Obviously, the only thing to do was to cease our adjurations, to get out our travelling rugs, mackintoshes, ulsters, short jackets, dress skirts, and such other garments as were available. With these for protection, and two umbrellas for further shelter, we found repose, again hoping to defy the terrors of the punkah until morning. Whereupon the punkah-wallah went blandly to sleep, and India returned to the torrid zone.

At seven A.M. came a knock at the ante-chamber door of our room. It was annoying; but Orthodocia said, 'Who is there?'

'*Chota Hazri!*'

'*Who?*' said Orthodocia.

'*Chota Hazri!*'

'Do you know anybody of that name?' Orthodocia inquired. And when I said I did not, 'Go away!' she commanded, and we slept again.

An hour afterwards another knock.

'Well?' said Orthodocia.

'*Chota Hazri*, memsahib!'

'I know no such person!' said Orthodocia; and again we slumbered.

It was after nine when the third knock came, and a voice, patient, gentle, and submissive, said once more:

'*Chota Hazri*, memsahib! Sala'am!'

Orthodocia declared that she would buy a Hindustani book that day, so that these people could no longer pretend they did not understand one when one told them to go about their business. But the interruption was becoming monotonous, so we arose, and by-and-by went forth into the ante-chamber to confront Chota Hazri and discover what he wanted. There sat our two servitors outside on the verandah, and on the table a tea-pot and some dry toast; but nobody corresponding to Chota Hazri. Ram Chan, who stuttered, came forward.

'Sala'am!' he said. '*Chota hazri* very c-c-c-cold!'

'Ram Chan,' said I sternly, for I saw that *chota hazri* meant the tea and toast, 'where did you get it?'

Lucky Beg and Ram Chan regarded one another intelligently, and then the round and unctuous little Hindoo responded with fluency. 'Down *bawarchi khana*.[1] I ask *chota hazri*[2] my memsahib. *Bawarchi*[3] he say no got *hukm*! Ram Chan he ask *chota hazri* his memsahib. *Bawarchi* say no got *hukm*.[4] I say "*atcha*!"[5] Ram Chan say "*atcha*!" Large, big verandah. Many *chota hazri*, sahibs not ready. Too plenty *chota hazri*——'

Lucky Beg paused, as if to leave the rest to my imagination, and though I failed to grasp the literal meaning of his words, their general import was scandalously obvious. Our zealous Prime Ministers had stolen our breakfast!

'Well!' I said to Orthodocia, who stood with horror and hunger painfully conflicting in her face; 'what are we to do about it?'

'It is too late, I am afraid,' said my friend, slowly and tentatively, 'to return it.' A pause. 'I think we had better——'

'Eat it!' I chimed in joyously. 'So do I!'

'But not in their presence!' she hastened to add, 'by no means in their presence! I could not be a party to *that*! You have done very, very wrong,' she said, impressively, addressing them both, 'though I dare say you meant well. I will explain this to you—

---

[1] Cook-room.   [2] Little breakfast.   [3] Cook.
[4] Order.   [5] All right.

ahem--another time.' And she sent them forth. And when Ram Chan and Lucky Beg had well departed to the market to buy our provisions for the day, I blush to record the fact that we fell upon the toast and tea of the unpunctual sahibs and utterly consumed it.

Anon, Ram Chan and Lucky Beg returned, having spent, as they informed us with scrupulous and consistent detail, four rupees seven annas and three 'picy' of the five rupees we had provided them with; producing a quarter of a pound of tea, a packet of brown sugar, a flat loaf of brownish native bread, four eggs, two oranges, six bananas, a lump of butter in an erstwhile marmalade pot, and the change. Orthodocia was touched by the scrupulousness of the account, and especially by the change. 'And yet,' she said, 'they say these people are dishonest.' And she immediately divided it between them.

'Orthodocia,' I said, with some timidity, 'we are not going *any*where to-day. Is—is that all?' You see in a rash moment I had made Orthodocia comptroller of the exchequer.

My friend looked at me in that patient long-suffering way with which we regard querulous weakness in those we love, and said that for her part she only wanted *one* egg.

But we boiled two for tiffin, after making tea in the same saucepan; and they had an imposing look, ranged one on each side of the spirit-lamp in the centre of the table, flanked by a banana and an orange, with the brown loaf as a *pièce de résistance* at one end, and the marmalade butter pot at the other. We took our places at this groaning board with much dignity, Lucky Beg and Ram Chan standing solemnly behind our chairs. There did not seem to be much active service for a butler, and at the stage of our repast when Orthodocia gave me half of her orange and I gave her half of my banana, I moved, in French, their adjournment to the verandah; but Orthodocia thought it would indicate laxity of discipline, and discipline among servants was a matter about which Orthodocia had been brought up to be particular.

> 'For lowly living and lofty thought
> Adorn and ennoble the poor man's cot.'

I quoted, unconsciously nibbling a section of orange-rind that happened to be left; but Orthodocia detected the spirit of ribaldry behind the words, and with a pained look said that there *was* another spoonful of butter, if I would like it. And when I declined, Orthodocia glanced at me with raised eyebrows, meaningfully, and rose with gentle precipitancy, as the ladies of Wigginton, Devon, do after adequate repasts, and swept into the inner apartment, I after her, Ram Chan and Lucky Beg drawing back our chairs and sala'aming as we went.

Orthodocia says that in justice to her I ought at this point to relate the incident of the duck. I think I ought, not in justice to Orthodocia, but for the benefit of any chance reader who may be planning a trip round the world and domestic economics in Calcutta, unaware that it is not a good place for them. Orthodocia said at the time, and has since maintained, that it was not a duck, but a fowl, and has never been able to see my very obvious reasoning that we might both be right about it. It was the morning of the third day, and I, having no exalted ideal to sustain me, was losing flesh rapidly. Orthodocia observed this, and being at heart not unmerciful, was moved, and despatched Ram Chan for a ready-roasted bird to the nearest restaurant. The moment after, as if in reward of virtue, came from a philanthropic memsahib we knew an invitation to tiffin. I hope the memsahib—who was largely instrumental, under Providence, in tempering the austerities of that week in which the necessaries of life were dispensed by Orthodocia- when she reads this will understand it was not wholly gross materialism which prompted the exclamation, '*Pillau!*'[1] that sprang to my lips on reading her note. It was not, really.

But Orthodocia could not conscientiously 'order up the fowl,' as she phrased it, that evening, on account of our having tiffined, so we dined upon *pan*[2] and *tiparri*[3] jam; and next day came a notable dinner *chez* another memsahib. The gloomy fact that we had no engagements for the next was lightened by the anticipation of our extravagance, and Orthodocia said she knew she wasn't justified in doing it, but sent Ram Chan to the restaurant for six annas' worth of bread sauce to go with it. The shades of even fell. We had resolved to dine at half-past seven, and make a modest private

---

[1] An Anglo-Indian delicacy.   [2] Native bread.   [3] Indian gooseberry.

carousal of it which should last far into the night ; say until nine. Practically, however, it was only seven when Orthodocia bade Ram Chan produce his purchase. I think if Ram Chan's complexion had allowed it he would have turned pale—as it was he looked desolate and hesitated. 'Go !' said Orthodocia. 'I g-g-g-go !' he replied miserably, and stood on the other leg, twisting his brown feet about, and went not. 'Well ?' said Orthodocia in her most awful accents, at which he and Lucky Beg regarded one another in an agonised manner and disappeared.

Shortly afterwards they reappeared with something in a covered dish. I do not say that they carried it between them, but I think they took turns. We were in our apartment preparing for the feast, and—*although* it was in a covered dish, and the door was shut— Orthodocia turned to me a few moments after with a certain pallor and said, 'I think the fowl is there.'

I answered her nothing, but went out into the verandah by another door, and besought them to take it away. And that night we dined mainly upon bread sauce and were thankful. But Orthodocia still mentions 'the fowl' in demonstrating that, although she did try to practise economy that week in Calcutta, she did it in moderation.

At the end of the week we gave up the idea, and returned thinner and wiser young women to Madame's long dining-table on the first floor, retaining, of the two bearers, only Ram Chan to be our attendant. I was sorry to lose my lucent Lucky, but friction arose in our personal staff, and it became so marked as to call for extreme measures. We frequently went out upon the verandah to find the long Ram Chan with his limbs coiled boa-constrictorwise round the body of my round Lucky Beg, whose convulsive fat fingers were full of Mahommedan locks. It was our initiation into the 'race difficulties' of India ; and it was to be regretted, inasmuch as it precipitated a transient coolness between Orthodocia and myself. For it was invariably her long Mahommedan who sat upon my round Hindoo, and one does not even like one's Hindoo to be always at the bottom.

And Orthodocia made a financial statement in her note-book on the eighth day, which showed a balance to the credit of her idea, of two annas and three pice.

XXVII

Boom-m-mm-m!
An interval.
Boom-m-mm-m!
'Ram Chan, what's that?' inquired Orthodocia.

It was in the brilliant heat of mid-morning in Calcutta, and we sat indolent with the burden of it on the broad upper verandah of our habitation there. Orthodocia's *dhurzie* squatted at the other end, drawing, when we looked at him, a long white thread in and out of the garment he was constructing, balmily asleep the rest of the time. Ram Chan also sat a little distance off, observing the *dhurzie*, who was fat, like a lean and hungry watch-dog, and occasionally prodding him to a sense of his duty, with much ostentation. It is not too much to say that we were entirely happy. The *dhurzie* alone constituted more than an average sum of human bliss for Orthodocia. She had been regarding him all morning, greatly to his inconvenience, murmuring tranquilly every now and then, 'Four annas—only four annas!' There was no doubt about his being cheap at the price, even to sleep on the verandah.

Boom-m-mm-m!

'Sala'am!' said Ram Chan, rising from his watch, whereat the *dhurzie* snored audibly. 'B-burra Lord Sahib go see Mm-Ma-Maharajah!'

Then Ram Chan took advantage of being on his legs to go and administer a well-calculated kick to the *dhurzie*, whose great toe instantly sought its seam again, while its owner named our servitor, softly, 'Son of a Pig.'

Burra Lord Sahib—great lord master—that was the Viceroy of these brown millions, going to make a return visit upon the ruler of a native principality—the Maharajah of Jeypoor. And the firing was one way in which the high and awful state of the Burra Lord Sahib was impressed upon his Oriental subjects. It was the echo, though, of past cannonading that had impressed them more.

We had read in *The Englishman* of the day before, how the Maharajah had been to pay his respects to the Viceroy, and how His Excellency had touched the gold mohur and permitted the presentation of the sirdars. And Orthodocia, whose knowledge of Anglo-Indian affairs, nurtured by *Punch* and the *Graphic*, was naturally of

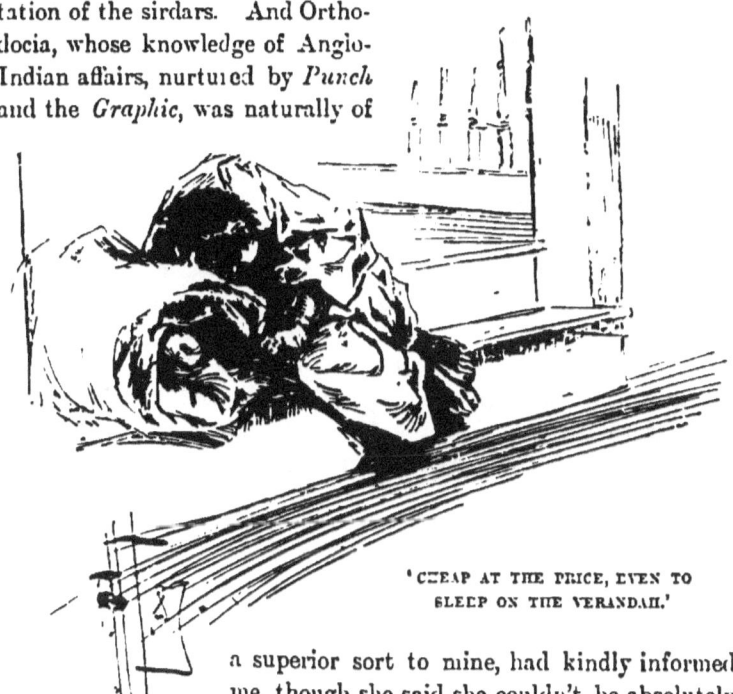

'CHEAP AT THE PRICE, EVEN TO SLEEP ON THE VERANDAH.'

a superior sort to mine, had kindly informed me, though she said she couldn't be absolutely certain, that the gold mohur was a Hindoo idol, and that the sirdars were the Maharajah's grandchildren. Using which information in the lavish way your tourist always does use acquired localisms, I had come to grief and confusion. Orthodocia was present at the scene of it; and 'Where in the world,' said Orthodocia, 'could you have heard *that*?'

And this was the stately compliment returned. We expected the booming to stop after a while, but it kept up steadily, at intervals of about three minutes, during the whole time, I should think, of His Excellency's call. 'It must be a rather depressing punctuation to their conversation,' Orthodocia remarked intelligently, at the thirteenth discharge. 'Fancy the Great White Rajah saying to the little Brown Rajah, "Lovely weather we're having!" and being obliged to hear that momentous statement cannonaded before he could follow it up with another to the effect that we haven't had much rain lately.' And we mused on the disadvantages of being a Viceroy.

Boom-m-mm-m! the fifteenth. At that moment we noticed a servant, with more than the usual amount of scarlet and gold about him, making his way through respectful groups in the compound below. The durwan called Ram Chan, and presently our servitor came up to us with a salver, a book, and an awed expression of countenance. 'Sala'am! Please sign book,' said Ram Chan. 'B-b-burra Lord Sahib!'

'Take it to the *chota memsahib*,'[1] said Orthodocia—there is the difference of an eighth of an inch between us—'while I'—obligingly —'open the envelope.'

It was a large square white envelope, and it contained a large square white card, from which Orthodocia read aloud, in an interested way, the fact that 'the Aide-de-Camp-in-Waiting' was 'commanded by His Excellency the Viceroy' to invite us to an 'Evening Party on the 28th of February at 9.30 o'clock.'

'How nice of them!' said I to Orthodocia. 'Ram Chan, you are not invited. Avaunt!'

'Of them?' she said inquiringly.

'Yes, dear! Of the Viceroy to command it, and the aide-de-camp to do it, you know. Shall we go?'

'Dear me!' exclaimed my friend, 'monarchical institutions *are* difficult to explain to the democratic mind! That's what aide-de-camps are *for*—to be commanded to do things. And this one was naturally delighted to obey.'

'All the nicer of him,' I responded cheerfully, 'considering that he never in his life saw either of us.' At which point I noticed an expression of resignation pass over my friend's countenance. 'But very likely'—as one who has an idea—'you'll find that a great-aunt-

[1] Little mistress.

in-law of his lives near Wigginton. Wigginton might be entirely populated with the relatives of people we've met thus far, and there must be some such explanation.' Orthodocia wearily fanned herself. 'So you think we'll go?'

'*Of course* we'll go!' said my dear friend, summarily. 'A Government House reception! All Calcutta, *and* the Viceroy, *and* the Maharajah! Why in the name of the Prophet shouldn't we?'

'Orthodocia, dear,' I said soothingly, 'consider—consider Ram Chan. Ram Chan is a dissenter, it is true, but even the aggravated Mahommedan sect of dissenters have feelings, and I have no doubt that your profane allusion has wounded several of Ram Chan's. I was only thinking of Pundit Krishna Kurshed Singh, who is coming, you know, by appointment, on the evening of the 28th of February, to give you notes for the Wigginton Dorcas Meetings on bi-metallism and the future of the rupee, structural and functional reforms of the Supreme Council, the repeal of the Arms Act, the ambiguous height to which the British Government has lifted the baboo, the philosophy of the Brahmo Somaj, the prospects for Home Rule in India, and a few other little matters like that.' I paused, for I was tired.

'Dear me!' said Orthodocia. 'So he *was*!' (the italics are hers). And then my friend went away and wrote a charming little perfumed note to Pundit Krishna Kurshed Singh, *Esq*.,' in which she informed him how deeply she regretted that an important unforeseen circumstance had intervened to prevent her availing herself of the most valuable information he had kindly proposed to give her on the evening of the 28th. How she would be delighted if he would name any other evening during our stay in Calcutta which might suit his convenience. How she trusted he might be able to do this, but in any case how he might believe her, 'Dear Mr. Pundit Khrisna Kurshed Singh,' very sincerely his, Orthodocia M. R. I. Love.

* * * * * *

'I will not go!' said Orthodocia, surveying the equipage drawn up under the smoky lamp that hung from the porch of our temporary habitation in Chowringhee. 'No! Nothing shall induce me!'

My friend and I gathered our fine raiment about us and looked round for Ram Chan, who had done this thing—who had brought,

to convey us to the unknown splendours of a Viceregal evening
reception, a wretched quadruped with one knee tied up, a cadaverous,
ragged, yellow driver, and a trap which had once been a victoria,
and still wore ends and fragments of its former luxury with a certain
lean-back air of abandon that gave it a thoroughly reckless and
depraved appearance. It was our second unhappy experience of the
unspeakableness of the Calcutta *ticca-gharri*, and it occurred with
painful inopportuneness. Ram Chan hid for a moment, then appeared to defend himself. 'Sala'am!' he said. 'Very b-bad
t-t-ticca-gharri!'

We made forcible statements of agreement, and ordered him
to get another *ek dum*, which, being interpreted, is 'in one breath.'

'Sala'am!' said Ram Chan. 'No m-m-more *ticca-gharris*. All
gone b-b-b-Burra Lord Sahib!'

'They won't let this one in!' Orthodocia said, almost tearfully,
as we arranged ourselves upon the ragged cushions, and disposed
Ram Chan on the box to cover as much space as his extremely
narrow personality would permit. 'I shall never be sorry for
Cinderella again. She only had to come home in her pumpkin, and
I have no doubt she had able-bodied rats.' And so, in sincere
repudiation of every principle of economy that ever animated the
heart of woman, we made our bumping, swaying, jolting progress
in the *gharri* rejected and contemned of all Calcutta, to His
Excellency the Viceroy's Evening Party. In the wide dim streets
we rattled through crowds of natives that stood to peer as the sahibs
and the memsahibs rolled by. We had imbibed enough Anglo-
Indianism not to mind the natives, though our state might have
provoked even an Aryan smile; the 'trying part,' as Orthodocia
said, was when our equipage twisted into place in the long, long lamp-
lit line of Calcutta's private carriages, that stretched far down the
darkness of the street, and gravely and solemnly advanced one step
at a time with the rest. That was indeed a linked torture long drawn
out. Orthodocia took the situation like Cæsar, in her mantle muffling
up her face, but mine was a dolman, so my sufferings were unmitigated.
But I cannot dwell upon them even now. Suffice it to say that they
had the clemency to let us in after all, that a benevolent memsahib
took us home, and that next day the *ticca-gharri* man presented us

'TO HIS EXCELLENCY THE VICEROY'S EVENING PARTY.'

with a bill for ten rupees, as compensation for the loss of his valuable time in vainly waiting for us—which Orthodocia paid with joy and thanksgiving.

As Orthodocia says, the mere preliminaries of that Evening Party blazed with light and colour—the lofty-ceiled entry hall guarded by portentous durwans, the palms and the flowers in the spacious corridors, the dazzling visions applying a last touch to hair and cheek in the dressing-room, where we met our friend the memsahib, the notes of the orchestra drifting out of the ball-room into the crimson-carpeted ante-chamber, where eddies of people came and went, the wide, cool, dimly-lighted verandahs looking out upon the mystery of a tropical garden, where the eddies never seemed to consist of more than two at a time. And the ball-room itself so scintillated before our unused Occidental eyes that Orthodocia very nearly upset a Mahārajah, and I took refuge upon the memsahib's train. A hundred gas jets shone back from the polished teak floor, white marble pillars made colonnades on either side, and against one wall ran a long buffet gay with roses and ferns, where already thirsty souls were drowning the sorrows of the Bengal Civil Service in tinkling champagne cup. As to the humanity gathered there, that met and parted, and bowed and smiled, and talked and passed on, I suppose for actual brilliancy, that sparkles in a jewel and glows in a rich fabric, and flashes where contrasting civilisations meet and mingle, nothing like it could be found out of the capital of the Indian Empire in the whole world. The body of it was, of course, Anglo-Indian, full of the fascinating oddities of Anglo-Indian speech and intercourse, with just a *nuance* of rich, tropical, easy unconventionality, full of gay talk and laughter with a spice of recklessness in it, full of uniforms and personalities and names. Very charmingly indeed do the Anglo-Indian ladies costume themselves, and neither in their clothes nor in their curtseys does one find the stiffness—now the saints give me courage !—that is occasionally laid to the charge of British femininity—but thou shalt not say I did it. Their pallor lends them shadows about the eyes, and an interesting look of ideality ; and perhaps it is the climate and the ubiquitous verandah chair that gives them such graceful reposeful ways. In fact, you delightful English people who stay at home haven't a conception of how much more delightful you sometimes become when you leave your leaky little island and get thoroughly warmed and dried abroad. But this is irrelevant.

We observed that the Anglo-Indian maids and matrons wore very little native jewellery, and were told that their British lords and masters, whose autocratic tendencies do not suffer in transplanting, I believe, disapprove; but an occasional shapely neck was enhanced by a single string of pearls. I cannot remember all the strange figures that seemed to make a stately carnival of the occasion, but the Archbishop of the Greek Church, tall and broad-shouldered, in his purple velvet and lace, was one; the conquering hero of Burmah, General Sir Harry Prendergast, another—a stalwart rugged soldier, his laurels not yet wilted, with a red face and bushy side whiskers, who seemed to divide the honours of the evening with a visiting German fairy prince, a tall, pale, goldenish creature with a wasp-like waist and the bluest of blue uniforms. It was getting late for celebrities, though; this was the last Evening Party of the season, and Calcutta would soon fly northward with the Viceroy, to dance at Simla the hot weather through, in the Himalayan heights. Nor were the celebrities half so attractive to our fresh enthusiasm as the dazzling brown Oriental part of the throng, that stood mostly by itself in a meditative way, or walked about with silent dignity and looked at the pictures. Certain persons whom we took to be Rajahs wore a strange mixture of barbaric and British in their garments, adopting what might be called the fundamentals of European costume, but clinging to all the bejewelled decorative parts of their own. The different degrees to which the foreign idea had prevailed were interesting, and I remember one potentate who had dispensed with all his traditions except his watch-chain. That hung about his neck, and was of gold-linked emeralds. It was a much-bejewelled prince of Upper India to whom I saw Orthodocia undergoing presentation; and so does the Western imagination riot concerning these things, I immediately expected her to be graciously invested with a ruby or two which the Rajah might have loose in his pocket, and experienced throes of envy. My friend allayed them afterwards when she told me that, after assuring her that he felt deeply honoured to make her acquaintance, the Rajah begged to know if she would like his photograph.

And here was the Afghan Ambassador, stately in his fur-trimmed turban, with nothing at all British about him, but habited for the most part in a garment that seemed made of a Paisley shawl. And a native judge of the High Court, the round and wrinkled impersonation of the liberality of British rule, and more than one native barrister and member of the Civil Service in smug evening dress. The only brown matrons were three or four Burmese princesses, very short and very squat, who stood in a stolid little glittering group and looked at the pageant, and a very occasional Indian matron of evident education and refinement, whose husband was 'advanced' enough to let her come. Herein, by the way, as perhaps is generally known, lies the main point of the reason Anglo-Indians give you for the non-intercourse between themselves and the educated natives in India. They cannot permit their wives and daughters social contact with men in whose eyes such contact is improper; and they say, very reasonably, that society must be upon equal terms. Hence it is only at an 'Evening Party,' when people do nothing but walk about and listen to the orchestra and eat ices, that one sees the Rajah or the Maharajah. His sense of propriety is not often further tried by an invitation to viceregal balls.

And there was the gracious aide-de-camp in his blue lapels doing his duty with supreme self-immolation by these dusky notables, steering for His Excellency, gently bored but valiant, with first one and then another complacent and unctuous craft in tow. The aide-de-camp, as he pervaded the ball-room with the sweet simplicity of those still significant lapels and the smiling intelligence of his exalted function, gave an inspired touch to the occasion—spoke mutely of the sacredness of institutions, and the conduct of affairs. Orthodocia asked me afterwards if I had picked out the special aide-de-camp who was kind about our invitation. Orthodocia was very sarcastic at times.

The evening after we were lucky enough to come in for the Investiture Durbar of the season. 'A grand *tamasho*!' said an old Anglo-Indian who had seen many Viceroys bestow the Queen's favours, *tamasho* being legal tender in Indian conversational currency for doings on any show scale. 'You oughtn't to miss it.' 'Me? Oh!' with a shrug, 'what have I done that I should be compelled to go and see a lot of old chaps make donkeys of themselves by Court process?' Which illustrates as well as anything I heard the mental attitude which Anglo-India would like you to think it takes toward certain things more covetable than pigeon's blood rubies.

'The bill of the play!' said Orthodocia, absently, as an A.D.C. handed us a large double sheet, with the order of the Ceremonial imposingly printed on it in letters of red and of blue; and there seemed, indeed, to be something in the heavy perfumed air like the suppressed excitement in a theatre before the curtain goes up. It was what the newspapers next day probably called a 'brilliantly representative assemblage' that picked its satin-shod way over the carpeting across the grass, and gathered under the great *shamiana*[1] in the grounds of Government House, to see Imperial honours done that night. The Lotus-eyed was there, waving her fan, the Heaven-born flashing his medals, nobles from Upper India, an envoy from Cabul, a dignitary from Nepaul, princes from Burmah, from Oudh and Mysore, and from Hyderabad Mr. Furdoonji Jamsedji.

And the Aide-de-Camp-in-Waiting, no longer a chrysalis of blue lapels, but winged in scarlet and gold, hovered over all.

An expectant instant, as the band outside struck up the National Anthem, and then all the people stood up, for the Viceroy and Grand Master of the Order of the Star of India, preceded by all his Secretaries and Knights-Commanders and Aides, was walking up the aisle. One thinks a Governor-General in the full panoply of his office rather well-dressed, until one has seen a Viceroy of India in the mantle and insignia of the Most Exalted Order of the Star of India. I am afraid I cannot be trusted for details, but the general effect was of gold-glowing, sword-flashing, ribbon-crossing, white silk knee-breeches and buckled shoes, three-cornered hat, and long pale blue silk mantle floating out behind, the ends carried by two tiny pages, all in pink and blue, with powdered heads and silk stockings. The procession walked as far as the throne chair, on a daïs under the Royal Arms, draped with the British flag, and parted, making reverent obeisance as the Grand Master passed through and took his seat. Then an Under-Secretary said something to the Grand Master, which purported, I believe, to tell him the purpose of the occasion,

[1] Tent.

and at a given signal the first gentleman to be decorated came forward three steps, with a Knight-Commander on either side of him and the Under-Secretary in front. Then they all four stopped and bowed, not to each other, but to the Grand Master, who looked pleasant, but, naturally, said nothing. The necessity of bowing at every three steps prolonged the process of getting within speaking distance of the Grand Master, but they all finally accomplished it. Then the two friendly Knights-Commanders who had supported the unfortunate gentleman to be decorated thus far, withdrew, and left him alone in his glory in the awful and immediate viceregal presence, under the analytic eye of all Calcutta. One would have needed a heart of stone not to feel sorry for that man.

Then the Grand Master did it with a very collected manner, and I thought in an extremely friendly and considerate way, but the unhappy old gentleman who had knelt plain 'Mr.' and arose 'Sir Knight' looked round him as helplessly as if he had just been given notice of his execution, until the other two friendly Knights-Commanders stepped forth again, one on each side of him, and together they retraced their steps backwards, pausing at every three to bow to the Grand Master on the throne, who could not show commiseration, though he must have felt it. It was agonising to look at, that backward progress, in its awful indetermination, its varying slips, and its terror-stricken sidelong glances at the politely-repressed audience. The ceremony was performed for another gentleman, who was made Companion, and then the audience came to its feet again as the procession went forth to the robing tent, where His Excellency changed his Star of India robes and insignia for those of the Order of the Indian Empire, not obviously less gorgeous, but representing a lower rank. Then I learned for the first time how that a C.S.I. and C.I.E. differ, not as one star differeth from another in glory, but as the sun and the moon in India. Not that C.I.E.'s are regarded the less, but that C.S.I.'s are regarded the more. For good works many 'natives' are exalted to be C.I.E.'s for one thing, whereas C.S.I. is not so easily attainable by drains and hospitals in the capital of the aspiring Rajah. The Rajah's possession of it does not appear to enhance an honour in Anglo-Indian eyes. Half a dozen Indian dignitaries sat expectant opposite at that moment, and presently it was our fortune to see the pleasure of the Queen towards them.

Up they came, the stately subjects, pacing with far more composure than their British fellows-in-honour. One wore a rose-coloured silk cap, with an aigrette in it of the hair-like tail-feathers of a bird of paradise, every one of which dropped heavy with a diamond. Round his swarthy neck hung seven rows of pearls like berries, clasped with an emerald the size of an egg. Another wore robes of pale blue silk with strings of twisted jewels hanging about his forehead. His eyes were limpid and beautiful under their drooping lids, but his face was fat and sensual, and under his little foppish, waxed moustache lurked a foolish, supercilious smile. We asked the name of this one, and were told it was the great visiting Maharajah—the Maharajah of Jeypoor.

The band played again; again His Excellency the Grand Master, this time at the head of the procession, went forth, and all the people stood up for the last time, and the guard presented arms. The spectacle was over: Her Majesty the Queen of Great Britain and Ireland and Empress of India had played another trump card. There was no denying its grandeur, its state, its impressiveness, and we were most glad we had seen it. My last glimpse I shall remember longest—of the trooping out through the great entrance-gates, under the Imperial arms, of His Excellency the Viceroy's mounted body-guard, tall, majestic, turbaned Sikhs, on splendid animals. Two by two they passed out of the nearer darkness through the lighted gate, and away into the further darkness, while all the people turned their heads to look, and again, and yet again, the band played 'God Save the Queen.'

XXVIII

I THINK I will let Orthodocia tell you this story as I heard her tell it to a lot of people who were roasting chestnuts round the fire in the last hours of 1889 at Love Lodge, St. Eve's-in-the-Garden, Wigginton, Devon.

'It was one night while we were in Calcutta,' she said. 'In the afternoon we had gone with the memsahib and a party to see the old Warren Hastings place in Alipore, which is a suburb of Calcutta, you know, once very fashionable. I don't know about its aristocratic pretensions now, but there was a chummery there'—here Orthodocia smiled an absent reminiscent smile—'and we had tea and ices and things at the chummery before we went, or after, I forget which. Such a dear little chummery, pink and green all over, like something iced in a confectioner's shop! In fact, I think it was a chum who organised the expedition—but that, of course, is a detail.

'It was a nice old place. We got in through a hole in the fence, or a little wicket-gate, or something that obliged us to go one by one, like sheep, and found ourselves in a big neglected compound full of tangled grass and ruined trees with strange creepers twisting and hanging about them. One of the creepers had clusters of long white trumpet-shaped flowers. Here is the spray I gathered!' and Orthodocia, with theatrical effect, opened her note-book where three dried brown crumpled scraps of vegetable matter had left a stain upon the opposite page. 'Of course, I wouldn't *say* that Warren Hastings planted that creeper, and probably wore its blossoms in his buttonhole, to anybody but you, but there's nothing to *prevent* his having done so,' said my friend earnestly, 'and it makes all the difference to one's impressions. Well, beyond the lawn, at the curve of the weedy drive, the house stood that we had come to see—a big square old place, rather dignified, but not a bit splendid, with a broad flight of stone steps up to the entrance-porch. It was very solitary—nobody about but a sala'aming *durwan*, who unlocked the shabby doors for us, and his three or four sly brown children, who followed us about at a distance. And natives in India,' said Orthodocia, ' always seem to make a place with English associations silenter and lonelier than when they're not there.

' Inside it was just a quaint old-fashioned house, with high ceilings and dusty walls, full of odd nooks and corners, and narrow passages, and little twirling staircases, and deep wells where staircases used to be. There was the Council Chamber of the great Indian Governor,' said Orthodocia, movingly, ' his dining-hall, the rooms he slept and danced and received in—all given over to silence and cobwebs and dust. One bare wall of the State assembly-room was covered half-way up with round spots that looked as if a great many people had played fives against it, but neither the memsahib nor the chums could explain this. The high ceiling was held up by wooden pillars, and up and down these, and all round the wainscoting and cornices, ran long, irregular, hollow streaks, that looked like dried clay. White ants,' Orthodocia said impressively, 'that are slowly eating into this monument of the past, and will some day bring it to the ground with a crash. One reads about the devastation of white ants, but one doesn't properly realise it until one stands under a ceiling they are known to be operating on. Well, it was a chum who told us about the white ants, and this led him on to talk about the ghost. We were awfully pleased, because we hadn't an idea that there was a ghost ; and there isn't a human being that doesn't love a ghost in the daytime. So, while we poked about the dusty passages and climbed the funny little stairs, and tried to imagine what viceregal housekeeping must have been like a hundred years ago, the chum went on talking, and, as far as I remember, this is what he said :

' "You see this old *Durbar* hall was a different place in those days to what it is now, and saw many a gorgeous gathering, and this little room we are in knew a good deal more of the State secrets of Warren Hastings' rule than ever came out in his trial. However, when he left the last time for England he thought he might some day come back and want to use a lot of papers he had accumulated—secret papers that showed how the affairs of the great East India Company had been managed to the profit of the directors, and how insecure were the titles of many a fat zemindar, who would gladly give up lakhs of his ill-gotten rupees to the Company in exchange for protection and patronage—that showed, too, many a shady transaction which had built the foundation of the empire that was to be, but which looked anything but straight considered unsympathetically. He didn't want to risk the papers on a voyage round the Cape, and still less to give his enemies a chance of showing them to Francis, so he built them up into one of these walls round us with his own hands, and plastered up the place so cunningly that nobody has been able to find it again. Warren Hastings never came back to Calcutta, and the great trial dragged on without the papers. And at last he died, poor, because he had been faithful to the Company, and had founded an empire, instead of looking after his own interests, and still honoured because the proofs of his crimes were and are safely hidden somewhere, perhaps within ten feet of us, and his accusers had no other evidence reliable enough."'

'AND PRESENTLY THERE IS A SCRAPING SOUND OF MOVING BRICKS AND FALLING PLASTER.'

Here Orthodocia interrupted herself so far as to say, 'Wasn't it interesting?' We all said it was, intensely.

'And then—where was I? Oh, yes. The chum went on : "But his spirit cannot rest while these papers are where they may any day be found, and sometimes in the dusk of the evening a sound of wheels is heard on the moss-grown drive, and an old-fashioned travelling carriage hurries up to the door, and out of it gets a faded old figure in a plum-coloured coat and high cravat, and the rusty hinges creak and the door flies open, in spite of the patent locks the owner tries to keep it shut with. And presently there is a scraping sound of moving bricks and falling plaster, and then the figure comes out again dusty and gloomy, for they say it can only stay for half an hour, and may not carry the papers away, so it comes again and again to see that they are safe. And meanwhile the old house gets more and more ruinous, and the white ants work silently on in the beams, so that soon it will fall down, and then, maybe, the papers will be found. For half a century the place belonged to an ancient dame who lived in a corner of it, and often saw the silent ghost flit along the passage where nobody else would venture after dark. She was not afraid, only she would never have the walls touched or repaired. Some years back she died, and the property has since passed into other hands. Every year it is said that it is to be repaired and let. An advertisement appears in the papers and people talk of taking it, for it is a fine old place and valuable here, for good houses bring enormous rents ; but somehow the negotiations for taking it always fall through, and the old place remains ruinous and desolate as you see it ; and the nor'-westers whistle through the broken casements, and the snakes creep in the *Durbar* hall, and the ghost comes and the secret papers are undisturbed, and people go by the other road at night." That's the way he put it as far as I can remember,' said Orthodocia, ' and I told him at the time I thought it was a very pretty ghost story. Then we all climbed up to the flat roof, where bushes and vines were growing in the cracks of the parapet, and walked about where that notable old Governor must often have walked, in the cool of the evening, only we saw the real spires and masts of the great city, with the sun going down behind, which he could only have seen in imagination. And before we came away we found a quaint old garden at the back of the house, and explored it. It had a narrow little path down the middle, with some scrappy box growing on each side, and a tumble-down arbour and some tangled petunias, and a deep round well with a mossy bricked edge half-way down the path. It made one think, somehow,' said Orthodocia, 'that English people had not always been content to live in " compounds " decorated with flower-pots from the market, but had tried, at first, to take their homes and their gardens with them to India.

'It had been rather an eventful day,' she went on, checking its events off on her fingers. 'First there had been breakfast with a memsahib who had a conjurer in to make a mango tree grow for us —a thing I haven't the slightest faith in—and then tiffin with another, who took us to see a Hindoo temple, then tea and this supernatural conversation, and in the evening a dance. I didn't feel at all equal to the walk to the old Hastings place afterwards, when we started, just the two of us—the Chronicler here and I—in the moonlight, and I kept constantly dropping this cluster of white flowers I gathered in the afternoon and wore at the dance. So we hailed a *ticca-gharri*, and it did not seem in any way remarkable that it should be driven by an aide-de-camp. He took us there quite safely, and only charged one anna three pice, which seemed very remarkable indeed, however, and we told him to wait.

'The *durwan* admitted us—or did we admit him ?—I don't remember; but inside it was very dark, except where the moonlight fell on the walls and the floor. We sat down in a corner of the State assembly-room and watched the lizards run across the moonlit places, and listened to the rustle of the trees outside; and suddenly the Chronicler remembered about the snakes, and went and asked the *durwan* if he would be kind enough to sweep the room out and syringe the corners with tobacco-water to kill them off, and he did. Then he went away, and we waited an immensity of time for something to occur. Nothing did, except more lizards, and the Chronicler said it was because we were expecting it, and only the unexpected happened; so she suggested that we should either discuss the problem of the Treasury surplus at Washington or go to sleep. I thought it would be nicer to get up charades, but the Chronicler had begun on the surplus, so I took the other alternative. About five minutes after that I heard the carriage rolling up outside, exactly as the chum said it did, and the Chronicler was gone. The Chronicler was always to be relied upon for getting ahead of one, and though I hardly expect you to believe it, I do assure you she had taken advantage of my being asleep and the excuse of the *durwan's* having retired to go and let the ghost in ! I heard them talking in the hall, or I would not have believed it ; and they came in together, she and an intellectual-looking little old gentleman with a high forehead and dark eyes, and a flowered waistcoat, and a longtailed coat, and black knee-breeches, and silk stockings, and a frill, carrying a travelling-bag, and looking awfully worried. And then she had the assurance to *introduce* me—nobody had introduced her !—and coolly went on to explain that, being on our first and probably our last trip round the world, we naturally wanted as many novel and original experiences and sensations as possible, the planet having become very commonplace since he left it—a thing I had fully intended to say myself ! And she trusted that His Excellency would consider, before pronouncing our visit an unpardonable intrusion, the difficulties that lay in the way of a formal presentation to him, just hinting, in a polite sort of way, that he could hardly expect to withdraw himself from society for so long, and not become to a certain extent unpopular. And then the old gentleman laid his hand on his heart and made a bow, and said that he was delighted to see us, and that it was very good of us to think of him when there must be so many more modern attractions. I could think of absolutely nothing to say, so I took out my dance programme and began to make notes on the back of it. I remember putting down quantities of interesting things, when the old gentleman looked at me in such an extraordinary way, and said, "I hope you are writing nothing invidious !" so sharply that I dropped it, and he quietly put his buckled shoe on it, so that I didn't get it again.

'I never saw the Chronicler so loquacious, or a ghost so curious. I should have asked questions, but she didn't—her sole thirst seemed to be to impart information. She talked so much that he asked her where she came from, and he seemed so deeply interested when she said America that she went volumes deep into the history and resources and future of her native continent. She ruffled him a little once by telling him the causes of the American Revolution, and I distinctly remember his saying, "My dear young lady, you needn't go back to Genesis ! I know all about that !"

'He became quite excited, for a ghost, when it transpired that we were travelling by ourselves, but he did not say approvingly, "How plucky of you!" which made him a great original exception to all the other people we met; and we both thanked him very sincerely for the omission. Neither did he say disapprovingly, "How very American!" But that, of course, he couldn't say, not knowing the full force of the expression. But he walked round both of us, and looked at us through a pair of gold-rimmed eyeglasses, and said with some astonishment: "So it has come to this! I must tell the elegant Marian. She would have enjoyed it!"

'By-and-by he began to take out his watch and to fidget about. "My time is extremely limited," he said, "extremely limited. And I don't care to come here often, because I tell you privately this house is Haunted, and the Apparition is nearly always about when I come. It is very inconvenient, not to say trying, and my nerves are not what they used to be. If you look through that doorway," he said in a great flurry, "you will see It now!" We looked, and there in the passage stood a tall, thin White Ant, with very full skirts, and a cap and apron, knitting. "She is always knitting!" said the old gentleman, irascibly. "It is a mere pretence—a mere pretence. But it reminds me," he said anxiously, looking at his watch again, "that my time is extremely limited."

'THE OLD GENTLEMAN MADE ANOTHER BOW.'

'I thought it would be polite to go then; but the Chronicler, with the most extraordinary assurance, nodded confidentially at the old gentleman. "They're all right, Your Excellency!" she said. "Don't worry!"

'"Dear me" he said, "I'm glad to hear that. Much obliged—much obliged. You see I'm still Viceroy of Upper India, where Nuncomar and the Princesses are quite as troublesome as ever, I assure you. And in the event of any displacement of my arrangements, the first newspaper man who died with the intelligence in his possession would doubtless take it straight to Mr. Pitt, which would be extremely inconvenient. I am indebted to you, really." And the old gentleman made another bow.

'"It is reasonably certain," he continued, "that you will be travelling alone again some day, without even the enviable solace of each other's society, in a direction in which I can be of service to you. I hope you will command me. Anything I can do to facilitate——"

'As a matter of fact,' said Orthodocia, 'I can't be certain that he said exactly that. It's a thing one hears so often on a trip round the world that I may only imagine he did.'

'Well,' said everybody round the fire, 'were you dreaming?'

'The Chronicler,' Orthodocia responded regretfully, 'says I was.'

XXIX

NOW it was our good fortune in Calcutta to come in the philanthropic path of a memsahib who knew people generally—who knew not only the gilded throng that came and went in the presence of the Burra Lord Sahib, but certain of the dusky under-world as well. With her, and by her good pleasure, we made two or three calls upon India proper.

The first was a visit to the family of Kirpa Singh, clerk to a great firm of sahibs in the city. The clerk spoke English, but had not otherwise departed from the ways of his forefathers. His wife was still *purdah-nashin*;[1] his daughter had just been married, at the age of seven, to the son of a brother clerk. He himself went at certain times, when his prosperity seemed waning, on a pilgrimage to Benares to see the gods about it. He was educating his son in English, but the son must get his education in India, for to cross the sea was to lose his caste, to disgrace his father, and

---

[1] Curtain-hidden.

to become a pariah in the orthodox circles of Hinduism. Besides which, it would send his grandfather mad, and his grandfather was quite the co-authority, if not the superior, of his father.

As we drove through the winding, perspiring, crowded streets of native Calcutta, the memsahib's coachman suddenly reined up and turned into a high-walled lane so narrow that the *beesti* had to stand close against the wall, with his dripping black *mussuck*, to escape a squeezing. The house stood at the end of the lane, glaringly whitewashed, high and narrow, with a few small windows irregularly dotted over it, and a general air of discouraging intrusions. We were expected, however, and the gate was open, the clerk standing at it in his long white draperies, rubbing his hands with an expression of rather troubled bliss. He did not often entertain memsahibs.

As we approached, our host hastened forward with polite joy. 'Sala'am!' he said, 'Sala'am! Sala'am! How do you to-day? You give me much honour to come. My house is yours.' He shook hands with Orthodocia and me as we were introduced, and one's first Aryan handshake is a thing to remember. The pale brown palms have no warmth in them, and the touch of the long slender fingers seems actually to lower one's temperature. Then he led the way to his domestic interior, and we followed curiously. A youth stood at the top of the half-dozen outer steps that brought us to the narrow passage leading inside, dressed like Kirpa Singh, but wearing shoes; and Kirpa Singh said, 'This is my son Ram.' The boy had nothing but 'Sala'am!' to respond to our salutations with; his English was still embryotic. 'My son Ram,' moreover, we could see in droves in the street any day. We kept our interest for the *purdah-nashin*, who had never yet gone from her father's or her husband's door except in a tightly-closed palanquin or carriage. We wanted to see how life was reflected from a face that knew it only behind these blank white walls.

The passage was flecklessly whitewashed and empty. Two doors opened off it into two rooms, both of which were also whitewashed and also empty, except for three wooden chairs arranged in a row in the middle. Kirpa Singh took us first into one of these, and then into the other. 'My house is yours,' he repeated with smiling dignity. 'Please to sit down; I will bring them, he said to the memsahib, who had been inquiring for his wife and daughter, and disappeared. Mrs. and Miss Singh had evidently been waiting to be brought, for he came back with them almost immediately. The wife was a shy-looking creature, with a soft, fat, brown face, full of pleasure and curiosity; a gentle, domestic animal in no way to be remarked; and we dismissed our romancing about her at a single glance. But little Miss Singh was a wonder to behold. In honour of our visit she had been literally put into her dowry, the dowry which orought her her ten-year-old husband in the son of the friend of Kirpa Singh. It glittered all over her, from the top of her small, sleek head to her little brown ankles and toes; the jewels of Ind as they had come to Kirpa Singh, and to the wife of Kirpa Singh, as they had been inherited, or bought, or bargained for in the bazaars. There is no decorative form known to civilisation which will describe them, so I can only tell you that they were things of beaten gold, and strung rubies, and emeralds, and sapphires, that fitted over her brow and connected in some way with her ears, so that whenever she turned her head a hundred stones danced and glanced with the movement. Her poor little ears were elongated past belief with the weight of the filagree and gems that hung down to her plump shoulders. Her nostrils were pierced three times with tiny gold hoops, each dangling a stone. Bracelets she wore on all parts of her arm; finger-rings, and toe-rings, and clashing ankle-rings half-way to the knee. Her single scanty garment under all this was of some barbaric embroidered stuff, chiefly gold and green. The little maiden looked very conscious and very proud. Evidently she knew that she was a good bargain to the husband she had married a week before, and that it was on her merits as a good bargain that she was exhibited. She gave us time to look at her, then offered her little hand to each of us in turn, saying gravely, thrusting her betel paste into her cheek for convenience, '*Atcha hai?*' '*Atcha hai?*' '*Atcha hai?*'[1]

Then Mrs. Kirpa came forward and took the memsahib gently by the hand; little Miss Singh gave her right to Orthodocia and her left to me; Kirpa led the way; his son Ram brought up the rear, and in this procession we sallied forth to see the domicile of the Singh family.

[1] Are you well?

'My house is yours,' said Kirpa again, turning on the staircase to give us this assurance.

We went up and up, noting absolutely nothing but whitewashed walls, except on a landing two or three brass *lotas* and flat dishes with milk in them. Another passage and more rooms, each with three chairs in the middle for our possible occupation. Never any

'MY HOUSE IS YOURS.'

other furniture, and only in one any further incident. That one was presumably the general reception-room ; it was provided with framed prints and a cupboard. The prints were coloured and interesting, as illustrating Kirpa Singh's art ideas, and reflecting to some extent the conditions of his life. They were chiefly representations in the three primaries of benign Hindoo gods and goddesses in sylvan surroundings, mixed up with the Princess of Wales in evening dress, an engraving of 'John Wesley's Deathbed,' and two or three pink and green lithographs of the baby and daisies order. The cupboard had glass doors, behind which the various idols affected by the Singh family grinned, squatting. There seemed to be no special protection for the idols, but a very solid-looking safety-lock and latest improvements iron safe stood in one corner for the jewels. We went up another winding staircase and emerged upon the roof, where Kirpa Singh descanted upon the view. He permitted Mrs. Kirpa to come out here in the evenings, he said, which was more than many of his friends allowed their wives to do. Mrs. Kirpa's parade ground for exercise was about ten feet by twelve, and commanded the back premises of other blankly-walled houses for some fifty yards around.

Then we descended, and were refreshed with bottled lemonade and round questionable-looking brown balls of confectionery that Mrs. Kirpa, her lord proudly stated, had made herself, and of which we partook with an inward prayer. And Kirpa Singh produced from somewhere three glass-stoppered bottles of perfume—'Violette,' 'White Rose,' and 'Mille-Fleurs,' and bestowed one upon each of us with graceful circumstance. 'In these scents you will keep my visit a long time,' he said, with poetry that would not have been awkward in his own language. And as we were about to depart, the crowning ceremony of the occasion was observed, and the girl-child threw about our necks the Hindoo wreath of felicitation—a thick, compact rope of sweet-smelling white flowers, something like guelder roses. The child and her mother pressed forward to the entrance in their innocent curiosity to see us go; but the arm of the husband and father pushed them gently back, and the door was shut with Kirpa Singh and his son Ram outside. There came the touch, the sudden pain of pity; and I think Kirpa Singh saw in our faces that our hearts were still behind the door. 'They would be afraid,' he said, looking at us deprecatingly. And so we came away.

It was a day or two later that we went with another memsahib to see a zenana. Our friend wrote M.D. after her name, and she made the visit in her official capacity. Otherwise I dare say a glimpse of this particular zenana would have been difficult to obtain. It was attached—at least one hopes so—to one Kun Jeer Bung, Bahadur Rana, who had confided it to the care of the doctor memsahib during his enforced temporary residence in Calcutta. Kun Jeer Bung was a Prince of a native State, which was not a comfortable place for him just then because of his detractors. His detractors were unkind enough to say that he had killed the old ruling Prince, his uncle; and Kun Jeer Bung was so sensitive to scandal of this sort that he had taken up his abode in Calcutta, where he could not hear it. Montreal, in much the same way, is popular with many unsuccessful American financiers. This often happens, and makes a pleasant excitement for Calcutta, especially when the detracted's enemies follow him secretly and poison him, vanishing, and leaving no trace; and it gives the newspapers something to talk about. Kun Jeer Bung, for instance, might have been declared a rascal unhung by *The Englishman*, while *The Statesman* believed him a deeply-wronged potentate, suffering cruel banishment for the crimes of others. We asked the medical memsahib her opinion as to whether Kun Jeer Bung had done this thing, but naturally she had none to offer. 'You must ask him about it,' she said, 'he doesn't mind.'

Evidently the exile and his establishment were expecting us; there was an air of preparation. It was a great bare room into which we were shown, but the empty champagne bottles along the walls were standing neatly in rows; two or three newspapers were lying folded on the table, and all the cigar ends and corks had been swept into a corner. The half-dozen chairs and one sofa were grouped round the table sociably. Three or four women, and as many more children, were presently peering out of the long, narrow apertures in the upper part of the wall. I don't know what we expected the princely alien to be like, but his appearance was decidedly surprising. He was a short, fat young man, with a slight moustache on the upper lip of his handsome, heavy, round face. He walked jauntily, in rather soiled white ducks, well made in the European way; but, of course, he wore no collar. The linen collar will be the last Aryan conquest of civilisation; we had given up expecting it, even from potentates. He shook hands with all of us politely, and begged us to sit down. He might have been, in looks and manner, a foppish mulatto waiter of a Broadway restaurant, a little down on his luck; and his English had very much the accent the waiter's would have. It was, however, rather more untrammelled. The natural man in

'THE PRINCE OF RISSOLES.'

Kun Jeer Bung, Bahadur Rana, was not accustomed to the restraints of polite society.

'*Damn* hot day!' said the Prince of Rissoles, with a warm sigh and an urbane smile, by way of opening the conversation.

Orthodocia jumped, recovered, and said, 'Yes, it is extremely hot.'

'Have a peg?' he inquired hospitably of the doctor memsahib. 'Rather think I will myself. Hi!' and the eunuch that crouched beside the door came forward. 'Bring some fizz for the ladies, and a B. and S. for me.'

It was rather early in the day for champagne, but the hospitality of Kun Jeer Bung was unacquainted with times and seasons.

'Any of the kids bad?' he asked the memsahib, which betrayed Orthodocia into the indiscreet commonplace of asking how many children he had.

Kun Jeer Bung thought a minute and then slapped his knee jocosely. 'Hanged if I know exactly,' he said. 'Twenty-three or four, ain't there, doctor?' The memsahib, with a reproving look at Orthodocia which my poor friend did not deserve, corroborated the last guess; but said they were all in good health the last time she reviewed them. She had come to see Kun Jeer Bung's youngest wife. He said something to the eunuch in his own tongue, who took a huge iron key from a fold in his gown and opened a heavy door at the end of the room, locking it again after him. The children in the gallery above became uproarious. 'Listen to the little devils!' said their fond parent, the Prince of Rissoles.

Presently the door reopened to the eunuch's key, and six black-eyed creatures appeared two and two—the most extraordinary little personalities it is possible to conceive. Every one of their tiny faces was whitened and rouged, every one of their queer little heads covered with short thin braids drawn to the front, that fell down over their cheeks and eyes. They wore silk embroidered bodices and muslin skirts, green and yellow and pink and blue, voluminous muslin skirts with a hundred yards in each of them, all gathered into a fan-like train which each little lady carried with much circumspection before her.

'You notice,' said Kun Jeer Bung, 'these ladies wear no jewels!' which was true. 'It is not the fashion now,' he added mendaciously, 'in Rissoles for ladies to wear jewellery.'

The humbug had pawned it all to raise money to buy rifles to shoot his detractors with.

The poor little souls—the youngest looked about fourteen—seemed glad enough to see the doctor memsahib, and one of them caressed her dress as she sat talking to them through the eunuch. This Prince took no further notice of them, but chatted away to us in his slangy English about the roller skating rink. He had taken, it seemed, a great fancy to roller skating. He asked us from what part of America we had sailed, and repeated 'Canada' thoughtfully. Suddenly he was inspired. 'Canada!' he said. 'Oh yes; I know, jolly well. The place the new Viceroy has just come from!'

He was a curious mixture of old heathenism and new civilisation, and our interest in him, though somewhat nervous, was so great that it did not occur to us until afterwards that we had quite forgotten to ask him whether he really killed his uncle.

But we were both distinctly of the impression that he did.

We felt that it was a leap over more than the fifty years of British influence upon social India from these primitive hospitalities to the 'At home' which we attended at the house of an Anglicised native, a barrister who pleaded in the High Court, and, with his wife, had been educated in England. This lady and gentleman, whom we found charming, were as favourable specimens as we could have met of pure natives on the very crest of the wave of progress that is lifting their race to the plane where men struggle and hope and pray as we do—specimens of the class that appreciates and lives up to the advantages of British rule, and is received and liked by the sahib and the memsahib accordingly. Mr. Chunder Dass (which wasn't his name, but that's of no consequence) was a tall, slender, graceful Indian with a delicate, sensitive face—intellectual, sympathetic. Mrs. Chunder Dass was a pretty oval-faced little woman, fair for her race, gentle mannered, a *pundita* of Girton or some such place. He wore European clothes as if his forefathers had evolved them; she wore the garb of the sect they both belonged to, the Brahmo Somaj. I think only feminine understandings can follow me when I say that the dress of Mrs. Chunder Dass was a compromise between the conventionalities of Europe and the easy draperies of the East. She wore a skirt and a plain high-necked long-sleeved bodice; but a white scarf, connected in some mysterious way with the skirt, and embroidered in gold, was draped before and behind to her left shoulder. The scarf was pink, and the dress was white; and this, they told us, was the costume prescribed for its women by the Brahmo Somaj—a sect that believes in their emancipation, education, and elevation. After Mrs. Chunder Dass had taken scholastic honours in England, she came to Calcutta to occupy a position in a

'BUT THE YOUNG BABOO SAT IN THE DRAWING-ROOM AND WAITED A LONG TIME FOR HIS ICE.'

school for Indian young ladies, and to disseminate such beneficent influence as she could; but she met Mr. Chunder Dass, and he, I think, called her in their own soft tongue 'The Lotus-eyed.' And after that the higher education of the young ladies of Bengal might have been despaired of in so far as the present Mrs. Chunder Dass is concerned—who wonders now, when she looks into the big brown eyes of the Dass baby, what she ever saw to admire in the differential calculus.

They lived in one of the nicest kind of Calcutta houses, with a large compound and a vine-clad verandah. Inside it was as European as possible. Mrs. Chunder Dass's library might have been anybody's, and Mrs. Chunder Dass's drawing-room was entirely correct as to the accepted facts of repoussé brass, hand-painted china, photographs, and draperies and casts. There were plenty of 'people' at Mrs. Chunder Dass's reception—a High Court Judge and his wife, a Member of Council and his, a stray Sir Knight. Numbers of brown faces were coming and going, all belonging to European clothes, though often some dash of colour or of character—an embroidered cap, or a crimson waistband—marked a lingering liking for things of India's gorgeous yesterday. They were all very polite, the Baboos and the Pundits, as well as interesting and impressive, and I think it was only the extreme shyness of a youth who talked to Orthodocia that victimised them both. Refreshments, the liberal pink ice, and frothing champagne-glass of India's lightest entertainment, were served in a marquee on the lawn, and gradually the drawing-room emptied in a steady stream towards these superior attractions. Orthodocia and the young Parsee were left by themselves. 'I think,' she said, insinuatingly, 'that they are having ices out there.' He said he thought they were, and asked her if she had seen the distribution of prizes at the Bethune School that day. Then Orthodocia inquired if he disliked ices, and he said he did not, did she? Orthodocia assured him that she adored them, and he smiled politely. Finally my unhappy friend asked him, as a crucial test, whether she might get him one, and he said she was very kind, and if it was not giving her too much trouble he should like it very much. Whereupon Orthodocia escaped and mingled with the crowd in the marquee, where some benevolent person took charge of her. But the young Baboo sat in the drawing-room and waited a long time for his ice.

XXX

CHUTTERSINGH—*bairagee*'—it ran in the register of the Kali-ghat. Ram Chan sat outside on the box of the *ticca-gharri*, visibly unhappy. Ram Chan, in life or death, objected to the Kali-ghat. He had perverted our instructions to the driver for three-quarters of an hour, hoping that we would finally believe it unattainable and go home. Only once before, when Orthodocia, in her eternal search for information, accidentally and amiably asked Ram Chan how old his wife was, had we seen our servitor in so protesting a state of mind. On that occasion he was stricken with violent toothache, and departed, nursing a hypothetical molar and very genuine wrath, for two days.

We saw the end of him, of this *bairagee*, this beggar of Calcutta, Orthodocia and I, one afternoon last March.

The beginning was seventy years ago, according to the register, on the sixth evening after he was born, while yet he and his Hindoo mother lay apart for purification, and the barber's wife kept watch over them both among the shadows of that separate place. Then through the music and the dancing outside, where all the people of the village had gathered to feast and drink on the sixth night of his life, great Brahma came, silent, invisible, and found the way to the dusky corner under the cocoanut thatch, and wrote upon the forehead of Chuttersingh in a fringe of Sanskrit characters all that life should mean for him. Nobody knew just when Brahma did this. The feasting crowd was oblivious, the mother slept in her tangle of black hair, and did not see; even the barber's wife, watching, was unaware. But next morning early, when the palmyra palms stood shadowed limpidly in the white light of the river, she, the mother, looked curiously at Chuttersingh's forehead as they went down to bathe, for she knew the writing was there.

At the end of a long day in the rice fields Chuttersingh felt a call from heaven to become a religious beggar, a *bairagee*. It was hot in the Indian jungle, and he had not the patience of the meek-eyed bullock whose tail he twisted for discipline as he walked beside his cart under the banyans to the village market. And so before another red sun went down behind the feathered palms and the pipal trees, Chuttersingh had gone out from his hut of baked mud and sticks, and had travelled far toward the city, leaving for those who had aught to say against it, '*Kopal me likkha!*'—'It is written upon my forehead!'

You might have met him soon after in the city streets, his black hair falling in matted ropes about his face, streaks of clay and lime across his forehead and down his nose, a single cotton garment wound about him. No glittering vanity of ear-rings or finger-rings; no dignity of turban

'HE HAD PERVERTED OUR INSTRUCTIONS TO THE DRIVER FOR THREE-QUARTERS OF AN HOUR.'

or jauntiness of *pagri*; not a pleasant picture—a picture of ostentatious squalor. And he would have 'sala'amed' to you, touching his forehead with his lean brown hand. Then, if you looked at him an instant, he would twang the single string of his *sittar*, and begin a song to Vishnu, not unmusical, and a tipsy dance in a semicircle, smiling all the time, and showing through his long black beard teeth reddened, as with blood, by the juice of the betel. And for the pice you might give him he would 'sala'am' again to you, with deeper reverence and added gentleness. Then, perhaps, before you turned away, you might see some trifling service, some little politeness, done with many sala'ams unto this *bairagee*, this beggar of Calcutta, by a rich man of lower caste than he.

Brahma and Vishnu, and Siva and Dirga, and Rama and Krishna, and all the nameless million gods that three thousand Hindoo years had accumulated for Chuttersingh, knew that he had vowed to make a pilgrimage to Benares, the sacred city where gods have lived for ages, and draw no inch nearer striding erect, in presumptuous dignity, as other men do, but falling flat on his face and measuring his length with his brass water-bottle, the whole hundred miles. Chuttersingh had confided it to Kali, the fire-goddess, before whom he meditated always the longest, and Kali had told the rest. So that they were looking for him there at Benares, on the ghats, the day that he should come, all dust and humility, prostrating himself to the end of his twelve months' journey.

Along the white highway he went in the blazing Indian noonday, meeting bearded Mahommedans who sneered at him, threading the jungle as the sun went down and the cool of the evening crept through the waving fronds of the date-palms. He heard the sunbirds in the morning, and the doves at night, high in the rustling bamboo branches that thrust pale green shadows between him and the sky. He crossed glistening streams that slid away through the rice fields to the sacred river; he crushed the dropped crimson blossoms of the silk cottons in his fall; he dreamed again, as he caught the fragrance of the creamy *frangi-panni*, of the ten thousand years of happiness which should reward him. He did not lack food or drink, or shelter; *pan* and *suttoo*, and rice straw mats to lie upon, Hindoo huts always had for him much or little—he was a *bairagee*; he helped to keep the world straight with the gods. At last one happy day, eyes bloodshot, feet blistered, he bowed before Kali again, having laved in the Ganges to all purification, and the priests—the *gurus*—looked upon him with recognition of his new holiness, and said one to another in their own tongue, 'It was written upon his forehead.'

There was a comely Hindoo widow in the house of Ramdaal, a merchant, who served her father and sisters-in-law with due wretchedness and humility until she gave alms to Chuttersingh. He, receiving them and looking upon her, suddenly heard a voice from heaven saying that she also must become a *bairagee*, and follow him in the ways of righteousness. There was no gainsaying a call from heaven for a superfluous widow, and she went with Chuttersingh, who was still a holy man.

I am afraid I do not know and cannot imagine anything further that happened to Chuttersingh, having heard his life only in a casual Calcutta half-hour, except the very last thing, which, as I told you, we saw ourselves that afternoon in March. We stood in an enclosure on the river bank in the city suburbs which was strange to us, an enclosure with high stone walls and steps leading down to the water. Shallow holes were scooped out of the beaten earth here and there, and at the other end

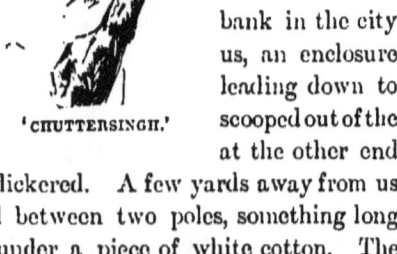

'CHUTTERSINGH.'

a long heap of coals glowed and flickered. A few yards away from us something lay upon the ground between two poles, something long and narrow and flat, outlined under a piece of white cotton. The wind blew over a corner of the white cotton, and we saw a thin brown face with great sunken eye-hollows, tense lips, and a wisp of gray hair behind—the face of Chuttersingh, dead that morning.

The bare-chested, bare-limbed Hindoos around us put their hands on their hips, chewed betel paste, talked and laughed and waited. Presently two more came in, carrying a bundle of wood. They made a pile of it over one of the holes. A tall Hindoo in a brown loin-

'HE, BENDING OVER THE DEAD MAN, TOUCHED FIRST THE LIPS WITH THE FIRE.'

cloth, threw some water upon the heap. He was a priest, they told us, and it was sacred water. Then two or three others picked up the poles with their burden and laid it upon the pile. As they did this Chuttersingh's lean brown arm fell down from his side upon the wood, and his bony fingers seemed to clasp it. The priest took rice and plantains, and put them to the beggar's lips, then upon his breast, saying something quickly in Sanskrit.

The Hindoos near us looked on, and still laughed. Chuttersingh was the eighteenth that day. If it had been a rich man, for whom sandal wood had been brought, and flowers, and many mourners, they might have been more curious.

Yet Chuttersingh was not quite without those things as he lay there before us in the midst of the faggots. Some one had put a wreath of yellow marigolds upon his feet, and this rag of affection clung there wilting in the sun. And an old man, another beggar, hovered about, rubbing quick tears away from his wrinkled cheeks, his lips trembling as he watched the work go on. Only another beggar! Yet I think that beggar's tears had more to do with Chuttersingh's eternal happiness than all the waters of the sacred river.

They piled the faggots closer round him and they laid a few upon his breast. The priest lighted a bundle of dry fibrous grasses and handed it to the other beggar, who was Chuttersingh's friend, and had come to do for him the service of brother or son. He, bending over the dead man, touched first the lips with the fire, according to the ritual, and then lighted the pile from below. Then standing back a little space, he folded his arms in his cotton chudder and looked on sadly.

The flames crept in and out, and little blue curls of smoke went up to the Indian sun. The cotton covering caught in a circle; we saw the loop of marigolds shrivel and blacken and drop. Chuttersingh was Kali's, her baptism upon his lips, the essence of her divinity wrapping him close. We turned away and left him there, with his strange indifference, in her embrace.

The other beggar turned away also, and as he brushed against us in the gate, we heard him murmur with a sob, '*Kopal me likkha!*'— 'It was written upon his forehead!'

XXXI

ORTHODOCIA and I did what struck a great many people as a singular thing in the arrangement of our trip so far as India was concerned. We went to Ceylon first, then up the Bay of Bengal to Calcutta, then down to Ceylon again, touching at Madras, then up to Bombay, and from Bombay up country to Agra and back again. Anybody who consults the map of India, or Cook's tourist guide-books, or any other indisputable authority, will discover that this was a most irrational tour; that the proper thing on the very face of it was to take rail from Calcutta across to Bombay, and so see 'Benares and all those places.' This was the unceasing burden of the cry of our fellow planet-pilgrims, to whom our conduct was usually painful to a degree. They pursued it with a remorseless interrogation point. 'Benares and all those places!' 'Darjiling and the Snows!' 'The marble angel over the well the murdered Englishwomen were thrown into at Cawnpore—the mutiny time, don't you know, when the British soldiers cut locks from the victims' heads and swore to kill a native for every hair of them. You are going to miss all that! Now do tell us your idea.'

It was the idea that worried them, the suspicion of a hidden motive that might possibly justify our course, a motive that had entirely escaped them in planning *their* tours round the world. This was acute torment, and our commonly evasive replies intensified it. We finally found it necessary to assume a brutal candour in order to escape at all; and I shall not soon forget the appalled look of a particularly pertinacious lady from Cincinnatti when Orthodocia fixed her with a glittering eye, and said:

'Madam, has it never occurred to you that possibly we might not have enough money?'

It never had—the notion that anybody could start on a journey round the world not financially equipped to explore every part of it was impossible to her. But we found this counter-inquiry so serviceable to us in warding off attack on the subject of our plans that we practised it in our cabins before the looking-glass, and were soon able to silence the most inquisitive and marvelling of our fellow-passengers at one shot, so to speak. Nothing is more discouraging to human curiosity than the revelation of penury, and the curio shops up to date had left us in possession of more penury than anything else. We found it very portable, however; we had no anxiety about losing it, and were not obliged to label it except under the circumstances I have described, so that it did not greatly inconvenience us. And we found it so useful at times in assisting us to dispense with the purchase of unnecessary objects that I should seriously advise you not to think of making any extended tour without a certain amount of it within easy reach.

And so on the *Khedive*—the P. and O. are as happy as the Royal Navy in the choice of names for their ships—we sailed away down the Hooghly again from Calcutta. It began to seem as if life were always to mean the changing from one great ship to another. The watching by day the soft southern seas break into chrysoprase about our bows; the listening by night to the deck piano as one reposed in one's Chinese chair, and observed flirtations, and imbibed lemon squashes through a straw; the fumbling to bed in the dark when one had forgotten, under luminous stars, that other lights were turned off promptly at half-past ten. Existence becomes identified, in a trip round the world, with the P. and O. It is difficult for the moment to imagine it taken up under less ideal conditions at the end. After all there is no end; once go round the world and you are a fated traveller. Life condenses itself ever after into a desire to go again.

The *Khedive* was our first crowded P. and O. ship. I don't know how many people were on her, but India was beginning to empty out for the hot weather, and every berth was taken. And life was amusing on the *Khedive*—it always is on a packed P. and O. homeward-bound from India—if you don't mind the very close company of your fellow beings, or the proof your conduct gives you that you belong very intimately to animal nature, still struggling for the survival of the fittest, 'red in tooth and claw.'

The 'general's wife'—there is always a general's wife—contributes as generously as anybody to make the trip interesting. She is usually a large, stalwart creature, very well preserved, with smooth dark-gray hair drawn back from a somewhat high-coloured countenance, and the air of a commander of cavalry. She promenades the deck on the general's arm *only*. She is the warlike personification of the domestic virtues. She wears a capacious sealskin coat when the night breeze is chilly, but you feel instinctively that it does her injustice, that to be properly appreciated her massive exterior deserves the revelation of dinner dress. She sits down unostentatiously, but where she sits she makes a Place, and everybody on deck is aware that that Place is occupied by the general's wife. It is also noticeable that nobody drops unconsciously in the general's wife's steamer-chair, as everybody does into the steamer-chairs of other people.

It is a novelty to the transatlantic feminine mind to encounter this lady in the ante-chamber of the bath when it is the turn of the transatlantic person belonging to it to go in first. Probably nine-tenths of the rest of the women on the ship would say, 'After you, madam!' and receive an icy bow of acknowledgment as the general's wife sailed in ahead, towels flying. But while seniority of years appeals to one's consideration, there is nothing infirm about the general's wife, and her assumption of seniority in the Army List is nettling. So the feminine democrat takes firm hold of her toilet bag and her right of priority, looks sweetly at the general's wife, and keeps an expectant eye upon the door. The stout stewardess fusses about in an anxious, unhappy way; consults with the thin stewardess in a corner; meditates admonishing the transatlantic female as to her duty; concludes that it would be better not—the door opens, letting out a shrinking creature in a dressing-gown — one convulsive gesture from the commandress herself, 'Don't be long, please, miss,' from the imploring stewardess; and the door closes again upon the feminine democrat, whose cheerful salt-water splashes relieve the monotony of the next ten minutes for the general's wife. The single glance she gets from that august countenance as she trips forth, cool and serene, is worth the exercise of much hardihood as a new sensation and a social revelation.

Another interesting lady is the Scandal of the ship, not so much on her own account, for she may be the most commonplace flirt imaginable, but as an illustration of the bias of the saloon in the matter of scandal. She is usually a pretty widow, fresh to her weeds. She has a nice little boy whom she tugs about like a poodle. For the first few days she takes little notice of anybody, but sits apart, hugs her grief, and plays plaintively with the little boy, often accompanied by a junior officer whom she has apparently known in a former state, and who has a brotherly care and regard for her. Meanwhile the passengers, gathered from every presidency and province in India, say 'all sorts of things' about her, which means really only one sort of thing, with details, and frescoes, and gilt edges, and many embroideries. The general's wife saith nothing; she is never known to speak to anybody but the general and the captain and the stewardess, but the temperature that she carries about with her goes down twenty degrees when the Scandal is anywhere in her vicinity. And everybody looks at the Scandal as she walks downcast through the crowded dining saloon to her place, the women commenting on the belladonna in her eyes and the powder on her cheeks, and the 'perfectly *awful*' way she laces. Noting with horror, too, that 'she's even got *him* in tow,' referring to some infatuated Commissioner of gray hairs and unimpeachable respectability who brings her afternoon tea to her in the very shadiest corner of the deck.

There is a climax of indignation when the Scandal is reported to have been seen smoking a cigarette with a junior officer—'that boy!'—on the hurricane deck at 10.30 P.M.

Then behold, there issueth forth from her cabin, where she hath been lying these four days with *mal de mer*, attended by her maid, who beareth rugs and a French novel, and the head-steward with burgundy and biscuits, a certain Honourable Mrs. Fitzomnipo. And the Honourable Mrs. Fitzomnipo beckoneth to the Scandal, who cometh trippingly, and they two embrace. Also the Scandal shareth the biscuits and the burgundy and laugheth with the Honourable Mrs. Fitzomnipo long, long laughs; and for two whole days the intimacy of the Scandal and the Honourable Mrs. Fitzomnipo is conspicuous. Now be it known that the Honourable Mrs. Fitzomnipo weareth a dickey and a slight moustache and smoketh cigarettes, not after dark, nor in secret places of the ship, but openly, aft of the smoking cabin, according to rules, in the broad afternoon, under the very noses of the scandalised, for she is the Honourable Mrs. Fitzomnipo of Grosvenor Square.

After the second day the intimacy of the Scandal with this lady is no longer noticeable because of her intimacies with quite two-thirds of the other ladies on the ship. The Hon. Mrs. Fitzomnipo whiffs and sniffs with the indifference of Grosvenor Square and will have none of them; but the Scandal is propitiable and walks the deck daily with her former calumniators, who still calumniate, but with caution and a smiling front. 'Oh yes! with pleasure!' one might have heard her say one day before the voyage was over, and turning beheld the

'THAT LOY!'

general's wife, urbane, majestic, smiling, and holding in her hand a Scripture text birthday book, and giving forth entreaty that the Scandal should write her name therein!

There is a large percentage of invalids, mostly ladies, in a state of collapse from the climate, but so glad to be going home that they bring no shadow with them and are brought up on deck every day in becoming *négligé* to receive compliments and inquiries. There are quantities of ayahs and babies, and ayahs and babies always make their immediate surroundings cheerful. They feed their small charges just outside your cabin at the gruesome hour of seven; and for really interesting sleep-barring conversation a dozen Anglo-Indian infants, ranging from six months to four years, talking Indo-Anglian, may be commended. After that all day long you can't ascend the companion-way without meeting a broad avalanche of smiling ayah, or descend without running into one, or step on deck in any quarter where babies are allowed without danger of personally damaging some fat brown figure wrapped in its muslins and crooning over its pale-faced little charge. It is a pleasure to see an ayah and a baby. The baby loves the ayah and the ayah would lie down and be trampled upon for the baby. She sings low monotonous Hindoo melodies to it, and the baby pulls the round gold hoops in her ears and pats her face and makes her very happy. The mother is rather out of it, but her turn comes later.

But I am dallying too long in the ship, as people are apt to do who write about P. and O. voyages, and yet have told you nothing of the dances in the evening on deck with late little suppers down below, dances managed with an anxious countenance by the ship's doctor, who is so desirous that everybody shall have a good time that he gives a personal polka to each young lady on board in turn. Then he retires behind the smoking cabin and heroically collapses into a puddle, for it is only the very, very young and light-hearted who can polka more than three times with impunity in the Bay of Bengal.

If you look in your old school geography at the map of India you will find about half-way down its eastern coast the city of Madras. One has unpleasant associations with Madras—it would be difficult to say precisely why, unless more than its share of famine and cholera reports have clustered about it—but one realises them all when one gets there. The *Khedive's* hot shipful spent two or three hours at Madras. People with two or three hours in port always behave in exactly the same way. The time of starting is invariably put up in the companion-way; but there are instances on record when the time of starting has been extended, and the first three-quarters of an hour is usually devoted to desultory inquiries as to the possibility of this. Then there are the peddlers to bargain with, to hesitate over, to dismiss. Then it becomes a question whether it is really worth while to go on shore at all 'in this sun.' Then, putting off from the ship's ladder, is seen a party of two or three people one knows. The example settles it, there is a hasty rush cabinward for pith helmet, parasol, gloves and umbrella, a speedily ungraceful descent of the ship's side; and the next sixty minutes are spent in a convulsive effort to see something through the holes in the sides of one's *ticca-gharri*, dashed with a morbid anxiety about the going off of the ship.

A ship some distance out in the harbour is a much more uncomfortable thing to have to do with than a ship well roped up to the wharf. There is absolutely no security about her. She may be slowly on the wing even while you stand on the shore and hail a sampan to take you out to her; and the vision of a chase is appalling. These were the emotions with which Orthodocia and I saw Madras in what seemed about five hours and a half, but was really only about thirty-seven minutes. One doesn't get a coherent idea of an Oriental city in thirty-seven minutes, feeling like this; and all I remember of our drive through Madras was the awful filth and apparent depravity of the place, with its imported 'public buildings' towering above, and the keen commiseration that we felt for such English people as fate ordained to live there. We saw a remnant of the old cruel days too, wheeled under a shed in an enclosure—a veritable Juggernaut's car, hideous beyond conception in barbarous red and yellow and green, with heavy wooden wheels, and a canopy, the erection about twelve feet high. The natives round about laughed when we stopped to look at the thing, and one or two of them grovelled before it, whereupon our driver pointed out our duty in the matter of backsheesh. All our recollections of Sunday-school literature failed to make Juggernaut's car impressive to us, and the burlesquing of the sacrificial rite completed the mockery. It seemed a grotesque old joke, and we laughed and drove on.

Two other things stand out in my memory of Madras. One is that the gentle, long-haired, human-looking Indian cattle had their horns painted red, and wore strings of blue beads round their necks. The other is that we saw in its mother's arms a year old Hindoo baby with light blue eyes. The effect was extraordinary and we thought our find unique at the time, but somebody told us afterwards that it was not uncommon in pure Hindoos, and that the blue-eyed one was thought a lucky baby.

They were selling famine pictures on the ship when we got hastefully back, three-quarters of an hour before she sailed, hideous groups of human skeletons, almost naked, every bone of their wretched bodies starting through its scanty covering of skin, photographed to show the awful possibilities of human endurance of hunger. The photographs were survivals of the last great famine. It seemed a sacrilegious thing to have caught and perpetuated such a horror; but there were people who bought the pictures at a rupee apiece, and I have no doubt they are adorning more than one West End album to-day—with violets and 'marguerites' hand-painted round the page.

XXXII

WE had only three fellow-passengers from Ceylon to Bombay : a Spanish gentleman who looked crossed in hopeless love, but had no English to reveal or disguise the fact ; a planter from the Himalayas, with sunstroke, who told us three times at every meal that Indian tea was the only beverage of the entire Royal Family of Russia, and that people who drank Chinese tea were mad ; and the planter's elderly wife. The tide of travel had turned the other way for the hot weather. The *Khedive*, heaving a sigh of relief as she dropped a small contingent at Ceylon, immediately groaned again with repletion as double the number of homesick exiles boarded her. And after the plentiful fat ayahs, and precocious babies, and inquisitive ladies' maids, and flirting couples that elbowed each other on the homeward-bound ship, diverting as they were at the time, the *Shannon's* cool spacious saloons and wide empty decks were full of solace and delight. We had all the captain's jokes and stories to ourselves, which was something, for the captain was a Welshman and witty ; and the attention of two stewards apiece. We could anchor our steamer-chairs anywhere undisturbed under the great canvas awnings ; and the only other specimens of womankind upon the ship besides ourselves and the old lady aforesaid were the stewardesses. To reckon this an advantage may seem disloyalty to the sex ; but an accident of travel will sometimes precipitate extreme views. Our accident of travel had been a young lady of the model Miss Mitford type, which in itself was nothing against her, except in so far as it aroused a spirit of envy and impossible emulation in Orthodocia and me. We had to share our three-berthed cabin with her, however, and one objects to extravagant virtue in a person one shares a cabin with in the Bay of Bengal. It was one of this young woman's little peculiarities, I remember, to pin a towel over the porthole, so that all the breeze blew down upon her berth below it; another, to ask us in a pained way if we would be good enough to let her have the cabin to herself every morning for an hour before breakfast 'for private devotion,' which we found slightly inconvenient. Her neatness was of the awful, unrelenting order, too, and one day she handed Orthodocia a fragment of paper on which curling-tongs had been rubbed, and which had somehow strayed to her side of the cabin, in frigid fear 'lest it might be lost.' It was wholly due to our experience with this young person, who belongs to a class the best-regulated steamship company in the world cannot avoid carrying, that we were so grateful for the exclusive society of the old lady-planter and the stewardesses. But it was a little like living alone in a very large, luxurious, floating hotel.

Early one misty morning came the rattling of chains, and the shouting of orders, and the blowing of steam-whistles, and then that sudden deathly stillness that told us we were in port at Bombay. There is an opulence about the very name of Bombay that stimulates one's imagination, and the expectations we took up on deck with us glowed with the colour and warmth of all the East Indian in merchandise or literature. The harbour-sight we saw was one of the kind that tempt people to the use of superlatives. We lay at anchor far out from shore in what seemed to be a wide shining space where the mist had lifted. In and out of this went heavy schooners and shrill steam tugs, and the slow-moving bulk of a great gunboat. Through the half transparent whiteness we saw far and near the spectral forms of scores of ships, some quite still, without a rope swaying from their high blurred rigging, others going silently about their shadowy business, threading their way through the most magnificently populous harbour in the world. The city on the shore made a fringed outline of spire and dome against the sky more darkly gray; and round about where the city was not went the protecting arms of the harbour, indistinctly high. An island loomed up in the middle of the basin, ringing with the hammers of fortification, they told us, though we were too far away to hear them. Suddenly, as we looked, a rosy flush came into the sky behind the city, which seemed to grow toward us; and the long three-cornered sail of a fishing boat that drifted near took on a touch of gold. Then one by one the great ships silhouetted themselves upon a sky that was gloriously blue and a sea that twinkled in the sun, and the mist fled raggedly to the hills round about, and Bombay, in all the beauty of her architecture and all the strength of her riches, lay before us.

We were put ashore at the 'Apollo Bunder,' probably the best known spot in India. It is a long, broad, stone-cased quay, with picturesque angles and slippery steps that you descend to reach the water's edge when the tide is out. The most notable of the clubs have quarters overlooking the Apollo Bunder. Here the yachts of the jaded civilians go forth, and here the band plays and the fashionable drive in the evenings. Here, too, the new Viceroy always makes his first utterance on Indian soil, which consecrated the spot long ago. Landing there, one is set down in the very midst of Bombay, among her finest churches, Government buildings, university colleges, shops, hotels. I decline to tell you anything about the remarkable public buildings of Bombay, except that they are massively proportioned and beautifully designed, which you have probably read books of travel enough to take for granted; but about the hotel at which we were presently domesticated—the best, by all report, in Bombay—I will be more communicative, for a bad hotel appeals to human interest the wide world over, while public buildings are a weariness to the flesh.

I believe that the hostelries of India are the worst in the world—in proportion to the luxury of the resident population indisputably the worst. The room that balanced a tariff of ten rupees a day was a tiny place in a tortuous passage, with disjointed wooden shutters opening on a court behind, grimy and dismal, and largely decorated with the cigar ends and torn papers and empty beer bottles of the last inhabitant. The bed might have been made of old red sandstone. The atmosphere was unsavoury. The passage was dark; we were in constant terror of stepping on native servants asleep outside their masters' rooms. When a gong resounded from the hall below we descended to be fed. The dining-room was full of long tables, and people hurrying to the chairs that private servants were guarding for them, or to those that were the common plunder of the masses. The people were of all nationalities under heaven, and seemed equally ravenous, Scythian or barbarian, bond or free. Quantities of worn-out tourists, scores of Anglo-Indians, homeward bound from all over the Empire, and thankfully starting by tomorrow's mail; a resident civil service contingent, with its wives, that lived in the hotel, and looked on calm, superior; a native prince, inclined to be drunk and disorderly; and a sprinkling of callow young subalterns, who looked as if they had just managed to pass their examination, and could be expected to do nothing further for the rest of their natural lives; not to speak of the crimson-faced old officer who bellowed for his nutriment, and threatened 'odds, curries, and chops!' to break every glass on the table over the head of the waiter if he took such a Pluto's abode of a time to get it. I have paraphrased the oaths, which didn't seem to shock anybody, however. The Anglo-Indians nearest looked up and smiled merely, and said one to another, 'Awful liver, poor chap!'

I cannot even now recall the hours Orthodocia and I spent in anxious suspense at that dining table without qualms of hunger, rising wrath, and an inward distress. We had not engaged a private servant. Some one of those kind philanthropic lunatics who go about distributing information they haven't got to people who don't want it had told us we should not need one in a hotel; and the pleasant boarding-house of Calcutta is practically unknown in Bombay. So we were at the mercy of the hotel waiters, of whom there were possibly two, liberally speaking, to every score of people; and who naturally selected the most gilded guests for their attentions. At this period of our trip round the world neither Orthodocia nor I looked particularly well gilded; so they passed us by on the other side, blind to the hungry glance, and deaf to appealing word. On one occasion we secured a vegetable dish full of potatoes, which made, divided between us, a substantial if somewhat monotonous meal. On another we were compelled to pass from soup to sour oranges without a single incident in the dreary waste between. On still another we were politely handed the bill of fare, and apparently expected to consume it, for we got nothing else during the entire repast. Orthodocia regarded it hungrily, but when I proposed to divide it she said no, she was sure such a mixture of English and

French would disagree with us. And perhaps she was right, though the self-denial was difficult at the time.

The world of Bombay rolled by below the balcony, when the sun was gone and a coolness crept in from the sea—Hindoo and Mahommedan babwos elbowing unctuous Parsees, palanquin-bearers elbowing both, water-carriers, peddlers, jugglers, beggars. It was the time of a Hindoo festival, and all the Hindoos of the street, men, women and children, were strangely splashed, as to their garments, with a bright magenta dye. It was absurdly funny in the children, who looked exactly as if some facetious person had dipped them into an ink-bottle and carefully wrung them out again. Carriages drove by with ladies in them, native ladies brightly attired, unveiled, and bareheaded, the wives and daughters of the Parsee merchant princes, who let their womankind look at the world unafraid. Half a dozen conjurers besought backsheesh below the balcony, heads thrown back, eyes appealing. They would do all they could for a four-anna bit. We held it up to one of the ragged creatures, and instantly he was seated upon the ground, unfastening the basket that contained his stock-in-trade. Out stole the twisting bodies of two or three yard long snakes, one of which immediately tried to escape across the street, to the intense terror of the *ticca-gharri* men opposite. The conjurer caught it and hung the three round his neck. One struck at his lean brown hand, and he held it up, bleeding, to increase the backsheesh. Then he put the snakes back, and brought forth two bags. From one he released a most alarming looking cobra, from the other a mongoose, tied by the neck with a string. The unfortunate little beast, which looked about the shape of a lemonade bottle and the size of a small kitten, made the most violent efforts to be off, and acted as if it had never had so much as a bowing acquaintance with a cobra in all its miserable life. The cobra, rising and undulating and swaying with majesty that defied the degradation of its circumstances, struck two or three times at the mongoose and finally did attract the wretched creature's attention. By that time, though, the conjurer thought he had shown us a generous four annas' worth, and unceremoniously bundled his possessions into their respective bags. We dropped the coin, and he went off, sucking his finger. We saw conjurers several times in India, but found them disappointing. They are clever enough, with their coins and their handkerchiefs and their rabbits, but they are not impressive, and in that country of occultism one naturally expects them to be impressive—necromantic, as Orthodocia said. Once we heard what struck our nerves as a really thrilling incantation, low, weird, suggestive of the most intimate connection with the Evil One. I bent and strained my ear to catch the syllables of that request for the assistance of the Prince of Darkness. What do you think they were?

<blockquote>
'Buffalo Bill come oudh <i>to-night</i>!
Buffalo Bill come <i>oudh</i> to-night!'
</blockquote>

Buffalo Bill seemed to have won an enviable reputation in the far East. It was the second time we had heard his name on the lips of a dweller there. And we concluded that since the days of the travellers who first told us of these things, conjuring had become a degraded art.

'Gymkana' sports were going on in an enclosure opposite the hotel that first day we spent in Bombay, and we fell in with the multitude to see the 'tent-pegging' by the officers of a regiment stationed near. With a vision in my mind of two gallant fellows flying past on horseback and picking up a tent on their spears between them as they went, which was the only form of tent-pegging that struck me as being adapted to warfare with native tribes, I asked a kindly old Anglo-Indian near me where the tents were. He smiled politely, and said there were no tents—I would see. And presently I did see, when a splendidly-sitting young officer came thundering by on a gallant Waler, and there was a flash toward the ground, and he rode on, lance erect, with a large wooden peg, the earth still clinging where it had been driven in, on the end of it. Then the next came, and the next, and the next, and some succeeded but most missed, for this is anything but an easy thing to do. And the sight was exhilarating, for some of the horses were Arabs, and some were 'barbs,' and both they and their riders were very fine animals indeed.

But I saw that Anglo-Indian go away and speak to three other Anglo-Indians, and they all turned their backs and laughed to rend themselves, and I had an extremely uncomfortable idea that I knew what it was about.

XXXIII

They looked so human with their gentle eyes, so like other people, whether they talk Guzerati or English, whether one saw them in the market-place or at meat, that it was difficult to believe this horror of them. Yet it was true, for there were the facts and statistics in a little handbook in the reading-room of the hotel, facts and statistics of to-day and yesterday, and not of any remote period of anti-civilisation. This, as to time; and as to place, not three miles from where we sat, on the topmost point of Malabar Hill, an eminence which also bore the residence of Lord Reay, Governor of the Bombay Presidency. We asked the hotel manager, who was a Parsee, if he had ever visited the spot. He shook his head and shrugged his shoulders just as an Englishman might have done talking of the churchyard or the family vaults. 'Parsees go only once,' he said, 'and then they are carried.' But he advised us to go; all tourists did, he said, and it was easy to get tickets. So we arranged to drive next morning very early to see the Towers of Silence on Malabar Hill, whither the Parsee living bear the Parsee dead, bidding them a stranger farewell than is conceived by any other people of any other creed on earth.

The city was full of warm mists and odours as we drove through it in the swathing gray of the Indian dawn. Men lay on the pavements, rows of them, in the stupor of sleep, their heads on their bony brown arms. The crows were visibly astir, flapping heavily from the trees to the streets in search of garbage, or sitting in lines on the shop verandahs, planning operations for the day. The tall, silent many-windowed, pink-and-yellow houses of native Bombay seemed to lean together above our heads across the narrow streets we rattled through; and their ragged little wooden balconies and casements looked like shreds of ancient finery, ready to drop at their feet. The Hindoo temples were all shut, but a few tall Mahommedans were threading their way to where a white mosque dome lifted itself above the squalid shops that clustered round it. We began to go uphill; and the city gathered together behind as we ascended, in its lordly magnificence, its conquering civilisation, and its outlying masses of barbarism that as yet knew civilisation only as a compelling law. The houses grew fewer and the gardens larger. We turned into the last gradual ascent, a broad white road, sending clouds of

'THE TOWERS OF SILENCE.'

dust up behind us, and we stopped at a flight of stone steps that led to an arched gate. Two native soldiers stood in the Queen's uniform at the gate, and looked at us with surprise. It was late in the season and early in the day for people who wanted to see the century-old sight they guarded from the over-curious.

Orthodocia went up to one of them with intrepidity and showed him our passes. He shook his head and said something in his own tongue. Neither of us understood it in the very least. I introduced a phrase which I had carefully concocted on the way from our Calcutta 'Handbook,' and which I intended to mean, 'We wish to see the Towers of Silence.' But the man only looked at his fellow and grinned. I tried another phrase, and yet another, but comprehension did not come. Then I reflected that perhaps the language of the Bengali baboo was not necessarily that of the native 'Tommy' of Bombay, and later investigation proved this to be the case. Finally one of the men pointed with his gun to a small house near by,-and nodded his head violently as Orthodocia made as if she would knock. So she knocked loudly, and presently there appeared, in blinking undress a very short, stout old Parsee, who instantly retreated again. We then sat down beneath a mango tree and awaited events.

The old Parsee was not long in reappearing, tall red cap and gown and girdle and all. In his hand he carried a large key, with which he beckoned to us to follow him. He went up the steps, unlocked the gate, and let us in. The road still ascended before us through the outskirts of a tropical garden, and we climbed to another iron gate, which the old Parsee unlocked. Then we stood in the dead calm of the morning, with the yellow light in the Eastern sky threatening every moment to break into flame, in a strange place. Flowers bloomed around us, those crimson and purple flowers of the tropics that are all sense and no soul. Bordered paths led in different directions, neatly kept, and clumps of trees did their best to give the spot shadow and sentiment. Below lay the city, fringed with cocoanut palms, gathering light, and the wide blue waters of the bay with its quiet fleet. Not a human being was in sight, and the stillness was absolutely unbroken, for the old Parsee gave up his efforts at English at last, finding us unresponsive, and stood apart with his arms folded. The sight that struck our Western eyes so strangely was nothing new to him.

For we were not looking at the flowers, or the city, or the sunrise, but at five strange round, white structures that rose at a little distance, divided from us by a wall, in the midst of heavy masses of trees. The oldest of them had been there two hundred years, with never a profanation of its name or office—a Tower of Silence all that time. The others had been added as they were needed. They were not vaults, and they were not cemeteries, yet their business was with the dead. Perhaps I need not tell you how they first arose among the Persian hills three thousand years ago by command of Zoroaster; how he, believing the elements to be sacred symbols, decreed that they should never be defiled. Neither earth, nor fire, nor water should serve a Parsee after death had made him a corrupt thing. His body should be placed on a tower high above all human habitations, that living men should escape its pollution, and no foot should enter there but those of its bearers who should leave it and come away. And the towers of Zoroaster's thought three thousand years ago were the towers with the latest sanitary improvements that stood before us in the month of March and the year of grace eighteen hundred and eighty-nine, which gives one an idea of the real meaning of conservatism.

There was a toy tower, a little model, in the garden for the amusement of visitors, and, as we contemplated it in the scientific spirit a model always inspires, the old Parsee gabbled his oft-told tale of filters and conduits. And even as we looked from this to the five real towers with a fascination that a horror sometimes has when it is slightly grotesque, and noted the square sixth one the old man pointed out as set apart for criminals, a commotion seemed to begin in the trees about them. Then one by one there flapped heavily out of the branches, dark, hideous birds, with fierce hooked claws and featherless heads and necks. They began to come in twos and threes, then in half-dozens, and settled closely together in high-shouldered rows, heads looking over, along the top of the stone parapet of the nearest tower. They knew the funeral was coming long before we did.

It was a child, the old Parsee said, as the procession wound up below us by a different road. The bearers carried it between them on a sort of trough with a sheet thrown over it. Before the funeral left the house, prayers had been said containing many moral precepts, and a dog had been made to look at the child, for the mystic sacred property of the dog's glance. The corpse-bearers wore pure white, as all the mourners did, who walked a long way behind the little draped heap in the trough, two and two. They carried a white handkerchief between them, but this emblem of grief was enough, it seemed—there was no weeping.

The strange procession passed on, and up, and reached the foot of the path that led to what looked like a black hole in the side of the tower. The vultures above crowded together more thickly, and stretched out their evil heads. The corpse-bearers entered with their burden; the mourners turned back and went into one of the Sagri, the prayer houses, where the sacred fire burns incense and sandal wood all day and all night, to pray.

A moment, and then all the air seemed full of the flapping of dark wings, and hoarse cries, and the parapet was quite empty. We turned away in unspeakable loathing, angry that we had come, and unable to rid ourselves of the imaginative carnage behind the great round wall; and as we turned a splendid wave of sunlight spread over the white towers and the palm-trees and the garden, and gave the horror a sardonic note. Descending, the old Parsee offered us bunches of flowers from the garden, but there should have been no flowers in such a place, since flowers grow on quiet graves, and we would have none of them. There was only one thing to do, and that was to get away as fast as possible from the ghoulish revelry behind us. So we hurried down the path and through the scarlet hibiscus bushes, putting many steps between it and us. We might have saved ourselves the trouble, for a turn in the road unexpectedly disclosed the towers again, and the vultures were flapping lazily back to their places.

XXXIV

THAT day in Bombay on which we made up our minds that we could not leave India without seeing its pearl of great price—the Taj—occurred rather later in the year than was advisable for a long trip by rail. People shook their heads when we talked about it, and advised us to be careful of what we ate and drank; told us stories, too, of unacclimatised Europeans who travelled in the hot weather, and were taken out dead at the end of the journey. And there would be hardly anybody in the up-country trains they said; all the world that could move at all was moving the other way. Agra would be very 'quiet.' One could hardly say it to people who made that bustling Bombay hotel the liveliest of all places, but privately we set down this last detraction from the tourist's pleasures at Agra to be an enhancement of the same; while we were grateful enough for the other cautions, and promised to bear them in mind. And so, about half-past six one hot evening in March, we were making acquaintance with the 'Bombay and Baroda' railway station, with our faces set towards the North-West Provinces of India, and our feet turned thither.

It was much like any other. Men were hanging about the platform selling newspapers and fruit, bells were ringing, engines shunting, *ticca-gharris* waiting, just as they do everywhere else, and if it were not for the complexion and clothes which prevailed it would have been hard to guess which continent we were travelling in. And the noise. The noise was frightful. Every piece of luggage was transported by at least four coolies, and they all talked at once, the possessor of the best lungs apparently demonstrating himself entitled to the most backsheesh. Our modest effects—two portmanteaux and a Japanese basket—were instantly hidden from view by a bawling multitude, and when we saw them again were surrounded by perspiring brown creatures in dirty loin-cloths, three deep. Quite fifteen of them demanded four annas apiece for carrying our effects, and it was in the midst of the problem of how to satisfy them with ten that a sahib, arriving to see us off, informed us that the proper thing was four annas to the lot. Then he stamped his foot and used some forcible Hindustani in the Anglo-Indian way, which the coolies evidently understood, for they all fled with one accord. The sahib's next proceeding was to cast ruthlessly out of the window a paper bag of fresh figs which we had provided for our refreshment, on hearing that we had bought them of a street hawker. This looked high-handed, but if, as he said, cholera was raging in the district they had probably come from, it was not wholly without justification. Then he inspected what he called our 'kit,' pronounced it incomplete, and disappeared. It consisted, beside our luggage, of a rug and a pillow apiece, flannel dressing-gowns, the contents of our hand-bags, half a dozen of Kipling's Indian stories, 'Twenty-one Days in India,' and two palm-leaf fans. The rugs were coarsely woven striped blankets, the pillows gaudy cotton bags stuffed with wool, sold in the hall of the hotel to all comers and goers; for Indian railway carriages are devoid of the stuffy comforts of Pullman cars, and from the Plains to the Hills it is far to go. The sahib came back with a box of ice and many lemonade bottles. We protested, saying that we expected to find all necessary nourishment and refreshment at the railway eating-houses by the way, but he assured us that we would often be attacked by thirst fifty miles from a lemon or anything related to it, and so it proved.

Night was coming on as we moved northward out of the station, and we could not see the Ghauts that frowned down upon the railway, except as great indistinct masses against the sky. The train ran slowly, and stopped occasionally at an outlying station where the lights revealed groups of Hindoos, Mussulmans, and Parsees, flashing on their white draperies and shining in their dark handsome faces, as they conferred or disputed, or walked about with slow graceful dignity, picturesque against the shadowy palms behind. Then came a long run into rumbling darkness that shut blankly down everywhere, warm, heavy, mysterious. India was outside—

India as we had not known it yet; but we could see only the lamp-lit carriage and each other. I remember wondering what an Indian railway carriage would be like—perhaps you have wondered too. This one, for eight people, was not luxurious, but big and well ventilated and comfortable, an English and American compromise, with the door and platform at one end, broad leather-covered seats running lengthwise, and a little toilet-room at the other end. The floor was bare, and upper berths might be let down from the walls of the carriage if they were wanted. There was no officious black porter to pull them down unnecessarily though. Railway authorities in India are willing to let you have all the comfort you can get for the price of your ticket. One thing more: the windows were fitted with *khus-khus tatties*, wheels woven of fragrant Indian grass, that revolved at a push through a tank below with water in it, and came up refreshingly cool and fragrant and dripping for the hot air to blow through at every turn. The *khus-khus tattie* is one of the hot weather housekeeping comforts of the memsahib also. It is an ingenious addition to a railway carriage, and beguiled hours of our two-day journey for Orthodocia and me. For neither Mr. Rudyard Kipling nor the lamented Ali Baba can be relied upon to cover the entire distance from Bombay to Agra, and they do not leave one, somehow, in a frame of mind to be appreciative of the more instructive authors one carries at the bottom of one's portmanteau.

We noted all these things, and then, with happy confidence and anticipation, went to sleep. I suppose it was three or four hours later that I became conscious of something unusual and electric in the air, and awoke to see my friend sitting bolt upright, frozen with horror, her eyes fixed upon the floor between our berths. For coolness we had chosen upper ones.

'Orthodocia!' I said, in as collected a manner as I could assume at such short notice, 'are you dreaming *again*?'

For answer she pointed where she looked. 'A tarantula!' she said.

The thing was on the floor, but kept making rapid, short, convulsive excursions, now in this direction, now in that. It was dark-coloured, and its body seemed about the size round of a teacup, legs in proportion.

'Throw your boot at it!' I suggested, in a terrified whisper.

'Throw your own!' returned Orthodocia, indignantly, '*I* don't want to attract its attention.'

But it did not seem to me that I did either, and the situation resolved itself into a prospect of sitting up all night to watch the erratic movements of the creature, with sudden and complete submersions in our blankets whenever it ran further than usual toward either of us. We tried to grasp the problem of what to do in case of being bitten by a tarantula, but found that the emergency had been wholly left out of our calculations. 'You should work a drowned person in and out under the arms,' said Orthodocia in a distracted effort of memory, 'and twist your handkerchief round with a stick above the place where an artery has been cut, and administer salt and warm water for arsenic; but I simply *can't* remember what to do for tarantula bites!'

'That is because nothing is ever done,' I responded, cheerfully; 'the bitten die at once!' Whereat, as the tarantula seemed taken with a desire to mount the wall on Orthodocia's side, she shrieked. The monster being over there, I felt at liberty to divert myself for a moment from the scene of his operations, and happened, vainly searching for a bell-rope for the purpose of stopping the train, to look at the lamp in the middle of the carriage roof. Then I laughed a long, large laugh, so that Orthodocia peeped out of her blanket with suppressed excitement. 'Is he gone?' cried she.

I pointed to the lamp, and there, where its rays were brightest, hung a small brown spider from a thread, behaving in the erratic manner which small brown spiders always assume at the end of threads, and blown this way and that by the currents of air that came in at the upper ventilators. My friend looked at it in silence for a moment, then she wrapped herself up in her blanket and turned her back upon the scene of our excitement. 'I wish,' she said tolerantly, 'that you wouldn't make such a fuss about nothing! Can't you see it's only the shadow of a harmless little spider?' and none of my revilings could elicit another word.

In the morning very early we had to change at Ahmedabad, and then we were in Guzerat, speeding north to Rajputana. And then, looking out from the carriage platform across the great levels that spread to the base of the far away Ghauts, all in a white glare of sunlight that left no twig or blade unindicated, we felt for the first time that we were in the India of belief and association, and books of travel illustrated by artists of imagination.

It was blindingly dusty, but not hot yet; the wind blew fresh across the track, and sent us shivering in for wraps. The country we saw was gaunt and dreary in all its outlines. Even the far mountains lacked the blue graciousness of mountains generally, and clave the air in hard aggressive masses, with no compromise in their tints. Occasionally we passed wheatfields and rice-paddies, but the land seemed chiefly low jungle and alkali plain. Now and then we saw, solitary in some tangled space, a tree with thick black, misshapen boughs, leafless, but bearing large flame-red flowers in thick profusion, a kind of magnolia. The Hindoos tell one that in the beginning, when all the trees were made, this one was over-vain —that it was decreed, therefore, never to bear leaves and flowers again at the same time. As we saw the tree it had a strange fierce air, as if its flowers consumed it.

Sometimes groups of huts gave the landscape a human look, and near these were always droves of the beautiful soft-coloured, soft-eyed Indian cattle, with their curving humps, that gathered in the hut yards and gazed meditatively at us as we passed, or worked the big water-wheel that sent little streams down through their master's furrows.

The station eating-houses were all alike—the inevitable curry, the inevitable breaded chop, the inevitable hurry. Almost every station had its trimly-kept flower-beds, and all the houses of the railway servants along the line were built like little white mosques, with arbours in front of them trailing purple bougainvilleas. More than once in the trees that overhung the railway buildings we fancied we saw men moving and climbing, till a great gray black-marked cunning head looked out from among the branches, and we beheld the personality Mr. Stevenson capitalises as Probably Arboreal. When we began to see these creatures oftener, going about their whimsically solemn business, dragging great tails behind them, clumsily gambolling, unafraid, within a stone's throw of the train, and camels turned out to graze the trees, and wild peacocks and parrots, and a dainty bird with a pink crest and a yellow bill, and a long hairlike white tail, that balanced itself on the telegraph wires, and an occasional skulking thing we did not know—it seemed as if we were travelling somewhere in Genesis, and that Adam might be expected to turn up anywhere along the line to name the animals.

The wide empty river-beds were strange to see, too, all sand and shale, winding for miles with a stream in the middle that a man might jump over. We rattled across the long bridges gaily enough, but in August, when 'the rains' have been pouring over India for a month, it is a different matter, and the sahibs and the memsahibs on the Bengal side are duly warned that they must post their 'home' letters a day or two earlier to allow for the whims of the watercourses.

As we entered Rajputana the country grew wilder and the colour effects more theatrical; yet in the course of the railway there seemed more huts and trees and waterwheels and pastures. Once or twice we saw a camel train, laden, crawling across the plain, or turned loose and cropping, while its turbaned masters lay under a clump of trees and rested in the heat of the day. Mount Aboo rose at our left, grim and stupendous, in the crisp dawn of the second day, and then the parched heights kept us company all the way. We had an unexpected three-quarters of an hour at Jeypoor, a delay which seemed to annoy a stately Rajput passenger who joined us there, wearing a jewelled chain and receiving many sala'ams. A little way behind the station stood his steed—he had ridden to meet the train—and his retinue of servants, dark-eyed and curious. The steed was not foam-flecked and panting; he looked rather calm and phlegmatic in fact, as if he had walked the whole way—a lordly elephant. He was richly caparisoned—why must one always say 'caparisoned' of an elephant?—and his trunk was a portable art gallery in red and blue and green. We gazed at him with a lively joy such as no exiled elephant had ever inspired, even when we were very young. He proved India to us, he illustrated it, he embodied it, annotated it, embroidered it, accompanied it in a major key. Indeed, that elephant, there on his native heath, was more thoroughly satisfactory to us than the entire Aryan contents, Sanskrit MSS. included, of Barnum and the British Museum.

He looked an amiable elephant, so Orthodocia ventured to caress his trunk with her parasol, the Rajput gentleman looking on amused. The elephant had not been accustomed, apparently, to attentions from European young ladies; at all events, he was not flattered by Orthodocia's. So he took the parasol away, gently but firmly, and with great dignity and presence of mind. It was a long-handled parasol with a large bow, and as the elephant twirled it lightly in the air in the way that elephants have with articles of the least consequence, it opened brilliantly in the sun. This annoyed the elephant still further, but he controlled himself wonderfully, merely depositing the offensive object gently upon the ground and putting his foot in it. Then he looked at Orthodocia in a fatherly way, and said something admonitory in the Rajput tongue. But an elephant, even an elephant of the best intentions, has a disagreeable accent, and we both fled incontinently behind the native gentleman, whose countenance by this time expressed acute distress. 'He no bite!' he said, reassuringly. 'Best esñalun—good, kind!' Then he went into paroxysms of grief about the parasol, and offered Orthodocia, so far as we could understand him, his entire worldly possessions in compensation. And it was with the liveliest pleasure

'MERELY DEPOSITING THE OFFENSIVE OBJECT GENTLY UPON THE GROUND AND PUTTING HIS FOOT IN IT.'

that he gathered from us that although neither houses, nor lands, nor bullocks, nor jewels would soothe our feelings, a little ride on the top of the elephant would be the balmiest consolation. 'If you are sure he won't object!' said Orthodocia.

So they brought chairs out of the station-house, and we were put up into the palanquin, and the native gentleman bowed on the platform, showing all his teeth with pleasure, and the servants walked alongside and explained matters to the elephant, and two corners of him started, followed, in the course of time, by the other two corners. It was a moment of very uncertain bliss. The motion was something like that of a Rocky Mountain on the billows of eternity, though Orthodocia says that is an exaggeration. It occupied our attention so completely, however, that I remember of the ride only a heaving dream of a wide, wide street, all pink and white, flushing and blushing in palaces and towers and arched gateways, and beautiful exceedingly—if we had only been walking. And we felt that we ought to return the animal very soon, as a matter of politeness. 'It isn't as if the gentleman had any *reason* to offer us a mount,' Orthodocia said. But afterwards we felicitated ourselves highly upon the adventure when we 'realised,' as Orthodocia remarked, the nature of it; and she has never regretted the parasol. 'Think,' she said, 'of the number of people who pass through India every year who would give *anything* to have it happen!'

The elephant dwarfed, as it were, the incidents of the rest of the journey, which not even he, nor Mr. Kipling, nor the expectation of the Taj at the end, nor the reminiscences of a trip half-way round the world, could make anything but a long, long journey. Orthodocia was delightful when she reminisced, though; it was a pleasure to hear her, especially about the prairies of the Canadian North-West. Her word-painting of Assiniboia would have made the fortune of an immigration agent. And one day, on this very journey to Agra, she said a thing which I found full of instruction. 'Haven't you often thought it funny,' my friend inquired, 'that all this time we've heard absolutely nothing from Jack?' I said no, it hadn't occurred to me. 'Well,' said she, 'I should have thought it awfully queer if I hadn't known the reason.' 'The reason?' quoth I. 'Yes—you remember that night—daisies and moonlight, and the

Aunt—at the farm ? Well, that night we quarrelled—*frightfully* !
About the crops ! And of course one doesn't expect him to write.
But I thought you must have wondered.' Now it did not require
much penetration to understand this statement of Orthodocia's,
though I rather wished she had made it sooner. One might have
invented consolations. As it was, there was nothing to do but look
out of the opposite window and pretend to take her seriously.

And so it went until the evening of the second day, when the
train rolled in between the great red ramparts of the Persian Akbar,
and Orthodocia and I, dusty and eyesore and deeply begrimed as to
our garments, set foot, rejoicing withal, in Agra, the City of the
Taj.

XXXV

Of that first night we were in Agra, I remember only a strange, fierce, confused picture. It was too late after dinner for any of the guide-book sights, so we took a *ticca-gharri* from the hotel and drove down into the city. On the way, set back somewhere among trees and gardens, we saw suggestions of scattered English bungalows, but these were few and did not obtrude themselves. We found Agra as 'native' of India as Tokio had been of Japan. Darkness was settling down over the masses of low-walled houses and narrow streets; but every squalid little open shop, chiefly holding tinselled gew-gaws, sent a flood of light into the road, which was full of people and cattle, and the gaudy little chariots, high, two-wheeled, fantastically painted, the shape of an old woman's poke bonnet, they call *ekkas*. Bullocks were harnessed to them, and wildly gesticulating black figures drove them, swinging long whips and uttering strange cries. The town seemed in a hubbub, the crowd surged in one direction—a mad grotesque crowd of men and women, boys and girls, in white and yellow and crimson scraps of drapery, gold glittering on their arms, silver at their ankles, jewels flashing in their nostrils. They crowded about our *gharri* and stared in; the children and beggars formed close about us demanding *back-*

INDIAN CATTLE.

sheesh. We were going with the crowd, and it became so dense that we could not turn. The driver struck out with his whip indiscriminately, and the syce behind used what we imagined to be voluble profanity, which scattered and silenced them for a moment; but immediately they closed in again more importunate than before. Presently we reached the end of the street, where the struggling mass was thickest and the uproar most deafening. Looking out, we saw a star-lit sky and palms waving against it. Under these a façade of duskily lighted houses, latticed and balconied, white and pink and yellow. The excited crowd swayed in front, waving torches, and from its midst into the semi-darkness rose, lofty and grotesque, and in some sort majestic, the head and neck of a camel ridden by two or three natives beating drums. The syce came round to the *gharri* window. 'See!' he shouted, 'nautch!' He turned the horse so that we saw at one side, on a sort of platform among the trees, two huge and hideous figures, blood red and grinning, for which we knew no better name than idols. Behind these something seemed to be going on. The syce invited us to descend, but we felt several degrees more comfortable in our *gharri* in that multitude. So, as we would not go to the nautch, the nautch came to us. The crowd parted, and a slender girl came through, with slow steps and passes, the drums and conches and flageolets playing with redoubled din and fury. She put her hands on her hips and looked at us. Her face was painted, and there was a charcoal addition to her eyelashes. Her features were delicately cut, and she was draped with much decency and some art; but there was a look of unutterable depravity in her round eyes, bold through their softness. We showed her a rupee and she began to dance for us.

The famous nautch! Orthodocia and I watched it begin with all the qualms and thrills that accompany a deliberate impropriety of behaviour; for many times we had heard of its iniquity, and now to witness it, alone—impromptu! But the qualms and thrills departed, one by one, leaving our consciences reprieved. For her performance was nothing more extraordinary than a succession of wrigglings and contortions, of putting one foot before and the other behind, of crossing her arms on her breast, or locking her fingers above her head. The crowd watched breathlessly, apparently with intense enjoyment, but our sense of the grace of motion was not cultivated to stand more than a very little of it, with the heat and the noise and the smells; and we were glad to escape from the inferno of which the girl with her bangles seemed the central figure and the climax.

We would not go to see the Taj, we decided next morning after breakfast, until the starlight of the early evening with the prospect of the moon at nine o'clock. After a certain point in a trip round the world one grows extremely nice about one's new sensations, most particular as to the circumstances one obtains them under. It is a sort of epicureanism of the imagination. At first one bolts things, as it were. And we knew that the Taj was the crown and glory of India, that all Indian vistas led up to it and melted away in it, that it had been the source of more extravagance of language in the people we had met who were going round the world the other way than anything else the guide-books had provided them with. We felt, therefore, that the Taj demanded a selection of circumstances and some preparation of the emotions. Orthodocia suggested dieting, but I thought it would do to abstain from any violent form of sight-seeing during the day and pass it in a state of anticipation. So we went for a quiet drive to the Fort.

'THE FORT.'

Akbar built the Fort, I find in Orthodocia's note-book—but Baedeker or Murray will tell you the same thing—one of the old conquering Moguls that left their art and religion all over India. He built it nearly three hundred years ago, of red sandstone many feet thick, and made it run half a mile along the high river-bank of the Jumna and a quarter of a mile in toward the town. India, Orthodocia remarks under this head, is not a country of old architectural monuments. It has added no Sphinx to the problems of modern humanity. (I *shall* enjoy telling you about Orthodocia and one we have!) Its peoples, she says, meaning India, builded for their time as a general thing, and the wave of the next century obliterated the traces of the last. So,

> 'Akbar's red bulwarks, shutting treasures in
> With league-long ramp of sandstone,'

gather more than their rightful share of interest and colour and feeling, as a survival showing exceptional breadth of conception and power of achievement. I'm not absolutely sure that Orthodocia is right about this; but I'm much obliged to her for the paragraph, which reads well. There is a good deal more of it; but when one is given an inch one doesn't always like to take an ell, and perhaps she will want to print it herself.

But Akbar builded and Victoria occupies. As we drove through the wide space in the tremendous walls where the iron gates used to be, a red-coated 'Tommy' lounging on guard at either side stood up very straight and importantly; and inside in an asphalt quadrangle we saw the careful white parallelograms of a British tennis-court. The roads inside the Fort were smooth and hard and wide; the sunlight lying in broad white masses over them and over the tiled roofs and shining domes that Akbar's Mussulman successors had gathered within it. Our driver, with the pertinacity of his kind, stopped half a dozen times at places which he knew all right-minded tourists wished to inspect; but we confused his notions of the desires of the *sahib-lok* [1] by declining to get out, and entirely upset them by sending him off when we reached the heart of the Fort—the scene of the extravagant domesticity of Akbar and Jahan and the rest— and strolling away through the curious old red place by ourselves.

We climbed innumerable shallow steps, glad of both topee and umbrella in the merciless sun, and then we were in a labyrinth of narrow winding passages and wide pillared chambers. A friendly hand painted on the walls pointed the way through for Europeans,

[1] Europeans.

or we should probably have been inspecting the household arrangements of Shah Jahan and his family still. It showed us first to the 'Dwan-i-Am,' that autocrat's Hall of Audience, and we entered a great roofless chamber as big as a London square, rows of pillars with arches between running along three sides of it. The sky shone blue overhead; the sun lay in a blinding square in the middle, lizards ran over the walls. The pillars had been painted in distemper once in curious designs, blue and red and yellow and green; but this early artistic effort had been obscured by a later one. The more modern artist had produced broader effects, one might say. He had a free hand, too, his massing was admirable, and there was no inequality in his treatment. He had stood sublimely on a step-ladder and dipped his brush in that pigment exalted in domestic economy all the world over—whitewash. The local authorities had done it in honour of

'THE MORE MODERN ARTIST HAD PRODUCED BROADER EFFECTS.'

some visiting dignitary years ago; then the Prince of Wales came, and the British Resident tried to let him see the pattern underneath, but the genius the pail-artist was still more *en évidence* than that of his predecessor. This is a mark of esteem, Orthodocia found out somewhere, still very popular in native India. For any guest of consideration the Rajah will whitewash all over—his house, his stables, his temples, any antiquities on the premises he thinks the stranger may be interested in, his record, his grandmother. It is ennobling, but monotonous in general effect.

We followed the hand, and it showed us into a wide empty raised terrace, columned like the other, looking into the garden, with a great black marble slab in it that once upheld Shah Jahan's golden throne and flashed back the stones that were set therein. Here he must have sat magnificently in his gold-embroidered robes inwrought with jewels, and heard petitions and dispensed justice, and looked upon slaves, and received tribute, and watched the feats of his courtier horsemen, and listened to the laughter of his dark-eyed harem peeping through the *grilles* in the wall above his head. The hand led on and we found ourselves in a maze of dusty corridors and twisted stairs, with here and there a mysterious windowless cell-like room that suggested what domestic insubordination must have meant in the establishment of Shah Jahan. We went through one of them gingerly enough, for it had been let to a family extremely resentful of intrusion—a thousand or so of Indian wild bees. If they had decided to put their minds to it they could have stung us to death in half an hour, but their attention was entirely occupied with their own affairs.

There seemed to be nobody in the place but an occasional native who followed us furtively in the hope of backsheesh. To such as these Orthodocia would turn with an air of majesty and say imperatively 'Jow!' I have not the least idea of the meaning of 'Jow!' I don't much think Orthodocia had either, and I am convinced that the natives had not; but usually when she had said it three times they went away.

The old pile was full of surprises. We stepped out once upon an open passage that ran along the top of the wall of the Fort. Little round-pillared balconies jutted out of this, and we sat down on the floor of one of these and looked away across below us at one of the most exquisitely-blended scenes one could find in the world. The sky was shimmering white at the horizon, growing bluer towards its dome. The Jumna slept among its sands and gave back the sky colour with scarcely a ripple. The river-bed lay in its windings— all pale grays and saffron-yellows, flat and wide, and across it came an endless train of slow-moving desultory cattle, that seemed accents of the colour about them, so perfectly the sand-tints were deepened and enriched in their soft dusky bodies. The drivers strolled and gossiped by the way, black-faced at this distance, white-turbaned, crimson-sashed. Along the shore the trees grew thickly, and out of them white domes and towers rose up. Closer below us lay the great ditch of the Fort, then an outer wall ; and sheer seventy feet down from our little balcony a tiny enclosed court full of palms and mango trees, and long rank grass, once made beautiful for the pleasaunce of the ladies who sat round their lord where we were sitting then, now abandoned to snakes and lizards, and the little swift green parrots that flew in and out in the sun like straight large-headed arrows about their noisy business. And all this we saw framed in the red sandstone pillars of the little balcony the Shahs had built with never a thought of us—entering into our part of the inheritance barbarism has handed down to civilisation the world over.

We left it all—the inlaid 'Dwan-i-Khas,' the bathing-house of mirrors, the chambers with long-necked holes in the walls where the slender-armed ladies of the zenana kept their jewels safely ; the whole quaint old place with its naïve grandeur and odd little tender bits of sentiment, feeling a certain gentle regret that did not attach to many scenes more pretentious and splendid. As we traced our way out again by more terraces and steps, we found in the heart of it still another garden, close-walled and impenetrable ; and high perched where no tourist foot might profane, we caught a glimpse of the flame spires of the three-domed white marble 'Gem Mosque'— 'Naginah Musjid'—where the beautiful Persians that ruled the Shahs with love's uncertain sceptre, entered the presence of Allah and swayed dreamily toward Mecca on their prayer carpets, and clasped their little henna-stained red palms in petition that they might bring sons, not daughters, to their lords.

We found a *gharri* to take us back whose driver simply declined to pass the Pearl Mosque. He spoke no English, and we no Hindustani ; and though Orthodocia said 'Jow !' in her best manner several times, it had not the least effect upon him. He remained entirely unmoved, and so did we. He presented an impassive, impenetrable back to our entreaties; he evidently knew our duty as well as his own, and was not going to have either shirked. So, as it was extremely warm sitting in a *ticca-gharri* in the March sun of the North-West Provinces of India, to say nothing of the heat of argument, we succumbed. I find in Mr. Murray's valuable 'Handbook' several columns of facts and statistics about the 'Moti Musjid'—the Pearl Mosque—but none of them seem to aid my memory much. I cannot remember, for instance, that I observed the 'trihedral projection' of the gateway, though it must have been there, or that there were fifty-eight pillars with twelve-

'THE MOTI MUSJID.'

sided shafts on square bases in the cloisters. But nobody who has ever entered this loveliest of sanctuaries can forget its sweet, cool purity, broad floor, slender pillars, arched colonnades ; every inch one's eye can make its own covered with glistening white marble, veined in gray and blue. We walked between long shadowy rows of pillars, under engrailed arches, on a platform raised somewhat above the great square central floor, and bounding it on three sides. Only this colonnade was roofed. The sun slanted dazzling white upon the marble floor and the tank for pious ablutions, and the old sun-dial in the corner, except for which the place would have been utterly empty. We wandered about it with a curious baffling sense of its meaninglessness. Wholly without incident, or sign, or emblem, it represented so high a religious abstraction that the Western eye lost sight of it, and perceived only beauty for the sake of the beautiful. The guide-book told us that 'they worshipped in the Western part.' From the opposite colonnade we could see three swelling white marble domes above this Western part, fair against the blue, and on the inner side a row of graceful minarets. We crossed the shining floor, the click of our footsteps sounding loud and clear through the emptiness of the place, to see why they worshipped in the Western part ; and we found the marble walls of the colonnade to be divided into panels, with flower wreaths sculptured on them in exquisite workmanship. We found at the end three doorways, too, one open, the others filled up with lattices of marble wonderfully cut. Beyond the open door were dusty passages and stairs that hinted so strongly of scorpions that we gave up our search for the Mussulman's religious idea in that direction.

We could not find it anywhere, but the pale, cool loveliness of the mosque itself—

> 'That gem
> Of holy places named the House of Pearl
> Moti-Musjid, where Archangels might pray
> And miss no grace of heaven, no purity!'

was enough to satisfy much deeper ascetic curiosity than possessed our nomad souls.

And so I have come to the end of the chapter before evening fell at the close of the day in Agra, and brought the stars that helped us to see that dream-wonder of the world, the Taj.

XXXVI

It came about this way, as of course you know, that the world has the Taj.

The Taj is a Queen's tomb, the most beautiful tomb of the most beautiful queen that ever, when her queenship crumbled away into the dust of common humanity, needed sepulchring like her subjects. The beauty of the queen lives in the beauty of the tomb, for without the immortalisation of the Taj, Arjamand Banu would have died like other 'dark stars' of the Orient, and when her lord, who only knew her face, followed her to another Paradise, her memory would have vanished from the palaces and pleasure grounds he made for her, and none of us perhaps would have known her name. But Shah Jahan, who called this lovely Persian wife of his 'Mumtaz-i-Mahal'—'Chosen of the Palace'—exalted her above all the rest in his love while she lived and his grief when she died, and thought her last wish for a tomb that would tell the world of her, when she lay in his arms 'that ill day in the camp at Burhanpur,' a light thing and easily fulfilled. So the Taj was conceived and begun, in a garden of roses and palms, on the right bank of the Jumna, high above its floods; and the queen was buried in the garden, where the bulbuls and the koils sang over her until it was finished.

From his lonely palace chamber in the Fort, with the blue river winding a mile between, Shah Jahan watched the wonderful white dome swelling and its four guardian towers rising to be the world's memorial of his love; and found more pleasure there than in the soft eyes of all from whom Arjamand had been the 'Chosen.' For seventeen years he watched it, teaching Arjamand's sons and daughters their mother's immortality, while the marble and the sandstone and the jewels came by toiling men and straining cattle 'over a thousand wastes, a hundred hills,' to perfect the symmetry and the grandeur and the inner loveliness of this most worshipful work that man has left upon the earth—the Taj. Then Shah Jahan died also, and was buried beside his queen, so that the great tomb tells of them both. Yet when one sees it, it seems eloquent only of her who desired it, and who was so dear a queen that her desire evoked it.

In the sweet, cool starlight that comes like a sudden benediction when the sun is gone in India, we drove to see the Taj. It was a long drive from Agra's one hotel, perched high in midtown, along a dusty, wide, red road that wound through the native bazaars and beyond the Fort, and past the shadowy bungalows where the memsahibs ruled. We met patient Indian cattle with their beautiful eyes and intelligent, confiding faces, and gaudy *ekkas* and pariah dogs and water-carriers, and now and then a group of white-draped natives or a trio of British 'Tommies,' but the drive had not many incidents, and I remember only the coolness and silence of it, and our eagerness. The driver stopped at last beneath some trees by the road-side, and we looked to the left and found ourselves before the high dark archway of the outer court. In a state of mental breathlessness we jumped from the *gharri* and went in. Was that the Taj?—that great majestic semi-dome of sandstone, arched and pillared, and written high on all its arches and pillars in white marble letters with stately script from the Koran—rising between massive walls adorned with graceful cupolas, and standing there before us in that mysterious light like a portal to all the East! For a moment we thought so, and felt the sensation of an ideal turned upside down. But if we could have read the Toghra text it would have said to us, 'Enter God's Garden,' even as it bade the poet enter who sat 'with Sa'di' there, as you have learned; and we would have known that this was only the screen of the Taj and the gate of Arjamand's garden. We could not read the Toghra text, but a dusky figure stole out from some lurking-place beneath, touched its forehead with the palm of its hand, and, pointing inwards, broke the stillness, saying, 'Sala'am!—The Taj!' Then the figure crept back into the shadows, and we went in together.

After the throbbing heat of the day, after the clattering *ekkas* and the crowded bazaars, we stood in a garden, all softly, tenderly green and full of silence, stretching into filmy darkness everywhere. Ghostly marble paths interlaced under the palms and the pipal trees; the stars could just tell the difference between the red roses and the yellow ones. The day would have shown us aloes and tulip-trees and waxen frangipanni,

> 'Sheets of fiery Indian marigolds,
> Moon-flowers and shell-flowers, crimson panoply
> Of the silk cottons and soft lilac lights,
> Where sunbeams sift through bougainvilleas.'

But in this sweet half-light we saw only the glamour of the garden, hiding in its arbours, straying across its paths. Rather, perhaps, we felt it, for as we stood there in our places in the long list of those whose feet have entered the portals of Arjamand, we had eyes only for the strange dream-thing that the garden made sanctuary for, rising phantasmal at its further end, beyond the roses and above the palms. The dropping of water came through the odorous air, and at our feet we saw the stars in a still, dark, glistening stretch, broken here and there by lily pads, troubled here and there where the fountain jets played, lying between the wide white marble pavements we stood upon. The pavements clove the garden, and led, the glistening water-tank always between, the roses shadowing over, and lines of dark mourning thuja trees on either side, by a long glimmering vista to the threshold of the dream-thing. We followed it with uncertain, quiet, timid footfalls; we could not be sure that it would suffer itself to be approached, or that a fugitive glance would find it on returning.

We reached wide, shallow steps and climbed them. Then we were on a sandstone platform, 'a thousand feet each way,' and closer to the phantasy, which curiously remained. So close, we could see that it rested lightly upon a great white marble level, that came down by many steps into the garden—steps that one might ascend, and so learn of a surety that the Taj was real. But for the moment we did not ascend them, preferring there in the sensuous mystery of that starlit Indian place, where was no voice or step but ours, the feeling of trespassing upon some old enchanted ground, that might vanish at any backward wand wave from before our eyes and under our feet.

The great tomb rose before us like a shapen cloud in the pallor of the starlight. It seemed to advance, it seemed to recede, it seemed to stand still. Here and there the pure whiteness of its swelling dome almost broke into a gleam, but never quite. The gleam would have fixed it—given it substance and surface, and it had not these. Whether a creation of the heavens above or the earth beneath, it hung poised between—a wonder unfamiliar to either. The great white dome lifted itself between two lesser domes, among attendant minarets, and the understructure that seemed to grow out of its snowy base to meet and support them, shaped like a square, 'the angles shorn,' was broken by a lovely lofty Saracenic arch in the middle, and another in each upspringing face. And from every corner of the broad white field it rested on sprang the slenderest pale minaret far towards the stars. Then trees, the bamboos and the palms, and out of the darkness of these the gentle glimmering curves of the shrine-mosques on either side. But no talk of plinths or arches, and no comparison—the world has nothing remotely like it—can make you see the Taj as we saw it there in the silent starlight of Shah Jahan's garden, the fountains rippling quietly in his marble watercourses, a drowsy bird stirring in his grieving thuja trees, the air a dream of perfume from the flowers that Arjamand loved. For the marvel and the spell of it lie over and beyond any conception of architecture. We did not think until afterwards of the beauty of the design, or the skill of the workmen, or the splendour of the material. Nobody does.

> 'You see it with the heart, before the eyes
> Have time to gaze!'

And to that subtler consciousness which receives it the Taj tells its own untranslatable story of Love and Death, and that strange brooding infinity, the shadow of whose wings falls over both Love and Death, which is the soul of the world. One may set down the majesty, the tenderness, the ideality of the Taj, and there seem to be no more words for this untold story. But that is because one is not the poet who sat with Sa'di there. He, with the wisdom of poets, calls it—

> 'A passion and a worship and a faith
> Writ fast in alabaster, so that earth
> Hath nothing anywhere of mortal toil
> So fine wrought, so consummate, so supreme,
> So, beyond praise, Love's loveliest monument
> As what, in Agra, upon Jumna's bank
> Shah Jahan builded for his lady's grave.'

Behind us, as we sat there mute with the marvel of it, and behind the furthest, duskiest palms at the garden's verge, had come a deepening yellow sky-rift; and there presently the slow beauty of the moon came up. It touched the gold finial of the fair white central dome, it crept down the curving sides, it reached the lesser domes and tipped the minarets—downward the sweet revelation spread, lovingly, graciously, marking the stern desolateness of the thuja trees, leaving pale flickering lights among the rose thickets. And as it lifted itself wan to the moon, with all its delicate traceries and inlayings, and bearing high scrolls of strange characters we knew to mean reverence to Allah and submission, we saw the Taj as the shrine of a tender human grief. And we fell to talking of Arjamand and of her Emperor's love.

* * * * * *

We sat there a long time, so long that a figure crouched on a lower step rose and stole up to us, and pointed down one of the paths and said something which we knew to mean, 'The Presence is there!' thinking that we awaited some sahib who was our escort. We had no words with which to tell him that we were alone, so he crept back and watched. And presently, as a quick silent black shadow fell across the path, he started forward again.

'The Presence comes!' he said.

The shadow stopped before us and removed its hands from its pockets. 'So it is you two!' the shadow's personality observed, taking off his hat. 'I thought you ought to turn up soon, in the ordinary course of things.' And Orthodocia said a great deal more than she knew in her little cry, '*Jack!*'

'THE TAJ.'

"'Yes!' he admitted, and then those extraordinary young people, wholly forgetting the Taj and the palms, and the roses, and the moon, forgetting everything except their two precious selves and the fact that they were profoundly interested in one another, said 'How do you do?' and shook hands with all the circumstance that might have been expected of them in Mayfair! It was too utterly absurd, and in contemplating the absurdity of it I did not observe that Mr. Jack Love entirely forgot to shake hands with me till afterward. Orthodocia informed me later that there was nothing at all extraordinary about our meeting him in that particular spot of that particular corner of the North-West Provinces of India (meaning that there was nothing at all extraordinary in *her* meeting him there), that it seemed to her altogether natural and a thing to be expected there of all places, as soon as he appeared; but nobody would have gathered this from the elaborately proper, but somewhat disjointed conversation that followed. And after Orthodocia had inquired tenderly and particularly for the Assiniboian Aunt, and made a few other references equally suitable to the time and place, she was inquired of as to whether she had seen the South-Eastern minaret yet; and they both prayed me to go with them to look at it. Whereupon I told them, with a fine inward scorn, that the Taj was all I wanted to see to-night, thank you, and they went away into the glamour of Arjamand's rose garden together.

Then, I remember, there stole out into the night from a spot in that garden place where the shadows were thickest and the moonlight fairest, a low sweet dropping melody, that fell, and ceased, and throbbingly fell again. It was the Bulbul singing to the Rose. If we may believe the poet he sang in Persian:

> 'Sweet, ever sweeter, sweetest Love hath been
> *Shirin, shirintar,* and *shirintarin!*'

And the Rose understood. And it seemed to me, although I was not versed in Persian, that I also understood.

* * * * * *

'Well?' said I to Orthodocia an hour later, in the privacy of our apartment, inquiringly.

'Well ?' she returned, with a transient defiance of my right to interrogate, and an inclination to tears.

'Do you mean to say that he *didn't* ?'—for I saw that the situation had to be taken by the horns, and with decision.

'I th—th—think he was *going to*,' my friend replied from the depths of her pillow, 'but we qua—qu—quarrelled again!'

'Crops this time ?' I asked, ironically, 'or freight rates, or the duty on binders and reapers ?'

'None of them,' said my friend, sitting up suddenly, with spirit and indignation. 'The tendencies of the age!'

'Which of you disapproved?'

'*He* did! and I think it was *extremely impertinent* of him. A person needn't *say* straight out what he means to make you understand very well! And if he didn't mean the tendency of girls to travel by themselves, why did he say he had been thinking about it ever since he saw us at Corona? And why did he think proper to start round the world the other way to meet us, and help us out of imaginary difficulties, and protect us from imaginary dangers, *pure* imagination——'

'Did he come for that?' I asked.

'He—he *insinuated* that he did.'

'It was a long way to come—for that, Orthodocia,' I remarked thoughtfully.

'I know it was!' rather miserably. 'Don't you see that's just the *thing* of it! When one knows the motive to be—unobjectionable—one can't resent the—the covert criticism of the act. I defy *you* to do it! I found it simply impossible; so I ignored it! But I *was* angry! So I told him—very politely and blandly, and quite ignoring his argument—what a delightful trip we'd had so far, and how kind everybody 'd been; and he said yes, he had no doubt of it; and that made me simply *furious*, so I said—not taking the slightest notice of what was in his mind—what a relief it was not to have a man bothering about the luggage labels, and feeling injured because he's kept waiting—which is all Uncle Robert ever did on the Continent; and then I distinctly saw him smile, and he changed the subject. Now, if there *is* an aggravating thing, it's to have one's subject changed that way! And he's at the club, and I know he means to call to-morrow afternoon, and I never told him we had to leave by the midday train to catch the *Oriental* at Bombay, and I *forbid* your doing it, and—well, that's all!'

'I can remember,' I said, 'a few occasions upon which I would have been—glad of a man.'

'So can I!' returned my friend instantly; 'but you wouldn't have had me *admit* it!'

'On the whole,' I said, 'perhaps it's as well that you didn't. It is difficult to say what the result might have been.'

I could see very plainly next morning by her eyelids that Orthodocia's stern resolution had dissolved in the night, so I sent a note privately to the club with an intimation of our departure. The bearer came back in half an hour to say that the sahib had gone forth with some other sahibs, and would not be back till two o'clock. So I did not tell Orthodocia that I had violated her commands, and together we went again, in the full glory of the sunlight, to see the Taj. Indeed, in flat disobedience to Murray's 'Handbook,' we bestowed no thought or care upon Futtehpur Sikri, the deserted city, or Sikandarah with its sculptures, or the tomb of Itimud Dowlah, 'Light of the World,' but jealously gave all the few hours we had left in Agra to Shah Jahan and Arjamand, grieving only that we could not learn the beauty of the Taj in the Eastern dawning, and under the soft long shadows of the waning day. What we would not see by impotent torch-light that first night in the garden—the interior of the Taj where the cenotaphs are—we saw next day, entering under the Saracenic arch and standing beneath the wonderful white dome. There we noted how exquisite the marble was, with its delicate veinings of rose and blue, that closed so tenderly far above our heads. How marvellous the many lattices, all wrought in marble, that so refined the Indian sun into a mystery of luminous twilight, falling gravely all about us on the texts from the Koran, and the jasper and the onyx, the crystal and the chalcedony, the jade and the lazulite, that twined in flower-fancies over and around the tomb of Arjamand. So that she

'Who loved her garden lieth now
Wrapped in a garden.'

But far most wonderful, most eloquent, most full of sweetest mystery, was the Voice of the Dome, a Voice that took up our lightest word, carried it to the coping-stone, and then sent it down, down, down, exquisitely softened and attuned, till the echo seemed to die away in the tomb, as if it had gone to talk with the queen there. Orthodocia lingered behind here, saying nothing, and as I

'MUMTAZ-I-MAHAL.'

turned to wait for her just outside the inner portal I heard the sweetest murmurings falling about her. She had evoked them herself, and she did not know I heard, so I shall not tell you the burden of them. But if ever you are in love, she advised me afterward, and want a faithful word about it, go to the Taj and ask Queen Arjamand.

So we gathered a red rose each in the garden, Orthodocia for the rose and I for the sweet sake of my friend, and came away

  * * * * * *

In the daytime they sell you slabs of marble in the outer court, inlaid in the manner of the cenotaphs, and loquats, yellow and luscious, and pictures of the Emperor and of Mumtaz-l-Mahal, which I shall borrow from Orthodocia to adorn this chapter with. And there are many whose forefathers bowed before Shah Jahan who now demand backsheesh of the pilgrim stranger, with other afflictions, all of which vanish when the stars come out. Therefore I adjure you, when you go to Agra, see the Taj by starlight, but look to it that your visit be upon no occasion of festivity, for I have it upon excellent authority that the Taj is then glorified by magnesium light and—ah, the atrocity !—the *band plays there !*

XXXVII

YET another ship, outward bound, steam up, flag flying, in the harbour of Bombay! Decks crowded with the going and the longing to go, the company's tug lying alongside, the sea swarming with lesser craft that cling to the big black sides of the *Oriental* while they may. A tall dark man, reluctant, embarrassed, beside his portmanteaux; a fair woman, *passée*, blondined, in widow's weeds, with red eyes, waiting for the last word. 'I will send for you,' he says, 'next hot weather.' She disbelieves him. 'You will have forgotten!'

And Orthodocia, restless, pacing, will not go down into the saloon for a cup of tea. 'People are so interesting,' she says, turning her head quickly as another pair of broad shoulders appears at the top of the companion-ladder. Poor dear Orthodocia! There had been just one chance of his getting back in time, and that, it seemed, he had missed, for the last bell rang, and the tug put off, waving handkerchiefs, and a belated box-wallah scrambled down the side amid the execrations of a quartermaster; and in the place where the *Oriental* had lain at anchor there was presently a blue waste with a few scattered sampans heaving upon it; and of the Presence in the Garden of the Taj there had been no trace or sign.

'Consider, Orthodocia,' I said, consolingly, 'we are in the Arabian Sea! It is something, under—under any circumstances, to be in the Arabian Sea! And there is tea going on below.'

Orthodocia put both her elbows on the taffrail and looked into the Arabian Sea with the remark that it was all in the name, and one body of water was exactly like another so far as she could observe; and where was the first place at which one could post letters? *A·len!* Aden—six days hence!

When a person casts her idealisations overboard, as it were, and finds a personal injury in the disposition of the earth's surface, and declines afternoon tea accompanied by cake with currants in it, her case requires strong measures.

'Orthodocia!' I said, 'do you remember that pink-

'YET ANOTHER SHIP, OUTWARD BOUND.'

cheeked woman at the breakfast-table at Agra who said she had travelled in the same compartment with Jack? She is going to Aden, too, apparently, and she looks immensely interested in you!'

'My dear,' said Orthodocia, with her most vivid smile, 'isn't it delightful to be off again? And don't you think, if we went below, we could get a steward to give us some tea?'

Two days afterwards, while we were dressing for dinner, I noticed a small corner of brown paper sticking out behind my looking-glass.

Orthodocia says four bells had just gone, but nobody but Orthodocia would remember that. I pulled it out with the idle curiosity that always prompts people to pull things out. It was an envelope with 'Indian Telegrams' printed across the top, and it was addressed— but Orthodocia had it before I had even an approximate idea to whom it was addressed

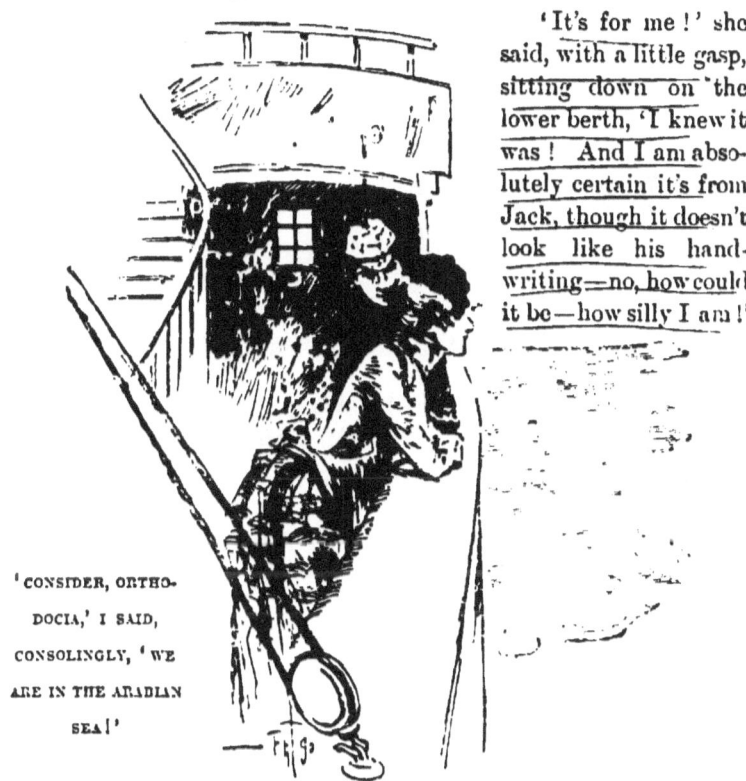

'It's for me!' she said, with a little gasp, sitting down on the lower berth, 'I knew it was! And I am absolutely certain it's from Jack, though it doesn't look like his handwriting—no, how could it be—how silly I am!'

'CONSIDER, ORTHODOCIA,' I SAID, CONSOLINGLY, 'WE ARE IN THE ARABIAN SEA!'

'Suppose you ascertain!' I suggested.

'Yes,' she said, 'I'm going to.' Nervously smoothing it out with both hands. 'Of *course*,' she added decisively, looking at the back of the envelope, 'there's something wrong. I am prepared for that' —growing paler, though still heroic. 'I only hope it isn't a tiger— *say* you don't think it's a tiger!'

'Don't be absurd, my dear,' I said, soothingly. 'How could he have telegraphed from the inside of a tiger? Open it.'

'No,' she answered, 'he wouldn't be in a position to do it—it's probably sunstroke.'

'Orthodocia,' I exclaimed, 'if you don't instantly open that telegram, which probably concerns some forgotten washing-bill'—witheringly—'I'll do it myself. I decline to be kept on the rack any longer.'

'I think,' returned my friend, with a strong effort at self-control, 'you might show a *little* feeling. C—can't you see I'm only—w—w—waiting for you to give me a hat-pin.'

Which showed that Orthodocia was bordering upon hysteria, for never before had I, or since have I, known her to apply an implement of this sort to any but its orthodox purpose. But she opened the telegram, read it once, twice, thrice; then handed it to me, lay flat down in the lower berth, and stared at the upper one with her arms under her head. It was rather a long telegram, dated at Agra, and ran thus:

'Lost 5.30 train wish offer heart and life came for purpose if consent wire here will follow next mail might marry Cairo if willing would prefer this as do not approve your travelling unprotected if refuse will go on and no answer expected forgive telegram no other resource very anxious kind regards to friend.'

I didn't know in the least what to say, so I counted them and said, 'Fifty-five words.'

'Fifty-four!' said Orthodocia.

I counted them again. 'This time I make seventy-three!' I said, for I was several degrees more nervous than Orthodocia, who looked at me with a quiver about her mouth, put both her hands to her face and began to laugh in a way that suggested to me that I should climb into the top berth and laugh too. And for the next five minutes the only comment upon Mr. John Love's proposal of marriage to Miss Orthodocia Love was a peal of hysterical mirth that brought the cabin steward to the door.

'Do you want anythink, Miss?'

'No—yes—ask him,' said Orthodocia, breathlessly. 'You're ready,'

'NERVOUSLY SMOOTHING IT OUT WITH BOTH HANDS.'

'Steward,' I said, confronting him with the brown envelope, 'when did this arrive?'

'Morning of the afternoon we sailed, Miss. You 'adn't come aboard, so I put it in the mirrir, where I thought you'd see it fust thing, Miss. I 'ope as you got it, Miss.'

'There!' I remarked, shutting the door after his retreating form. 'It wasn't his fault. Reasonable people always come down to their cabins to see about things before the ship goes; and you would *not* leave the deck, Orthodocia——'

'Don't,' commanded my unhappy friend, so I didn't, and we silently pondered the situation.

'You can telegraph from Aden,' I suggested.

'Where?'

An interval.

'Ceylon,' I said. 'He *must* go there. Care P. and O.'

'There is a yacht,' Orthodocia responded, 'at Calcutta—a friend's yacht. He said he *might* go on in her, and I think now he meant if he—if I——'

'Said "No,"' I supplemented, and Orthodocia nodded.

'Name of yacht?'

'I forget. And I think she was going up the Yang-Tse-Kiang. Oh,' with a burst of emotion, 'I *wish* you'd stop talking! Can't you see I'm perfectly miserable?' And Orthodocia turned her face to the ship's side. I went out to dinner and sent her in the most comforting things on the bill of fare, maintaining an unbroken absence till nine o'clock. By that time I had such philosophical reflections as the situation admitted ready for her, and as we paced the hurricane deck together in the moonlight I gave her the benefit of them. I begged her to ask herself what she would have telegraphed. To which the only reply I got was a small squeeze immediately above my right elbow. Then I said that for my part I was not prepared for the results. At which Orthodocia asked me why, in a tone that suggested that I, if you please, had no concern in the results! Whereupon I was obliged to point out to her that if Mr. John Love turned his face westward and took the next home mail it would be for the purpose of joining us in Cairo, wouldn't it? Acquiescence—calm, blissful. Then if matrimony ensued—interruption. Orthodocia wouldn't *think* of such a thing! What would they say at home?—if matrimony ensued, I had to contemplate the prospect of finishing up our free untrammelled trip under the eye of a chaperon, for one thing; and I asked Orthodocia to reflect upon the austerity of her probable development, under the influence of Mr. John Love, in that character. I begged her to consider whether it would be fair and honourable behaviour on her part to take deliberate measures to become a person qualified to order me about, and entitled to a supreme opinion under all circumstances, in view of the good faith in which we started. I brought the matter home to her by asking her what she would think of me if I were to turn chaperon on *her* hands! to say nothing of the alluring possibility of coming in at the end of one's journey round the world, a very bad second in a honeymoon! And set down, 'even by you, Orthodocia,' in the category of strangers and railway guards and undesirable people who are always looking on. I have some imagination in an emergency, and I think I made Orthodocia see what this would be to me. And if matrimony did not ensue—further interruption, unnecessary to record—one must draw the line somewhere, and I thought it ought to be drawn at the travelling companionship, on any pretext whatever, of a young man who was in love with Orthodocia—with the young man on the other side. Moreover, to be personal again, had Orthodocia ever heard of a 'gooseberry?' and did I *look* like an individual who would enjoy that personation? And so, on the whole, especially in view of the absurdity of believing that Mr. John Love would accept such a doubtful ultimatum, also in view of how greatly travel would enhance the young man's desirability as a companion in Assiniboia, didn't she think things had turned out for the best?

And Orthodocia, though she implied that the philosophy was all on my side, gave a dubious assent, which she amused herself by qualifying and contradicting all the way to Aden.

You know Aden, military station, south coast of Arabia, population 34,711, area 66 square miles, acquired 1838. You have seen many photographs and heard much talk of Aden, and need not be told how it is a symbol for all desolation. How the sun smites down upon the gaunt gray heights that come trending forward from the horizon to stand in the coolness of the sea; how they darken and crowd together thunderously; how the wind blows white curling whiffs of rock-dust in their faces out of the roads leading up to the bare, hard-faced little cluster of roofs and walls that men have had the temerity to build there. Not a leaf, not a tree, no trace of the tenderness or gentleness of the human world—yes, one. We saw it as we turned an angle in the sharp, zigzag road up-hill—it lay in a hollow, softly green, the grim, torn rocks threatening it all round about, a tiny place where the people who must always stay in Aden are comforted with grass and flowers.

Orthodocia had spent a good deal of the time between Bombay and Aden in the exclusive society of her pen and a big, flat-bottomed cabin inkstand—so much, indeed, that it began to be rumoured on deck that she was writing a book, and people became shy of expressing themselves before her for fear their statements might be reproduced in print with names attached. Which leads me to say, by the way, that people who go round the world really to write a book ought to keep the fact profoundly to themselves, simply out of consideration for the other passengers, most of whom are thoroughly persuaded that none of their little ways and words are safe from being held up to a scoffing public marked as belonging to Mr. J—n—s or Mrs. S—i—h, in the manner of *Punch*. It is entirely an unnecessary fear, but it makes them quite pathetically nervous. I suppose the P. and O. must carry literary people as well as Jews, Turks, infidels, and heretics, when such persons demand transport; but the commanders ought to take measures with an author as with a funeral on board, to keep the matter quiet for the sake of the sensibilities of the saloon. Orthodocia could not convince anybody but me that she was not a literary character, her note-book being circumstantial evidence of the most damaging description; but I knew that the volumes she wrote between tiffin and afternoon tea were intended for the most limited private circulation only, and were addressed in various indefinite ways that seemed to offer a chance of reaching Mr. John Love before he left India. It was an occupation for Orthodocia, and it freed her mind so that when she came up on deck again we could talk about something else occasionally. Therefore I approved it, but I was not at all surprised when she decided, after sealing and stamping them very carefully at Aden, not to post any of them. The idea of a reply to a proposal by telegraph falling into any hands but those for whom it was intended *was* a little trying; some of the missives were sure to go to the Dead Letter Office; and there was no reason to send one more than another of them. So Orthodocia cast them in little bits into the Red Sea, and resigned herself, she told me, in so far as Jack was concerned, to faith for the present, hope for the future, and charity for the past. I do not feel at liberty to give you the extracts I heard from the letters that went into the Red Sea; but if I could, I think you would agree with me that Orthodocia might have sent them harmlessly either to Mr. Love or to the clerks in the Dead Letter Office; for, beyond a general expression of forgiveness and goodwill, they conveyed to the ordinary intelligence nothing whatever. But there may have been tangibilities in extracts that I did not hear.

I defy you to arrive at the Red Sea in a journey round the world without a sensation of surprise. One hardly knows what one expects, but it is something that has survived one's childish idea of a really red sea and associations with Moses and the hosts of Pharaoh that is nonplussed a little by a commonplace body of salt water just like any other. Orthodocia declared that her chief disappointment lay in being out of sight of land, which is clearly traceable to Moses. Everybody was astonished in the Red Sea, however, the novices as aforesaid, and the Anglo-Indian comers and goers, because of the temperature. For the whole saloon had made up its mind to sleep on deck in the Red Sea, old and young, squeamish and unsqueamish. 'Of course one *must* do it there, you know; the cabins will be insupportable!' And the gentleman with a tendency to apoplexy had been dieting for two days, and the lady with asthma had confided to several of the passengers that she wouldn't be in the least surprised if she didn't 'come through it'; and the 'First' had told us how sometimes they had to 'put back' to get a breath of air, and everybody had listened to the person who had once come through the Red Sea when there had been 'three deaths' from the appalling heat. And every soul on board appeared that first morning of the Red Sea in the most gossamer-like and coolest garments his or her wardrobe afforded, and privately believed himself or herself the victim of fever and ague, with the fever left out, for shivering in them. It was actually not until after dinner, when we had begun to go about clad in ulsters and travelling rugs, seeking the corners nearest to the engines and envying the stokers down below, that a deputation was formed to wait upon the captain and request some justification for the conduct of the weather, regarding which he seemed to consider himself irresponsible. We succeeded in making him say, however, that he had 'never seen it fresher this time of year,' which was something. And nobody was warm until we got to Suez and set foot in Egypt.

It seemed to be a pale, water-colour country, full even to this outer edge, which had suffered somewhat from foreign usage, as outer edges in the East are apt to do, of delicate charm. There was a gray, well-baked wall with a gate in it, that threw blocks of shadow upon the dust lying white in the sunlight. In the gate an old Arab sold little flat oranges, yellow like flame; a waterway slipped past giving back the tender sky; in the near distance the tall, tilted masts of some dahabeehs grew out of the sand. The Arab was cross-eyed, and behind the gate were only the Company's offices; but in the soft illusion of one's first quarter of an hour in Egypt commonplaces have no consequence. One does not even object to them. They are not to be accounted.

We sauntered through the dusty little town after our luggage to the railway station, where it was a shock to find ourselves enlightened in French as to our movements. Up to this point in our journey round the world, the alternate language had been English. Orthodocia thought it extremely ungrateful of the Khedive after all 'we' had done for him, but I suppose that is a matter about which the Khedive is entitled to an opinion. At the railway station, too, we made acquaintance with the little virtuous silver piastre, and the big unprincipled leaden piastre, which is the first thorn in the flesh in Egypt—carefully paying all the little virtuous ones away in backsheesh, and cherishing the big unprincipled ones to settle hotel bills with, and other matters of financial magnitude. And so we started for Cairo, in a railway-carriage better calculated to afford passengers every discomfort than any of our previous experience. The seats were narrow and hard, the backs straight and uncompromising, the floor unclean; the windows rattled and let in the dust as a blanket; there was no solace anywhere. And a little, black-eyed Frenchman, with long hair and a drooping moustache, and a shabby coat, and a wife and daughter, rather disconsolately *débonnaire*, shared the carriage—which, in justice to the Khedive, I must admit to have been a second-class carriage—with us. The little Gaul carried a large framed crayon portrait of himself. It was set carefully on the seat opposite him and evidently represented his profession. In the portrait though, the long hair waved glossily, and there was an affecting ideality under the pensive eyelids, and the moustache was waxed to correspond, and there was something like a decoration in the trim button-hole, which, however, may have been only an artistic detail—without doubt the counterfeit of Monsieur in a former and more prosperous state. He regarded it affectionately now and then, absently twisting the original moustache and running his fingers through the original locks, to approximate the ideal opposite. The fat, easily amused, philosophical wife glanced at it proudly, and the little precocious theatrical daughter stood before it lost in profound admiration. They did not speak of it—perhaps as a topic it had been exhausted—but they made it an object of interest to Orthodocia and me with a pretended unconsciousness and *naïveté* which was delightful. It was an intimate glimpse of France as we seemed often afterwards to find her in Egypt, a little seamy and frayed, with the more ornamental morals a suspicion the worse for wear, usually travelling in search of better fortunes, happy in the sun that eases poverty, always bowing, politely, self-respectfully, to the presence of the ages. The family of the artist, he himself and his astral body, got out at Zag-a-Zig, and it was an occupation for a while to wonder what scope and what returns a crayon genius might find in Zag-a-Zig.

One crosses a bit of desert between Suez and Cairo, with the white, shifting, wasting sand piled so high beside the track that it becomes a marvel how it is kept off the rails. One sees the sharp line between green life and gray death where the little fields of rice and lucerne lie bravely against the waste, smiling in the sun, and plainly thanking Heaven for the old, old gift of the Nile; and waterways that feed the little fields, with deeper greens and a fringe of palms along their edges, looking as simple and as unrelated to modern engineering as if Joseph had dug them out himself. And little clay-built, flat-roofed cities, with a mosque dome rising up, and a tamarisk clump drooping over, and pale-brown heaps of roofless walls and broken pottery that were little clay-built cities once, and stood on other heaps that little clay-built cities have crumbled away into since the days when Nitetis was beautiful and Phanes sailed over from Greece. The train stops at a little station bearing on a common wooden signboard 'Tel-el-Kebir,' and immediately the carriage window fills up with newspaper cablegrams and medalled heroism, and Lord Wolseley; and one looks eagerly through all this to find, as one always finds with illogical disappointment, looking for battle sites, only a peaceful sky and pleasant fields, and people going about their businesses as if history had never touched them. There are people at all the stations, the people of the little clay-built cities, and some are Nubians, and some are Turks, and some are Jews, and a few are Arabs, while the Egyptians seem fewest of all. One judges, of course, from the outer man, knowing neither tongue nor custom. Little boys and hideously old women sell water in clay water-bottles, and dates in shallow wicker trays, and leeks and eggs hard-boiled and painted a reddish-purple. Orthodocia bought eggs, for there was a famine in our compartment, offering three or four little silver piastres. The wife of Achmed handed up three, and three more, and three more. I came to Orthodocia's assistance. The wife of Achmed continued to hand up eggs. I passed them on to Orthodocia, who laid them in a careful line along the back of the seat. When we had received fifteen eggs I tried to discourage the wife of Achmed, whose tray was nearly empty. She seemed to understand, and handed up the last egg, nodding and smiling to reassure me. Then she ran off to colloquy with the wife of Yusef, returning with an air of integrity and one more egg! Orthodocia said it reminded her of the *demi-saison* sales in Oxford Street, when one gets so much more than the value of one's money. This suggestion, as applied to the eggs, made us very liberal with them to outsiders.

Another slow and dirty little train, and we rattled away through more sand-drifts, with only two hours to wait for Cairo; and Orthodocia went to sleep over 'An Egyptian Princess,' which everybody takes to Egypt, but never by any chance reads there.

'Land of Goshen!' I ejaculated to myself as the green fields came again, and the pleasant palms, and there spread a fatness over all the landscape.

'Another of those awful Americanisms of yours!' my friend disturbed herself to say. 'Why can't you exclaim in English! What is the matter?'

'Nothing!' I responded with outraged dignity. 'Only it *is* the land of Goshen—out of the windows.'

'I don't believe it!' said Orthodocia, flatly. 'How can anybody know?' And she slumbered again, despising Baedeker and all that is written.

And presently, when the two hours had waned to twenty minutes I saw against a yellow sunset sky, away to the right, where the pale lines of the desert wandered and wavered, a little gray triangle, and woke Orthodocia, pointing to it. My friend rubbed her eyes. 'It's a *Pyramid*!' she cried, in accents of mortified desolation, 'and you've gone and seen it first!'

We went to Shepheard's, of course. Shepheard's is no longer Shepheard's, I believe. There is another name on the corners of the table-napkins and the handles of the spoons and the bottoms of the soup plates. But Shepheard's cannot be divorced from its original godfather; it is an institution, like the Pyramids, and I doubt if any of the Ramses enjoy the personal identification with a winter in Egypt that seems to have fallen to the lot of the obscure and possibly departed Shepheard.

It is always interesting at Shepheard's—the place is full of a rare, fine, distilled essence of the world. The world loves Cairo, and is happy at Shepheard's. It is always smiling there, always indolent, half curious, disposed to make acquaintance, charmingly dressed, a little relaxed, entertaining, cosmopolitan. We met Rubicundo—it had become no matter of surprise to meet Rubicundo on any part of the earth's surface—on the steps leading from the wide piazza into the street. Rubicundo, not lost, but gone before—Rubicundo, bubbling over with enthusiasm about the cutlets, the donkeys, the Sphinx, the climate, the Arabian ladies, everything.

'You're late for dinner,' he cried with excitement, as we shook hands, 'but try an obelisk if you can get one—superb!' Whereat Orthodocia looked at me gravely, and said it was evident that Rubicundo, at least, had dined.

Inside, people were moving about with an easy familiarity that was a little dazzling at first—ladies in low-necked evening dresses, officers in uniform, little groups bending and whispering and softly laughing so evidently over the last bit of Court scandal—it reminded one with something of a shock that there was, after all, a modern Egypt. The walls were hung with photographs of young ladies and gentlemen taken in Egyptian dress for the mystification of their friends, of a dark-eyed Roumanian, done with great folds across her forehead, and before her ears, a travesty *à la Sphinx*, of the Khedive and the son of the Khedive, of Generals, and Pashas, and Beys. We wrote our names under Count Teleki's, newly parched from Africa, in the register where Stanley the other day wrote his. A Duke and a Duchess hobnobbed with John Smith on the same page. We longed to turn it over and find other distinguished autographs; but with a lobby full of people all wondering—nothing could shake your belief in that—who you are and how you came there, you are not disposed to flights of inquisitiveness. At the top of the wide easy-going stairs we were given over to a wrinkled, ambling, bowing old Frenchman, major-domo of the corridor, whose very coat tails, as he led the way to our apartment, waggled a deferential sense of the position of major-domos. Down in the big white dining-room, with its old-fashioned panels and cornices and groups of palms in the corners, plenty of people were dining still—a lowering beer-baronet, with his handsome young son, and newly-acquired pretty young wife, a comedy of three—a pair of high-coloured, high-spirited Irish girls, with a tiny old chaperon and a couple of uniforms attached, the latter attachment much the closer of the two, if one could believe appearances. We romanced about the little chaperon, whom we decided to be engaged at a salary, because she looked depressed and said nothing, even when one of the young women ate raisins with her elbows on the table. And I was glad afterward, for the sake of my native continent, to verify the fact that they were *not* Americans, as Orthodocia said they must be, with reference to this slight unconventionality. Opposite us a gentleman, with three medals on his coat (two Victoria's, one the Khedive's), told stories of active service under Gordon. An American lady at our elbow pointed out another with blue eyes and fair hair who she said was Captain Haggard. 'It was *so* embarrassing!' she gossiped. 'When Captain Haggard was introduced to me, I said, *quite* thoughtlessly, "I suppose you are very tired of being asked if you are any connection of Rider Haggard's?" and he said, "Yes, as I happen to be his brother!" He is literary, too. I don't see how he could *help* being so with such a brother, do you? But he writes poetry chiefly.' Then she indicated Mr. Cope Whitehouse, and his plan for redeeming a great desert tract, 'which he declares was thought of in the Bible,' and a black-haired blue-eyed Russian notability, impervious, imperious, who swept out past us with a very lofty head, her suite after her, and the young lady artist who was painting the portrait of the Khedivia, and a Polish princess, with pale gray eyes and hair tightly drawn back from a prim narrow forehead. We picked out for ourselves the people who were just starting for, or who had just returned from, the Holy Land. They were unmistakable, not only the three fat priests from Chicago and the Presbyterian minister with his little Scotch wife, and the distinguished Ritualist and party, but all the little lay brethren and sisters as well. Clothes, manners, physiognomy—something of the three and yet not any single characteristic—wrote 'Holy Land' all over them. One might have challenged them to produce their tickets, if it had been proper, with perfect security. The world of the baronet and the Polish princess was not going to the Holy Land—it had always been told that Jerusalem was disappointing—but to the races. It was a world that moved in a different orbit that was minded to make this pilgrimage —a great many middle-aged ladies in it, and superannuated clergymen, and quiet family parties and shy young men who taught in Sunday-school at home. And here and there a face telling a pathetic story of pinching and saving that a disciple, nineteen centuries after, might look upon the fields and the skies of the Master's country.

We passed a little smoking-room on our way to the *salon*, where sat our old-maid Princess in the blue clouds of her cigarette. Perhaps the drawing-room, to critical and satiated eyes, might be a little aggressively Egyptian; but Orthodocia and I found its divans and its potteries a revelation of the arts of Cairo and the history of dynasties, and walked about and looked at them with all the pleasure of the uncritical and the unsatiated. Scraps of low talk, of street music, the tinkle of glasses, and the fragrance of real 'Egyptiennes' floated past the palms and between the curtains from the piazza outside, where the world in low-cut waistcoats bent over the world in embroidered opera-cloaks, where turbaned dragomans and donkey-boys, and the sellers of great bunches of pink roses at a piastre apiece, hovered thick as near as they dared, and the gentle air caressed one in the darkness, full of soft sounds and odours. We found the little American in a corner out there, and while Orthodocia dropped into her usual train of meditation in another, the little American gossiped to me about the Khedivia, and didn't say I was not to tell. It had been quite recently that the first man except the Khedive had seen the Khedivia's face—and he was a photographer! Her Highness had been immensely amused at the interview, and had mimicked the fortunate professional afterward to all her Court. 'Dear no! she never receives with the Khedive, or dines, or anything of that sort, and when he gives a ball she has to stand behind a gauze curtain to look on, poor thing!

'Oh, yes! she receives *ladies*—on certain days, when she sits on a daïs and all the ladies in a semicircle round her; and one never knows *who* she may address in French, and one *must* answer, you know—before all the rest—and it's *so* embarrassing!' The semicircle being fortified, however, by coffee and sweetmeats. Very much 'petted and spoiled' is this Turkish princess, according to our little friend who seemed to know—speaking French but not English, and being withal an 'intelligent' princess, good-natured and easily amused. One sometimes met her with the whole *harim*, driving in close carriages out towards the desert. To contemplate the monumental Pyramids and guess at the riddle of the Sphinx? Dear no! To sit and eat bon-bons, each out of her own embroidered bag! She is thirty-one, complains of getting 'fat and very old,' but is still happy and still queen. Next day I had a privy glimpse of the portrait the young lady was at work upon, between sittings at the

Palace, in her studio—a rich warm colour scheme of golden-browns in the fur-edged velvet robe, with yellow lace inside ; pearls in the dark braided hair, a pomegranate face—a little while ago. Still lovely enough, in a slightly heavy way, with liquid brown eyes, a pretty pouting mouth, and a dimple in the chin—unmistakably, however, a double chin !

But I am retailing scandal. Let me hasten to inform you that Egypt reached the very highest point of its historical prosperity in the reign of Amasis, the successor of Apries. I can't say this comes to me at first-hand, and you know a story never loses, but I got it from the Rev. Barham Zincke, and the Rev. Barham Zincke got it from Herodotus—so it ought to be true !

XXXVIII

IT was ten o'clock in the morning on the piazza at Shepheard's. The air was full of wine and sunlight. Cairo was all astir. From the gardens of the Esbekeeyah came dainty odours of new budding things. We had come through India's endless summer to find the spring in Egypt.

The street we looked out into was broad and pleasant and European. The signboards spoke of France, the cafés of Italy, the saunterers of all countries, nothing of Egypt except the Arab guides and the donkey boys, loitering among the comers and goers, and an occasional ass trotting, or camel pacing beside the carts and carriages in the highway. The real Cairo was—I have asked Orthodocia, and she says five minutes' walk straight on and turn to your left; but I should describe the distance as a thousand miles and several centuries from this Cairo of Shepheard's and the shops and the gardens of the Esbekeeyah, which it was the boast and delight of the ruler Ismail, twenty years ago, to make into an imitation Paris.

Orthodocia and I were consultatively putting on our gloves. You may put on your gloves on the piazza at Shepheard's. It is one of the advantages of that famous hostelry. Nobody suspects you of not knowing better.

'There is the Citadel,' said I, out of my Baedeker.

'Sunset for that!' returned Orthodocia.

'The Mosques—Sultan Hassan—Kait Bey——'

'I don't feel like Mosques.'

'Tombs of the Caliphs?'

'Gloomy.'

'Ostrich Farm?'

'Commonplace! Isn't there anything else?'

'The Pyramids, if we may believe this author, have been for some time located in Egypt. Could you summon up a transient interest in the Pyramids?'

'The one single sensation—*genuine* sensation—we have left! And you would take it casually, in the middle of the morning, like a glass of Apollinaris!'

'I DON'T FEEL LIKE MOSQUES.'

Orthodocia reproached me with all her soul. 'We must plan for the Pyramids.'

'Bazaars then—the Mousky—attar of roses——'

'Frivolous!' cavilled my friend, and took the guide-book from my unresisting hand. This conversation is registered to show the parlous state into which one may fall in the course of a journey round the world, especially when one has failed, at any point, to make proper connections.

Orthodocia glanced over the pages of Herr Baedeker's 'Lower Egypt' with an indifference which was not assumed. 'It's quite time we were beginning to improve our minds,' she said. 'Let us go to the Museum at Boulak. There are the very beginnings of history at Boulak, and we can go by tram. Besides, they've got Pharaoh there. I should love to see Pharaoh.'

So we went to the Museum at Boulak, crossing the ages 'by tram.'

A dusty disordered quarter, squalid but for the sun, of low houses and straggling streets, tenanted chiefly by poor Europeans—this is Boulak, where Egypt has lodged Mariette's museum. A portal, where they sit at the receipt of piastres, and you go through to an outer court, which looks a little, just at first, if I might be permitted the sacrilege, like premises where they put you up—

'Marble urns and cherubims
Very low and reasonable.'

This is the effect of King Usertesen I., much larger than life, of four lion-headed goddesses from Karnak, a double statue of the god Ammon and an Ethiopian queen, and some fragments, all in granite, standing about in that undecided way which is always characteristic of stonecutters' monuments; and it is a pity, because, as Orthodocia says, it interferes with one's impression.

Beyond this there is a garden, at least Baedeker says it is a garden. I saw only a clump of acacia trees and some grass. The little low-roofed unpretending museum, all painted blue and green and red in the Egyptian manner, opens into the garden; and Mariette lies buried there in a stone sarcophagus for the confusion of posterity, that will not understand the compliment, and will trace through it the direct connection of the Hyksos with the French

Revolution. The Nile slips past, dreaming of the days of Mena, King of This—surely of That, Father Nile, since it is six thousand eight hundred and ninety-four years since the shadow of his sceptre fell upon the land, according to Baedeker! And under the acacias, with the grass springing about them, are gathered together a company of those strange imperishable imperturbable teachers of antiquity who will still be talking of Ramses II. and Thothmes III. and Psammetikh, when you and I are the dust that blows upon their eyelids and about their feet. There is something pathetically inconsistent about the effort to embower these granite Things with their prodigious memories. They have seen the sweet grasses wither and the tall trees die so many times. They belong to the desert, gray and grim like it, to the time-desert too, that lies out and away beyond the furthest verge that is green with any touch of common human sympathy. Orthodocia didn't say all that, but I saw her looking at a tiny red 'ladybird' creeping between the paws of a rose-coloured sphinx, and I am certain she was preparing an Impression very like it, which I hereby plagiarise.

My own impressions were less valuable. There was a delightful old thing described by Baedeker as a fragment because it had lost its head, that stood in an iron support with its hands clasped in front of it, and wore its hieroglyphics in a tablet down its back, exactly like a Watteau pleat, that charmed me immensely; and I was deeply interested in the official French label attached to the sarcophagi in 'gray granite from Sakkâra, belonging to two brothers named Takhos, who were high officials in the time of the first Ptolemies' (see B.). We would have printed, brutally 'Sarcophagi of the Brothers Takhos,' as we speak of the Cæsars or Shakespeare. But the dear French people understand much better than we the deference that is due to 'high officials,' even to high officials who obtained decorations from the Ptolemies, and inform the public of Victoria and the Khedive that these are sarcophagi 'du General Takhos' and 'du General en chef Takhos'! It is sweetly polite of them.

We went inside, under the winged disc of the sun; and to go inside the museum at Boulak is to enter a strange soulless elder world, peopled with stones instead of shadows, with dried and crackling Realities, beside which a ghost of times we know would seem reasonable and comprehensible and pleasant to meet. At least we would understand his tastes, and his ways, and his prejudices, and his political opinions ; he would be no ghost if we couldn't, but an essence, a vapour, something that would not frighten us. But from these stony immutabilities who can gather anything ? From what they have left us, and what we have guessed, we can see the Cave Men, fighting, grovelling, gambolling, on the beaches of a silent world. We understand and pity them as crude beginners—a little imagining easily fills out their lives. But how shall we begin to imagine about these mocking old personalities that the sands round the Fayoum have been flowing over for three thousand years, and that yet reflect in their wonderful faces, motives and scruples and passions and pleasures complex as our own ! Not the 'steles'—the picture-slabs—they, when Baedeker explains them, seem comprehensible enough. There is a proper artistic primitiveness about the triangular petticoats and the impossible legs of the kings and queens arriving to sacrifice before the Dog-Headed Ape of Thoth. They belong naturally to a time a great distance off, the casual gazer at Boulak does not trouble himself any further than that. But King Khafra, in diorite, might be met to-day sauntering through Piccadilly from his club with a silk hat on—Tih might have looked up from the 'Sporting Intelligence' of a daily newspaper. I found Orthodocia wringing her hands before the wooden man. 'Six thousand years old !' she cried. 'And so like *us* !' This is the startling difficulty—I am talking always of the Baedeker-person at Boulak who doesn't know anything. I can't say how it is with learned people—this is what throws one's imagination back upon itself, and makes conjecture impossible and printed facts vain things. This club-land Khafra and sporting Tih, this intellectual wooden man, who speculated as we do on the riddle of the Sphinx, six thousand years closer to the answer. Khafra built the Second Pyramid—how could he have been a club man ? Tih perhaps talked with Abraham—how could he have been frivolous ? The wooden man lived sixty centuries before Herbert Spencer, and wore an apron ; why should he have suffered unrest about the Wherefore of things ?

And all the walls of the little *salles* are lined with picture-slabs of painted limestone, telling in fresh colours how this desert-drowned world lived, and fought, and died, and worshipped, and even loved, while round about sit its strange old inhabitants with their hands on their granite knees, and read their own history. A green basalt coffin of a woman named Betaita! The jewels of Queen Aah-hoteb, who must have been a queen indeed to wear these golden lions and jackals and lapis-lazuli winged vultures upon her breast and arms, and to count a fierce axe and a wicked dagger among her precious possessions. Yet she was a woman too, with soft moods and vanities, for here are her gilded fan and her tarnished mirror. I caught Orthodocia regarding the mirror of Queen Aah-hoteb from every possible angle. How little we change!

Best of all, I remember a cluster of leaves that is lying in the *Salle du Centre* of the Museum at Boulak. Somebody broke it off where it drooped in an olive-garden of Thebes, I think, one sunny yesterday—some woman, I know. One can see her, reaching up, pale with grief, and failing to understand the red of the pomegranate blossoms and the playing of the fountains and the song of the blind harper on the other side of the wall; for the cluster is to lie through the centuries beside her beloved dead. And there, in the Museum at Boulak, it holds its graceful form and slender substance—one can hear the soft wind rustle in it—still telling of that sunny morning, outliving grief, outdying death.

'Pharaoh!' said Orthodocia, with a little shudder of expectancy, as we entered the *Salle des Momies Royales*.

We walked across to where three or four great coffins stood in the bright light of the eastern windows. The attendant drew the loose cover of one of them away, and there, under the glass, with his long fingers loosely crossed upon his breast, and a wisp of red hair visible behind his ears—black and shrivelled, but tall and kingly still—lay Pharaoh, whose heart the Lord hardened so that he would not let the Children of Israel go.

Not a dead man. Death had been here once, ages and ages ago, and had gone away again, discouraged, discomfited, cheated, leaving little permanent impression. Death was a phase to Pharaoh—he lived through it, so to speak. And now he has nothing further to do with it. A country churchyard, full of friendly people you knew before they went to stay there, would be a much more alarming place to walk through at night than the *Salle des Momies Royales* of the Boulak Museum, who lie in their ragged Egyptian cerements, their wide mouths stuffed with gummy drugs, and smile, the world's sincerest cynics, at both death and life.

He was placarded 'Ramses II.,' but we did not care about him as Ramses II. or 'The Sesostris of the Greeks,' and the fact that he encouraged culture and the arts and presented a library to Thebes, had no weight with us. How should it matter what Herodotus said about him! He held our eyes as the stubborn old Pharaoh of a hundred sermons and Bible stories—distinctly, as I looked at him, I saw the scratched paint on the back of a Presbyterian pew in Canada, and my own small boot, and felt the emotions of a culprit—and we stared, shocked and angry with the defiant old mummy, in spite of Herodotus, thinking of the tale of bricks. It was *those* lips that said to the oppressed of Israel, 'Ye are idle! Ye are idle!'—*that* arm that pointed, imperial, 'Get you to your burdens!'

'You wicked old man!' said Orthodocia. Then, thinking of his slain first-born, when there was a great cry in Egypt and not a house where there was not one dead, she softened. Just then, I remember, came up the Scotch elder and his wife who were going to the Holy Land. A nice old gentleman leaning on his cane, a dear old lady known to her friends, I'm sure, as 'a real practical body.' We had a breakfast-table acquaintance with them. 'Not Pharaoh!' she exclaimed.

Her husband explained that there was 'no dout whateffer aboot it.'

'The Pharaoh that commanded the same day the taskmasters o' the people and their officers, saying: "Ye shall no more give the people straw to mak' brick, as heretofore—they must go and find it for theirsels!—and o' the tale o' brick ye s'all not diminish owt"— the verra same?'

The old gentleman reiterated his conviction.

'Weel,' said she, inspecting the oppressor with the keenest disapprobation, 'I could quite believe him capable o' doin' it!'

Poor old Pharaoh! It was very crushing, and it excited Orthodocia to valorous pity. 'Dear Madam,' she said, deprecatingly, 'this—gentleman—has been preserved three thousand years! One

'I COULD QUITE BELIEVE HIM CAPABLE O' DOIN' IT!'

does go off in one's looks in that time—it's only natural! Don't you think you do him some injustice in not considering what he might have been when he was—newer? For my part, I think he wears wonderfully—and at his age one couldn't expect him to be prepossessing, really!'

'"Gentleman!"' responded the old lady, with a sharp rap of her fan on the sarcophagus. 'The Lord hasna made me a judge nor a divider over him, but I'd no call him a *gentleman*!'

Orthodocia smiled sweetly, but I saw the sparkle of enthusiasm in her eye, and as I did not care about being involved in a dispute about fore-ordination as Pharaoh illustrated it, I took her away to see his papa, who occupies a sarcophagus adjoining. She went back, however, while I was looking at Thothmes II. and Queen Hest-em-Sekhet and the other people, and I find in her note-book a page which explains what she was doing. It tells me that she heard matters made up to Pharaoh while she was there, by a lady who came and clasped her hands, and regarded him with that sad resignation which comparative strangers always use at coffinsides, and said in an undertone, 'What a perfectly natural expression!'

XXXIX

ORTHODOCIA maintains that we walked straight on for five minutes and turned to our left when we went to the real Cairo, and you may believe her if you like. I am not certain, and I can't find anything in Baedeker about it. But it is not important. When you go to Cairo anybody except a policeman will tell you the way to the Mousky, and after you get there you will not care how you came. 'Mousky,' you will observe, and not 'Muski,' which is the modern, orthodox, and accepted version. 'Mousky' is disreputable, odorous, tattered, picturesque, abounding in fleas. 'Muski' might be anything.

No, we had seen nothing like this. Cairo is nowhere duplicated; nowhere even suggested. Orthodocia went the length of admitting that we had felt nothing like it, that Cairo was a distinct and genuine sensation, entirely apart from what she expected of the Sphinx and the Pyramids.

The sun was warm and life was light. The Mousky was full of cheerfulness, of sweet rascality, delightful to breathe. It has become ambitious lately, and is Europeanising; but it is still more

Eastern than respectable, and it is hard to believe that it can ever
be very snug or very clean. We sauntered along among Jews, and
Copts, and Arabs, and Egyptians, and Frenchmen, and Greeks, and
Italians, and Turks, and bold black stalwart creatures from inner
Africa, with happy placidity, having nothing to do, and feeling
exactly like doing it, which is the charm of Egypt. Baedeker told
us who the people were, but their commingling was dazzling, and we
could not apply Baedeker. To us they were an endless twisting
throng in sandals and tarboosh, and floating robes of blue and
yellow and white, that moved against the dusky mystery of the
shops, and made fascinating bits of colour where the shadows deepened in the distance. Their faces had as much of the pallor of the
East as of its deeper tints, and differed, of course, in type, but they
all wore the dignity that seems to be the Oriental substitute for a
soul, and were full of that agreeable unconcern which, after our con-
science-wrangles of the West, it is worth travelling a few thousand
miles to look upon. Only the negroes we could tell—they were so
black, and so big, and so supercilious, and so gay of vestment. To
turn a corner of old Cairo and come upon a large, self-satisfied
negro, habited as he knows nature intended him to be, and expanding
in the sun he loves, is not a matter to be looked over in noting the
pleasures of El Kahir.

Women, too—we regarded them curiously ; and they looked at
us often with a smile in their eyes—conscious, tantalising eyes that
shine lustrous between their blackened fringes, with a gilt wooden
tube between and a yard long strip of *yashmak* hanging from it,
making a mystery of nose and lips and chin. They may all be
beautiful—the presumption is against it, but the possibility is always
there, and until crow's-feet gather too palpably above the *yashmak*,
the eyes express the possibility in the most alluring manner—knowing very well that you are thinking of it, secure in the knowledge
that you can't find out. Otherwise the ladies of Cairo are not attractive. Their figures express more than a suspicion of *embonpoint*,
and their garments carry out the idea. A dame we saw in the
Mousky that morning seems to have passed my elbow this minute.
She was loftily mounted on a very superior donkey, whose ornaments
jingled as he went. Her own ears and arms and fingers were heavy

with bedeckments, and as she trotted by her copious swathings took the wind and bellowed out about her like a sombre cloud. But her eyes shone forth from it like stars, and started Orthodocia upon a theory that if for generations and generations one were allowed to exhibit only one's eyes, one's eyes would, in the course of time—without the slightest effort or desire upon one's own part—become very charming indeed, which I suppose is true. And at the stage of natural development which the orbs of the Cairene ladies have reached already, one can easily imagine a susceptible person's first walk in the Mousky to be, from beginning to end, a sympathetic study of eyes.

But I have not told you of the indescribable din of this street of Cairo; how the carriages dash recklessly—whips cracking—among the people; how the water-sellers clash their brass vessels and cry, 'Drink, O Faithful!' and the pedlars of lemons and of lupins, of dates and sweet cakes, call upon Allah to make their baskets light; and the money-changers sit at the corners of the streets endlessly chaffering and clinking, and the donkeys bray, and the people talk in many tongues, and the camel joins the chorus in his own distinctive voice. Ah, the camel of Cairo! I tremble on the verge of a paragraph about him; I know I cannot do him justice, but the emotions that came with the first one that gladdened us in the Mousky that morning crowd back upon me and will not be dismissed. He was immediately behind us—we turned suddenly and saw him, a great pack of green clover on his back, looking down at us with a bland and level condescension which seemed intended to allay our nervousness, though it had not precisely that effect. We had grown used to the donkeys. They trotted, and obeyed a stick from the rear. When they elbowed us it was with apology, and when we turned to speak to each other and found an asinine countenance close to our own it was always full of deference. They occupied the human plane, moreover; their joys and sorrows were, in a manner, ours; they shared the common lot. And one didn't get out of their way; one kept them waiting. But this slow, strange beast, with his lofty and deliberate assertion of precedence—we made room for him at once, and without cavil, as he mutely requested us to do, and as he passed we stood and looked at him. We saw that everybody made room for him, as if he were incarnate fate. He went quietly and comfortably through the narrowest lanes and the densest crowds by the mere force of his personality. He was the most impressive living thing we saw in Egypt, not excepting two Pashas and a Bey.

'WE NEVER SAW ONE THAT WAS NOT INDISPUTABLY SECOND-HAND.'

He was engaged with large philosophies, one could see that, and the superciliousness in the curve of his neck was unavoidable. Ages ago he had tried to make up for it by a smile, a smile of the simple primary sort, acquired before the world learned smiling hatred, a mere pulling up of the corners of the mouth, expressing pure amiability, and from generation to generation the smile had become a fixture, though he gives one the impression that he would dispense with it now if he could. For he thinks and remembers and compares. The people have changed and have divided their inheritance; he is a solitary survival, and has preserved his. Their traditions are his history: he knew the desert world; he walked in the train of the Queen of Sheba; he could retail scandals of the Court of Solomon. And he bends his back to the modern burden, neither more nor less than he carried then, because it is, and has always been, part of the formula of life for him. When they took it off I suppose he was relieved, but he did not show it in any way; when they made it too heavy he simply looked round communicatively and declined to get up. He did what was required of him with a superior leisurely dignity that was elevating to observe. He never hurried; I did not see him beaten. As to his personal appearance, it is difficult to say that he is beautiful; but I defy you to go to Cairo and thereafter call him ugly. He seems to belong to a world of different standards in these matters. His skin is the most interesting thing about him, to a lover of the antique. It seems to have been in constant use since the original camel took it out of the ark with him, it is so battered and tattered, so seamy and patched, so disreputably parchment-coloured. Orthodocia did not love this Egyptian as I did; she said he was known to have a vicious bite, and his airs were insupportable. 'Moreover,' she remarked, 'I want to see a *new* camel!' But, though we gazed on many clover-laden trains winding through many *sharia* of Cairo, we never saw one that was not indisputably second-hand.

Our feet turned naturally with the shuffling multitude's into the bazaars, where the throng grew thicker and the babel less, for a donkey in the Khan el Khaleel is a serious matter, and

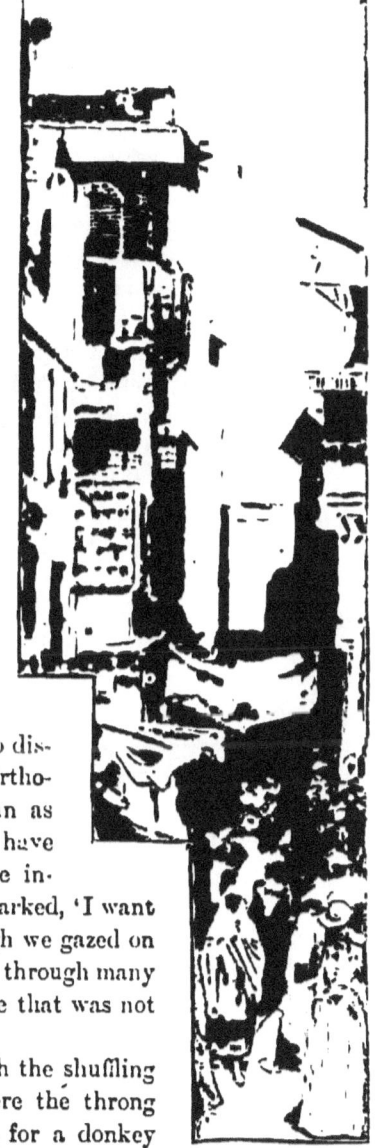

'INTO THE BAZAARS.

two donkeys, properly applied, bar the way. The only merchants in the world live in the Khan el Khaleel, where the sunlight comes seldom, and from a great distance, down through the ruined flapping brown awnings that stretch across from the dilapidated lattices on one side to the dilapidated lattices on the other, and falls in flecks and patches on the green turban of a descendant of the Prophet as he chaffers with a Jew in yellow about the price of a keffiyah. The only merchants in the world, though they cannot show you the jewels of India, or make you the bows of Japan, nor have yet mastered the significance of 'clearing' sales. Though their shops are only cubes in the wall, wherein they sit cross-legged, and draw at their coiled 'hubble-bubbles,' and stroke their long beards and smile in your face, and cry, 'Take it! I give it thee! Allah will recompense me!' when you dispute their conscienceless prices. There is somewhat about themselves of a subtler essence of barter and somewhat about their goods, which are not gorgeous or wonderful, but full of quaint colour and conscious charm, that makes the only true merchandise of them in a most satisfying way. Though, as Orthodocia says, it may be only an after-glow of 'The Arabian Nights.'

'But one can see it all in Regent Street!' No, dear lady. Not the piles and piles of pointed Turkish sandals, red and yellow, flaming out against the shadows where one mysterious vista twists into another. Not the pale embroidered stuffs that age has withered into fancies more exquisite than any modern loom could imagine. Not the queer little saucerless coffee services, in brass and blue enamel, with their slender, long-necked urns and thimble cups! And if you can by chance buy a koran-holder, a set of doyleys, a gold-embroidered vest, a brass lamp studded with coloured glass, in London, what is it? You miss the profusion, the people, the bargaining, the delicious sense of making a tiny bit of all that picturesqueness your own. And your Regent Street things will never have the smell of Cairo that mine have.

One sees them all at work, that is another charm. Fashioning the bright slippers, pulling the gold thread in and out of the dragoman's vest, hammering and chasing the brazen lamp, laying each completed thing on the shelf to be sold and beginning another on the spot—the very poetry of commerce. There were the little people who sat outside, a foot from the ground, and tinkered and gossiped, and cheated and smiled, and praised Allah. There were richer merchants, whose possessions filled two rooms. Of these was Abu-el-Hassan. Abu-el-Hassan, portly and courtly, speaking French, producing, with much grace, a box of Turkish Delight to assist our deliberations on his inlaid cabinets, his heaped-up embroideries, his Persian antiquities. As we sat in the tempting little back room of Abu-el-Hassan, and wondered how much overcharge one was honourably bound to submit to after partaking of the double confection of his politeness and his sweets, he showed us his chiefest treasure. It was a soft, rich carpet, deep piled and velvety, full of flickering colours, with here and there a sparkle of gold. Its price was one hundred and fifty pounds. Abu-el-Hassan stroked it fondly. There came a real, beautiful pleasure into his face. 'It is my lofe!' said he. On account of which sentiment Orthodocia paid him, I am convinced, a great many unnecessary piastres.

Coming out and away, we stopped before handsome young Abdallah, a seller of perfumes, of kohl for blackening the eyelashes, and henna for staining the finger nails, and bought tiny heart-shaped green bottles of attar of roses. As we bought, a friend of Abdallah's came that way—such a dainty young lady with tripping little feet, and a piquant face, unveiled. Her dress and her chatter were French; but she was a Spaniard, we thought. And we learned, from her conversation with Abdallah that she wished to borrow his clothes for a romantic rendezvous that evening under the acacias in the garden of the Esbekeeyah. And Abdallah, assenting, kissed her lightly on both cheeks, whereat she nodded at him smilingly and was gone. Much we wondered who she was and how the escapade would end; and she made a vivacious little contrasting episode, passing lightly through the mazes of the Khan el Khaleel, that stays in my memory of it.

Many mosques saw we that afternoon, with a 'guide'; but there is getting to be a great paucity of material in Orthodocia's notebook, and I can find out from it only the more or less uninteresting fact that one mosque was striped. As I remember them, they were all great gaunt places, extremely brown and ragged and hollow, and usually splashed with the blood of a person we had never heard of before. The guide was invaluable. He never failed to tell us to take our shoes off, or missed an opportunity of making us pay piastres. For the rest, he walked round the places we visited with the deepest interest, and showed an intelligent curiosity on a number of points, which, by means of Baedeker, we were happily able to gratify. In the black, oily water of a fountain in the Mosque of Hassan some women were washing their faces and their feet. As we came in, they hurried on their *yashmaks*—the guide was a man—but went on bathing their extremities with serene composure. And then the guide made the one illuminative remark in his répertoire. 'Sultan Hassan very good doctor!' he said, and that was all. Neither the gate whereon the faithful leave their toothaches and their cares, with molars that grind no more and wisps of hair and other personal tributes, nor the tombs of the Caliphs, nor eke of the Mamelukes, nor any other object of interest or of admiration, could elicit a further statement from him. Orthodocia told him that he was a most original and interesting type of guide—so willing to learn—and that he might come again to-morrow; but as it was a little fatiguing to support the entire burden of the conversation for so long, he might go then, if he could find the way home alone. So he went, but we saw nothing of him next day. He was probably unable to ascertain the whereabouts of the hotel.

And we drove alone to the strange little Coptic church that rises out of tenements and potteries and dilapidations all round about, with its tarnished interior and quaint Byzantine saints, once gilt and red. A boy in priestly garments showed us the trough where these later Christians bathe their feet, as they did who listened to Paul and Apollos, and the divisions for the men, and the women, and the children, and the inscription in strange characters on the right of the high altar, 'Greetings to the Temple of the Father.' Then he led the way down a dark narrow stone stair into a vaulted crypt, at one end of which stood an altar like a tomb-niche, to mark the spot where, in the early light that came before the full dawning, rested the Mother and the Child. Perhaps if we had been in Palestine and had had a surfeit of traditions, this one would not have impressed us—there were plenty of scoffers at the hotel who told us it was humbug. But there is one consoling thing about being disillusionised—it presupposes the illusion ; and both Orthodocia and I were glad we had gone down, credulous, into that quiet little place, and thought, believing, of the sweet eyes with the motherhood of Christ in them, that looked upon it when the chronicles of time, for us, had just begun.

The British 'Tommy,' in uniform, is not imposing upon a donkey. His legs hang stiffly to within a few inches of the ground, he holds himself with the martial erectness of a Life Guardsman, and he reflects an idea that his character justifies any position in life which even the donkey finds amusing. We met numbers of him mounted thus trotting down out of the Citadel, wearing a notable air of occupying Egypt, which did not go well with the donkey either.

And there, when the day was done, lay Cairo all about our feet. Cairo, the city of the genii, and of our dreams, always farthest away of all the cities in the magical distance beyond the rim o' the world which edges the fields of home—for did not the way thither lie through the air on wishing carpets? Cairo, pale and fair in the glow of sunset, brooding over her rich stuffs and her dead Caliphs, still cherishing and exhaling, there in her tranquil beauty, the foolish old thought that she is the Mother of the World ! The mosque-bubbles rose into the mellow light, and the slim minarets pierced it, and mingling with the old, old hum of humanity that rose from her bosom and floated up to us in her high Citadel came the voices of her blind mueddin in the minarets, calling the people to their sunset prayers. Eastward the sheer high lines of the Mokattum Hills, unsoftened even by this yellowed air ; then Cairo in their valley, her old Nile lover still at her feet, slipping between Arabia and Libya to the sea ; and beyond and about it all the gray-white speechless desert with the Pyramids on its verge.

Immediately beneath us, and in full view, was the spot where the Mamelukes were massacred ; but I could not get Orthodocia to pay any attention to it. Her excuse was that so far as she knew there was no record whatever of such an event in the 'Arabian Nights'

—and what other historical records of Cairo had we that could possibly be depended upon?

* * * * *

'One always hears,' said I, 'that it is the proper thing to do.'

'I have only seen one lady doing it,' said Orthodocia, 'and she looked like a cook.'

We were discussing how we should go to Heliopolis to see the obelisk there, and I was urging the donkey way of going. Up to this time we had been spending what was left of our substance at an alarming rate upon victorias.

From the first I had regarded the donkeys longingly, feeling instinctively that I should adorn one; that I, who am no horsewoman, would sit a donkey with composure and grace. They inspired me with a confidence and a desire to get on which I had never felt in connection with any other quadruped. But up to this time Orthodocia had said it was '*infra dig.*,' and when Orthodocia used Latin I knew that there was nothing for it but to accept the situation. On this particular morning, however, I confronted her with serious considerations of finance, and donkeys are as cheap in Cairo as carriages are dear. Just then Rubicundo passed at full trot, with an hilarious *hammar*[1] behind, an inspiriting sight to see. 'Dear man!' said I, with enthusiasm, 'what a glorious time he is having! Do, Orthodocia!' I did not then suspect my friend of any ulterior motive in thus setting her face against the national animal. Orthodocia was usually so straightforward. But as we have often told each other since, people must travel round the world with their friends to know them.

'Do, Orthodocia!' I supplicated, restating the argument of the exchequer. And Orthodocia did.

We found a group of donkey-boys round the corner from the hotel. Orthodocia said that the amount of our entire expenses in Cairo would not induce her to mount in front of the piazza. The boys were tossing coppers, and the donkeys stood about a little distance off in a three-legged, *néglige* manner, apathetically nosing the ground. Boys and donkeys surrounded us in a moment with an enthusiasm which made a choice difficult to me.

[1] Donkey-boy.

'My donkey numb' one donkey, lady! He name Lily Langtry!'
'Lily Langtry he kick!'—confidentially from a rival—'my donkey she go easy; she name sometime "Gran' Ole Man" sometime "Granny!"'

I hesitated for pleasure and delight. I deeply desired each donkey in turn. Had time permitted I would have taken a gay and fanciful excursion into the unknown on the back of every one of them. But time did not permit, so I selected, for his serious deportment and other excellent features, an ass named Mark Twain. Orthodocia vacillated also, but not from love. She regarded the lot with frowning criticism, and considered the testimonials, spoken and written, with stern incredulity. Her final decision was a meek little white quadruped, 'Rose of Sharon.' 'Rose of Sharon' had a 'character' from an English nobleman of distinction—I think it was the Duke of Hamilton—in which a certain prominence was given to her tractability and sweetness of disposition. Then the elect donkey-boys scuttled off to change the trappings for side-saddles. 'Not that it will make much difference!' remarked Orthodocia, with something very like a groan.

'Get on first, dear!' said my friend persuasively, when the quartette came back, stroking her white donkey on the neck and nose. 'I'll follow you in a minute. I like to—to get them to know me!' At this the white donkey tossed his head and made an 'allemande left,' Orthodocia going patiently after it.

I may say, in no boastful spirit, that I vaulted lightly into the saddle, and that Mark Twain and I participated in a spirit of perfect good-fellowship from the beginning. He was my very, very first donkey, and the emotions he inspired were of that deliciously pristine character that one loves to look back upon in after life. No other donkey can ever be to me what Mark was—I called him Mark. We were on terms that permitted the use of his baptismal name at the end of the first half-mile. There was something about the manner of his going that combined the exaltation of a tandem with the security of a tram, and gave one a joyous thrill of daring, together with the divine feeling of mistress-ship and the opportunity of looking round. His pace was steady and serene. He required nothing in the saddle, no tugging at the bridle-rein, no whip, no voice of command. Indeed, the bridle-rein was a mockery, and the whip a vain thing; he recognised no authority except his master's, who ran behind and discoursed to him; and his rider had no care or responsibility on his account. This is what made donkey-riding so superior an attraction to me. I had only to bounce naturally and be happy. Some people, especially equestrians, would not have liked it, I know. For instance, when it became apparent that Orthodocia was not catching up, and I wanted to go back to look for her, I communicated my desire to the donkey in the usual way. He did not take the slightest notice of me. I exhorted him, and clung with both hands to one rein. He trotted on with that composure which is the special talent of his kind. I was obliged finally to ask the donkey-boy to turn him round. He said one word —I have always been sorry not to remember the word; in going through life one meets so many of Mark Twain's connections who are difficult to persuade—and the donkey swerved round as if he had been arranged on a pivot. An equestrian doubtless would have considered this humiliating. I am not an equestrian, and I thought it satisfying to a degree. It so thoroughly relieved one from all complicity in case of accident.

I found Orthodocia still stroking the nose of the Rose of Sharon; and there were some fragments of biscuits lying about which she did not explain.

'I *think* she knows me now!' my friend remarked uncertainly; then, diplomatically, 'How beautifully you sit, dear! Do go on! I'll be with you in one moment.'

Thus flatteringly adjured I trotted off again, and gave myself up to the delirium of my first donkey without restraint until Orthodocia's voice from the rear, full of woe, smote me upon the heart. 'Ha-ow —very fast—you go!' quoth she, quothing shrill and breathlessly. Then when I looked upon Orthodocia I could by no means refrain from laughter, of such prodigious sort that Mark Twain, taking it in some personal way, broke into a gallop and left the Rose of Sharon further behind than ever. My dear friend occupied her saddle with what might be called distressed decorum, in which was written plainly the air of being accustomed to better things. She held her bridle-rein to a nicety, and her elbows might have been glued to her side. But the Rose was doing her best in the way of pace, and the motion somehow did not harmonise with the lady's bearing. Moreover, she wore an inexplicable expression—I mean Orthodocia—in which grief and awe and terror were blended in a way that is funny in connection with a donkey. And her eyes were fixed, to the utter disregard of the landscape, upon the Rose of Sharon's left ear.

'Why,' said she, as Mark Twain, entirely of his own accord, obligingly waited for the Rose, 'does she lay it down that way?' referring to the ear. 'Do you think she's got any tricks—does she *look* as if she had? If she has, I think it was positively *criminal* of the Duke of Hamilton not to mention them?'

The Rose was probably the most inoffensive and amiable little ass in Cairo, and I assured Orthodocia of this, I fear a little witheringly, for I felt very superior.

'It's all very well for you!' she responded. 'You seem *born* to ride donkeys'—crushingly—'but'—here came the revelation—'I know exactly how it will be. I've tried them at Mentone, at Capri, everywhere—*do* walk a little!—my friends are always donkey-mad like you —*and I never can stay on!*' This in a tone of real melodrama.

'I observe,' I said, 'that when these *hammars* wish these *homars* —I speak according to Baedeker—to stop, they say "Bus!" to go on faster, "*Ha'arga!*" This is not according to Baedeker; but perhaps our *hammars* have not been brought up by a well-principled guidebook. If you can master these two terms you are safe, for though your *homar* will pay no attention to them, your *hammar* will heed, and thus it shall be as you desire.'

'Thanks!' replied Orthodocia. "Bus!" "*Ha'ar-ga!*" "Bus!" "*Ha'ar-ga!*" Not at all difficult to remember.'

'No!' said I; 'and now, since we are well outside the city'— we were throwing grotesque shadows on the yellow white road that winds past the barracks, high above a crumbling waste of old potteries and dusty olive trees—'suppose we "*ha'ar-ga*" a little. What do you say to a race?'

'No—*no*—no!' cried Orthodocia, explosively; and indeed I would not have insisted, though I was highly incredulous of her disabilities, but the donkey-boys, catching my idea, laid forthwith about the flanks of Mark Twain and the Rose in a spirit of wild exultation; and instantly we were off, all six of us, in a shouting, gesticulating, dusty, delirious whirl. I do not know the pleasures of the chase. I had never before ridden anything that went at the rate of x^n as Mark Twain did, keeping always a good neck ahead of the Rose, who also exhibited wonders. To me it was pure, undiluted happiness, and I patted Mark Twain softly on the neck, and whispered my applause into his large and receptive ear.

This was all in the course of the first sixty seconds, at the end of which I looked round to cheer and encourage Orthodocia. She sat erect as ever, pale and determined of countenance, a world of concentration in her eyes, but bumping in such a hysterical and highly-agonised manner that it was impossible to predict by three square feet, when she rose, where she would come down. I called aloud to her in her distress, 'Orthodocia !'

'*Ha'ar-ga !*' she answered wildly. '*Ha'ar-ga! Ha'ar-ga !*' bumping more convulsively than ever, and clutching madly at the Rose of Sharon's ear. Her *hammar* hammared with renewed zeal, and the Rose galloped ear and ear with Mark. 'Don't be rash, Ortho-

'TO HELIOPOLIS.'

docia !' I cried ; and *'Ha'ar ga !'* screamed my friend despairingly for answer.

'All right !' I returned. 'Good for the Rose ! Go on, Rosy ! Get up, Mark ! *Ha'ar-ga !*'

The donkeys galloped against one another, and just then Orthodocia, swerving, made an impetuous attempt to sit down in my saddle. 'Oh, what an ass !' cried she. 'Can't you keep to your own side of the road ?' And to this day I can't be certain whether she meant Mark Twain or me. Orthodocia is so excitable. 'What *are* you encouraging them for ! *Ha'ar-ga !* you young lunatic !' to the donkey-boy.

Mark was leading again, and Orthodocia's *hammar* said the last word of persuasion to the Rose of Sharon, who literally kicked up her heels—at least Orthodocia said she did, but I don't consider that she was in a position to see—in her effort to overtake us. Three more distressful communications reached me from Orthodocia at this point. They came in rapid succession. 'I'm going off!' con expressione—'*I'm going off!*' crescendo—'I'm OFF!' forte.

After that silence reigned for a space while Orthodocia rearranged her draperies and removed the lime dust from her front teeth with her handkerchief. After having ascertained that she had suffered no fracture anywhere I fear that I gave myself up to tearful and uncontrollable hilarity. Orthodocia received it in silence which was more than cold—it was Arctic.

'THE ROSE OF SHARON.'

'Would you mind telling me,' she said frigidly after an interval, 'if you had any special reason for *not* ha'argaing, when I so particularly desired it?'

Whereupon the truth dawned over me, and I very nearly perished untimely. 'You wanted to *stop*!' I said, leaning against Mark Twain, who had come up for his share of the humour of the situation. 'Then "*Bus!*" was the proper expletive, my dear—"*Bus!*"'

'Oh!' said Orthodocia; 'don't you think we had better be getting on to Heliopolis?'

Orthodocia had such lovely ways—to borrow a phrase from the Irish politicians—of burking the situation.

So we went on to Heliopolis, under the acacias, and past the labouring dripping water-wheels in pale green fields, where graceful white ibises were bowing and stepping—on to Heliopolis in the caressing sunlight, in much the same circumstance as people went in those early days when Heliopolis was there to see. Occasionally we met other donkeys, with whom Mark Twain and the Rose invariably exchanged the statement that it was a fine day in their own musical tongue, and a way that was highly embarrassing to us, for we did not know any of the tourists attached to the other donkeys. We did all we could to prevent it; but you couldn't

'I'M OFF!'

prevent a donkey with a genuinely emotional nature from giving expression to his feelings by Act of Parliament, much less by moral suasion. I had learned in my natural history that when a donkey wants to bray he always twists his tail round in the instinctive way in which we put our hands to our mouths when we yawn, and that if anybody interfered with the first part of the function it would be impossible for him to carry out the second. I mentioned this to Orthodocia, who might have interrupted Mark Twain in this way very conveniently if she had chosen to do so, but she said she didn't like to be interrupted herself, and she was quite sure he would be annoyed about it. And it was not a thing that one cared to urge.

When we arrived at Heliopolis we found an obelisk there, set up some time ago by Ra-Kheper-Ka Usertesen, Lord of the Diadems and Son of the Sun, the like of which can be seen only on the Thames Embankment in London, or in Central Park in New York. But the interest that remains in my mind about Heliopolis concentrates itself upon the way we got there.

XL

I was an unhappy white slave of Baghdad, and a genii of benevolent intention had just arisen before me out of a sodawater bottle, when I heard a repressed voice in my ear and saw an unnatural shining through my eyelids. 'Get up!' said Orthodocia. 'It's long after three!'

We were not on the point of departure, as you may think, by any unnatural train or ship. We were only going to see the Sphinx and the Pyramids, at the hour Orthodocia considered most fitting for the last Impression of our trip which she intended to capitalise —the hour of dawn. To see the day break upon the countenance of the Sphinx, however, at Orthodocia's rate of going, though we had only seven miles to ride, it was necessary to start at least two hours earlier. I recognised the situation, therefore, especially when I saw upon the table in the dim and ghastly gaslight the revolver which Orthodocia had borrowed from Rubicundo the night before for our protection in the event of brigands by the way—and with an internal malediction upon all impressions of an unseasonable nature, I arose.

A quarter of an hour later, we slipped past the sleeping chamberlains in the upper corridors and down the wide staircases to the outer portals, which the drowsy Luigi guarded alone. He started up when we indicated our desire to be let out, and stared at us, Orthodocia said afterwards, as if we had been guilty of some unconventionality. Orthodocia also says that he shuddered as the cold light of the hall lamp fell upon the silver barrels of her revolver; but I did not see the shudder. I suppose he concluded that since we were not taking our luggage with us, it could be no concern of his or Shepheard's, for he let us out without comment.

It was very dark and silent out on the broad verandah; a little chilly wind rustled among the palms; nothing stirred or spoke but that. Cairo was asleep under a sprinkling of stars. There were no lights anywhere in the tall houses that stood obscurely against the sky. 'Let us go back, Orthodocia!' said I, for I am not a brave person, and I did not expect it to be so dark.

'Never!' returned Orthodocia. Then, leaning over the verandah, 'Achmed!' she called, softly; 'Achmed!'

A little figure rose up in the street and stole quickly to the verandah steps. 'I here,' it said; 'I go bring donkey!' and it sped away into the night. Achmed's faith in his appointment with us had not been absolute. In a quarter of an hour he was back, however, with Mark Twain and the Rose, and an apology for the other hammar, who, he said, had gone to visit his grandfather in Alexandria—in other words, did not approve the expedition.

We mounted and stole away into the deeper shadows of Cairo. There came gray breadths between them as we went, and the stars in the narrow spaces above our heads grew fewer; but we could see only that we were riding into a high-walled mystery of lattices and casements and *mush*-*aribekeyahs*. The stillness was very soft and mean-

'AWAY INTO THE DEEPER SHADOWS OF CAIRO.'

ingful, and the pattering of the donkeys' hoofs, which seemed to be the only sound abroad in all the city, made it a palpable thing, so that we said nothing to break it. Achmed, behind, ran silently. Occasionally there floated out to us from a dark garden thicket some scent that told of roses and pomegranates.

We left the tall old clustering houses and rode through the wider streets of Ismail's city, where the grayness was lighter and fell upon white walls and yellow ones, and upon the dark indistinctness of olive trees, and so across the great bridge, with the *dahabeeyahs* sleeping under it, that spans the Nile—it was in itself a curious thing to be crossing the Nile. Then we looked back from the other side at Cairo, crowding wan along the shore, and saw by the paling sky behind her minarets that we must make haste.

The path twisted through dusky sand heaps piled on the edge of a little river that wound its way to the Nile. From behind one and another of these, dark figures began to steal forth, turbaned, mysterious, with long robes flung over one shoulder. They seemed to grow out of the sand and to slip back into it again, so silently they went; and in that creeping Eastern half-light they suggested all the romance of Arabia. Nevertheless they made me nervous.

'Orthodocia,' said I, 'is that revolver loaded?'

'Certainly *not*!' responded my friend. 'Do you think I would *touch* such a thing? What would prevent its going off at any moment, and then, with this animal, where should I be?'

'The Rose is excitable,' I concurred; 'but I suppose you've brought cartridges?'

'Yes,' said Orthodocia, 'a dozen and a half!'

Then she turned very pale and suddenly reined up. 'It has just struck me, my dear,' she said, 'that I've got them *in my pocket*!'

'Well!'

'*Well!*' Orthodocia repeated with concentration, 'don't you know that cartridges will go off, as well as pistols, with sufficient concussion! You haven't the slightest idea of how this donkey concusses! I've been running the most frightful danger all this time! And you laugh! I consider you inhuman!'

'No, my love!' I responded, with an effort at self-control, and in proof of my sincerity I offered to carry the cartridges. Orthodocia said that she thought it would be more prudent to throw them away. I asked her if she thought she had any right to throw away a dozen and a half of Rubicundo's cartridges, probably all he had; whereat Orthodocia consented to hand them over to me. 'After all,' she said, 'it is really only fair that we should divide our ammunition.' And the Rose made a detailed statement of relief as Orthodocia emptied her pocket.

We were trotting under the long avenue of acacias that leads to the Pyramids, and already we could see them, away to the left, in glimpses between the tree trunks, for the day was growing. We began to meet camels, clover-laden, pacing silently to find the sun in Cairo's market-places, and to catch the fragrance of their burdens as they passed. Their masters and Achmed exchanged grave salutations.

The still morning air was a dream of peace. Behind us, where Cairo was, the sky gleamed white and silver; nearer, fields of young grasses, tenderly green, with the reedy river winding through bearing the dawn in its bosom; and by the river the palm-shadowed dusky huts of the fellaheen. Tranquil beyond all telling—even the white ibises flew softly in the rice fields—with no rejoiceful tint of rose and gold, but brooding and fair, the soul of that Eastern dawning came on before its sun. We gazed and gazed at the sweet wonder of it; then, remembering our chief desire, adjured Achmed, so that the donkeys sped with one accord and ceased not to speed until we all arrived at the Desert of Sahara, and picked our way past the Great Pyramid, through the sandy *débris* of the desert's edge, to where, in a wide hollow, scooped out of the sand, the great gray Sphinx upreared itself, watching for the sun.

We were not a moment too soon. Even as we dismounted, all the east, behind the river and the cloudy palms, trembled in faint pale yellow, and the desert world grew full of light, so that we saw very plainly the majestic form before us, that also waited, in infinite silence, in infinite patience.

'Ah!' said Orthodocia, as we sat down together in the sand and watched the face of the marvel.

There had come a sudden joy upon it with the rays that struck golden on the unblinking eyeballs. They regarded each other, the great Sphinx and the great Sun, exulting, understanding—the only changeless ones, who had known it all from the beginning, old comrades who had yet to fail each other. As the sunlight spread splendidly down over her the solemn gladness grew in the face of the Sphinx, and we saw also in her shattered features their strange divinity, their power to comprehend, their tender human sympathy.

'THE SOLEMN GLADNESS GREW IN THE FACE OF THE SPHINX.'

She seemed to carry the mystery of life in her heart, to have knowledge of it, to answer our feeble 'Wherefore?' with an inscrutable 'Therefore!' yet to brood always upon the pity of it. Somewhere about her strong, calm lips an answer shaped itself for every bubbling question of ours; a grief might have slept in the shadow of her breast. With her face and her soul the Sphinx led me to believe that she was the foster-mother of all humanity. Yet she is only a great stone image, sixty-six feet high, badly mutilated, crouching upon the edge of the Desert of Sahara, with her paws half buried in its sands.

'Orthodocia,' said I, 'what is your Impression?'

My friend, sitting in the sand two paces off, regarded the Sphinx earnestly a little longer. Then, 'I think she is a woman,' said Orthodocia, 'and I think she Made the World!'

Whereafter there was nothing for a considerable space, I being scientifically unable to contradict Orthodocia; and we both sat on the edge of the sand-hollow and gave ourselves up to thought, each believing the other to be wrapped in sacred idealisations which neither would venture to intrude upon. We confided to one another afterwards that most of the vague sentiments that inspired us after a time bore upon our breakfasts; but both Orthodocia and myself would have been ashamed to confess that such material considerations could dwell with us for a moment in the presence of the Sphinx. So we sat there before her, turning a deaf ear to our inward complainings, doing our best to feel properly; each believing that any word of hers would break the spell that bound the other. If Mark Twain had been equally considerate, I really don't know when we should have got away, but he was not. He knew no concealment of the emotions, and respected none. He stood silhouetted against the flaming Eastern sky alone; Achmed and the Rose had wandered off. He felt the silence, the impressiveness, the loneliness of the situation, and he stretched out his neck, and curled up his tail, and brayed bitterly. Not an ordinary bray, a bray that ran up and down the chromatic scale and knew all the chords of woe—a genuinely emotional bray, proceeding from the most badly-oiled donkey interior in Cairo; a long, long lyric that sounded far out upon the waste and returned again, burdened with tears. I suppose it was because of Orthodocia's instinctive aversion to his kind that she could never see anything fine or pathetic in a donkey's bray, and she looked at Mark Twain with some annoyance while he relieved his feelings.

'What a voice!' said she.

I retorted that I thought Mark had a very nice voice indeed for a donkey; and in the discussion which followed we suddenly began to descend the sandbank. We went with a certain rapidity to the bottom, and by the time we reached it our desire for elevating sentiments seemed to have disappeared for ever. Orthodocia declared, as she shook the sand out of her hair, that the Sphinx looked like an Irish washerwoman from that point of view, and I considered the washerwoman libelled by the comparison. This did not lead me to consider Orthodocia's first impression less valuable, but it confirmed my belief in the instability of all sentiment evolved out of its proper connection with meals.

Pieces of the paws of the Sphinx, with rough, primitive mortar attached, were lying about in the sand. If there was a person jointly considered by Orthodocia and myself a thoroughly disreputable individual with a small mind, it was the person who carries off 'relics' of famous objects he sees in foreign countries. This severe opinion not being upon the surface of our minds, however, we carefully picked up and cherished lumps of the Sphinx's paws, not, I think, because of the Sphinx, but because of the mortar. It brought us—we fancied we could see the very finger prints in it —into such close, homely, intimate relation with the people who laid it on the other side of the centuries; it seemed to tell us more than Mariette had at Boulak. And, indeed, was it not very likely, as Orthodocia said, if Pharaoh had fancied any alterations in the Sphinx at that time, that Moses himself might have spread it!

If it had not been for our misadventure, we would doubtless have resented the uncomprehending sacrilege of the smiling Arabs waiting at the top to offer us 'coffywi'thespinx'—thick, hot, black Turkish stuff, in tiny cups. That had left us in so frivolous a state of mind, however, that we pledged her with the most impertinent sentiments, bestowing much backsheesh for the opportunity. How grotesque it all was—the wide, gray desert, the imperturbable Guardian of Secrets staring triumphantly at the sun, the Pyramids standing a little way off in their eternal angle against the sky, and we two, in exuberant foolishness, in happy, mocking ignorance, with our feet in her shifting sands, wishing the Sphinx and ourselves 'Many happy returns!'

There had been nobody at all but the Sphinx when we arrived, but at the clink of the first piastre the desert began to give forth her inhabitants, and in ten minutes the place was alive with Bedouins. They said nothing, except the vendor of coffee, but stood about in groups which suggested every possible form of backsheesh, and kept a furtive watch upon our movements. Presently we saw, approaching from the direction of Gizeh, two camels, of insinuating deportment. They were ridden by Arab youths, who guided them straight to the group formed by Orthodocia, Mark Twain, the Rose of Sharon, Ach-med, and me.

'Like ride camel, lady?'

'No,' said Orthodocia, firmly.

'Every lady like dis camel, lady! He best quality camel, low'st price!'

'IT WAS A PROUD MOMENT FOR ORTHODOCIA.'

Orthodocia carefully untied the brown paper parcel which contained the revolver—I omitted to state that she had done it up thus on the way as soon as there was light enough to see it. The knots took her some little time. Then she folded the brown paper into a neat parallelogram, put it in her pocket, and grasped the revolver determinedly with her left hand.

'No!' she said again, and with repressed significance. 'Go away!'

The camel-boys said no further word of persuasion but went away immediately, and we noticed a slight simultaneous movement of departure in the groups looking on. It was a proud moment for Orthodocia. 'This is Bedouin bravery!' she said scornfully. Then she unfolded the brown paper again, and tied the revolver nicely up in it, using the same piece of string. 'One should never waste anything!' said Orthodocia. 'I always keep my pieces of paper and string. You see how valuable the habit is!'

'Yes, Orthodocia,' said I, 'but aren't you going to ride the camel?'

'Certainly not! Would you like me to make *another* exhibition of myself?'

'Orthodocia,' said I, solemnly, 'one ought not to consider *any-thing*—in connection with an Impression!'

'I will not be coerced!' responded my friend with firmness.

'Then lend me the revolver,' I requested. Orthodocia lent me it. I put it in my pocket, and beckoned to the camel-boys reassuringly. I found an approximately clean place near one camel's shoulder, and patted him on it. Presently I saw him looking at me from the other end of his neck, and desisted. In the meantime the camel-boys came up.

'Are *you*?' said Orthodocia.

'I am.'

'How are you going to get on?' she inquired.

'He will come down,' I responded confidently. 'He will bring his upper flats to the ground floor. I've seen them do it.'

'Well,' said Orthodocia, 'I should certainly come off.'

I sighed heavily. 'I will not coerce you, Orthodocia,' said I, 'but I cannot lose the opportunity, occurring perhaps once in a lifetime, of riding the ship of the desert over his native element! Bring him down!' to the camel-boy.

If you care to ascertain accurately how that camel came down, I must ask you to look in your book of natural history. Orthodocia and I cannot agree upon the matter. She says he took his back legs down first, and I am almost certain he folded up his front ones and sat down on them, as it were, before he effected any re-arrangement to the rear. It is not a point upon which there ought to be any difference of opinion among commentators; however, you will have no difficulty in settling it for yourself. He came down in sections, at all events, and it took him some little time, during which Orthodocia vacillated. I took no notice of her vacillation, but calmly sat down upon the sheepskins which formed his saddle. The camel looked round and told me to get off, but I would not. 'Send him up!' said I to the elevator-boy—as we say in America—in attendance.

The boy went through one formula, and the camel went through another. I can't describe it, because of the same difference of opinion between Orthodocia and me about the order of his going up, as about the order of his coming down. I know there were two angles of forty-five degrees and a remarkably sudden transition from one to the other, together with such a rise in the world as it had not been my lot to experience before. But when I reached the climax, and looked down upon Orthodocia in the sand below, from the camel's third story, the sensation was delightful.

'THE SCENE THAT FOLLOWED.'

'To the hotel by the Pyramids, for breakfast,' I commanded the camel-boy. 'I suppose you will follow on your white donkey!' to Orthodocia.

'Thank you!' said Orthodocia, with prodigious sarcasm. 'If you can ride a camel, I can!'

D D

Of the scene that followed I possess a jumbled, tearful, hysterical mental picture with which I would not part, as people say of other amateur canvases, for many times its value. In the camel-back mode of transport there is a swing and a toss and a thud, chaos, the lost chord, the ragged edge of despair. Worst of all there was Orthodocia, bleating piteously a little way ahead that it **was no use**—she could *not* stay on. The camels ambled faster—I embraced **my** camel's neck—we rounded the Great Pyramid at an alarming gait.

'WE ALL WENT UP TOGETHER.'

The world reeled, the Great Pyramid stood on its apex. 'I can't help it!' I heard Orthodocia say, as in a dream. . . . The sand was very soft where I descended, and I much preferred my fate to Orthodocia's. As she said, dear girl, she couldn't help it, but it is possible, for safety's sake, to assume positions that are forcibly inelegant on a camel. Happily, however, the sight of my misfortunes induced her camel-boy to stop before they got to the hotel, so that nobody saw but the Sphinx and me—and neither of us will ever tell.

OUR JOURNEY ROUND THE WORLD

Some people we knew had driven out from Cairo to climb the Great Pyramid, and after breakfast we all went up together. As you are probably aware, this remarkable old pile covers thirteen acres. The blocks of which it is built are usually about three feet high, and one climbs a slope of five hundred and sixty-eight feet to the top. Ascending pyramids is rather a violent form of exercise,

'HE HAD LEFT HIS WHITE TIE AND HIS DIGNITY EIGHTY FEET BELOW.'

therefore, for people weighing more than ten stone. Two old ladies answering this description were of our party, and they preferred the view from the bottom, they said.

The rest of us took a couple of swarthy Bedouins apiece and started. Others followed, carrying water in bottles of hard-baked Nile mud. One guide went ahead and pulled us up by the arms, the other came behind and lifted us from stone to stone. It was not a comfortable mode of ascent—'hot, risky, and fatiguing,' as a clerical gentleman of the party remarked at the first resting-place, one-third of the way up. He had left his white tie and his dignity eighty feet below, and didn't care about losing either. The guides told us all that we were the heaviest people that had ever made the ascent in safety, and suggested an instalment of backsheesh on that account. We were dragged up another third, and rested again; and this second halting-place two or three gasping and perspiring scalers found the height of their ambition. Not, I am proud to say, either Orthodocia or your chronicler. We, with a struggling remnant, got to the top.

There was room enough up there to dance a quadrille. That was our first astonishment. We had expected the Pyramid, somehow, to be pointed, as it is in the pictures. Then came a sense of its awful rugged vastness, spreading down on four sides of us, block outedging block, into the waste lapping round its thirteen acres. It was a little like standing on a symmetrical pile of the centuries.

'Remarkable view!' said the cleric of High Church tendencies and the advanced opinions of 1889 A.D., tapping with his stick the capstone Cheops laid upon his Pagan tomb somewhere about 3,070 B.C. 'Remarkable view!'

Two deserts that rolled, gray and yellow and white, as far as one could see beneath the sky, the Libyan at our feet, the Arabian beyond, Cairo, lying fair between the two under her palms, beside her Nile. Rising round us out of the restless Libyan sands, the time-defying monuments of those old, old kings who made their immortality with stones, and the half-buried Sphinx, gazing with that strange eager joy eastward. And sharp on the white heaving waste below, a great triangular western shadow. It was, after all, not the view but the shadow that was so notably worth climbing to the top of the Pyramid to look down upon; and the shadow, strangely enough, as we gazed, grew more significant than the Pyramid. Cheops had stood in it, and Moses, the shepherd kings, the Ptolemies, Herodotus, Mahomet perhaps, and it had gradually lessened and withdrawn itself from them, even as it did before our eyes. It was only a shadow, and we were beings, young and strong and human, who could think, and yet for thousands of years before we saw the sun it had travelled silently from west to east in those two exact long lines, darkening just that desert section and no more, and would travel for other thousands after we who mock at shadows should be less than shadows. It talked of immutable, inscrutable law and of eternity, and we felt ourselves, looking down at it there, pathetically ill-equipped to understand it.

'A remarkable view!' said the cleric, dusting a place upon the capstone of Cheops, adjusting his coat-tails, and sitting down on it. 'A very remarkable view!'

Orthodocia wishes me to ask you, when you go to the top of the Great Pyramid, please to look for our initials somewhere near 'Jenny Lind,' which is cut very deeply in the stone. If there was a person severely reprobated by Orthodocia and myself as a thoroughly disreputable person with a small mind, it was the person who goes about the world disfiguring everything in it with his uninteresting name. This opinion did not occur to us at the time, however, and now that we've done it Orthodocia says it will be a comfort to know that somebody has seen it. And yet it is commonly believed that the feminine mind is not logical!

XLI

I PLEADED for another week of Cairo, the place was so seductive, even then when the Nile was at its lowest, the sun growing hot, and the hotel emptying day by day—but Orthodocia denied me absolutely. She said by way of excuse, that she knew it was simply silly and ridiculous, and that she was sure I couldn't understand it; but that in spite of all the pleasures of the Orient and my delightful society, she was getting homesick! I had observed a diminution in Orthodocia's interest in most things for some little time, so I begged to know since when. And she replied, 'Oh, for the past three or four weeks!' which space, though a little indefinite, dated back quite conclusively enough to Agra. So I mused upon the nature of impressions, and mourned inly; but packed my trunk, and said no more. With a motive power dating from Agra in Orthodocia's mind, probably located close to founts of tears, resistance would have been imbecile. But I little thought, when I contemplated our journey round the world, that it could be wrecked, so to speak, by a little thing like the Wigginton Post-Office.

Orthodocia's spirits rose all the way to Ismailia to such an extent that she was quite willing to gratify me during the two or three hours we had to wait for the ship there, by looking at the place from my favourite point of view—the top of a donkey. This fact registers her state of mind as well as anything could, I fancy. So we had a cup of tea in a vacant little room of a vacant little hotel, with the usual Frenchman's fat wife in charge, and sallied forth. I regret that I cannot set down much that is favourable regarding the Ismailia donkey. He does not compare in any one particular with his aristocratic connections of Cairo—he is altogether a different quadruped, smaller, feebler, very ragged, without any self-respect whatever. He has resources of cunning, however, that have not yet occurred to his

Cairo brethren. When I, with many compunctions, finally decided upon my donkey and mounted him, he said nothing at all in protest, but calmly, systematically, and with beautiful unanimity, he gave way. What I mean by 'unanimity' is that he did not tumble down in any rickety or hysterical manner, but reached the ground by a gradual and general subsidence. I felt it to be considerate on the donkey's part, but it did not add to my sense of the dignity of the situation, or I may say, to Orthodocia's, who laughed in a most unbecoming manner. She was more fortunate, but I had to go through this mortifying process in connection with three donkeys before I found one that avowed himself equal to me.

Fortunately, though, there seemed nobody to see. With the exception of the donkeys and the donkey-boys, the streets of the sandy little town were almost empty. The sun struck down hotly, there were no trees to speak of, and the flat colourless houses belonged very properly to their flat, colourless surroundings. But a delicious breeze had stolen up from the Mediterranean, and gave the air a sweet exhilaration.

We clattered through the main street, that had some insignificant shops in it, whose somewhat slatternly proprietors chattered with one another in the doors; there seemed to be no customers. Here we stopped to buy those odds and ends that are always the last things one thinks of on embarking; and from the startling experience of paying for them, I should say that Ismailia is probably the most expensive commercial centre in the world. After which, with the donkey-boys at our heels, we took a long canter out upon a road that led to the Canal, a road moderately shaded, straight and hard, where we met three or four beings of a superior order upon horseback. This convinced us that people did live in the bare bright little town behind us, but we were not disposed to envy them.

The Canal, from a point of view on land, is a great surprise. There is no understanding, a hundred yards off, whence it comes, whither it goes, or even where it is. A great smoke-stack slants itself into the air a little way to the left, growing apparently out of a dusty tangle of sycamore trees, and a line of masts have somehow pushed up through a long sand-heap to the right. Your donkey trots a little further on, scrambles over a heap of sifting *débris* that

"THE CANAL."

rises before you, and there at your feet, stretching this way and curving that—the smoke-stack still seems an abnormal growth of the sycamore trees—lies the Suez Canal. It is more radiantly blue and more extraordinarily narrow, cleaving the wide, white desert on either side, than any body of water you have ever seen before. The gigantic task of making it seems altogether out of relation to this simple ribbon brightening the waste, and the marvel of it is that it should be a marvel.

It was quite night when our little company of belated tourists huddled themselves on board the tug beside the wharf, and steamed away to where a great black hulk lay indistinctly outlined by the electric light at her prow. The wind blew cold across from the sea, I remember, and the dreariness of Ismailia had grown upon us so that we were glad to climb the *Peninsular's* companion ladder and find ourselves again among the familiar Lascars and quartermasters and home-going Anglo-Indians of the P. and O. We had grown to feel at home in these great steamships, and to learn to depend upon the kindness and courtesy, and even protection, which unfailingly met us on board them. There was no special reason why this should have been the case—neither Orthodocia nor I were anybody in particular, only two young women of good constitution and sanguine temperament who had elected to go round the world by themselves —but it so invariably was the case that I think in this last chapter I should like to say so. And as I have said, it was pleasant to step into the warmth and brightness of the saloon, where dinner lay in waiting for us, to find our cabin with happy confidence and fill it with the pink roses of Cairo ; and afterwards, among the groups gathered on deck, watching the great white shaft of electric light on the dark narrow water-way, to discover friends of other journeys and hear and tell many things.

The Mediterranean toward the middle of last April was ambitiously Atlantic in its tendencies, and Orthodocia and I were solidly comforted in the thought of all the unnecessary pieces of baggage we had had labelled, 'WANTED AT BRINDISI.' We had looked for balmy breezes from the gardens of Theocritus, with other anticipations more or less accurately classic, and warm sunlight behind Mount Ida ; but our path round the planet thus far had been strewn, as it were, with shattered expectations, so we were not surprised to leave a few in the Mediterranean. Orthodocia found the cold wind 'bracing,' she said, and paced the deck with a demeanour that grew daily more joyous. Her exuberance of feeling let itself off in various ways, noticeably in dragging steamer chairs about for old ladies, and

'AND BORROWING SMALL WHITE PULPY BABIES.'

borrowing small white pulpy babies from their ayahs to dance up and down deck with before breakfast, and singing 'White Wings' to herself in her upper berth at an entirely unnecessary hour of the morning. The organ-grinders have got 'White Wings' now; it has become a noise and abhorrent; yet in whatsoever alley way I hear it, I stop a moment and listen for some note in its rickety rendition that reminds me of Orthodocia's homeward voyage.

It was Easter-tide when we got to Brindisi, and my first vision of Italy was a very shaky and very *bouffante* Virgin in black and white, carried by men in scarlet with long white masks in a procession along the wharf, and followed by little girls in flimsy white and paper flowers. A ragged, brown-eyed little crowd brought up the rear, and they all disappeared in the warm sunlight that lay for them as it did for Claudius over the Appian Way. The loungers on the wharf seemed rather disreputably cosmopolitan—Brindisi is another battered outer edge—but there were swarthy ones among them who cried oranges, and two or three *insouciant* in the brave and boasted attire of Customs' officers that made Italy enough of the place to be a pleasant picture in one's memory. Nobody could tell us of anything in particular to see at Brindisi; but we found for ourselves the pillars that commemorate that march to Rome, and the market-place, gay with fruits and kerchiefs, and an ancient moat and castle, where we sat and let the sun warm us through and through, while Orthodocia counted the days between that point and the Royal Albert Docks and made a daisy chain. My friend renewed her extreme youth to such an extent upon this voyage that I hourly expected to see her sucking her thumb. This, however, was spared me. She unblushingly proposed that we should go home by the mail train from Brindisi. 'Simply to escape the Bay of Biscay, dear!' but I found matter for strenuous protest in missing Malta and Gibraltar; and she withdrew the proposition, watching the departure of the people who did get off at Brindisi, however, with a pathetic resignation which I found aggravating.

And by-and-by, sailing southward, we came to Malta, where the *Peninsular* found the most geometrical haven that could be imagined, all hard straight lines and parallelograms and sharp angles. Malta, cherishing her old Crusaders high up from the sparkling sea, and throwing back the strong white sunlight from the tops of her huddling roofs. The *Peninsular* waited an obligingly long time at Malta, and we were able to be rowed ashore and climb the steep, narrow, stone street-stairways into the town, and there engage a vehicle and a guide, a pleasant, broad-faced, smiling old soldier guide, whose lack of English to convey information with was made up for by the superior quality of the politeness that was thrown in. He took us first to the shops in the Strada Reale, but beyond photographs, and silver Maltese crosses, and thick Maltese lace, and serpent bracelets made of pink sea-shell, the shops had no particular fascinations. Moreover, it was Sunday, and it is impossible to shop deliberately on Sunday with any degree of enjoyment. As Orthodocia said, however, when we clattered off among the church-goers to St. John's, it was a satisfaction to have seen what they were like, and it freed our minds for the contemplation of higher things.

Service was just about to begin at the famous old church when we reached it. Already it was half-full of people with serious faces. The men were chiefly in ordinary English clothes, but many of the women were picturesque in the Maltese dress of their foremothers—full black silk skirts and plain bodices, with sombre capes gathered half-way round the edge of a large stiff hood so as to partly conceal the face inside. As a costume it was rigorous and select. It almost talked of sanctity. It was the most unmistakably 'Sunday' dress either of us had ever seen.

I have no words for architectural description, but the Church of St. John's at Malta is a lovely place to be in. Not only that the vaulted roof glows in all the imaginative colour that the art of other times invested the Saviour's life with ; or that the world has brought tribute of all her treasure of porphyry and silver and gold for the chapel sanctuaries ; or that grave old pictures glow with the candle-light that gleams everywhere on pale sculptures and rich fashionings in wood and precious metals. All this, and more ; but beside, the place is so full of knightly memories, lying under their quaint old Latin inscriptions on the floor, that it seems almost to hold its service for a solemn congregation that look over the heads of the frivolous human interlopers of to-day—kneeling unseen, responding unheard. I cannot believe that there is a church anywhere so full of distinct, dignified, important old personalities, all governed by the same idea, all holding their earthly character and mission in such noble conceit as this Church of the Knights at Malta. Walking over them from chapel to chapel, reading the lofty phrase of what they had to say for themselves deep-set in the paving stones, and regarding the *naïf* sentiments and types of death inwrought there before men learned to accept the mystery of it in silence, one ﬁnds something very like envy of the life that ended so. It must ——— in the simple and self-respecting and unqu——— high necessity of its creation, or the su——— sion, and knowing little but that. And th——— satisfactory than our great knowledge and little ——— sal interest spread out thin, our self-pity, our growi——— we should be at all, and whether it is quite worth w——— Orthodocia thought so.

The skeletons were a most interesting and amusing study in themselves, done as they were in black marble and white and coloured, draped and undraped, uttering all sorts of convictions that go with skeletons. One, which must have represented the understructure of a very frivolous person indeed, wore a bow under its chin. Orthodocia did not consider that an advantageous way, however, of having one's skeleton done. This year, she said, bows were worn under the left ear; next year, perhaps, no bows would be worn at all. She said she thought skeletons ought to be represented quite simply, in unaffected positions, and with natural expressions, which would make the whims of fashion in millinery a matter of indifference to them. She could not quite understand the depth of reality of my interest in them—I, who had never seen such a thing on a tombstone in my life—and remarked that she sat under one every Sunday in church at Wigginton. I stated that the skeleton was not a popular form of church decoration in America. 'Of course,' replied my friend, sweetly, 'you are such a young country, I suppose you haven't got any!'

Just as we passed Count Beaujolais's effigy, in purest white marble, the young man lying gracefully, breathing softly, his head on his hand, 'serenissimus et dulcissimus,' a chant arose in the distance, muffled, sonorous, as if the old knights beneath once more called the people to armed prayer, and they listened quiet in their places but would not go. And then with slow ceremony came the white-haired bishop up the aisle, in gold-broidered alb and cope and chasuble and trailing purple, the crozier going before, a train of priestly youths with fine pale Greek faces coming after. The chant grew louder ceased; a voice raised itself in the Latin tongue. Then we ... left the ... with their descendants to pray. At ... ...docia looking back with a sentiment in her ..., I saw, high upon the southern wall, and ... splendour, the arms and the flag of England. ... across the wide moat and drawbridge, where great ... in the corners and weedy grasses were growing on the walls, ... the Church of the Capuchins, to see the dead monks in their vault-niches there. We had the expectation of being much horrified and a little afraid, as we followed the guide down the dark passage into the vault; but Brother Carlo Somebody, who was the first we met, dispelled this idea entirely. His demeanour was thoroughly reassuring, and apart from that he was much too absurdly dry and musty to affect anybody's nerves. Like the rest, he laughed, a wide, noiseless laugh. He was almost doubled up with mirth, was Brother Carlo, and leaning forward to chuckle with his neighbour in the next niche. They were all gowned, these old Capuchins, and one or two of them were bearded. Their hands were crossed on their ancient breasts, and, so far as possible, their superiors of the present day had endeavoured to give them an appearance of respectability. But the attempt was quite futile and did not impose upon one in the least. They were all arrantly and inherently disreputable, and when they weren't convulsed with mirth over jokes that were not holy, they stared with the most impudent curiosity in their empty eye-sockets at people who came to look at them. There were seventeen altogether in the vault we saw. One was confined behind a wire netting, doubtless not without good reason—probably for the enormity of his puns. They stood in a sardonic row on each side of a narrow dark passage, down which our single candle shone flickeringly, and they were not decorative from any point of view. There was also that quality in the air which the presence of a well-kept mummy alone can impart. And so, in spite of their having given us such a cordial welcome, as it were, and having made us feel so entirely at home, we spent very little time in making our adieux; and Orthodocia declared that she had never seen anything so utterly horrid as a preserved Capuchin.

Then came the day we sailed under the frowning front of Gibraltar, quaking a little. It was quite unreasonable, but there was not a passenger on deck that morning as we slowly steamed under the guns bristling in the face of that mighty rock, that did not look subdued by the situation. Once inspected and admitted, the prevailing feeling changed at once, and everybody began to say to everybody else, 'Do you know the description of Gibraltar in the Spanish geographies? No? An important fortification of Spain, *in the temporary occupation* of the Queen of England!' I think the captain started it, but it was one of those active jokes that skip restlessly from mouth to mouth; and I am sure it came to my own personal ear at least eleven times—and I say 'eleven' because, so near the end of this chronicle, I wish to avoid exaggeration. Orthodocia revenged herself by answering the question : 'Do you know what the Spanish geographies say about Gibraltar?'—its form varied—by a bland 'Yes,' which was disconcerting and annoying, and I am sure made her enemies ; but she didn't seem to mind.

We had only a brief two hours to stay, so we spent them in a desultory drive about the town and the Alameda gardens, and the outer fortifications. Arum lilies and geraniums looked over the private garden walls, and acacias gave what shade there was. As I remember the market-place it seemed to hold nothing but roses and Jerusalem artichokes, which must be incorrect. Perhaps though, at this point, you will be willing to excuse a few vegetables—it would be an act of kindness that you would never have reason to repent of. The narrow streets were full of colour and picturesqueness, chiefly Spanish, and across a long narrow sandy tract came an endless stream of market-folk from Spain, shawls over their heads, baskets on their arms. The shops were altogether delightful, and full of the East, from Japan hitherward ; but we looked sadly upon the Moorish potteries, and Morocco cushions, and tasselled Spanish hats, and fans with the gay *bolero* painted on them, and turned away. I leave the reason to your sympathetic intuition.

Gibraltar, Orthodocia said, did not inspire her happily. It spoke, she complained, always of war and demolition—nowhere of anything else. Even through the climbing roses of the beautiful public gardens there pointed down upon the harbour a gun, and a gun of a hundred tons. It was inhumanly strong and massive and impregnable, and Orthodocia couldn't say she liked it. But I had to set down against that the fact that a delay occurred at Gibraltar which retarded our arrival at the Royal Albert Docks by an hour and a half.

*　　*　　*　　*　　*　　*

I think I see her now, with those letters. She was very pretty to look at, and so absorbed in them that she didn't mind my looking at her a good deal. They were handed to her by the purser at Plymouth; and though they must have been written in the space of a week, under unfavourable conditions, they would have made a volume of respectable dimensions, and, if Orthodocia's face was anything to go by, of an interesting nature. We were passing Margate or Ramsgate, or some such place, when she told me in a rapt manner, which neither your choppy Channel nor your English east wind had any effect upon, something of what they contained. And I understood that Mr. John Love had determined, after two days and nights of reckless despair, to go round the world the other way as rapidly as possible to Wigginton, where he would arrive, Orthodocia calculated, in about three weeks, and where *he was expected*—with an emphasis that made me understand in what capacity. She also stated that when he did arrive he felt confident that he would be able to persuade her to telegraph properly; but that may have been a slight excitement in Orthodocia's mind. And if he did, and she would, they were to live in Vancouver, where Jack had some new interests, which would be ever so much nicer than Assiniboia, wouldn't it? And Jack, though he entirely disapproved of her speculation there, had managed to buy the very lot that once was hers to build their house upon, and could anything be more idyllic! And much more which my regard for Orthodocia, and charity for her state of mind at the time, induces me to suppress. You may be interested, however, to know the leading points.

A few hours later a motherly lady, driving Orthodocia and me in a pony-carriage through St. Eve's-in-the-Garden, where the japonica was beginning to redden the walls of the cottages and spring had come to stay in the hedges, reproached me for my lack of experience and gray side-curls. She was so gratified to get Orthodocia back again alive that the reproaches were not very bitter; and she said we would say nothing more about it if I would give her a candid opinion upon one point. '*Do* you think,' said she, 'as the result of all your experiences, that it is entirely safe and wise for young ladies to travel by themselves?'

'Dear Mrs. Love!' I equivocated, 'I am afraid the wisdom of it must always depend upon the young ladies themselves; and as to the danger—you see what befell Orthodocia!'

'Yes,' put in my friend at my side, thoughtfully, 'but then—that might have happened anywhere!'

And I suppose it might.

THE END

PRINTED BY
SPOTTISWOODE AND CO., NEW STREET SQUARE
LONDON

OPINIONS OF THE PRESS
ON
A SOCIAL DEPARTURE.
By SARA JEANNETTE DUNCAN.

With 111 Illustrations by F. H. TOWNSEND.

'The book is throughout one of the cleverest, and freshest, and funniest books of travel ever written. The key of humour is struck in Miss Duncan's first page, and the fun never flags to the last. A book containing hundreds of such things needs no recommendation in the holiday season, or any other.'—SCOTTISH LEADER.

'A bright and pleasant book. . . . We have not seen for a long time any sketches more truly artistic, more picturesque, more lifelike, more delicately humorous, more full of touches and tones of beauty. . . . The whole impresses the reader as a pleasant enterprise out of which has come a pleasant record.'—DAILY NEWS.

'The reader who does not have "a good time" over "A Social Departure" must have a blunted appreciation of fun and pluck. There is not a dull page in it. . . . The story is told with wonderful dash and cleverness; and the illustrations are as good as the text.'—SCOTSMAN.

'It is a long time since anything so freshly and brightly written has come into our hands. . . . An amazingly original book. . . . It is not too much to say that there is not a single dull page in it.'—WORLD.

'It is because Miss Duncan has written what most of us like to read that we admire her book so much. . . . It seems to us more than likely that this volume will become one of the books of the season.'—WHITEHALL REVIEW.

'That delightfully refreshing book, "A Social Departure" . . . amusing and withal instructive. . . . There is not a dull page in the whole book.'—WOMAN.

'Globe-trotting, undertaken in a novel manner, and with a cargo of excellent spirits, is the foundation on which rests the fascinating volume entitled "A Social Departure." . . . The story is told in the raciest style, and possesses the sovereign recommendation of not including a dull page. . . . It is profusely illustrated.'—DAILY TELEGRAPH.

'The narrative of a real journey, as interesting and instructive as any we remember reading. . . . It is impossible to read more than a page of this delightful book without coming upon something that calls up a broad smile, if not, indeed, a hearty laugh.'—GLASGOW HERALD.

'One of the brightest and most readable books of the season. . . . A thoroughly unconventional and delightful book.'—COURT JOURNAL.

'This is about the most charming book of travels it has been our good fortune to come across.'—PALL MALL GAZETTE.

'The characters of the two girls are not only attractively drawn, but their individuality is well and carefully sustained; the illustrations, which are for the most part very clever, skilfully bearing out the text. . . . There is a stream of fun running through the entire volume, rarely forced, and often decidedly amusing.'—ATHENÆUM.

'This charming volume. . . . No greater treat could we bespeak for all who in this sorry world love at times to be amused as well as interested than the perusal of "A Social Departure."'—TORONTO GLOBE.

'In the way of a holiday book, full of the most delightful humour, set off with innumerable charmingly picturesque touches, and illustrated with singular felicity, we do not remember to have encountered for a good many years anything quite so fresh and enticing as this altogether unconventional volume.'—TIMES OF INDIA.

'The book is fascinating from cover to cover. It reads like a fairy-tale, only the fairies are real and the story is true.'—ATALANTA.

'Readers will be at a loss whether most to admire the charming descriptions or the clever style to be found in this notable book of travel. . . . The volume is full of countless good things, bright, clever, fanciful, and, once read, never to be forgotten.'—NORTHERN WHIG.

'Here is the most amusing record of "globe-trotting" that has yet been penned in English. . . . It is fresh, sparkling, and feminine.'—SCOTS OBSERVER.

'There are few readers blessed with any sense of humour who will not be delighted with this book. The East, whether China, Japan, or India, is sketched from a thoroughly feminine as well as humorous point of view.'—MORNING POST.

London: CHATTO & WINDUS, 214 Piccadilly, W.

OPINIONS OF THE PRESS
ON
AN AMERICAN GIRL IN LONDON.
By SARAH JEANNETTE DUNCAN.
With 80 Illustrations by F. H. TOWNSEND. Crown 8vo. cloth extra, 7s. 6d.

'"An American Girl" is full of humorous observation and pleasant fun. Miss Duncan is known to English readers as the author of the brightest, merriest book of travel that has appeared for many a long day. This book has the same constant flow of good spirits. Her observations upon the things, the persons, the manners, and above all the women she sees are delightfully fresh, keen, instructive, and amusing. . . . This is admirably done, and the book ought to be read by everyone who can enjoy a good-humoured satirical exposure of our peculiarities.'—SCOTSMAN.

'The "American Girl's" impressions of London and the people she met there are written with a graceful badinage and a genial satire which are very attractive. . . . The book is characterised by evidences of acute power of observation and by a bright, fresh, lively style.'.—VANITY FAIR.

'"An American Girl" is one long sweet smile. It breaks into chuckles here and there; it becomes the sardonic grin here and there; but in one form or another it is full of laughter which does good to man's soul, from beginning to end. For her bright and charming book we are exceedingly grateful.'—GRANTA.

'The book is thoroughly fresh and amusing, and affords some very pleasant reading.'—GRAPHIC.

'This is a very entertaining account of England from a visitor's point of view.'—SPECTATOR.

'It is a book to be read—lively, shrewd, and humorous.'—ST. JAMES'S GAZETTE.

'"An American Girl" comes upon us with a delightful freshness. The writer, a clever young Canadian lady, possesses a keen sense of the humorous, a ready wit, and a ready pen, and her descriptions have all the charms of actuality, accentuated by the power of recognising and reproducing the fun which underlies even the most solemn of society functions. The book is one of great freshness and piquancy—one of the brightest books of the season.—COURT JOURNAL.

'"An American Girl" is quite the best book about London society, its manners and customs, that we have read. Lady Torquilin is a delightful and lovable old lady, and Miss Peter Corke is a very entertaining and witty individual. This is certainly a book to read.'—THE LADY.

'With admirable humour and archness the "American Girl" relates all that befell her during her stay in London. . . . Lively, rattling, full of good spirits and good taste, there is not a dry page in the book. It is interspersed with abundance of illustrations, the humour of which adds distinctly to the zest of the text.'—SCOTTISH LEADER.

'A clever and lively book, showing that the writer retains the stock of spirits of which she had such abundance when she made "A Social Departure." . . . The writer is a shrewd observer, and satirises, with much liveliness and considerable truth, Londoners and London ways.'—ATHENÆUM.

'In "An American Girl" Miss Duncan makes fun, smartly yet good-naturedly, of English ways. Her clever sketch of what a Chicago girl thought and saw during a London season is distinctly amusing. She is very observant, and her descriptions are fair as well as lively; and there is a humour and freshness about her book that is entertaining—and something more.'—ANTI-JACOBIN.

'Miss Duncan's book contains numerous good sketches of life in London, and, besides being distinctly fresh and lively in style, is adorned by some vivacious pictures.'—DAILY TELEGRAPH.

'One of the brightest books we have read for some time. The sketches are full of humour, and it is a humour which has the very rare quality of being quite kindly. Miss Duncan's portraits of typical English girls are quite wonderful in their accuracy. The book is racy and entertaining from beginning to end.'—WESTERN DAILY MERCURY.

'Remarkably entertaining, bright, and interesting.'—GLASGOW HERALD.

'It is not very often that a reviewer comes across so bright and charming a book as "An American Girl." . . . She records her observations with delightful humour, good temper, and perfect fairness. The characters are described with truth and clearness. It is a brilliant book, and deserves to be read widely.'—SPEAKER.

'The present volume displays Miss Duncan's charming gifts perhaps to even more perfection than did "A Social Departure." . . . She must be congratulated on being fortunate in creating a volume which will add lustre to her name, while it will doubtless be very widely read on account of its humorous and taking qualities.'—THE WEEK.

'The book is very lightly and pleasantly written.'—GUARDIAN.

'The author of "A Social Departure" is certainly to be congratulated on having written another book quite equalling her first . . . The story is as full of genuine humour as her last, and it really is a pleasure to come across a book that is so brimful of sunshine. . . . " An American Girl " is an exhilarating book, it is so entirely fresh and unconventional.'—WOMAN.

London: CHATTO & WINDUS, 214 Piccadilly, W.

Telegraphic Address—BOOKSTORE, LONDON.   Telephone No.—3524 CENTRAL.

AN ALPHABETICAL CATALOGUE
OF BOOKS IN FICTION AND GENERAL LITERATURE
PUBLISHED BY
CHATTO & WINDUS
111 ST. MARTIN'S LANE
CHARING CROSS
LONDON, W.C.
[JUNE, 1904.]

A B C (The) of Cricket: a Black View of the Game. (26 Illustrations.) By HUGH FIELDING. Demy 8vo, 1s.

Adams (W. Davenport), Works by.
A Dictionary of the Drama: A Guide to the Plays, Playwrights, Players, and Playhouses of the United Kingdom and America, from the Earliest Times to the Present. Vol. I. (A to G). Demy 8vo, cloth, 10s. 6d. net. [Shortly.
Quips and Quiddities. Selected by W. DAVENPORT ADAMS. Post 8vo, cloth limp, 2s. 6d.

Agony Column (The) of 'The Times,' from 1800 to 1870. Edited, with an Introduction, by ALICE CLAY. Post 8vo, cloth limp, 2s. 6d.

Alden (W. L.).—Drewitt's Dream. Crown 8vo, cloth, gilt top, 6s.

Alexander (Mrs.), Novels by. Post 8vo, illustrated boards, 2s. each.
Maid, Wife, or Widow? | Blind Fate.
Crown 8vo, cloth, 3s. 6d. each; post 8vo, picture boards, 2s. each.
Valerie's Fate. | A Life Interest. | Mona's Choice. | By Woman's Wit.
Crown 8vo, cloth 3s. 6d. each.
The Cost of her Pride. | Barbara, Lady's Maid and Peeress. | A Fight with Fate.
A Golden Autumn. | Mrs. Crichton's Creditor. | The Step-mother.
A Missing Hero.

Allen (F. M.).—Green as Grass. Crown 8vo, cloth, 3s. 6d.

Allen (Grant), Works by. Crown 8vo, cloth, 6s. each.
The Evolutionist at Large. | Moorland Idylls.
Post-Prandial Philosophy. Crown 8vo, art linen, 3s. 6d.
Crown 8vo, cloth extra, 3s. 6d. each; post 8vo, illustrated boards, 2s. each.
Babylon. 12 Illustrations. | The Devil's Die. | The Duchess of Powysland.
Strange Stories. | This Mortal Coil. | Blood Royal.
The Beckoning Hand. | The Tents of Shem. | Ivan Greet's Masterpiece.
For Maimie's Sake. | The Great Taboo. | The Scallywag. 24 Illusts.
Philistia. | Dumaresq's Daughter. | At Market Value.
In all Shades. | Under Sealed Orders.
The Tents of Shem. POPULAR EDITION, medium 8vo, 6d.

Anderson (Mary).—Othello's Occupation. Crown 8vo, cloth, 3s. 6d.

Andrews (E. Benjamin).—The United States in Our Own Time.
With 500 Illustrations. Royal 8vo, cloth, gilt top, 16s. net.

Antrobus (C. L.), Novels by. Crown 8vo, cloth, gilt top. 6s. each.
Quality Corner. | Wildersmoor. | The Wine of Finvarra.

Appleton (G. W.), Novels by.
Rash Conclusions. Crown 8vo, cloth, 3s. 6d.
The Lady in Sables. Crown 8vo, cloth, gilt top, 6s.

Arnold (Edwin Lester), Stories by.
The Wonderful Adventures of Phra the Phœnician. Crown 8vo, cloth extra, with 12 Illustrations by H. M. PAGET, 3s. 6d.; post 8vo, illustrated boards, 2s.
The Constable of St. Nicholas. With Frontispiece by S. L. WOOD. Crown 8vo, cloth, 3s. 6d.; picture cloth, flat back, 2s.

Ashton (John), Works by.
English Caricature and Satire on Napoleon the First. With 115 Illustrations. Crown 8vo, cloth, 7s. 6d.
Social Life in the Reign of Queen Anne. With 85 Illustrations. Crown 8vo, cloth, 3s. 6d.
Crown 8vo, cloth, gilt top, 6s. each.
Social Life under the Regency. With 90 Illustrations.
Florizel's Folly: The Story of GEORGE IV. With Photogravure Frontispiece and 12 Illustrations.

Brewster (Sir David), Works by. Post 8vo, cloth, 4s. 6d. each.
More Worlds than One: The Creed of the Philosopher and Hope of the Christian. With Plates.
The Martyrs of Science: GALILEO, TYCHO BRAHE, and KEPLER.
Letters on Natural Magic. With numerous Illustrations.

Bright (Florence).—A Girl Capitalist. Cr. 8vo, cloth, gilt top, 6s.

Brillat-Savarin.—Gastronomy as a Fine Art. Translated by R. E. ANDERSON, M.A. Post 8vo, half-bound, 2s.

Bryden (H. A.).—An Exiled Scot: A Romance. With a Frontispiece, by J. S. CROMPTON, R.I. Crown 8vo, cloth, 3s. 6d.

Brydges (Harold).—Uncle Sam at Home. With 91 Illustrations. Post 8vo, illustrated boards, 2s.; cloth limp, 2s. 6d.

Buchanan (Robert), Poems and Novels by.
The Complete Poetical Works of Robert Buchanan. 2 vols., crown 8vo, buckram, with Portrait Frontispiece to each volume, 12s.

Crown 8vo, cloth, 3s. 6d. each; post 8vo, illustrated boards, 2s. each.
The Shadow of the Sword. | Love Me for Ever. With Frontispiece.
A Child of Nature. With Frontispiece. | Annan Water. | Foxglove Manor.
God and the Man. With 11 Illustrations by | The New Abelard. | Rachel Dene.
Lady Kilpatrick. [FRED. BARNARD. | Matt: A Story of a Caravan. With Frontispiece.
The Martyrdom of Madeline. With | The Master of the Mine. With Frontispiece.
Frontispiece by A. W. COOPER. | The Heir of Linne. | Woman and the Man.

Crown 8vo, cloth, 3s. 6d. each.
Red and White Heather. | Andromeda: An Idyll of the Great River.
The Shadow of the Sword. POPULAR EDITION, medium 8vo, 6d.
The Charlatan. By ROBERT BUCHANAN and HENRY MURRAY. Crown 8vo, cloth, with a Frontispiece by T. H. ROBINSON, 3s. 6d.; post 8vo, picture boards, 2s.

Burgess (Gelett) and Will Irwin.—The Picaroons: A San Francisco Night's Entertainment. Crown 8vo, cloth, 3s. 6d.

Burton (Robert).—The Anatomy of Melancholy. With Translations of the Quotations. Demy 8vo, cloth extra, 7s. 6d.
Melancholy Anatomised: An Abridgment of BURTON'S ANATOMY. Post 8vo, half-cl., 2s. 6d.

Caine (Hall), Novels by. Crown 8vo, cloth extra, 3s. 6d. each; post 8vo, illustrated boards, 2s. each; cloth limp, 2s. 6d. each.
The Shadow of a Crime. | A Son of Hagar. | The Deemster.

Also LIBRARY EDITIONS of the three novels, set in new type, crown 8vo, bound uniform with The Christian, 6s. each; and CHEAP POPULAR EDITIONS, medium 8vo, portrait-cover, 6d. each.— Also the FINE-PAPER EDITION of The Deemster, pott 8vo, cloth, gilt top, 2s. net; leather, gilt edges, 3s. net.

Cameron (Commander V. Lovett).—The Cruise of the 'Black Prince' Privateer. Post 8vo, picture boards, 2s.

Canada (Greater): The Past, Present, and Future of the Canadian North-West. By E. B. OSBORN, B.A. With a Map. Crown 8vo, cloth, 3s. 6d.

Captain Coignet, Soldier of the Empire: An Autobiography. Edited by LOREDAN LARCHEY. Translated by Mrs. CAREY. With 100 Illustrations. Crown 8vo, cloth, 3s. 6d.

Carlyle (Thomas).—On the Choice of Books. Post 8vo, cl., 1s. 6d.

Carruth (Hayden).—The Adventures of Jones. With 17 Illustrations. Fcap. 8vo, cloth, 2s.

Chambers (Robert W.), Stories of Paris Life by.
The King in Yellow. Crown 8vo, cloth, 3s. 6d.; fcap. 8vo, cloth limp, 2s. 6d.
In the Quarter. Fcap. 8vo, cloth, 2s. 6d.

Chapman's (George), Works. Vol. I., Plays Complete, including the Doubtful Ones.—Vol. II., Poems and Minor Translations, with Essay by A. C. SWINBURNE.—Vol. III., Translations of the Iliad and Odyssey. Three Vols., crown 8vo, cloth, 3s. 6d. each.

Chaucer for Children: A Golden Key. By Mrs. H. R. HAWEIS. With 8 Coloured Plates and 30 Woodcuts. Crown 4to, cloth extra, 3s. 6d.
Chaucer for Schools. With the Story of his Times and his Work. By Mrs. H. R. HAWEIS A New Edition, revised. With a Frontispiece. Demy 8vo, cloth, 2s. 6d.

Chess, The Laws and Practice of. With an Analysis of the Openings. By HOWARD STAUNTON. Edited by R. B. WORMALD. Crown 8vo, cloth, 5s.
The Minor Tactics of Chess: A Treatise on the Deployment of the Forces in obedience to Strategic Principle. By F. K. YOUNG and E. C. HOWELL. Long fcap. 8vo, cloth, 2s. 6d.
The Hastings Chess Tournament. Containing the Authorised Account of the 230 Games played Aug.-Sept., 1895. With Annotations by PILLSBURY, LASKER, TARRASCH, STEINITZ, SCHIFFERS, TEICHMANN, BARDELEBEN, BLACKBURNE, GUNSBERG, TINSLEY, MASON, and ALBIN; Biographical Sketches of the Chess Masters, and 22 Portraits. Edited by H. F. CHESHIRE. Cheaper Edition. Crown 8vo, cloth, 5s.

CHATTO & WINDUS, Publishers, 111 St. Martin's Lane, London, W.C. 5

Chapple (J. Mitchell).—The Minor Chord: The Story of a Prima Donna. Crown 8vo, cloth, 3s. 6d.

Clare (Austin), Stories by.
For the Love of a Lass. Post 8vo, illustrated boards, 2s.; cloth, 2s. 6d.
By the Rise of the River: Tales and Sketches in South Tynedale. Crown 8vo, cloth, 3s. 6d.
Crown 8vo, cloth, gilt top, 6s. each.
The Tideway. | Randal of Randalholme.

Clive (Mrs. Archer), Novels by.
Post 8vo, cloth, 3s. 6d. each; picture boards, 2s. each.
Paul Ferroll. | Why Paul Ferroll Killed his Wife.

Clodd (Edward, F.R.A.S.).—Myths and Dreams. Cr. 8vo, 3s. 6d.

Coates (Anne).—Rie's Diary. Crown 8vo, cloth, 3s. 6d.

Cobban (J. Maclaren), Novels by.
The Cure of Souls. Post 8vo, illustrated boards, 2s.
The Red Sultan. Crown 8vo, cloth extra, 3s. 6d.; post 8vo, illustrated boards, 2s.
The Burden of Isabel. Crown 8vo, cloth extra, 3s. 6d.

Collins (C. Allston).—The Bar Sinister. Post 8vo, boards, 2s.

Collins (John Churton, M.A.), Books by. Cr. 8vo, cl., 3s. 6d. each.
Illustrations of Tennyson.
Jonathan Swift. A Biographical and Critical Study.

Collins (Mortimer and Frances), Novels by.
Crown 8vo, cloth extra, 3s. 6d. each; post 8vo, illustrated boards, 2s. each.
From Midnight to Midnight. | Blacksmith and Scholar.
You Play me False. | The Village Comedy.
Post 8vo, illustrated boards, 2s. each.
Transmigration. | Sweet Anne Page. |
A Fight with Fortune. | Sweet and Twenty. | Frances.

Collins (Wilkie), Novels by.
Crown 8vo, cloth extra, many illustrated, 3s. 6d. each; post 8vo, picture boards, 2s. each;
cloth limp, 2s. 6d. each.
*Antonina. | My Miscellanies. | Jezebel's Daughter
*Basil. | Armadale. | The Black Robe.
*Hide and Seek. | Poor Miss Finch. | Heart and Science
*The Woman in White. | Miss or Mrs.? | 'I Say No.'
*The Moonstone. | The New Magdalen. | A Rogue's Life.
*Man and Wife. | The Frozen Deep. | The Evil Genius.
*The Dead Secret. | The Law and the Lady. | Little Novels.
After Dark. | The Two Destinies. | The Legacy of Cain.
The Queen of Hearts. | The Haunted Hotel. | Blind Love.
No Name. | The Fallen Leaves. |
** Marked * have been reset in new type, in uniform style.
POPULAR EDITIONS, medium 8vo, 6d. each.
The Moonstone. | Antonina. | The Dead Secret. | No Name.
The Woman in White. | The New Magdalen. | Man and Wife. | Armadale.
The Woman in White. LARGE TYPE, FINE PAPER EDITION. Pott 8vo, cloth, gilt top, 2s. net; leather, gilt edges, 3s. net.

Colman's (George) Humorous Works: 'Broad Grins,' 'My Nightgown and Slippers,' &c. With Life and Frontispiece. Crown 8vo, cloth extra, 3s. 6d.

Colquhoun (M. J.).—Every Inch a Soldier. Crown 8vo, cloth, 3s. 6d.; post 8vo, illustrated boards, 2s.

Colt-breaking, Hints on. By W. M. HUTCHISON. Cr. 8vo, cl., 3s. 6d.

Compton (Herbert), Novels by.
The Inimitable Mrs. Massingham. Crown 8vo, cloth, 3s. 6d.
The Wilful Way. Crown 8vo, cloth, gilt top, 6s.

Cooper (Edward H.).—Geoffory Hamilton. Cr. 8vo, cloth, 3s. 6d.

Cornish (J. F.).—Sour Grapes: A Novel. Cr. 8vo, cloth, gilt top, 6s.

Cornwall.—Popular Romances of the West of England; or, The Drolls, Traditions, and Superstitions of Old Cornwall. Collected by ROBERT HUNT, F.R.S. With two Steel Plates by GEORGE CRUIKSHANK. Crown 8vo, cloth, 7s. 6d.

Cotes (V. Cecil).—Two Girls on a Barge. With 44 Illustrations by F. H. TOWNSEND. Crown 8vo, cloth extra, 3s. 6d.; post 8vo, cloth, 2s. 6d.

Craddock (C. Egbert), Stories by.
The Prophet of the Great Smoky Mountains. Crown 8vo, cloth, 3s. 6d.; post 8vo, illustrated boards, 2s.
His Vanished Star. Crown 8vo, cloth, 3s. 6d.

Crellin (H. N.).—Romances of the Old Seraglio. With 28 Illustrations by S. L. WOOD. Crown 8vo, cloth, 3s. 6d.

6 CHATTO & WINDUS, Publishers, 111 St. Martin's Lane, London, W.C.

Cresswell (Henry).—A Lady of Misrule. Cr. 8vo, cloth, gilt top, 6s.

Crim (Matt.).—Adventures of a Fair Rebel. Crown 8vo, cloth extra, with a Frontispiece by DAN. BEARD, 3s. 6d.; post 8vo, illustrated boards, 2s.

Crockett (S. R.) and others.—Tales of Our Coast. By S. R. CROCKETT, GILBERT PARKER, HAROLD FREDERIC, 'Q.,' and W. CLARK RUSSELL. With 2 Illustrations by FRANK BRANGWYN. Crown 8vo, cloth, 3s. 6d.

Croker (Mrs. B. M.), Novels by. Crown 8vo, cloth extra, 3s. 6d. each; post 8vo, illustrated boards, 2s. each; cloth limp, 2s. 6d. each.

Pretty Miss Neville.
Proper Pride.
A Bird of Passage.
Diana Barrington.
Two Masters.

Interference.
A Family Likeness.
A Third Person.
Mr. Jervis.

Village Tales & Jungle Tragedies.
The Real Lady Hilda.
Married or Single?

Crown 8vo, cloth extra, 3s. 6d. each.

Some One Else.
In the Kingdom of Kerry.
Terence. With 6 Illustrations by SIDNEY PAGET.
The Cat's-paw. With 12 Illustrations by FRED. PEGRAM.
'To Let,' &c. Post 8vo, picture boards, 2s.; cloth limp, 2s. 6d.

Miss Balmaine's Past.
Jason, &c.

Beyond the Pale.
Infatuation.

POPULAR EDITIONS, medium 8vo, 6d. each.

Diana Barrington. | Pretty Miss Neville.

Cruikshank's Comic Almanack. Complete in Two SERIES: The FIRST, from 1835 to 1843; the SECOND, from 1844 to 1853. A Gathering of the Best Humour of THACKERAY, HOOD, MAYHEW, ALBERT SMITH, A'BECKETT, ROBERT BROUGH, &c. With numerous Steel Engravings and Woodcuts by GEORGE CRUIKSHANK, HINE, LANDELLS, &c. Two Vols., crown 8vo, cloth gilt, 7s. 6d. each.
The Life of George Cruikshank. By BLANCHARD JERROLD. With 84 Illustrations and a Bibliography. Crown 8vo, cloth extra, 3s. 6d.

Cumming (C. F. Gordon), Works by. Large cr. 8vo, cloth, 6s. each.
In the Hebrides. With an Autotype Frontispiece and 23 Illustrations.
In the Himalayas and on the Indian Plains. With 42 Illustrations.
Two Happy Years in Ceylon. With 28 Illustrations.
Via Cornwall to Egypt. With a Photogravure Frontispiece.

Cussans (John E.).—A Handbook of Heraldry; with Instructions for Tracing Pedigrees and Deciphering Ancient MSS., &c. Fourth Edition, revised, with 408 Woodcuts and 2 Coloured Plates. Crown 8vo, cloth extra, 6s.

Daudet (Alphonse).—The Evangelist; or, Port Salvation. Crown 8vo, cloth extra, 3s. 6d.; post 8vo, illustrated boards, 2s.

Davenant (Francis, M.A.).—Hints for Parents on the Choice of a Profession for their Sons when Starting in Life. Crown 8vo, cloth, 1s. 6d.

Davidson (Hugh Coleman).—Mr. Sadler's Daughters. With a Frontispiece by STANLEY WOOD. Crown 8vo, cloth extra, 3s. 6d.

Davies (Dr. N. E. Yorke-), Works by. Cr. 8vo, 1s. ea.; cl., 1s. 6d. ea.
One Thousand Medical Maxims and Surgical Hints.
Nursery Hints: A Mother's Guide in Health and Disease.
Foods for the Fat: The Dietetic Cure of Corpulency and of Gout.
Aids to Long Life. Crown 8vo, 2s.; cloth limp, 2s. 6d.

Davies' (Sir John) Complete Poetical Works. Collected and Edited, with Introduction and Notes, by Rev. A. B. GROSART, D.D. Two Vols., crown 8vo, cloth, 3s. 6d. each.

De Guerin (Maurice), The Journal of. Edited by G. S. TREBUTIEN. With a Memoir by SAINTE-BEUVE. Translated from the 20th French Edition by JESSIE P. FROTHINGHAM. Fcap. 8vo, half-bound, 2s. 6d.

De Maistre (Xavier).—A Journey Round my Room. Translated by HENRY ATTWELL. Post 8vo, cloth limp, 2s. 6d.

De Mille (James).—A Strange Manuscript found in a Copper Cylinder. Crown 8vo, cloth, with 19 Illustrations by GILBERT GAUL, 3s. 6d.; post 8vo, illustrated boards, 2s.

Derby (The): The Blue Ribbon of the Turf. With Brief Accounts of THE OAKS. By LOUIS HENRY CURZON. Crown 8vo, cloth limp, 2s. 6d.

Dewar (T. R.).—A Ramble Round the Globe. With 220 Illustrations. Crown 8vo, cloth extra, 7s. 6d.

De Windt (Harry), Books by.
Through the Gold-Fields of Alaska to Bering Straits. With Map and 33 full-page Illustrations. Cheaper Issue. Demy 8vo, cloth, 6s.
True Tales of Travel and Adventure. Crown 8vo, cloth, 3s. 6d.

Dickens (Charles), About England with. By ALFRED RIMMER. With 57 Illustrations by C. A. VANDERHOOF and the AUTHOR. Square 8vo, cloth, 3s. 6d.

Dictionaries.
The Reader's Handbook of Famous Names in Fiction, Allusions, References, Proverbs, Plots, Stories, and Poems. By Rev. E. C. BREWER, LL.D. A New Edition, Revised. Crown 8vo, cloth, 3s. 6d.
A Dictionary of Miracles: Imitative, Realistic, and Dogmatic. By the Rev. E. C. BREWER, LL.D. Crown 8vo, cloth, 3s. 6d.
Familiar Short Sayings of Great Men. With Historical and Explanatory Notes by SAMUEL A. BENT, A.M. Crown 8vo, cloth extra, 7s. 6d.
The Slang Dictionary: Etymological, Historical, and Anecdotal. Crown 8vo, cloth, 6s. 6d.
Words, Facts, and Phrases: A Dictionary of Curious, Quaint, and Out-of-the-Way Matters. By ELIEZER EDWARDS. Crown 8vo, cloth extra, 3s. 6d.

Dilke (Rt. Hon. Sir Charles, Bart., M.P.).—The British Empire. Crown 8vo, buckram, 3s. 6d.

Dobson (Austin), Works by.
Thomas Bewick and his Pupils. With 95 Illustrations. Square 8vo, cloth, 3s. 6d.
Four Frenchwomen. With Four Portraits. Crown 8vo, buckram, gilt top, 6s.
Eighteenth Century Vignettes. IN THREE SERIES. Crown 8vo, buckram, 6s. each.
A Paladin of Philanthropy, and other Papers. With 2 Illusts. Cr. 8vo, buckram, 6s.
Side-walk Studies. With 5 Illustrations. Crown 8vo, buckram, gilt top, 6s.

Dobson (W. T.).—Poetical Ingenuities and Eccentricities. Post 8vo, cloth limp, 2s. 6d.

Donovan (Dick), Detective Stories by.
Post 8vo, illustrated boards, 2s. each; cloth limp, 2s. 6d. each.
The Man-Hunter. | Tracked to Doom. | Suspicion Aroused. | Riddles Read.
Caught at Last. | Link by Link. | A Detective's Triumphs.
Tracked and Taken. | In the Grip of the Law.
Who Poisoned Hetty Duncan? | From Information Received.
Crown 8vo, cloth extra, 3s. 6d. each; post 8vo, illustrated boards, 2s. each; cloth, 2s. 6d. each.
The Mystery of Jamaica Terrace. | The Chronicles of Michael Danevitch.
Crown 8vo, cloth, 3s. 6d. each.
The Records of Vincent Trill, of the Detective Service.—Also picture cloth, flat back, 2s.
The Adventures of Tyler Tatlock, Private Detective.
Deacon Brodie; or, Behind the Mask. | Tales of Terror.
Dark Deeds. Crown 8vo, cloth limp, 2s. 6d; picture cloth, flat back, 2s.
Wanted! Crown 8vo, picture cloth, flat back, 2s.; post 8vo, illust. boards, 2s.; cloth limp, 2s. 6d.
The Man from Manchester. With 23 Illustrations Crown 8vo, cloth, 3s. 6d.; picture cloth, flat back, 2s.; post 8vo, picture boards, 2s; cloth limp, 2s. 6d.

Dowling (Richard).—Old Corcoran's Money. Crown 8vo, cl., 3s. 6d.

Doyle (A. Conan).—The Firm of Girdlestone. Cr. 8vo, cl., 3s. 6d.

Dramatists, The Old. Cr. 8vo, cl. ex., with Portraits, 3s. 6d. per Vol.
Ben Jonson's Works. With Notes, Critical and Explanatory, and a Biographical Memoir by WILLIAM GIFFORD. Edited by Colonel CUNNINGHAM. Three Vols.
Chapman's Works. Three Vols. Vol. I. contains the Plays complete; Vol. II., Poems and Minor Translations, with an Essay by A. C. SWINBURNE; Vol. III., Translations of the Iliad and Odyssey.
Marlowe's Works. Edited, with Notes, by Colonel CUNNINGHAM. One Vol.
Massinger's Plays. From GIFFORD'S Text. Edited by Colonel CUNNINGHAM. One Vol.

Dublin Castle and Dublin Society, Recollections of. By A NATIVE. Crown 8vo, cloth, gilt top. 6s.

Duncan (Sara Jeannette: Mrs. EVERARD COTES), Books by.
Crown 8vo, cloth extra, 7s. 6d. each.
A Social Departure. With 111 Illustrations by F. H. TOWNSEND.
An American Girl in London. With 80 Illustrations by F. H. TOWNSEND.
The Simple Adventures of a Memsahib. With 37 Illustrations by F. H. TOWNSEND.
Crown 8vo, cloth extra, 3s. 6d. each.
A Daughter of To-Day. | Vernon's Aunt. With 47 Illustrations by HAL HURST.

Dutt (Romesh C.).—England and India: A Record of Progress during One Hundred Years. Crown 8vo, cloth, 2s.

Early English Poets. Edited, with Introductions and Annotations, by Rev. A. B. GROSART, D.D. Crown 8vo, cloth boards, 3s. 6d. per Volume.
Fletcher's (Giles) Complete Poems. One Vol.
Davies' (Sir John) Complete Poetical Works. Two Vols.
Sidney's (Sir Philip) Complete Poetical Works. Three Vols.

Edgcumbe (Sir E. R. Pearce).—Zephyrus: A Holiday in Brazil and on the River Plate. With 41 Illustrations. Crown 8vo, cloth extra, 5s.

Edwardes (Mrs. Annie), Novels by.
A Point of Honour. Post 8vo, illustrated boards, 2s. | A Plaster Saint. Cr. 8vo, cl., 3s. 6d.
Archie Lovell. Crown 8vo, cloth, 3s. 6d.; illustrated boards, 2s.

Edwards (Eliezer).—Words, Facts, and Phrases: A Dictionary of Curious, Quaint, and Out-of-the-Way Matters. Cheaper Edition. Crown 8vo, cloth, 3s. 6d.

Egerton (Rev. J. C., M.A.). — Sussex Folk and Sussex Ways. With Introduction by Rev. Dr. H. WACE, and Four Illustrations. Crown 8vo, cloth extra, 5s.

8 CHATTO & WINDUS, Publishers, 111 St. Martin's Lane, London, W.C.

Eggleston (Edward).—Roxy: A Novel. Post 8vo, illust. boards, 2s.

Englishman (An) in Paris. Notes and Recollections during the Reign of Louis Philippe and the Empire. Crown 8vo, cloth, 3s. 6d.

Englishman's House, The: A Practical Guide for Selecting or Building a House. By C. J. RICHARDSON. Coloured Frontispiece and 534 Illusts. Cr. 8vo, cloth, 3s. 6d.

Eyes, Our: How to Preserve Them. By JOHN BROWNING. Cr. 8vo, 1s.

Familiar Short Sayings of Great Men. By SAMUEL ARTHUR BENT, A.M. Fifth Edition, Revised and Enlarged. Crown 8vo, cloth extra, 7s. 6d.

Faraday (Michael), Works by. Post 8vo, cloth extra, 4s. 6d. each.
   The Chemical History of a Candle: Lectures delivered before a Juvenile Audience. Edited by WILLIAM CROOKES, F.C.S. With numerous Illustrations.
   On the Various Forces of Nature, and their Relations to each other. Edited by WILLIAM CROOKES, F.C.S. With Illustrations.

Farrer (J. Anson).—War: Three Essays. Crown 8vo, cloth, 1s. 6d.

Fenn (G. Manville), Novels by.
   Crown 8vo, cloth extra, 3s. 6d. each; post 8vo, illustrated boards, 2s. each.
   The New Mistress. | Witness to the Deed. | The Tiger Lily. | The White Virgin.

Crown 8vo, cloth 3s. 6d. each.
A Woman Worth Winning. | Double Cunning. | The Story of Antony Grace
Cursed by a Fortune. | A Fluttered Dovecote. | The Man with a Shadow.
The Case of Ailsa Gray. | King of the Castle. | One Maid's Mischief.
Commodore Junk. | The Master of the Ceremonies. | This Man's Wife.
Black Blood. | | In Jeopardy.

Crown 8vo, cloth, gilt top, 6s. each.
The Bag of Diamonds, and Three Bits of Paste.
Running Amok: a Story of Adventure.
The Cankerworm: being Episodes of a Woman's Life. | Black Shadows.
A Crimson Crime. Crown 8vo, cloth, gilt top, 6s.; picture cloth, flat back, 2s.

Fiction, A Catalogue of, with Descriptive Notices and Reviews of over NINE HUNDRED NOVELS, will be sent free by Messrs. CHATTO & WINDUS upon application.

Fin-Bec.—The Cupboard Papers: Observations on the Art of Living and Dining. Post 8vo, cloth limp, 2s. 6d.

Firework-Making, The Complete Art of; or, The Pyrotechnist's Treasury. By THOMAS KENTISH. With 267 Illustrations. Crown 8vo, cloth, 3s. 6d.

First Book, My. By WALTER BESANT, JAMES PAYN, W. CLARK RUSSELL, GRANT ALLEN, HALL CAINE, GEORGE R. SIMS, RUDYARD KIPLING, A. CONAN DOYLE, M. E. BRADDON, F. W. ROBINSON, H. RIDER HAGGARD, R. M. BALLANTYNE, I. ZANGWILL, MORLEY ROBERTS, D. CHRISTIE MURRAY, MARY CORELLI, J. K. JEROME, JOHN STRANGE WINTER, BRET HARTE, 'Q.,' ROBERT BUCHANAN, and R. L. STEVENSON. With a Prefatory Story by JEROME K. JEROME, and 185 Illustrations. A New Edition. Small demy 8vo, art linen, 3s. 6d.

Fitzgerald (Percy), Works by.
   Little Essays: Passages from the Letters of CHARLES LAMB. Post 8vo, cloth, 2s. 6d.
   Fatal Zero. Crown 8vo, cloth extra, 3s. 6d.; post 8vo, illustrated boards, 2s.

Post 8vo, illustrated boards, 2s. each.
Bella Donna. | The Lady of Brantome. | The Second Mrs. Tillotson.
Polly. | Never Forgotten. | Seventy-five Brooke Street.
Sir Henry Irving: Twenty Years at the Lyceum. With Portrait. Crown 8vo, cloth, 1s. 6d.

Flammarion (Camille), Works by.
   Popular Astronomy: A General Description of the Heavens. Translated by J. ELLARD GORE, F.R.A.S. With Three Plates and 288 Illustrations. Medium 8vo, cloth, 10s. 6d.
   Urania: A Romance. With 87 Illustrations. Crown 8vo, cloth extra, 5s.

Fletcher's (Giles, B.D.) Complete Poems: Christ's Victorie in Heaven, Christ's Victorie on Earth, Christ's Triumph over Death, and Minor Poems. With Notes by Rev. A. B. GROSART, D.D. Crown 8vo, cloth boards, 3s. 6d.

Forbes (Hon. Mrs. Walter R. D.).—Dumb. Crown 8vo, cl., 3s. 6d.

Francillon (R. E.), Novels by.
   Crown 8vo, cloth extra, 3s. 6d. each; post 8vo, illustrated boards, 2s. each.
One by One. | A Real Queen. | A Dog and his Shadow. | Ropes of Sand. Illust

Post 8vo, illustrated boards, 2s. each.
Queen Cophetua. | Olympia. | Romances of the Law. | King or Knave?
Jack Doyle's Daughter. Crown 8vo, cloth, 3s. 6d.

Frederic (Harold), Novels by. Post 8vo, cloth extra, 3s. 6d. each; Illustrated boards 2s. each.
Seth's Brother's Wife. | The Lawton Girl.

CHATTO & WINDUS, Publishers, 111 St. Martin's Lane, London, W.C. 9

Fry's (Herbert) Royal Guide to the London Charities, 1904.
Edited by JOHN LANE. Published Annually. Crown 8vo, cloth, 1s. 6d.

Gardening Books. Post 8vo, 1s. each; cloth limp, 1s. 6d. each.
A Year's Work in Garden and Greenhouse. By GEORGE GLENNY.
Household Horticulture. By TOM and JANE JERROLD. Illustrated.
The Garden that Paid the Rent. By TOM JERROLD.

Gaulot (Paul), Books by:
The Red Shirts: A Tale of "The Terror." Translated by JOHN DE VILLIERS. With a Frontispiece by STANLEY WOOD. Crown 8vo, cloth, 3s. 6d.; picture cloth, flat back, 2s.
Crown 8vo, cloth, gilt top, 6s. each.
Love and Lovers of the Past. With a Frontispiece. Translated by C. LAROCHE, M.A.
A Conspiracy under the Terror. With Illustrations and Facsimiles.

Gentleman's Magazine, The. 1s. Monthly. Contains Stories, Articles upon Literature, Science, Biography, and Art, and 'Table Talk' by SYLVANUS URBAN.
** *Bound Volumes for recent years kept in stock, 8s. 6d. each. Cases for binding, 2s. each.*

German Popular Stories. Collected by the Brothers GRIMM and Translated by EDGAR TAYLOR. With Introduction by JOHN RUSKIN, and 22 Steel Plates after GEORGE CRUIKSHANK. Square 8vo, cloth, 6s. 6d.; gilt edges, 7s. 6d.

Gibbon (Chas.), Novels by. Cr. 8vo, cl., 3s. 6d. ea.; post 8vo, bds., 2s. ea.
Robin Gray. With Frontispiece.   The Braes of Yarrow.
The Golden Shaft. With Frontispiece.   Of High Degree.
The Flower of the Forest.   Queen of the Meadow.

Post 8vo, illustrated boards, 2s. each:
The Dead Heart.	In Pastures Green.	Loving a Dream.
For Lack of Gold.	In Love and War.	In Honour Bound.
What Will the World Say?	A Heart's Problem.	Heart's Delight.
For the King.	By Mead and Stream.	Blood-Money.
A Hard Knot.	Fancy Free.	

Gibney (Somerville).—Sentenced! Crown 8vo, cloth, 1s. 6d.

Gilbert's (W. S.) Original Plays. In 3 Series, post 8vo, 2s. 6d. each.
The FIRST SERIES contains: The W".ked World—Pygmalion and Galatea—Charity—The Princess—The Palace of Truth—Trial by Jry—Iolanthe.
The SECOND SERIES: Broken Hearts—Engaged—Sweethearts—Gretchen—Dan'l Druce—Tom Cobb—H.M.S.' Pinafore'—The Sorcerer—The Pirates of Penzance.
The THIRD SERIES: Comedy and Tragedy—Foggerty's Fairy—Rosencrantz and Guildenstern—Patience—Princess Ida—The Mikado—Ruddigore—The Yeomen of the Guard—The Gondoliers—The Mountebanks—Utopia.

Eight Original Comic Operas written by W. S. GILBERT. Two Series, demy 8vo, cloth, 2s. 6d. each. The FIRST SERIES contains: The Sorcerer—H.M.S.' Pinafore '—The Pirates of Penzance—Iolanthe—Patience—Princess Ida—The Mikado—Trial by Jury.
The SECOND SERIES contains: The Gondoliers—The Grand Duke—The Yeomen of the Guard—His Excellency—Utopia, Limited—Ruddigore—The Mountebanks—Haste to the Wedding.
The Gilbert and Sullivan Birthday Book: Quotations for Every Day in the Year, selected from Plays by W. S. GILBERT set to Music by Sir A. SULLIVAN. Compiled by ALEX. WATSON. Royal 16mo, cloth, 2s. 6d.

Gilbert (William).—James Duke, Costermonger. Post 8vo, illustrated boards, 2s.

Gissing (Algernon), Novels by. Crown 8vo, cloth, gilt top, 6s. each.
A Secret of the North Sea. | The Wealth of Mallerstang.
Knitters in the Sun. | An Angel's Portion. | Baliol Garth. [Shortly.

Glanville (Ernest), Novels by.
Crown 8vo, cloth extra, 3s. 6d. each; post 8vo, illustrated boards, 2s. each.
The Lost Heiress: A Tale of Love, Battle, and Adventure. With Two Illustrations by H. NISBET.
The Fossicker: A Romance of Mashonaland. With Two Illustrations by HUME NISBET.
A Fair Colonist. With a Frontispiece by STANLEY WOOD.

The Golden Rock. With a Frontispiece by STANLEY WOOD. Crown 8vo, cloth extra, 3s. 6d.
Kloof Yarns. Crown 8vo cloth, 1s. 6d.
Tales from the Veld. With Twelve Illustrations by M. NISBET. Crown 8vo, cloth, 3s. 6d.
Max Thornton. With 8 Illustrations by J. S. CROMPTON, R.I. Large crown 8vo, cloth, gilt edges, 5s.; cloth, gilt top, 6s.

Glenny (George).—A Year's Work in Garden and Greenhouse: Practical Advice as to the Management of the Flower, Fruit, and Frame Garden. Post 8vo, 1s.; cloth, 1s. 6d.

Godwin (William).—Lives of the Necromancers. Post 8vo, cl., 2s.

Golden Treasury of Thought, The: A Dictionary of Quotations from the Best Authors. By THEODORE TAYLOR. Crown 8vo, cloth, 3s. 6d.

Goodman (E. J.).—The Fate of Herbert Wayne. Cr. 8vo, 3s. 6d.

Gore (J. Ellard, F.R.A.S.).—The Stellar Heavens: an Introduction to the Study of the Stars and Nebulæ. Crown 8vo, cloth, 2s. net.

Grace (Alfred A.).—Tales of a Dying Race. Cr. 8vo, cloth, 3s. 6d.

10 CHATTO & WINDUS, Publishers, 111 St. Martin's Lane, London, W.C.

Greeks and Romans, The Life of the, described from Antique Monuments. By ERNST GUHL and W. KONER. Edited by Dr. F. HUEFFER. With 545 Illustrations. Large crown 8vo, cloth extra, 7s. 6d.

Greenwood (James): "The Amateur Casual").—The Prisoner in the Dock; My Four Years' Daily Experiences in the London Police Courts. Cr. 8vo, cl., 3s. 6d.

Grey (Sir George).—The Romance of a Proconsul: Being the Personal Life and Memoirs of Sir GEORGE GREY, K.C.B. By JAMES MILNE. With Portrait. SECOND EDITION. Crown 8vo, buckram, 6s.

Griffith (Cecil).—Corinthia Marazion: A Novel. Crown 8vo, cloth extra, 3s. 6d.

Gunter (A. Clavering, Author of 'Mr. Barnes of New York').— A Florida Enchantment. Crown 8vo, cloth, 3s. 6d.

Guttenberg (Violet), Novels by.
Neither Jew nor Greek. | The Power of the Palmist.

Hair, The: Its Treatment in Health, Weakness, and Disease. Translated from the German of Dr. J. PINCUS. Crown 8vo, 1s.; cloth, 1s. 6d.

Hake (Dr. Thomas Gordon), Poems by. Cr. 8vo, cl. ex., 6s. each.
New Symbols. | Legends of the Morrow. | The Serpent Play.
Maiden Ecstasy. Small 4to, cloth extra, 8s.

Halifax (C.).—Dr. Rumsey's Patient. By Mrs. L. T. MEADE and CLIFFORD HALIFAX, M.D. Crown 8vo, cloth, 3s. 6d.

Hall (Mrs. S. C.).—Sketches of Irish Character. With numerous Illustrations on Steel and Wood by MACLISE, GILBERT, HARVEY, and GEORGE CRUIKSHANK. Small demy 8vo, cloth extra, 7s. 6d.

Hall (Owen), Novels by.
The Track of a Storm. Crown 8vo, picture cloth, flat back, 2s.
Jetsam. Crown 8vo, cloth, 3s. 6d.
Crown 8vo, cloth, gilt top, 6s. each.
Eureka. | Hernando.

Harte's (Bret) Collected Works. Revised by the Author. LIBRARY EDITION, in Ten Volumes, crown 8vo, cloth extra, 6s. each.
Vol. I. COMPLETE POETICAL AND DRAMATIC WORKS. With Steel-plate Portrait.
 „ II. THE LUCK OF ROARING CAMP—BOHEMIAN PAPERS—AMERICAN LEGEND.
 „ III. TALES OF THE ARGONAUTS—EASTERN SKETCHES.
 „ IV. GABRIEL CONROY. | Vol. V. STORIES—CONDENSED NOVELS, &c.
 „ VI. TALES OF THE PACIFIC SLOPE.
 „ VII. TALES OF THE PACIFIC SLOPE—II. With Portrait by JOHN PETTIE, R.A.
 „ VIII. TALES OF THE PINE AND THE CYPRESS.
 „ IX. BUCKEYE AND CHAPPAREL.
 „ X. TALES OF TRAIL AND TOWN, &c.
Bret Harte's Choice Works, in Prose and Verse. With Portrait of the Author and 40 Illustrations. Crown 8vo, cloth, 3s. 6d.
Bret Harte's Poetical Works, including "Some Later Verses." Crown 8vo, buckram, 4s. 6d.
Some Later Verses. Crown 8vo, linen gilt, 5s.
In a Hollow of the Hills. Crown 8vo, picture cloth, flat back, 2s.
Condensed Novels. (The Two Series in One Volume.) Pott 8vo, cloth, gilt top, 2s. net; leather, gilt edges, 3s. net.
Crown 8vo, cloth, 6s. each.
On the Old Trail. | From Sandhill to Pine.
Under the Redwoods. | Stories in Light and Shadow.
Mr. Jack Hamlin's Mediation.
Crown 8vo, cloth extra, 3s. 6d. each; post 8vo, picture boards, 2s. each.
Gabriel Conroy.
A Waif of the Plains. With 60 Illustrations by STANLEY L. WOOD.
A Ward of the Golden Gate. With 59 Illustrations by STANLEY L. WOOD.
Crown 8vo, cloth extra, 3s. 6d. each.
Susy: A Novel. With Frontispiece and Vignette by J. A. CHRISTIE.
Sally Dows, &c. With 47 Illustrations by W. D. ALMOND and others.
The Bell-Ringer of Angel's, &c. With 39 Illustrations by DUDLEY HARDY and others
Clarence: A Story of the American War. With Eight Illustrations by A. JULE GOODMAN.
Barker's Luck, &c. With 39 Illustrations by A. FORESTIER, PAUL HARDY, &c.
Devil's Ford, &c. With a Frontispiece by W. H. OVEREND.
The Crusade of the "Excelsior." With a Frontispiece by J. BERNARD PARTRIDGE.
Three Partners; or, The Big Strike on Heavy Tree Hill. With 8 Illustrations by J. GULICH.
Tales of Trail and Town. With Frontispiece by G. P. JACOMB-HOOD.
New Condensed Novels: Burlesques.
Crown 8vo, cloth, 3s. 6d. each; picture cloth, flat back, 2s. each.
The Luck of Roaring Camp, and Sensation Novels Condensed.
A Sappho of Green Springs. | Colonel Starbottle's Client.
A Protegee of Jack Hamlin's. With numerous Illustrations.
Post 8vo, illustrated boards, 2s. each.
An Heiress of Red Dog. | The Luck of Roaring Camp. | Californian Stories.
Post 8vo, illustrated boards, 2s. each; cloth, 2s. 6d. each.
Flip. | Maruja. | A Phyllis of the Sierras.

Halliday (Andrew).—Every-day Papers. Post 8vo, picture bds., 2s.

Hamilton (Cosmo), Stories by. Crown 8vo, cloth gilt, 3s. 6d. each.
The Glamour of the Impossible. | Through a Keyhole.
*** The two stories may also be had bound together in one volume, crown 8vo, cloth, 3s. 6d.

Handwriting, The Philosophy of. With over 100 Facsimiles and Explanatory Text. By DON FELIX DE SALAMANCA. Post 8vo, half-cloth, 2s. 6d.

Hanky-Panky: Easy and Difficult Tricks; White Magic, Sleight of Hand, &c. Edited by W. H. CREMER. With 200 Illustrations. Crown 8vo, cloth extra, 4s. 6d.

Hardy (Rev. E. J., Author of 'How to be Happy though Married').—Love, Courtship, and Marriage. Crown 8vo, cloth, 3s. 6d.

Hardy (Iza Duffus), Novels by. Crown 8vo, cloth, gilt top, 6s. each.
The Lesser Evil. | Man, Woman, and Fate.
A Butterfly: Her Friends and her Fortunes.

Hardy (Thomas).—Under the Greenwood Tree. Post 8vo, cloth extra, 3s. 6d.; Illustrated boards, 2s.; cloth limp, 2s. 6d.—Also the FINE PAPER EDITION, pott 8vo, cloth, gilt top, 2s. net; leather, gilt edges, 3s. net.

Haweis (Mrs. H. R.), Books by.
The Art of Beauty. With Coloured Frontispiece and 91 Illustrations. Square 8vo, cloth bds., 6s.
The Art of Decoration. With Coloured Frontispiece and 74 Illustrations. Sq. 8vo, cloth bds., 6s.
The Art of Dress. With 32 Illustrations. Post 8vo, 1s.; cloth, 1s. 6d.
Chaucer for Schools. With the Story of his Times and his Work. A New Edition, revised. With a Frontispiece. Demy 8vo, cloth, 2s. 6d.
Chaucer for Children. With 38 Illustrations (8 Coloured). Crown 4to, cloth extra, 3s. 6d.

Haweis (Rev. H. R., M.A.).—American Humorists: WASHINGTON IRVING, OLIVER WENDELL HOLMES, JAMES RUSSELL LOWELL, ARTEMUS WARD, MARK TWAIN, and BRET HARTE. Crown 8vo, cloth, 6s.

Hawthorne (Julian), Novels by.
Crown 8vo, cloth extra, 3s. 6d. each; post 8vo, illustrated boards, 2s. each.
Garth. | Ellice Quentin. | Beatrix Randolph. With Four Illusts.
Fortune's Fool. | Dust. Four Illusts. | David Poindexter's Disappearance.
The Spectre of the Camera.

Post 8vo, Illustrated boards, 2s. each.
Miss Cadogna. | Love—or a Name.
Sebastian Strome. Crown 8vo, cloth, 3s. 6d.

Healy (Chris).—Confessions of a Journalist. With a Portrait. Crown 8vo, cloth, gilt top, 6s.

Heckethorn (C. W.), Books by. Crown 8vo, cloth, gilt top, 6s. each.
London Souvenirs. | London Memories: Social, Historical, and Topographical.

Helps (Sir Arthur), Books by. Post 8vo, cloth limp, 2s. 6d. each.
Animals and their Masters. | Social Pressure.
Ivan de Biron: A Novel. Crown 8vo, cloth extra, 3s. 6d.; post 8vo, illustrated boards, 2s.

Henderson (Isaac).—Agatha Page: A Novel. Cr. 8vo, cl., 3s. 6d.

Henty (G. A.), Novels by.
Rujub, the Juggler. Post 8vo, cloth, 3s. 6d.; illustrated boards, 2s.
Colonel Thorndyke's Secret. With a Frontispiece by STANLEY L. WOOD. Small demy 8vo, cloth, gilt edges, 5s.

Crown 8vo, cloth, 3s. 6d. each.
The Queen's Cup. | Dorothy's Double.

Herman (Henry).—A Leading Lady. Post 8vo, cloth, 2s. 6d.

Hertzka (Dr. Theodor).—Freeland: A Social Anticipation. Translated by ARTHUR RANSOM. Crown 8vo, cloth extra, 6s.

Hesse-Wartegg (Chevalier Ernst von).—Tunis: The Land and the People. With 22 Illustrations. Crown 8vo, cloth extra, 3s. 6d.

Hill (Headon).—Zambra the Detective. Crown 8vo, cloth, 3s. 6d.; picture cloth, flat back, 2s.; post 8vo, picture boards, 2s.

Hill (John), Works by.
Treason-Felony. Post 8vo, boards, 2s. | The Common Ancestor. Cr. 8vo, cloth, 3s. 6d.

Hinkson (H. A.), Novels by. Crown 8vo, cloth, gilt top, 6s. each.
Fan Fitzgerald. | Silk and Steel.

Hoey (Mrs. Cashel).—The Lover's Creed. Post 8vo, boards, 2s.

Holiday, Where to go for a. By E. P. SHOLL, Sir H. MAXWELL, Bart., M.P., JOHN WATSON, JANE BARLOW, MARY LOVETT CAMERON, JUSTIN H. MCCARTHY, PAUL LANGE, J. W. GRAHAM, J. H. SALTER, PHOEBE ALLEN, S. J. BECKETT, L. RIVERS VINE, and C. F. GORDON CUMMING. Crown 8vo, cloth, 1s. 6d.

12 CHATTO & WINDUS, Publishers, 111 St. Martin's Lane, London, W.C.

Holmes (Oliver Wendell), Works by.
The Autocrat of the Breakfast-Table. Illustrated by J. GORDON THOMSON. Post 8vo cloth limp, 2s. 6d. Another Edition, post 8vo, cloth, 2s.
The Autocrat of the Breakfast-Table and The Professor at the Breakfast-Table. In One Vol. Post 8vo, half-bound, 2s.

Hood's (Thomas) Choice Works in Prose and Verse. With Life of the Author, Portrait, and 200 Illustrations. Crown 8vo, cloth, 3s. 6d.
Hood's Whims and Oddities. With 85 Illustrations. Post 8vo, half-bound, 2s.

Hook's (Theodore) Choice Humorous Works; including his Ludicrous Adventures, Bons Mots, Puns, Hoaxes. With Life and Frontispiece. Crown 8vo, cloth, 3s. 6d.

Hopkins (Tighe), Novels by.
For Freedom. Crown 8vo, cloth, 6s.
Crown 8vo, cloth, 3s. 6d. each.
'Twixt Love and Duty. With a Frontispiece. | The Incomplete Adventurer.
The Nugents of Carriconna. | Nell Haffenden. With 8 Illustrations by C. GREGORY.

Horne (R. Hengist).—Orion: An Epic Poem. With Photograph Portrait by SUMMERS. Tenth Edition. Crown 8vo, cloth extra, 7s.

Hornung (E. W.).—The Shadow of the Rope. Crown 8vo, cloth, gilt top, 6s.

Hugo (Victor).—The Outlaw of Iceland (Han d'Islande). Translated by Sir GILBERT CAMPBELL. Crown 8vo, cloth, 3s. 6d.

Hume (Fergus), Novels by.
The Lady from Nowhere. Crown 8vo, cloth, 3s. 6d.; picture cloth, flat back, 2s
The Millionaire Mystery. Crown 8vo, cloth, 3s. 6d.
The Wheeling Light. Crown 8vo, cloth, gilt top, 6s.

Hungerford (Mrs., Author of 'Molly Bawn'), Novels by.
Crown 8vo, cloth extra, 3s. 6d. each; post 8vo, illustrated boards, 2s. each; cloth limp, 2s. 6d. each.
A Maiden All Forlorn. | Peter's Wife. | An Unsatisfactory Lover.
In Durance Vile. | Lady Patty. | The Professor's Experiment.
Marvel. | Lady Verner's Flight. | The Three Graces.
A Modern Circe. | The Red-House Mystery. | Nora Creina.
April's Lady. | | A Mental Struggle.
Crown 8vo, cloth extra, 3s. 6d. each.
An Anxious Moment. | The Coming of Chloe. | A Point of Conscience. | Lovice.

Hunt's (Leigh) Essays: A Tale for a Chimney Corner, &c. Edited by EDMUND OLLIER. Post 8vo, half-bound, 2s.

Hunt (Mrs. Alfred), Novels by.
Crown 8vo, cloth extra, 3s. 6d. each; post 8vo, illustrated boards, 2s. each.
The Leaden Casket. | Self-Condemned. | That Other Person.
Mrs. Juliet. Crown 8vo, cloth extra, 3s. 6d.

Hutchison (W. M.).—Hints on Colt-breaking. With 25 Illustrations. Crown 8vo, cloth extra, 3s. 6d.

Hydrophobia: An Account of M. PASTEUR'S System; The Technique of his Method, and Statistics. By RENAUD SUZOR, M.B. Crown 8vo, cloth extra, 6s.

Idler Magazine (The). Edited by ROBERT BARR. Profusely Illustrated. 6d. Monthly.

Impressions (The) of Aureole. Post 8vo, cloth, 2s. 6d.

Indoor Paupers. By ONE OF THEM. Crown 8vo, 1s.; cloth, 1s. 6d.

Inman (Herbert) and Hartley Aspden.—The Tear of Kalee. Crown 8vo, cloth, gilt top, 6s.

In Memoriam: Verses for every Day in the Year. Selected and arranged by LUCY RIDLEY. Small square 8vo, cloth, 2s. 6d. net; leather, 3s. 6d. net.

Innkeeper's Handbook (The) and Licensed Victualler's Manual. By J. TREVOR-DAVIES. A New Edition. Crown 8vo, cloth, 2s.

Irish Wit and Humour, Songs of. Collected and Edited by A. PERCEVAL GRAVES. Post 8vo, cloth limp, 2s. 6d.

Irving (Sir Henry): A Record of over Twenty Years at the Lyceum. By PERCY FITZGERALD. With Portrait. Crown 8vo, cloth, 1s. 6d.

James (C. T. C.).— A Romance of the Queen's Hounds. Post 8vo, cloth limp, 1s. 6d.

Jameson (William).—My Dead Self. Post 8vo, cloth, 2s. 6d.

Japp (Alex. H., LL.D.).—Dramatic Pictures, &c. Cr. 8vo, cloth, 5s

Jefferies (Richard), Books by.
The Open Air. Post 8vo, cloth, 2s. 6d.
Crown 8vo, buckram, 6s. each ; post 8vo, cloth limp, 2s. 6d. each.
Nature near London. | The Life of the Fields.
Also, the LARGE TYPE, FINE PAPER EDITION of **The Life of the Fields.** Pott 8vo, cloth gilt top, 2s. net; leather, gilt edges, 3s. net.
The Eulogy of Richard Jefferies. By Sir WALTER BESANT. With a Photograph Portrait. Crown 8vo, cloth extra, 6s.

Jennings (Henry J.), Works by.
Curiosities of Criticism. Post 8vo, cloth limp, 2s. 6d.
Lord Tennyson: A Biographical Sketch. With Portrait. Post 8vo, cloth, 1s. 6d.

Jerome (Jerome K.).—Stageland. With 64 Illustrations by J. BERNARD PARTRIDGE. Fcap. 4to. picture cover, 1s.

Jerrold (Douglas).—The Barber's Chair; and The Hedgehog Letters. Post 8vo, printed on laid paper and half-bound. 2s.

Jerrold (Tom), Works by. Post 8vo, 1s. ea. ; cloth limp, 1s. 6d. each.
The Garden that Paid the Rent.
Household Horticulture: A Gossip about Flowers. Illustrated.

Jesse (Edward).—Scenes and Occupations of a Country Life. Post 8vo, cloth limp, 2s.

Johnston (R.).—The Peril of an Empire. Cr. 8vo, cloth, gilt top, 6s.

Jones (William, F.S.A.), Works by. Cr. 8vo, cl. extra, 3s. 6d. each.
Finger-Ring Lore: Historical, Legendary, and Anecdotal. With Hundreds of Illustrations.
Crowns and Coronations: A History of Regalia. With 91 Illustrations.

Jonson's (Ben) Works. With Notes Critical and Explanatory, and a Biographical Memoir by WILLIAM GIFFORD. Edited by Colonel CUNNINGHAM. Three Vols. crown 8vo, cloth extra, 3s. 6d. each.

Josephus, The Complete Works of. Translated by WILLIAM WHISTON. Containing 'The Antiquities of the Jews' and 'The Wars of the Jews.' With 52 Illustrations and Maps. Two Vols., demy 8vo, half-cloth, 12s. 6d.

Kempt (Robert).—Pencil and Palette: Chapters on Art and Artists. Post 8vo, cloth limp, 2s. 6d.

Kershaw (Mark). — Colonial Facts and Fictions: Humorous Sketches. Post 8vo, illustrated boards, 2s.; cloth, 2s. 6d.

King (R. Ashe), Novels by. Post 8vo, illustrated boards, 2s. each.
'The Wearing of the Green.' | Passion's Slave. | Bell Barry.
A Drawn Game. Crown 8vo, cloth, 3s. 6d. ; post 8vo, illustrated boards, 2s.

Kipling Primer (A). Including Biographical and Critical Chapters, an Index to Mr. Kipling's principal Writings, and Bibliographies. By F. L. KNOWLES, Editor of 'The Golden Treasury of American Lyrics.' With Two Portraits. Crown 8vo, cloth, 3s. 6d.

Knight (William, M.R.C.S., and Edward, L.R.C.P.). — The Patient's Vade Mecum: How to Get Most Benefit from Medical Advice. Cr. 8vo, cloth, 1s. 6d.

Knights (The) of the Lion: A Romance of the Thirteenth Century. Edited, with an Introduction, by the MARQUESS OF LORNE, K.T. Crown 8vo, cloth extra, 6s.

Lambert (George).—The President of Boravia. Crown 8vo, cl., 3s. 6d.

Lamb's (Charles) Complete Works in Prose and Verse, including 'Poetry for Children' and 'Prince Dorus.' Edited, with Notes and Introduction, by R. H. SHEPHERD. With Two Portraits and Facsimile of the 'Essay on Roast Pig.' Crown 8vo, cloth, 3s. 6d.
The Essays of Elia. Post 8vo, half-cloth, 2s.
Little Essays: Sketches and Characters by CHARLES LAMB, selected from his Letters by PERCY FITZGERALD. Post 8vo, cloth limp, 2s. 6d.
The Dramatic Essays of Charles Lamb. With Introduction and Notes by BRANDER MATTHEWS, and Steel-plate Portrait. Fcap. 8vo, half-bound, 2s. 6d.

Landor (Walter Savage).—Citation and Examination of William Shakspeare, &c. before Sir Thomas Lucy, touching Deer-stealing, 19th September, 1582. To which is added, **A Conference of Master Edmund Spenser** with the Earl of Essex, touching the State of Ireland, 1595. Fcap. 8vo, half-Roxburghe, 2s. 6d.

Lane (Edward William).—The Thousand and One Nights, commonly called in England **The Arabian Nights' Entertainments.** Translated from the Arabic, with Notes. Illustrated with many hundred Engravings from Designs by HARVEY. Edited by EDWARD STANLEY POOLE. With Preface by STANLEY LANE-POOLE. Three Vols., demy 8vo, cloth. 7s. 6d. ea.

Larwood (Jacob), Works by.
Anecdotes of the Clergy. Post 8vo, laid paper, half cloth, 2s.
Theatrical Anecdotes. Post 8vo, cloth limp, 2s. 6d.
Humour of the Law: Forensic Anecdotes. Post 8vo, cloth, 2s.

14 CHATTO & WINDUS, Publishers, 111 St. Martin's Lane, London, W.C.

Lehmann (R. C.).—Harry Fludyer at Cambridge, and Conversational Hints for Young Shooters. Crown 8vo, turned-in cover, 1s.; cloth, 1s. 6d.

Leigh (Henry S.).—Carols of Cockayne. Printed on hand-made paper, bound in buckram, 5s.

Leland (C. Godfrey).—A Manual of Mending and Repairing. With Diagrams. Crown 8vo, cloth, 5s.

Lepelletier (Edmond). — Madame Sans-Gène. Translated from the French by JOHN DE VILLIERS. Post 8vo, cloth, 3s. 6d.; picture boards, 2s.

Leys (John K.), Novels by.
The Lindsays. Post 8vo, picture bds., 2s. | A Sore Temptation. Cr. 8vo, cloth, gilt top, 6s.

Lilburn (Adam).—A Tragedy in Marble. Crown 8vo, cloth, 3s. 6d.

Lindsay (Harry, Author of 'Methodist Idylls'), Novels by.
Crown 8vo, cloth, 3s. 6d. each.
Rhoda Roberts. | The Jacobite: A Romance of the Conspiracy of 'The Forty.'
Crown 8vo, cloth, gilt top, 6s. each.
Judah Pyecroft, Puritan. | The Story of Leah.

Linton (E. Lynn), Works by.
An Octave of Friends. Crown 8vo, cloth, 3s. 6d.
Crown 8vo, cloth extra, 3s. 6d. each; post 8vo, illustrated boards, 2s. each.
Patricia Kemball. | Ione. | Under which Lord? With 12 Illustrations.
The Atonement of Leam Dundas. | 'My Love!' | Sowing the Wind.
The World Well Lost. With 12 Illusts. | Paston Carew, Millionaire and Miser.
The One Too Many. | Dulcie Everton. | With a Silken Thread.
The Rebel of the Family.
Post 8vo, cloth limp, 2s. 6d. each.
Witch Stories. | Ourselves: Essays on Women.
Freeshooting: Extracts from the Works of Mrs. LYNN LINTON.

Lowe (Charles, M.A.).—Our Greatest Living Soldiers. With 8 Portraits. Crown 8vo, cloth, 3s. 6d.

Lucy (Henry W.).—Gideon Fleyce: A Novel. Crown 8vo, cloth extra, 3s. 6d.; post 8vo, illustrated boards, 2s.

McCarthy (Justin), Works by.
The Reign of Queen Anne. 2 vols., demy 8vo, cloth, 12s. each.
A History of the Four Georges and of William the Fourth. By JUSTIN MCCARTHY and JUSTIN HUNTLY MCCARTHY. Four Vols., demy 8vo, cloth extra, 12s. each.
A History of Our Own Times, from the Accession of Queen Victoria to the General Election of 1880. LIBRARY EDITION. Four Vols., demy 8vo, cloth extra, 12s. each.—Also a POPULAR EDITION, in Four Vols., crown 8vo, cloth extra, 6s. each.—And the JUBILEE EDITION, with an Appendix of Events to the end of 1886, in Two Vols., large crown 8vo, cloth extra, 7s. 6d. each.
A History of Our Own Times, Vol. V., from 1880 to the Diamond Jubilee. Demy 8vo, cloth extra, 12s.; or crown 8vo, cloth, 6s.
A History of Our Own Times, Vol. VI., from the Diamond Jubilee, 1897, to the Accession of King Edward VII. Demy 8vo, cloth, 12s. [Shortly.
A Short History of Our Own Times. One Vol., crown 8vo, cloth extra, 6s.—Also a CHEAP POPULAR EDITION, post 8vo, cloth limp, 2s. 6d.
Reminiscences. With a Portrait. Two Vols., demy 8vo, cloth, 24s.
The Story of an Irishman. Demy 8vo, cloth, 12s. [Shortly.
Crown 8vo, cloth extra, 3s. 6d. each; post 8vo, illustrated boards, 2s. each; cloth limp, 2s. 6d. each
The Waterdale Neighbours. | Donna Quixote. With 12 Illustrations.
My Enemy's Daughter. | The Comet of a Season.
A Fair Saxon. | Linley Rochford. | Maid of Athens. With 12 Illustrations.
Dear Lady Disdain. | The Dictator. | Camiola: A Girl with a Fortune.
Miss Misanthrope. With 12 Illustrations. | Red Diamonds. | The Riddle Ring.
Crown 8vo, cloth, 3s. 6d. each.
The Three Disgraces, and other Stories. | Mononia: A Love Story of 'Forty-eight.'
'The Right Honourable.' By JUSTIN MCCARTHY and Mrs. CAMPBELL PRAED. Crown 8vo, cloth extra, 6s.

McCarthy (Justin Huntly), Works by.
The French Revolution. (Constituent Assembly, 1789-91). Four Vols., demy 8vo, cloth, 12s. each.
An Outline of the History of Ireland. Crown 8vo, 1s.; cloth, 1s. 6d.
Ireland Since the Union: Sketches of Irish History, 1798-1886. Crown 8vo, cloth, 6s.
Hafiz in London: Poems. Small 8vo, gold cloth, 3s. 6d.
Our Sensation Novel. Crown 8vo, picture cover, 1s.; cloth limp, 1s. 6d.
Doom: An Atlantic Episode. Crown 8vo, picture cover, 1s.
Dolly: A Sketch. Crown 8vo, picture cover, 1s.
Lily Lass: A Romance. Crown 8vo, picture cover, 1s.; cloth limp, 1s. 6d.
A London Legend. Crown 8vo, cloth, 3s. 6d.

MacColl (Hugh), Novels by.
Mr. Stranger's Sealed Packet. Post 8vo, illustrated boards, 2s.
Ednor Whitlock. Crown 8vo, cloth extra, 6s.

Macdonell (Agnes).—Quaker Cousins. Post 8vo, boards, 2s.

CHATTO & WINDUS, Publishers, 111 St. Martin's Lane, London, W.C. 15

MacDonald (George, LL.D.), Books by.
Works of Fancy and Imagination. Ten Vols., 16mo, cloth, gilt edges, in cloth case, 21s.; or the Volumes may be had separately, in Grolier cloth, at 2s. 6d. each.
Vol. I WITHIN AND WITHOUT.—THE HIDDEN LIFE.
" II. THE DISCIPLE.—THE GOSPEL WOMEN.—BOOK OF SONNETS.—ORGAN SONGS.
" III. VIOLIN SONGS.—SONGS OF THE DAYS AND NIGHTS.—A BOOK OF DREAMS.—ROADSIDE POEMS.—POEMS FOR CHILDREN.
" IV. PARABLES.—BALLADS.—SCOTCH SONGS
" V. & VI. PHANTASTES: A Faerie Romance. | Vol. VII. THE PORTENT.
" VIII. THE LIGHT PRINCESS.—THE GIANT'S HEART.—SHADOWS.
" IX. CROSS PURPOSES.—THE GOLDEN KEY.—THE CARASOYN.—LITTLE DAYLIGHT.
" X. THE CRUEL PAINTER.—THE WOW O' RIVVEN.—THE CASTLE.—THE BROKEN SWORDS. —THE GRAY WOLF.—UNCLE CORNELIUS.
Poetical Works of George MacDonald. Collected and Arranged by the Author. Two Vols. crown 8vo, buckram, 12s.
A Threefold Cord. Edited by GEORGE MACDONALD. Post 8vo, cloth, 5s.
Phantastes: A Faerie Romance. With 25 Illustrations by J. BELL. Crown 8vo, cloth extra, 3s. 6d.
Heather and Snow: A Novel. Crown 8vo, cloth extra, 3s. 6d.; post 8vo, illustrated boards, 2s.
Lilith: A Romance. SECOND EDITION. Crown 8vo, cloth extra, 6s.

MacGregor (Robert).—Pastimes and Players: Notes on Popular Games. Post 8vo, cloth limp, 2s. 6d.

Machray (Robert), Novels by. Crown 8vo, cloth, gilt top, 6s. each.
A Blow over the Heart. | **The Mystery of Lincoln's Inn.**

Mackay (Charles, LL.D.).—Interludes and Undertones; or, Music at Twilight. Crown 8vo, cloth extra 6s.

Mackenna (Stephen J.) and J. Augustus O'Shea.—Brave Men in Action: Thrilling Stories of the British Flag. With 8 Illustrations by STANLEY L. WOOD. Small demy 8vo, cloth, gilt edges, 5s.

Maclise Portrait Gallery (The) of Illustrious Literary Characters: 85 Portraits by DANIEL MACLISE; with Memoirs—Biographical, Critical, Bibliographical, and Anecdotal—illustrative of the Literature of the former half of the Present Century, by WILLIAM BATES, B.A. Crown 8vo, cloth extra, 3s. 6d.

Macquoid (Mrs.), Works by. Square 8vo, cloth extra, 6s. each.
In the Ardennes. With 50 Illustrations by THOMAS R. MACQUOID.
Pictures and Legends from Normandy and Brittany. 34 Illusts. by T. R. MACQUOID.
Through Normandy. With 92 Illustrations by T. R. MACQUOID, and a Map.
About Yorkshire. With 67 Illustrations by T. R. MACQUOID.

Magician's Own Book, The: Performances with Eggs, Hats, &c. Edited by W. H. CREMER. With 200 Illustrations. Crown 8vo, cloth extra, 4s. 6d.

Magic Lantern, The, and its Management: Including full Practical Directions. By T. C. HEPWORTH. With 10 Illustrations. Crown 8vo, 1s.; cloth, 1s. 6d.

Magna Charta: An Exact Facsimile of the Original in the British Museum, 3 feet by 2 feet, with Arms and Seals emblazoned in Gold and Colours, 5s.

Mallory (Sir Thomas).—Mort d'Arthur: The Stories of King Arthur and of the Knights of the Round Table. (A Selection.) Edited by B. MONTGOMERIE RANKING. Post 8vo, cloth limp, 2s.

Mallock (W. H.), Works by.
The New Republic. Post 8vo, cloth, 3s. 6d.; picture boards, 2s.
The New Paul and Virginia: Positivism on an Island. Post 8vo, cloth, 2s. 6d.
Poems. Small 4to, parchment, 8s. | **Is Life Worth Living?** Crown 8vo, cloth extra, 6s.

Margueritte (Paul and Victor), Novels by.
The Disaster. Crown 8vo, cloth, 3s. 6d.
The Commune. Translated by F. LEES and R. B. DOUGLAS. Crown 8vo, cloth, gilt top, 6s.

Marlowe's Works. Including his Translations. Edited, with Notes and Introductions, by Colonel CUNNINGHAM. Crown 8vo, cloth extra, 3s. 6d.

Mason (Finch).—Annals of the Horse-Shoe Club. With 5 Illustrations by the AUTHOR. Crown 8vo, cloth, gilt top, 6s.

Massinger's Plays. From the Text of WILLIAM GIFFORD. Edited by Col. CUNNINGHAM. Crown 8vo, cloth extra, 3s. 6d.

Masterman (J.).—Half-a-dozen Daughters. Post 8vo, picture boards, 2s.

Matthews (Brander).—A Secret of the Sea, &c. Post 8vo, illustrated boards, 2s.; cloth limp, 2s. 6d.

Max O'Rell, Books by. Crown 8vo, cloth, 3s. 6d. each.
Her Royal Highness Woman. | **Between Ourselves.**
Rambles in Womanland.

Merivale (Herman).—Bar, Stage, and Platform: Autobiographic Memories. With a Portrait. Crown 8vo, cloth, gilt top, 6s.

16 CHATTO & WINDUS, Publishers, 111 St. Martin's Lane, London, W.C.

Meade (L. T.), Novels by.
A Soldier of Fortune. Crown 8vo, cloth, 3s. 6d.; post 8vo, illustrated boards, 2s.
Crown 8vo, cloth, 3s. 6d. each.
With 8 Illustrations.
The Voice of the Charmer. | On the Brink of a Chasm. | An Adventuress.
In an Iron Grip. | The Way of a Woman. | The Blue Diamond.
The Siren. | A Son of Ishmael. | A Stumble by the Way.
Dr. Rumsey's Patient.
Crown 8vo, cloth, gilt top, 6s. each.
This Troublesome World. | Rosebury.

Merrick (Leonard), Novels by.
The Man who was Good. Post 8vo, picture boards, 2s.
Crown 8vo, cloth, 3s. 6d. each.
This Stage of Fools. | Cynthia: A Daughter of the Philistines.

Miller (Mrs. F. Fenwick).—Physiology for the Young; or, The
House of Life. With numerous Illustrations. Post 8vo, cloth limp, 2s. 6d.

Milton (J. L.).—The Bath in Diseases of the Skin. Post 8vo,
1s.; cloth, 1s. 6d.

Minto (Wm.).—Was She Good or Bad? Crown 8vo, cloth, 1s. 6d.

Mitchell (Edmund), Novels by.
The Lone Star Rush. With 8 Illustrations by NORMAN H. HARDY. Crown 8vo, cloth, 3s. 6d.
Crown 8vo, cloth, gilt top, 6s. each.
Only a Nigger. | The Belforts of Culben.
Crown 8vo, picture cloth, flat backs, 2s. each.
Plotters of Paris. | The Temple of Death. | Towards the Eternal Snows.

Mitford (Bertram), Novels by. Crown 8vo, cloth extra, 3s. 6d. each.
The Gun-Runner: A Romance of Zululand. With a Frontispiece by STANLEY L. WOOD.
Renshaw Fanning's Quest. With a Frontispiece by STANLEY L. WOOD.
The Triumph of Hilary Blachland.
Crown 8vo, cloth, 3s. 6d. each; picture cloth, flat backs, 2s. each.
The Luck of Gerard Ridgeley.
The King's Assegai. With Six full-page Illustrations by STANLEY L. WOOD.
Haviland's Chum. Crown 8vo, cloth, gilt top, 6s.

Molesworth (Mrs.).—Hathercourt Rectory. Crown 8vo, cloth,
3s. 6d.; post 8vo, illustrated boards, 2s.

Moncrieff (W. D. Scott-).—The Abdication: An Historical Drama.
With Seven Etchings by JOHN PETTIE, W. Q. ORCHARDSON, J. MACWHIRTER, COLIN HUNTER, R. MACBETH and TOM GRAHAM. Imperial 4to, buckram, 21s.

Montagu (Irving).—Things I Have Seen in War. With 16 full-
page Illustrations. Crown 8vo, cloth, 6s.

Moore (Thomas), Works by.
The Epicurean; and **Alciphron.** Post 8vo, half-bound, 2s.
Prose and Verse; including Suppressed Passages from the MEMOIRS OF LORD BYRON. Edited by R. H. SHEPHERD. With Portrait. Crown 8vo, cloth extra, 7s. 6d.

Murray (D. Christie), Novels by.
Crown 8vo, cloth extra, 3s. 6d. each; post 8vo, illustrated boards, 2s. each.
A Life's Atonement. | A Model Father. | Bob Martin's Little Girl.
Joseph's Coat. 12 Illusts. | Old Blazer's Hero. | Time's Revenges.
Coals of Fire. 3 Illusts. | Cynic Fortune. Frontisp. | A Wasted Crime.
Val Strange. | By the Gate of the Sea. | In Direst Peril.
Hearts. | A Bit of Human Nature. | Mount Despair.
The Way of the World. | First Person Singular. | A Capful o' Nails.
The Making of a Novelist: An Experiment in Autobiography. With a Collotype Portrait. Cr. 8vo, buckram, 3s. 6d.
My Contemporaries in Fiction. Crown 8vo, buckram, 3s. 6d.
His Own Ghost. Crown 8vo, cloth, 3s. 6d.; picture cloth, flat back, 2s.
Crown 8vo, cloth, 3s. 6d. each.
This Little World. | A Race for Millions. | The Church of Humanity.
Tales in Prose and Verse. With a Frontispiece by ARTHUR HOPKINS.
V. C.: A Chronicle of Castle Barfield and of the Crimea.
Crown 8vo, cloth, gilt top, 6s. each.
Despair's Last Journey. | Verona's Father.
Joseph's Coat. POPULAR EDITION, medium 8vo, 6d.

Murray (D. Christie) and Henry Herman, Novels by.
Crown 8vo, cloth extra, 3s. 6d. each; post 8vo, illustrated boards, 2s. each.
One Traveller Returns. | The Bishops' Bible.
Paul Jones's Alias, &c. With Illustrations by A. FORESTIER and G. NICOLET.

Murray (Henry), Novels by.
Post 8vo, cloth, 2s. 6d. each.
A Game of Bluff. | A Song of Sixpence.

CHATTO & WINDUS, Publishers, 111 St. Martin's Lane, London, W.C. 17

Morris (Rev. W. Meredith, B.A.).—British Violin-Makers,
Classical and Modern. With numerous Portraits, Illustrations, and Facsimiles of Labels. Demy 8vo, cloth, gilt top. 10s. 6d. net.

Morrow (W. C.).—Bohemian Paris of To-Day. With 106 Illustrations by EDOUARD CUCUEL. Small demy 8vo, cloth, gilt top, 6s.

Muddock (J. E.), Stories by. Crown 8vo, cloth, 3s. 6d. each.
Basile the Jester. With Frontispiece by STANLEY WOOD.
Young Lochinvar. | The Golden Idol.
Post 8vo, illustrated boards, 2s. each.
The Dead Man's Secret. | From the Bosom of the Deep.
Stories Weird and Wonderful. Post 8vo, illustrated boards, 2s.; cloth, 2s. 6d.
Maid Marian and Robin Hood. With 12 Illustrations by STANLEY L. WOOD. Crown 8vo, cloth, 3s. 6d.; picture cloth, flat back, 2s.

Nisbet (Hume), Books by.
'Ball Up.' Crown 8vo, cloth extra, 3s. 6d.; post 8vo, illustrated boards, 2s.
Dr. Bernard St. Vincent. Post 8vo, illustrated boards, 2s.
Lessons in Art. With 21 Illustrations. Crown 8vo. cloth extra, 2s. 6d.

Norris (W. E.), Novels by. Crown 8vo, cloth, 3s. 6d. each ; post 8vo, picture boards, 2s. each.
Saint Ann's. | Billy Bellew. With a Frontispiece by F. H. TOWNSEND.
Miss Wentworth's Idea. Crown 8vo, cloth, 3s. 6d.

Ohnet (Georges), Novels by. Post 8vo, illustrated boards, 2s. each.
Doctor Rameau. | A Last Love.
A Weird Gift. Crown 8vo, cloth, 3s. 6d.; post 8vo, picture boards, 2s.
Crown 8vo, cloth, 3s. 6d. each.
Love's Depths. | The Woman of Mystery.
The Money-Maker. Translated by F. ROTHWELL. Crown 8vo, cloth, gilt top, 6s.

Oliphant (Mrs.), Novels by. Post 8vo, illustrated boards, 2s. each.
The Primrose Path. | The Greatest Heiress in England.
Whiteladies. Crown 8vo, cloth, with 12 Illustrations by ARTHUR HOPKINS and HENRY WOODS, 3s. 6d.; post 8vo, picture boards, 2s.
The Sorceress. Crown 8vo, cloth, 3s. 6d.

Orrock (James), Painter, Connoisseur, Collector. By BYRON WEBBER. In Two Handsome Volumes, small folio, Illustrated with nearly One Hundred Photogravure Plates and a profusion of Drawings reproduced in half-tone, in a binding designed by Sir J. D. LINTON, P.R.I. Price, in buckram gilt, Ten Guineas net.

O'Shaughnessy (Arthur), Poems by:
Fcap. 8vo, cloth extra, 7s. 6d. each.
Music and Moonlight. | Songs of a Worker.
Lays of France. Crown 8vo, cloth extra, 10s. 6d.

Ouida, Novels by. Cr. 8vo, cl., 3s. 6d. ea.; post 8vo, illust. bds., 2s. ea.
Held in Bondage. | A Dog of Flanders. | In Maremma. | Wanda.
Tricotrin. | Pascarel. | Signa. | Bimbi.
Strathmore. | Chandos. | Two Wooden Shoes. | Frescoes. | Othmar.
Cecil Castlemaine's Gage | In a Winter City. | Princess Napraxine.
Under Two Flags. | Ariadne. | Friendship. | Guilderoy. | Rufino.
Puck. | Idalia. | A Village Commune. | Two Offenders.
Folle-Farine. | Moths. | Pipistrello. | Santa Barbara.
POPULAR EDITIONS, medium 8vo, 6d. each.
Under Two Flags. | Moths. | Held in Bondage. | Puck. | Strathmore. | Tricotrin.
Syrlin. Crown 8vo, cloth, 3s. 6d.; post 8vo, picture cloth, flat back, 2s.; Illustrated boards, 2s.
The Waters of Edera. Crown 8vo, cloth, 3s. 6d.; picture cloth, flat back, 2s.
Wisdom, Wit, and Pathos, selected from the Works of OUIDA by F. SYDNEY MORRIS. Post 8vo, cloth extra, 5s.—CHEAP EDITION, illustrated boards, 2s.

Pain (Barry).—Eliza's Husband. Fcap. 8vo, picture cover, 1s.; cloth, 1s. 6d.

Palmer (W. T.), Books by. Crown 8vo, cloth, gilt top, 6s. each.
Lake Country Rambles. With a Frontispiece.
In Lakeland Dells and Fells. With a Frontispiece.

Pandurang Hari; or, Memoirs of a Hindoo. With Preface by Sir BARTLE FRERE. Post 8vo, illustrated boards, 2s.

Paris Salon, The Illustrated Catalogue of the, for 1904. (Twenty-sixth Year.) With over 300 Illustrations. Demy 8vo. 3s.

Pascal's Provincial Letters. A New Translation, with Historical Introduction and Notes by T. M'CRIE, D.D. Post 8vo, half-cloth, 2s.

Paternoster (G. Sidney).—The Motor Pirate. With 12 Illustrations by C. R. SYKES. Crown 8vo, cloth, 3s. 6d.

18   CHATTO & WINDUS, Publishers, 111 St. Martin's Lane, London, W.C.

Paston Letters (The), 1422-1509. Containing upwards of 600 more Letters than appeared in the original 5-volume issue in 1787-1823. Edited, with Introduction and Notes, by JAMES GAIRDNER, of the Public Record Office. A NEW EDITION, in 6 Volumes, square demy 8vo, art linen, gilt top, 12s. 6d. net per volume. (Sold only in sets.)

Paul (Margaret A.).—Gentle and Simple. Crown 8vo, cloth, with Frontispiece by HELEN PATERSON, 3s. 6d.; post 8vo, illustrated boards, 2s.

Payn (James), Novels by.
Crown 8vo, cloth extra, 3s. 6d. each; post 8vo, illustrated boards, 2s. each.
Lost Sir Massingberd.   The Family Scapegrace.
A County Family.   Holiday Tasks.
Less Black than We're Painted. The Talk of the Town. With 12 Illusts.
By Proxy.   For Cash Only. The Mystery of Mirbridge.
High Spirits.   The Word and the Will.
A Confidential Agent. With 12 Illusts. The Burnt Million.
A Grape from a Thorn. With 12 Illusts. Sunny Stories. | A Trying Patient.

Post 8vo, illustrated boards, 2s. each.
Humorous Stories. | From Exile.   Found Dead. | Gwendoline's Harvest.
The Foster Brothers.   Mirk Abbey. | A Marine Residence.
Married Beneath Him.   The Canon's Ward.
Bentinck's Tutor. | Walter's Word. Not Wooed, But Won.
A Perfect Treasure.   Two Hundred Pounds Reward.
Like Father, Like Son.   The Best of Husbands.
A Woman's Vengeance.   Halves. | What He Cost Her.
Carlyon's Year. | Cecil's Tryst.   Fallen Fortunes. | Kit: A Memory.
Murphy's Master. | At Her Mercy.   Under One Roof. | Glow-worm Tales.
The Clyffards of Clyffe.   A Prince of the Blood.
Some Private Views.

A Modern Dick Whittington; or, A Patron of Letters. With a Portrait of the Author. Crown 8vo, cloth, 3s. 6d.; picture cloth, flat back, 2s.
Notes from the 'News.' Crown 8vo, cloth, 1s. 6d.
Walter's Ward. POPULAR EDITION, medium 8vo, 6d.

Payne (Will).—Jerry the Dreamer. Crown 8vo, cloth, 3s. 6d.

Pennell-Elmhirst (Captain E.).—The Best of the Fun. With 8 Coloured Illustrations by G. D. GILES, and 48 in Black and White by J. STURGESS and G. D. GILES. Medium 8vo, cloth, gilt top, 16s.

Pennell (H. Cholmondeley), Works by. Post 8vo, cloth, 2s. 6d. ea.
Puck on Pegasus. With Illustrations.
Pegasus Re-Saddled. With Ten full-page Illustrations by G. DU MAURIER.
The Muses of Mayfair: Vers de Société. Selected by H. C. PENNELL.

Penny (F. E.).—The Sanyasi: An Indian Romance. Crown 8vo, cloth, gilt top, 6s.

Phelps (E. Stuart), Books by.
Beyond the Gates. Post 8vo, picture cover, 1s.; cloth, 1s. 6d.
Jack the Fisherman. Illustrated by C. W. REED. Crown 8vo, cloth, 1s. 6d.

Phil May's Sketch-Book. Containing 54 Humorous Cartoons. Crown folio, cloth, 2s. 6d.

Phipson (Dr. T. L.), Books by. Crown 8vo, canvas, gilt top, 5s. each.
Famous Violinists and Fine Violins. | The Confessions of a Violinist.
Voice and Violin: Sketches, Anecdotes, and Reminiscences.

Pilkington (Lionel L.).—Mallender's Mistake. Crown 8vo, cloth, gilt top, 6s.

Planche (J. R.), Works by.
The Pursuivant of Arms. With Six Plates and 209 Illustrations. Crown 8vo, cloth, 7s. 6d.
Songs and Poems, 1819-1879. With Introduction by Mrs. MACKARNESS. Crown 8vo, cloth, 6s.

Plutarch's Lives of Illustrious Men. With Notes and a Life of Plutarch by JOHN and WM. LANGHORNE, and Portraits. Two Vols., demy 8vo, half-cloth 10s. 6d.

Poe's (Edgar Allan) Choice Works: Poems, Stories, Essays. With an Introduction by CHARLES BAUDELAIRE. Crown 8vo, cloth, 3s. 6d.

Pollock (W. H.).—The Charm, and other Drawing-room Plays. By Sir WALTER BESANT and WALTER H. POLLOCK. With 50 Illustrations. Crown 8vo, cloth gilt, 6s.

Praed (Mrs. Campbell), Novels by. Post 8vo, illust. bds., 2s. each.
The Romance of a Station. | The Soul of Countess Adrian.

Crown 8vo, cloth, 3s. 6d. each; post 8vo, boards, 2s. each.
Outlaw and Lawmaker. | Christina Chard. With Frontispiece by W PAGET.
Mrs. Tregaskiss. With 8 Illustrations by ROBERT SAUBER.

Crown 8vo, cloth, 3s. 6d. each.
Nulma. | Madame Izan. | 'As a Watch in the Night.'

Price (E. C.).—Valentina. Crown 8vo, cloth, 3s. 6d.

Princess Olga.—Radna: A Novel. Crown 8vo, cloth extra, 6s.

Proctor (Richard A.), Works by.
Flowers of the Sky. With 55 Illustrations. Small crown 8vo, cloth extra, 3s. 6d.
Easy Star Lessons. With Star Maps for every Night in the Year. Crown 8vo, cloth, 6s.
Familiar Science Studies. Crown 8vo, cloth extra, 6s.
Saturn and its System. With 13 Steel Plates. Demy 8vo, cloth extra, 10s. 6d.
Mysteries of Time and Space. With numerous Illustrations. Crown 8vo, cloth extra, 6s.
The Universe of Suns, &c. With numerous Illustrations. Crown 8vo, cloth extra, 6s.
Wages and Wants of Science Workers. Crown 8vo, 1s. 6d.

Pryce (Richard).—Miss Maxwell's Affections. Crown 8vo, cloth, with Frontispiece by HAL LUDLOW, 3s. 6d.; post 8vo, illustrated boards, 2s.

Rambosson (J.).—Popular Astronomy. Translated by C. B. PITMAN. With 10 Coloured Plates and 63 Woodcut Illustrations. Crown 8vo, cloth, 3s. 6d.

Randolph (Col. G.).—Aunt Abigail Dykes. Crown 8vo, cloth, 7s. 6d.

Richardson (Frank), Novels by.
Crown 8vo, cloth, 3s. 6d. each.
The Man who Lost his Past. With 50 Illustrations by TOM BROWNE, R.I.
The Bayswater Miracle.
Crown 8vo, cloth, gilt top, 6s. each.
The King's Counsel. | Semi-Society.

Riddell (Mrs. J. H.), Novels by.
A Rich Man's Daughter. Crown 8vo, cloth, 3s. 6d.
Weird Stories. Crown 8vo, cloth extra, 3s. 6d.; post 8vo, illustrated boards, 2s.
Post 8vo, illustrated boards, 2s. each.
The Uninhabited House. | Fairy Water.
The Prince of Wales's Garden Party. | Her Mother's Darling.
The Mystery in Palace Gardens. | The Nun's Curse. | Idle Tales.

Reade's (Charles) Novels.
The Collected LIBRARY EDITION, in Seventeen Volumes, crown 8vo, cloth, 3s. 6d. each.
1. Peg Woffington; and Christie Johnstone.
2. Hard Cash.
3. The Cloister and the Hearth. With a Preface by Sir WALTER BESANT.
4. 'It is Never Too Late to Mend.'
5. The Course of True Love Never Did Run Smooth; and Singleheart and Doubleface.
6. The Autobiography of a Thief; Jack of all Trades; A Hero and a Martyr; and The Wandering Heir.
7. Love Me Little, Love me Long.
8. The Double Marriage.
9. Griffith Gaunt.
10. Foul Play.
11. Put Yourself in His Place.
12. A Terrible Temptation.
13. A Simpleton.
14. A Woman-Hater.
15. The Jilt, and other Stories; and Good Stories of Man and other Animals.
16. A Perilous Secret.
17. Readiana; and Bible Characters.

In Twenty-one Volumes, post 8vo, illustrated boards, 2s. each.
Peg Woffington. | Christie Johnstone.
'It is Never Too Late to Mend.'
The Course of True Love Never Did Run Smooth.
The Autobiography of a Thief; Jack of all Trades; and James Lambert.
Love Me Little, Love Me Long.
The Double Marriage.
The Cloister and the Hearth.
Hard Cash. | Griffith Gaunt.
Foul Play. | Put Yourself in His Place.
A Terrible Temptation.
A Simpleton. | The Wandering Heir.
A Woman-Hater.
Singleheart and Doubleface.
Good Stories of Man and other Animals.
The Jilt, and other Stories.
A Perilous Secret. | Readiana.

LARGE TYPE, FINE PAPER EDITIONS. Pott 8vo, cl., gilt top, 2s. net ea.; leather, gilt edges, 3s. net ea.
The Cloister and the Hearth. | 'It is Never Too Late to Mend.'

POPULAR EDITIONS, medium 8vo, 6d. each.
'It is Never Too Late to Mend.' | The Cloister and the Hearth. | Foul Play.
Peg Woffington; and Christie Johnstone. | Hard Cash. | Griffith Gaunt.
Put Yourself in His Place.

Christie Johnstone. With Frontispiece. Choicely printed in Elzevir style. Fcap. 8vo, half-Roxb. 2s. 6d.
Peg Woffington. Choicely printed in Elzevir style. Fcap. 8vo, half-Roxburghe, 2s. 6d.
The Cloister and the Hearth. EDITION DE LUXE, with 16 Photogravure and 84 half-tone Illustrations by MATT B. HEWERDINE. Small 4to, cloth gilt and gilt top, 10s. 6d. net.—Also in Four Vols., post 8vo, with an Introduction by Sir WALTER BESANT, and a Frontispiece to each Vol., buckram, gilt top, 6s. the set.
Bible Characters. Fcap. 8vo, leatherette, 1s.
Selections from the Works of Charles Reade. With an Introduction by Mrs. ALEX. IRELAND. Post 8vo, cloth limp, 2s. 6d.

Rimmer (Alfred), Works by. Large crown 8vo, cloth, 3s. 6d. each.
Rambles Round Eton and Harrow. With 52 Illustrations by the Author.
About England with Dickens. With 58 Illustrations by C. A. VANDERHOOF and A. RIMMER.

Rives (Amelie), Stories by. Crown 8vo, cloth, 3s. 6d. each.
Barbara Dering. | Meriel: A Love Story.

Robinson Crusoe. By DANIEL DEFOE. With 37 Illustrations by GEORGE CRUIKSHANK. Post 8vo, half-cloth, 2s.

Robinson (Phil), Works by. Crown 8vo, cloth extra, 6s. each.
The Poets' Birds. | The Poets' Beasts. | The Poets' Reptiles, Fishes, and Insects.

Robinson (F. W.), Novels by.
Women are Strange. Post 8vo, illustrated boards, 2s.
The Hands of Justice. Crown 8vo, cloth extra, 3s. 6d.; post 8vo illustrated boards, 2s.
The Woman in the Dark. Crown 8vo, cloth, 3s. 6d.; post 8vo, illustrated boards, 2s.

Roll of Battle Abbey, The: A List of the Principal Warriors who came from Normandy with William the Conqueror, 1066. Printed in Gold and Colours, 5s.

Rosengarten (A.).—A Handbook of Architectural Styles. Translated by W. COLLETT-SANDARS. With 630 Illustrations. Crown 8vo, cloth extra, 7s. 6d.

Ross (Albert).—A Sugar Princess. Crown 8vo, cloth, 3s. 6d.

Rowley (Hon. Hugh). Post 8vo, cloth, 2s. 6d. each.
Puniana: or, Thoughts Wise and Other-wise; a Collection of the Best Riddles, Conundrums, Jokes, Sells, &c., with numerous Illustrations by the Author.
More Puniana: A Second Collection of Riddles, Jokes, &c. With numerous Illustrations.

Runciman (James), Stories by.
Schools and Scholars. Post 8vo, cloth, 2s. 6d.
Skippers and Shellbacks. Crown 8vo, cloth, 3s. 6d.

Russell (Dora), Novels by.
A Country Sweetheart. Post 8vo, picture boards, 2s.; picture cloth, flat back, 2s.
The Drift of Fate. Crown 8vo, cloth, 3s. 6d.; picture cloth, flat back, 2s.

Russell (Herbert).—True Blue. Crown 8vo, cloth, 3s. 6d.

Russell (Rev. John) and his Out-of-door Life. By E. W. L. DAVIES. A New Edition, with Illustrations coloured by hand. Royal 8vo, cloth, 16s. net.

Russell (W. Clark), Novels, &c., by.
Crown 8vo, cloth, gilt top, 6s. each.
Overdue. | Wrong Side Out.
Crown 8vo, cloth extra, 3s. 6d. each; post 8vo, illustrated boards, 2s. each; cloth limp, 2s. 6d. each.
Round the Galley-Fire. | An Ocean Tragedy.
In the Middle Watch. | My Shipmate Louise.
On the Fo'k'sle Head. | Tale of the Ten. | Alone on a Wide Wide Sea.
A Voyage to the Cape. | The Good Ship 'Mohock.'
A Book for the Hammock. | The Phantom Death.
The Mystery of the 'Ocean Star.' | Is He the Man? | The Convict Ship.
The Romance of Jenny Harlowe. | Heart of Oak. | The Last Entry.
Crown 8vo, cloth, 3s. 6d. each.
A Tale of Two Tunnels. | The Death Ship.
The Ship: Her Story. With 50 Illustrations by H. C. SEPPINGS WRIGHT. Small 4to, cloth, 6s.
The 'Pretty Polly'; A Voyage of Incident. With 12 Illustrations by G. E. ROBERTSON. Large crown 8vo, cloth, gilt edges, 5s.
The Convict Ship. POPULAR EDITION, medium 8vo, 6d.

Saint Aubyn (Alan), Novels by.
Crown 8vo, cloth extra, 3s. 6d. each; post 8vo, illustrated boards, 2s. each.
A Fellow of Trinity. With a Note by OLIVER WENDELL HOLMES and a Frontispiece.
The Junior Dean. | The Master of St. Benedict's. | To His Own Master.
Orchard Damerel. | In the Face of the World. | The Tremlett Diamonds.
Crown 8vo, cloth, 3s. 6d. each.
The Wooing of May. | A Tragic Honeymoon. | A Proctor's Wooing.
Fortune's Gate. | Gallantry Bower. | Bonnie Maggie Lauder.
Mary Unwin. With 8 Illustrations by PERCY TARRANT. | Mrs. Dunbar's Secret.

Saint John (Bayle).—A Levantine Family. Cr. 8vo, cloth, 3s. 6d.

Sala (George A.).—Gaslight and Daylight. Post 8vo, boards, 2s.

Scotland Yard, Past and Present: Experiences of Thirty-seven Years. By Ex-Chief-Inspector CAVANAGH. Post 8vo, illustrated boards, 2s.; cloth, 2s. 6d.

Secret Out, The: One Thousand Tricks with Cards: with Entertaining Experiments in Drawing-room or 'White' Magic. By W. H. CREMER. With 300 Illustrations. Crown 8vo, cloth extra, 4s. 6d.

Seguin (L. G.), Works by.
The Country of the Passion Play (Oberammergau) and the Highlands of Bavaria. With Map and 37 Illustrations. Crown 8vo, cloth extra, 3s. 6d.
Walks in Algiers. With Two Maps and 16 Illustrations. Crown 8vo, cloth extra, 6s.

Senior (Wm.).—By Stream and Sea. Post 8vo, cloth, 2s. 6d.

Sergeant (Adeline), Novels by. Crown 8vo, cloth, 3s. 6d. each.
Under False Pretences. | Dr. Endicott's Experiment.

Seymour (Cyril).—The Magic of To-Morrow. Cr. 8vo, cloth, 6s.

Shakespeare the Boy. With Sketches of the Home and School Life, the Games and Sports, the Manners, Customs, and Folk-lore of the Time. By WILLIAM J. ROLFE, Litt.D. A New Edition, with 42 Illustrations, and an INDEX OF PLAYS AND PASSAGES REFERRED TO. Crown 8vo, cloth gilt, 3s. 6d.

Sharp (William).—Children of To-morrow. Crown 8vo, cloth, 6s.

CHATTO & WINDUS, Publishers, 111 St. Martin's Lane, London, W.C. 21

Shelley's (Percy Bysshe) Complete Works in Verse and Prose.
Edited, Prefaced, and Annotated by R. HERNE SHEPHERD. Five Vols., crown 8vo, cloth, 3s. 6d. each.
Poetical Works, in Three Vols.:
- Vol. I. Introduction by the Editor; Posthumous Fragments of Margaret Nicholson; Shelley's Correspondence with Stockdale; The Wandering Jew; Queen Mab, with the Notes; Alastor, and other Poems; Rosalind and Helen; Prometheus Unbound; Adonais, &c.
- " II. Laon and Cythna; The Cenci; Julian and Maddalo; Swellfoot the Tyrant; The Witch of Atlas; Epipsychidion; Hellas.
- " III. Posthumous Poems; The Masque of Anarchy; and other Pieces.

Prose Works, in Two Vols.:
- Vol. I. The Two Romances of Zastrozzi and St. Irvyne; the Dublin and Marlow Pamphlets; A Refutation of Deism; Letters to Leigh Hunt, and some Minor Writings and Fragments.
- II. The Essays; Letters from Abroad; Translations and Fragments, edited by Mrs. SHELLEY. With a Biography of Shelley, and an Index of the Prose Works.

Sherard (R. H.).—Rogues: A Novel. Crown 8vo, cloth, 1s. 6d.

Sheridan's (Richard Brinsley) Complete Works, with Life and
Anecdotes. Including Drama, Prose and Poetry, Translations, Speeches, Jokes. Cr. 8vo, cloth, 3s. 6d.
The Rivals, The School for Scandal, and other Plays. Post 8vo, half-bound, 2s.
Sheridan's Comedies: The Rivals and The School for Scandal. Edited, with an Introduction and Notes to each Play, and a Biographical Sketch, by BRANDER MATTHEWS. With Illustrations. Demy 8vo, buckram, gilt top, 12s. 6d.

Shiel (M. P.), Novels by. Crown 8vo, cloth, gilt top, 6s. each.
The Purple Cloud. | **Unto the Third Generation.**

Sidney's (Sir Philip) Complete Poetical Works. With Portrait.
Edited by the Rev. A. B. GROSART, D.D. Three Vols., crown 8vo, cloth, 3s. 6d. each.

Signboards: Their History, including Anecdotes of Famous Taverns and
Remarkable Characters. By JACOB LARWOOD and JOHN CAMDEN HOTTEN. With Coloured Frontispiece and 94 Illustrations. Crown 8vo, cloth extra, 3s. 6d.

Sims (George R.), Works by.
Post 8vo, illustrated boards, 2s. each; cloth limp, 2s. 6d. each.
The Ring o' Bells. | **My Two Wives.** | **Memoirs of a Landlady.**
Tinkletop's Crime. | **Tales of To-day.** | **Scenes from the Show.**
Zeph: A Circus Story, &c. | **The Ten Commandments:** Stories.
Dramas of Life. With 60 Illustrations.

Crown 8vo, picture cover, 1s. each; cloth, 1s. 6d. each.
The Dagonet Reciter and Reader: Readings and Recitations in Prose and Verse.
The Case of George Candlemas. | **Dagonet Ditties.** (From *The Referee*.)
Young Mrs. Caudle.

How the Poor Live; and Horrible London. With a Frontispiece by F. BARNARD. Crown 8vo, leatherette, 1s. | **Dagonet Dramas of the Day.** Crown 8vo, 1s.
Rogues and Vagabonds. Crown 8vo, cloth, 3s. 6d.; picture cloth, flat back, 2s.; post 8vo, illustrated boards, 2s.; cloth limp, 2s. 6d.

Crown 8vo, cloth, 3s. 6d. each; post 8vo, picture boards, 2s. each; cloth limp, 2s. 6d. each.
Mary Jane's Memoirs. | **Mary Jane Married.** | **Dagonet Abroad.**

Crown 8vo, cloth, 3s. 6d. each.
Once upon a Christmas Time. With 8 Illustrations by CHARLES GREEN, R.I.
In London's Heart: A Story of To-day.—Also in picture cloth, flat back, 2s | **A Blind Marriage.**
Without the Limelight: Theatrical Life as it is. | **The Small-part Lady, &c.**
Biographs of Babylon: Life Pictures of London's Moving Scenes.
Among My Autographs. With 70 Facsimiles.

Sinclair (Upton).—Prince Hagen: A Phantasy. Cr. 8vo, cl., 3s. 6d.

Sister Dora. By M. LONSDALE. 4 Illusts. Demy 8vo, 4d.; cloth, 6d.

Sketchley (Arthur).—A Match in the Dark. Post 8vo, boards, 2s.

Slang Dictionary (The): Etymological, Historical, and Anecdotal.
Crown 8vo, cloth extra, 6s. 6d.

Smart (Hawley), Novels by.
Crown 8vo, cloth, 3s. 6d. each; post 8vo, picture boards, 2s. each.
Beatrice and Benedick. | **Long Odds.** | **Without Love or Licence** | **Master of Rathkelly**

Crown 8vo, cloth, 3s. 6d. each.
The Outsider. | **A Racing Rubber.**
The Plunger. Post 8vo, picture boards, 2s.

Smith (J. Moyr), Works by.
The Prince of Argolis. With 130 Illustrations. Post 8vo, cloth extra, 3s. 6d.
The Wooing of the Water Witch. With numerous Illustrations. Post 8vo, cloth, 6s.

Snazelleparilla. Decanted by G. S. EDWARDS. With Portrait of
G. H. SNAZELLE, and 65 Illustrations by C. LYALL. Crown 8vo, cloth, 3s. 6d.

Society in London. Crown 8vo, 1s.; cloth, 1s. 6d.

Somerset (Lord Henry).—Songs of Adieu. Small 4to, Jap. vel., 6s.

Spenser for Children. By M. H. TOWRY. With Coloured Illustrations
by WALTER J. MORGAN. Crown 4to, cloth extra, 3s. 6d.

Speight (T. W.), Novels by.
Post 8vo, illustrated boards, 2s. each.
The Mysteries of Heron Dyke. | The Loudwater Tragedy.
By Devious Ways, &c. | Burgo's Romance.
Hoodwinked ; & Sandycroft Mystery. | Quittance in Full.
The Golden Hoop. | Back to Life. | A Husband from the Sea.

Post 8vo, cloth limp, 1s. 6d. each.
A Barren Title. | Wife or No Wife?

Crown 8vo, cloth extra, 3s. 6d. each.
The Grey Monk. | The Master of Trenance.
A Minion of the Moon : A Romance of the King's Highway | Her Ladyship.
The Secret of Wyvern Towers. | The Doom of Siva. | The Web of Fate.
The Strange Experiences of Mr. Verschoyle. | As it was Written.
Stepping Blindfold. Crown 8vo, cloth, gilt top, 6s.

Sprigge (S. Squire).—An Industrious Chevalier. Crown 8vo, cloth, gilt top, 6s.

Spettigue (H. H.).—The Heritage of Eve. Crown 8vo, cloth, 6s.

Stafford (John), Novels by.
Doris and I. Crown 8vo, cloth, 3s. 6d. | Carlton Priors. Crown 8vo, cloth, gilt top, 6s.

Stanley (Winifred).—A Flash of the Will. Cr. 8vo, cl., gilt top, 6s.

Starry Heavens (The): POETICAL BIRTHDAY BOOK. Roy. 16mo, cl., 2s. 6d.

Stag-Hunting with the 'Devon and Somerset:' Chase of the Wild Red Deer on Exmoor. By PHILIP EVERED. With 70 Illustrations. Crown 4to, cloth, 16s. net.

Stedman (E. C.).—Victorian Poets. Crown 8vo, cloth extra, 9s.

Stephens (Riccardo, M.B.).—The Cruciform Mark: The Strange Story of RICHARD TREGENNA, Bachelor of Medicine (Univ. Edinb.) Crown 8vo, cloth, 3s. 6d.

Stephens (Robert Neilson).—Philip Winwood: A Sketch of the Domestic History of an American Captain in the War of Independence. Crown 8vo, cloth, 3s. 6d.

Sterndale (R. Armitage).—The Afghan Knife: A Novel. Post 8vo, cloth, 3s. 6d. ; illustrated boards, 2s.

Stevenson (R. Louis), Works by.
Crown 8vo, buckram, gilt top, 6s. each.
Travels with a Donkey. With a Frontispiece by WALTER CRANE.
An Inland Voyage. With a Frontispiece by WALTER CRANE.
Familiar Studies of Men and Books.
The Silverado Squatters. With Frontispiece by J. D. STRONG.
The Merry Men. | Underwoods: Poems. | Memories and Portraits.
Virginibus Puerisque, and other Papers. | Ballads. | Prince Otto.
Across the Plains, with other Memories and Essays.
Weir of Hermiston. | In the South Seas.
Songs of Travel. Crown 8vo, buckram, 5s.
New Arabian Nights. Crown 8vo, buckram, gilt top, 6s. ; post 8vo, illustrated boards, 2s.
—POPULAR EDITION, medium 8vo, 6d.
The Suicide Club ; and The Rajah's Diamond. (From NEW ARABIAN NIGHTS.) With Eight Illustrations by W. J. HENNESSY. Crown 8vo, cloth, 3s. 6d.
The Stevenson Reader : Selections from the Writings of ROBERT LOUIS STEVENSON. Edited by LLOYD OSBOURNE. Post 8vo, cloth, 2s. 6d. ; buckram, gilt top, 3s. 6d.
The Pocket R.L.S. : Favourite Passages. Small 16mo, cloth, 2s. net ; leather, 3s. net.
LARGE TYPE, FINE PAPER EDITIONS. Pott 8vo, cl., gilt top, 2s. net each ; leather, gilt edges, 3s. net each.
Virginibus Puerisque, and other Papers. | New Arabian Nights.
Familiar Studies of Men and Books.
R. L. Stevenson : A Study. By H. B. BAILDON. With 2 Portraits. Crown 8vo, buckram, 6s.

Stockton (Frank R.).—The Young Master of Hyson Hall. With 36 Illustrations by V. H. DAVISSON and C. H. STEPHENS. Crown 8vo, cloth, 3s. 6d. ; picture cloth, 2s.

Strange Secrets. Told by PERCY FITZGERALD, CONAN DOYLE, FLORENCE MARRYAT, &c. Post 8vo, illustrated boards, 2s.

Strutt (Joseph). — The Sports and Pastimes of the People of England. Edited by WILLIAM HONE. With 140 Illustrations. Crown 8vo, cloth, 3s. 6d.

Sundowner, Stories by.
Told by the Taffrail. Cr. 8vo, cl., 3s. 6d. | The Tale of the Serpent. Cr. 8vo, cl., flat back, 2s.

Surtees (Robert).—Handley Cross ; or, Mr. Jorrocks's Hunt. With 79 Illustrations by JOHN LEECH. Post 8vo, cloth, 2s.

Sutro (Alfred).—The Foolish Virgins. Fcap. 8vo, picture cover, 1s. ; cloth, 1s. 6d.

Swift's (Dean) Choice Works, in Prose and Verse. With Memoir, Portrait, and Facsimiles of the Maps in 'Gulliver's Travels.' Crown 8vo, cloth, 3s. 6d.
Gulliver's Travels, and A Tale of a Tub. Post 8vo, half-cloth, 2s.
Jonathan Swift : A Study. By J. CHURTON COLLINS. Crown 8vo, cloth extra, 8s.

Swinburne's (Algernon Charles) Works.

Selections from the Poetical Works of A. C. Swinburne. Fcap. 8vo 6s.
Atalanta in Calydon. Crown 8vo, 6s.
Chastelard: A Tragedy. Crown 8vo, 7s.
Poems and Ballads. FIRST SERIES. Cr.8vo,9s.
Poems and Ballads. SECOND SER. Cr.8vo,9s.
Poems & Ballads, THIRD SERIES. Cr. 8vo, 7s.
Songs before Sunrise. Crown 8vo, 10s. 6d.
Bothwell: A Tragedy. Crown 8vo, 12s. 6d.
Songs of Two Nations. Crown 8vo, 6s.
George Chapman. (See Vol. II. of G. CHAPMAN'S Works.) Crown 8vo, 3s. 6d.
Essays and Studies. Crown 8vo, 12s.
Erechtheus: A Tragedy. Crown 8vo, 6s.
A Note on Charlotte Brontë. Cr. 8vo, 6s.
A Study of Shakespeare. Crown 8vo, 8s.
Songs of the Springtides. Crown 8vo, 6s

Studies in Song. Crown 8vo, 7s.
Mary Stuart: A Tragedy. Crown 8vo, 8s.
Tristram of Lyonesse. Crown 8vo, 9s.
A Century of Roundels. Small 4to, 8s.
A Midsummer Holiday. Crown 8vo, 7s.
Marino Faliero: A Tragedy. Crown 8vo, 6s.
A Study of Victor Hugo. Crown 8vo, 6s.
Miscellanies. Crown 8vo, 12s.
Locrine: A Tragedy. Crown 8vo, 6s.
A Study of Ben Jonson. Crown 8vo, 7s.
The Sisters: A Tragedy. Crown 8vo, 6s.
Astrophel, &c. Crown 8vo, 7s.
Studies in Prose and Poetry. Cr. 8vo, 9s.
The Tale of Balen. Crown 8vo, 7s.
Rosamund, Queen of the Lombards: A Tragedy. Crown 8vo, 6s.
A Channel Passage, &c. Cr. 8vo, 7s. [*Shortly.*

The Collected Poems of Algernon Charles Swinburne. In 6 Vols., crown 8vo, 36s. net the Set. The volumes will be issued at short intervals at 6s. net each. (Can be subscribed for only in Sets.)

Taine's History of English Literature. Translated by HENRY VAN LAUN. Four Vols., demy 8vo, cloth, 30s.—POPULAR EDITION, Two Vols., crown 8vo, cloth, 15s.

Taylor (Bayard).—Diversions of the Echo Club. Post 8vo, cl., 2s.

Taylor (Tom).—Historical Dramas: 'JEANNE DARC,' 'TWIXT AXE AND CROWN,' 'THE FOOL'S REVENGE,' 'ARKWRIGHT'S WIFE,' 'ANNE BOLEYNE,' 'PLOT AND PASSION.' Crown 8vo, 1s. each.

Temple (Sir Richard, G.C.S.I.).—A Bird's-eye View of Picturesque India. With 32 Illustrations by the Author. Crown 8vo, cloth, gilt top, 6s.

Thackerayana: Notes and Anecdotes. With Coloured Frontispiece and Hundreds of Sketches by WILLIAM MAKEPEACE THACKERAY. Crown 8vo, cloth extra, 3s. 6d.

Thames, A New Pictorial History of the. By A. S. KRAUSSE. With 340 Illustrations. Post 8vo, cloth, 1s. 6d.

Thomas (Annie), Novels by.
The Siren's Web: A Romance of London Society. Crown 8vo, cloth, 3s. 6d.
Comrades True. Crown 8vo, cloth, gilt top, 6s.

Thomas (Bertha), Novels by. Crown 8vo, cloth, 3s. 6d. each.
The Violin-Player. | In a Cathedral City.
Crown 8vo, cloth, gilt top, 6s. each.
The House on the Scar: a Tale of South Devon. | The Son of the House.

Thomson's Seasons, and The Castle of Indolence. With Introduction by ALLAN CUNNINGHAM, and 48 Illustrations. Post 8vo, half-cloth, 2s.

Tompkins (Herbert W.).—Marsh-Country Rambles. With a Frontispiece. Crown 8vo, cloth, gilt top, 6s.

Twain's (Mark) Books.
Author's Edition de Luxe of the Works of Mark Twain, in 23 Volumes (limited to 600 Numbered Copies), price 12s. 6d. net per Volume (Sold only in Sets.)
UNIFORM LIBRARY EDITION. Crown 8vo, cloth extra, 3s. 6d. each.
Mark Twain's Library of Humour. With 197 Illustrations by E. W. KEMBLE.
Roughing It; and The Innocents at Home. With 200 Illustrations by F. A. FRASER.
The American Claimant. With 81 Illustrations by HAL HURST and others.
*The Adventures of Tom Sawyer. With 111 Illustrations.
Tom Sawyer Abroad. With 26 Illustrations by DAN BEARD.
Tom Sawyer, Detective, &c. With Photogravure Portrait of the Author.
Pudd'nhead Wilson. With Portrait and Six Illustrations by LOUIS LOEB.
*A Tramp Abroad. With 314 Illustrations.
*The Innocents Abroad; or, The New Pilgrim's Progress. With 234 Illustrations. (The Two Shilling Edition is entitled Mark Twain's Pleasure Trip.)
*The Gilded Age. By MARK TWAIN and C. D. WARNER. With 212 Illustrations.
*The Prince and the Pauper. With 190 Illustrations.
*Life on the Mississippi. With 300 Illustrations.
*The Adventures of Huckleberry Finn. With 174 Illustrations by E. W. KEMBLE.
*A Yankee at the Court of King Arthur. With 220 Illustrations by DAN BEARD.
*The Stolen White Elephant. | *The £1,000,000 Bank-Note.
A Double-barrelled Detective Story. With 7 Illustrations by LUCIUS HITCHCOCK.
The Choice Works of Mark Twain. Revised and Corrected throughout by the Author. With Life, Portrait, and numerous Illustrations.
※ The books marked * may be had also in post 8vo, picture boards, at 2s. each.

Crown 8vo, cloth, gilt top, 6s. each.
Personal Recollections of Joan of Arc. With Twelve Illustrations by F. V. DU MOND.
More Tramps Abroad.
The Man that Corrupted Hadleyburg, and other Stories and Sketches. With a Frontispiece.

Mark Twain's Sketches. Pott 8vo, cloth, gilt top, 2s. net; leather, gilt edges, 3s. net.

24 CHATTO & WINDUS, Publishers, 111 St. Martin's Lane, London, W.C.

Thornbury (Walter), Books by.
The Life and Correspondence of J. M. W. Turner. With Eight Illustrations in Colours and Two Woodcuts. New and Revised Edition. Crown 8vo, cloth, 3s. 6d.
Tales for the Marines. Post 8vo, illustrated boards, 2s.

Timbs (John), Works by. Crown 8vo, cloth, 3s. 6d. each.
Clubs and Club Life in London: Anecdotes of its Famous Coffee-houses, Hostelries, and Taverns. With 41 Illustrations.
English Eccentrics and Eccentricities: Stories of Delusions, Impostures, Sporting Scenes, Eccentric Artists, Theatrical Folk, &c. With 48 Illustrations.

Treeton (Ernest A.).—The Instigator. Cr. 8vo, cloth, gilt top, 6s.

Trollope (Anthony), Novels by.
Crown 8vo, cloth extra, 3s. 6d. each; post 8vo, illustrated boards, 2s. each.
The Way We Live Now. | Mr. Scarborough's Family.
Frau Frohmann. | Marion Fay. | The Land-Leaguers.
Post 8vo, illustrated boards, 2s. each.
Kept in the Dark. | The American Senator. | The Golden Lion of Granpere.

Trollope (Frances E.), Novels by.
Crown 8vo, cloth extra, 3s. 6d. each; post 8vo, illustrated boards, 2s. each.
Like Ships upon the Sea. | Mabel's Progress. | Anne Furness.

Trollope (T. A.).—Diamond Cut Diamond. Post 8vo, illust. bds., 2s.

Tytler (C. C. Fraser-).—Mistress Judith: A Novel. Crown 8vo, cloth extra, 3s. 6d.; post 8vo, illustrated boards, 2s.

Tytler (Sarah), Novels by.
Crown 8vo, cloth extra, 3s. 6d. each; post 8vo, illustrated boards, 2s. each.
Buried Diamonds. | The Blackhall Ghosts. | What She Came Through.
Post 8vo, illustrated boards, 2s. each.
The Bride's Pass. | The Huguenot Family. | Noblesse Oblige. | Disappeared.
Saint Mungo's City. | Lady Bell. | Beauty and the Beast.
Crown 8vo, cloth, 3s. 6d. each.
The Macdonald Lass. With Frontispiece. | Mrs. Carmichael's Goddesses.
The Witch-Wife. | Rachel Langton. | Sapphira. | A Honeymoon's Eclipse.
A Young Dragon.
Citoyenne Jacqueline. Crown 8vo, picture cloth, flat back, 2s.
Crown 8vo, cloth, gilt top, 6s. each.
Three Men of Mark. | In Clarissa's Day. | Sir David's Visitors.
The Poet and his Guardian Angel.

Upward (Allen).—The Queen Against Owen. Crown 8vo, cloth, 3s. 6d.; picture cloth, flat back, 2s.; post 8vo, picture boards, 2s.

Vandam (Albert D.).—A Court Tragedy. With 6 Illustrations by J. BARNARD DAVIS. Crown 8vo, cloth, 3s. 6d.

Vashti and Esther. By 'Belle' of *The World*. Cr. 8vo, cloth, 3s. 6d.

Vizetelly (Ernest A.), Books by. Crown 8vo, cloth, 3s. 6d. each.
The Scorpion: A Romance of Spain. With a Frontispiece. | The Lover's Progress.
With Zola in England: A Story of Exile. With 4 Portraits.
A Path of Thorns. Crown 8vo, cloth, gilt top, 6s.
Bluebeard: An Account of Comorre the Cursed and Gilles de Rais; with a Summary of various Tales and Traditions. With 9 Illustrations. Demy 8vo, cloth, 9s. net.

Wagner (Leopold).—How to Get on the Stage, and how to Succeed there. Crown 8vo, cloth, 2s. 6d.

Waller (S. E.).—Sebastiani's Secret. With 9 Illusts. Cr. 8vo, cl., 6s.

Walton and Cotton's Complete Angler. With Memoirs and Notes by Sir HARRIS NICOLAS. Post 8vo, cloth, gilt top, 2s. net; leather, gilt edges, 3s. net.

Walt Whitman, Poems by. Edited, with Introduction, by WILLIAM M. ROSSETTI. With Portrait. Crown 8vo, hand-made paper and buckram, 6s.

Warden (Florence), Novels by.
Joan, the Curate. Crown 8vo, cloth, 3s. 6d.; picture cloth, flat back, 2s.
A Fight to a Finish. Crown 8vo, cloth, 3s. 6d.
Crown 8vo, cloth, gilt top, 6s. each.
The Heart of a Girl. With 8 Illustrations. | What ought she to do?

Warman (Cy).—The Express Messenger. Crown 8vo, cloth, 3s. 6d.

Warner (Chas. Dudley).—A Roundabout Journey. Cr. 8vo, cl., 6s.

Wassermann (Lillias).—The Daffodils. Crown 8vo, cloth, 1s. 6d.

Warrant to Execute Charles I. A Facsimile, with the 59 Signatures and Seals. Printed on paper 22 in. by 14 in. 2s.
Warrant to Execute Mary Queen of Scots. A Facsimile, including Queen Elizabeth's Signature and the Great Seal. 2s.

CHATTO & WINDUS, Publishers, 111 St. Martin's Lane, London, W.C. 23

Weather, How to Foretell the, with the Pocket Spectroscope. By F. W. CORY. With Ten Illustrations. Crown 8vo, 1s.; cloth, 1s. 6d.

Webber (Byron).—Sport and Spangles. Crown 8vo, cloth, 2s.

Werner (A.).—Chapenga's White Man. Crown 8vo, cloth, 3s. 6d.

Westbury (Atha).—The Shadow of Hilton Fernbrook: A Romance of Maoriland. Crown 8vo, cloth, 3s. 6d.

Westall (William), Novels by.
Trust Money. Crown 8vo, cloth, 3s. 6d.; post 8vo, Illustrated boards, 2s.

Crown 8vo, cloth, 6s. each.
As a Man Sows. | As Luck would have it. | The Sacred Crescents.
The Old Bank. | Dr. Wynne's Revenge.

Crown 8vo, cloth, 3s. 6d. each.
A Woman Tempted Him. | Nigel Fortescue. | The Phantom City.
For Honour and Life. | Ben Clough. | Birch Dene. | Ralph Norbreck's Trust.
Her Two Millions. | The Old Factory (also at 6d.) | A Queer Race.
Two Pinches of Snuff. | Sons of Belial. | Red Ryvington.
With the Red Eagle. | Strange Crimes. | Roy of Roy's Court.
A Red Bridal. | Her Ladyship's Secret.

Wheelwright (E. Gray).—A Slow Awakening. Crown 8vo, 6s.

Whishaw (Fred.), Novels by. Crown 8vo, cloth, 3s. 6d. each.
A Forbidden Name | Many Ways of Love. With 8 Illustrations.

Crown 8vo, cloth, gilt top, 6s. each.
Mazeppa. | Near the Tsar, near Death. | A Splendid Impostor.

White (Gilbert).—Natural History of Selborne. Post 8vo, 2s.

Wilde (Lady).—The Ancient Legends, Mystic Charms, and Superstitions of Ireland; with Sketches of the Irish Past. Crown 8vo, cloth, 3s. 6d.

Williams (W. Mattieu, F.R.A.S.), Works by.
Science in Short Chapters. Cr. 8vo, cl. 7s. 6d. | Chemistry of Cookery. Cr. 8vo, cloth, 6s.
A Simple Treatise on Heat. With Illustrations. Crown 8vo, cloth, 2s. 6d.

Williamson (Mrs. F. H.).—A Child Widow. Post 8vo, bds., 2s.

Wills (C. J.), Novels by.
An Easy-going Fellow. Crown 8vo, cloth, 3s. 6d. | His Dead Past. Crown 8vo, cloth, 6s.

Wilson (Dr. Andrew, F.R.S.E.), Works by.
Chapters on Evolution. With 259 Illustrations. Crown 8vo, cloth extra, 7s. 6d.
Leisure-Time Studies. With Illustrations. Crown 8vo, cloth extra, 6s.
Studies in Life and Sense. With 36 Illustrations. Crown 8vo, cloth, 3s. 6d.
Common Accidents: How to Treat Them. With Illustrations. Crown 8vo, 1s.; cloth, 1s. 6d.
Glimpses of Nature. With 35 Illustrations. Crown 8vo, cloth extra, 3s. 6d.

Winter (John Strange), Stories by. Post 8vo, 2s. ea.; cloth, 2s. 6d. ea.
Cavalry Life. | Regimental Legends.
Cavalry Life and Regimental Legends. Cr. 8vo, cloth, 3s. 6d.; picture cloth, flat back, 2s.

Wissmann (Hermann von).—My Second Journey through Equatorial Africa. With 92 Illustrations. Demy 8vo, cloth, 16s.

Wood (H. F.), Detective Stories by. Post 8vo, boards, 2s. each.
The Passenger from Scotland Yard. | The Englishman of the Rue Cain.

Woolley (Celia Parker).—Rachel Armstrong. Post 8vo, cloth, 2s. 6d.

Wright (Thomas, F.S.A.), Works by.
Caricature History of the Georges; or, Annals of the House of Hanover. Compiled from Squibs, Broadsides, Window Pictures, Lampoons, and Pictorial Caricatures of the Time. With over 300 Illustrations. Crown 8vo, cloth, 7s. 6d.
History of Caricature and of the Grotesque in Art, Literature, Sculpture, and Painting. Illustrated by F. W. FAIRHOLT, F.S.A. Crown 8vo, cloth, 7s. 6d.

Wynman (Margaret).—My Flirtations. With 13 Illustrations by J. BERNARD PARTRIDGE. Post 8vo, cloth limp, 2s.

Zangwill (Louis).—A Nineteenth Century Miracle. Cr. 8vo, 2s.

Zola's (Emile) Novels. UNIFORM EDITION. Translated or Edited, with Introductions, by ERNEST A. VIZETELLY. Crown 8vo, cloth, 3s. 6d. each.
His Masterpiece. | The Joy of Life. | The Dram-Shop.
Germinal: Master and Man. | The Fat and the Thin. | Money.
The Honour of the Army. | His Excellency. | The Dream.
Abbe Mouret's Transgression. | The Downfall. | Doctor Pascal.
The Fortune of the Rougons. | Lourdes. | Rome. | Paris.
The Conquest of Plassans. | Fruitfulness. | Work. | Truth.

POPULAR EDITIONS, medium 8vo, 6d. each.
The Dram-Shop. | The Downfall. | Rome.

With Zola in England. By ERNEST A. VIZETELLY. With Four Portraits. Crown 8vo, cloth, 3s. 6d.

26 CHATTO & WINDUS, Publishers, 111 St. Martin's Lane, London W.C.

SOME BOOKS CLASSIFIED IN SERIES.

The St. Martin's Library. Pott 8vo, cloth, 2s. net each; leather, 3s. net each
London. By Sir WALTER BESANT. | The Woman in White. By WILKIE COLLINS.
All Sorts and Conditions of Men. By Sir WALTER BESANT.
The Cloister and the Hearth. By CHAS. READE. | 'It is Never Too Late to Mend.' By CH. READE.
Familiar Studies of Men and Books. By ROBERT LOUIS STEVENSON.
Virginibus Puerisque, and other Papers. By R. LOUIS STEVENSON.
The Pocket R.L.S.: Favourite Passages from STEVENSON'S Works.
New Arabian Nights. By ROBERT LOUIS STEVENSON. | The Deemster. By HALL CAINE.
Under the Greenwood Tree. By THOMAS HARDY. | The Life of the Fields. By RICHARD JEFFERIES.
Walton and Cotton's Complete Angler | Mark Twain's Sketches.
Condensed Novels. (The Two Series in one Volume.) By BRET HARTE.

The Mayfair Library. Post 8vo, cloth limp, 2s. 6d. per Volume.
Quips and Quiddities. By W. D. ADAMS. | Little Essays: from LAMB'S LETTERS.
The Agony Column of 'The Times.' | Forensic Anecdotes. By JACOB LARWOOD.
A Journey Round My Room. By X. DE MAISTRE. | Theatrical Anecdotes. By JACOB LARWOOD.
Poetical Ingenuities. By W. T. DOBSON. | Ourselves. By E. LYNN LINTON.
The Cupboard Papers. By FIN-BEC. | Witch Stories. By E. LYNN LINTON.
Songs of Irish Wit and Humour. | Pastimes and Players. By R. MACGREGOR.
Animals and their Masters. By Sir A HELPS. | New Paul and Virginia. By W. H. MALLOCK.
Social Pressure. By Sir A. HELPS. | Puck on Pegasus. By H. C. PENNELL.
Autocrat of Breakfast-Table. By O. W. HOLMES. | Pegasus Re-saddled. By H. C. PENNELL.
Curiosities of Criticism. By H. J. JENNINGS. | The Muses of Mayfair. By H. C. PENNELL.
Pencil and Palette. By R. KEMPT. | By Stream and Sea. By WILLIAM SENIOR.

The Golden Library. Post 8vo, cloth limp, 2s. per Volume.
Songs for Sailors. By W. C. BENNETT. | Scenes of Country Life. By EDWARD JESSE.
Lives of the Necromancers. By W. GODWIN. | La Mort d'Arthur: Selections from MALLORY.
The Autocrat of the Breakfast Table. By OLIVER WENDELL HOLMES. | Diversions of the Echo Club. BAYARD TAYLOR.

My Library. Printed on laid paper, post 8vo, half-Roxburghe, 2s. 6d. each.
The Journal of Maurice de Guerin. | Christie Johnstone. By CHARLES READE.
The Dramatic Essays of Charles Lamb. | Peg Woffington. By CHARLES READE.
Citation of William Shakspeare. W. S. LANDOR.

The Pocket Library. Post 8vo, printed on laid paper and hf.-bd., 2s. each.
Gastronomy. By BRILLAT-SAVARIN. | The Essays of Elia. By CHARLES LAMB.
Robinson Crusoe. Illustrated by G. CRUIKSHANK | Anecdotes of the Clergy. By JACOB LARWOOD.
Autocrat and Professor. By O. W. HOLMES. | The Epicurean, &c. By THOMAS MOORE.
Provincial Letters of Blaise Pascal. | Plays by RICHARD BRINSLEY SHERIDAN.
Whims and Oddities. By THOMAS HOOD. | Gulliver's Travels, &c. By Dean SWIFT.
Leigh Hunt's Essays. Edited by E. OLLIER. | Thomson's Seasons. Illustrated.
The Barber's Chair. By DOUGLAS JERROLD. | White's Natural History of Selborne.

POPULAR SIXPENNY NOVELS.
By GRANT ALLEN.
The Tents of Shem
By WALTER BESANT.
Children of Gibeon. | The Orange Girl.
All Sorts and Conditions of Men.
For Faith and Freedom.
By BESANT and RICE.
The Golden Butterfly. | Ready-Money Mortiboy.
The Chaplain of the Fleet.
By ROBERT BUCHANAN.
The Shadow of the Sword.
By HALL CAINE.
A Son of Hagar. | The Deemster.
The Shadow of a Crime.
By WILKIE COLLINS.
Armadale. | The Woman in White.
Man and Wife. | The Dead Secret.
Antonina. | The New Magdalen.
The Moonstone. | No Name.
By B. M. CROKER.
Diana Barrington. | Pretty Miss Neville.

By D. CHRISTIE MURRAY.
Joseph's Coat.
By OUIDA.
Puck. | Moths. | Strathmore. | Tricotrin.
Held in Bondage. | Under Two Flags.
By JAMES PAYN.
Walter's Ward.
By CHARLES READE.
Griffith Gaunt. | Put Yourself in His Place.
Peg Woffington: and Christie Johnstone.
The Cloister and the Hearth. | Foul Play.
It is Never Too Late to Mend. | Hard Cash.
By W. CLARK RUSSELL.
The Convict Ship.
By ROBERT LOUIS STEVENSON.
New Arabian Nights.
By WILLIAM WESTALL.
The Old Factory.
By EMILE ZOLA.
The Downfall. | The Dram-Shop. | Rome.

THE PICCADILLY NOVELS.
LIBRARY EDITIONS OF NOVELS, many Illustrated, crown 8vo, cloth extra, 3s. 6d. each.
By Mrs. ALEXANDER.
Valerie's Fate. | Barbara.
A Life Interest. | A Fight with Fate.
Mona's Choice. | A Golden Autumn.
By Woman's Wit. | Mrs. Crichton's Creditor.
The Cost of Her Pride. | The Step-mother.
A Missing Hero.
By M. ANDERSON.—Othello's Occupation.
By G. W. APPLETON.
Rash Conclusions.
By F. M. ALLEN.—Green as Grass.

By GRANT ALLEN.
Philistia. | Babylon. | The Great Taboo.
Strange Stories. | Duchess of Powysland.
For Maimie's Sake. | Blood Royal.
In all Shades. | I. Greet's Masterpiece.
The Beckoning Hand. | The Scallywag
The Devil's Die. | At Market Value.
This Mortal Coil. | Under Sealed Orders.
The Tents of Shem.
By ARTEMUS WARD.
Artemus Ward Complete.

CHATTO & WINDUS, Publishers, 111 St. Martin's Lane, London, W.C. 27

THE PICCADILLY (3/6) NOVELS—*continued.*

By EDWIN L. ARNOLD.
Phra the Phœnician. | Constable of St. Nicholas.

By ROBERT BARR
In a Steamer Chair. | A Woman Intervenes.
From Whose Bourne. | Revenge!

By FRANK BARRETT.
A Prodigal's Progress. | Under a Strange Mask.
Woman of Iron Bracelets. | A Missing Witness.
Fettered for Life. | Was She Justified?
The Harding Scandal.

By 'BELLE.'—Vashti and Esther.

By ARNOLD BENNETT.
The Gates of Wrath. | The Grand Babylon Hotel.

By Sir W. BESANT and J. RICE.
Ready-Money Mortiboy. | By Celia's Arbour.
My Little Girl. | Chaplain of the Fleet.
With Harp and Crown. | The Seamy Side.
This Son of Vulcan. | The Case of Mr. Lucraft.
The Golden Butterfly. | In Trafalgar's Bay.
The Monks of Thelema. | The Ten Years' Tenant.

By Sir WALTER BESANT.
All Sorts & Conditions. | S. Katherine's by Tower
The Captains' Room. | Verbena Camellia, &c.
All in a Garden Fair. | The Ivory Gate.
Dorothy Forster. | The Rebel Queen.
Uncle Jack. Holy Rose | Dreams of Avarice.
World Went Well Then. | In Deacon's Orders.
Children of Gibeon. | The Master Craftsman.
Herr Paulus. | The City of Refuge.
For Faith and Freedom. | A Fountain Sealed.
To Call Her Mine. | The Changeling.
The Revolt of Man. | The Fourth Generation
The Bell of St. Paul's. | The Charm.
Armorel of Lyonesse. | The Orange Girl.

By AMBROSE BIERCE—In Midst of Life.

By HAROLD BINDLOSS. Ainslie's Ju-Ju.

By M. McD. BODKIN.
Dora Myrl. | Shillelagh and Shamrock.
Patsy the Omadaun.

By PAUL BOURGET.—A Living Lie.

By J. D. BRAYSHAW.—Slum Silhouettes.

By H. A. BRYDEN.—An Exiled Scot.

By ROBERT BUCHANAN.
Shadow of the Sword. | The New Abelard.
A Child of Nature. | Matt. | Rachel Dene
God and the Man. | Master of the Mine.
Martyrdom of Madeline | The Heir of Linne.
Love Me for Ever. | Woman and the Man.
Annan Water. | Red and White Heather.
Foxglove Manor. | Lady Kilpatrick.
The Charlatan. | Andromeda.

By GELETT BURGESS and WILL IRWIN.—The Picaroons.

R. W. CHAMBERS.—The King in Yellow.

By J. M. CHAPPLE.—The Minor Chord.

By HALL CAINE.
Shadow of a Crime. | Deemster. | Son of Hagar.

By AUSTIN CLARE.—By Rise of River.

By Mrs. ARCHER CLIVE.
Paul Ferroll. | Why Paul Ferroll Killed his Wife.

By ANNE COATES.—Rie's Diary.

By MACLAREN COBBAN.
The Red Sultan. | The Burden of Isabel.

By WILKIE COLLINS.
Armadale. | AfterDark. | The New Magdalen.
No Name. | Antonina | The Frozen Deep.
Basil. | Hide and Seek. | The Two Destinies.
The Dead Secret. | 'I Say No.'
Queen of Hearts. | Little Novels.
My Miscellanies | The Fallen Leaves.
The Woman in White. | Jezebel's Daughter.
The Law and the Lady. | The Black Robe.
The Haunted Hotel. | Heart and Science.
The Moonstone. | The Evil Genius.
Man and Wife. | The Legacy of Cain.
Poor Miss Finch. | A Rogue's Life.
Miss or Mrs.? | Blind Love.

By MORT. & FRANCES COLLINS.
Blacksmith & Scholar. | You Play me False.
The Village Comedy. | Midnight to Midnight.

M. J. COLQUHOUN.—Every Inch Soldier.

By HERBERT COMPTON.
The Inimitable Mrs. Massingham.

By E. H. COOPER.—Geoffory Hamilton.

By V. C. COTES.—Two Girls on a Barge.

By C. E. CRADDOCK.
The Prophet of the Great Smoky Mountains.
His Vanished Star.

By H. N. CRELLIN.
Romances of the Old Seraglio.

By MATT CRIM.
The Adventures of a Fair Rebel.

By S. R. CROCKETT and others.
Tales of Our Coast.

By B. M. CROKER.
Diana Barrington. | The Real Lady Hilda.
Proper Pride. | Married or Single?
A Family Likeness. | Two Masters.
Pretty Miss Neville. | In the Kingdom of Kerry
A Bird of Passage. | Interference.
Mr. Jervis. | A Third Person.
Village Tales. | Beyond the Pale.
Some One Else. | Jason. | Miss Balmaine's Past.
Infatuation. | Terence.
The Cat's-paw.

By ALPHONSE DAUDET.
The Evangelist; or, Port Salvation.

H. C. DAVIDSON.—Mr. Sadler's Daughters.

By JAS. DE MILLE.
A Strange Manuscript Found in a Copper Cylinder.

By HARRY DE WINDT.
True Tales of Travel and Adventure.

By DICK DONOVAN.
Man from Manchester. | Tales of Terror.
Records of Vincent Trill | Chronicles of Michael
The Mystery of | Danevitch. | Detective.
Jamaica Terrace. | Tyler Tatlock, Private
Deacon Brodie.

By RICHARD DOWLING.
Old Corcoran's Money.

By A. CONAN DOYLE.
The Firm of Girdlestone.

By S. JEANNETTE DUNCAN.
A Daughter of To-day. | Vernon's Aunt.

By ANNIE EDWARDES.
Archie Lovell. | A Plaster Saint.

By G. S. EDWARDS.—Snazelleparilla.

By G. MANVILLE FENN.
Cursed by a Fortune. | A Fluttered Dovecote.
The Case of Ailsa Gray | King of the Castle
Commodore Junk. | Master of Ceremonies.
The New Mistress. | The Man with a Shadow
Witness to the Deed. | One Maid's Mischief.
The Tiger Lily. | Story of Antony Grace.
The White Virgin. | This Man's Wife.
Black Blood. | In Jeopardy. 'ning
Double Cunning. | A Woman Worth Win-

By PERCY FITZGERALD.—Fatal Zero

By Hon. Mrs. W. FORBES.—Dumb.

By R. E. FRANCILLON.
One by One. | Ropes of Sand.
A Dog and his Shadow. | Jack Doyle's Daughter.
A Real Queen.

By HAROLD FREDERIC.
Seth's Brother's Wife. | The Lawton Girl.

By PAUL GAULOT.—The Red Shirts.

By CHARLES GIBBON.
Robin Gray. | The Braes of Yarrow.
Of High Degree | Queen of the Meadow.
The Golden Shaft. | The Flower of the Forest.

By E. GLANVILLE.
The Lost Heiress. | The Golden Rock.
Fair Colonist | Fossicker | Tales from the Veld.

By E. J. GOODMAN.
The Fate of Herbert Wayne.

By Rev. S. BARING GOULD.
Red Spider. | Eve.

By ALFRED A. GRACE.
Tales of a Dying Race.

CECIL GRIFFITH.—Corinthia Marazion.

THE PICCADILLY (3/6) NOVELS—continued.

By A. CLAVERING GUNTER.
A Florida Enchantment.

By BRET HARTE.
A Waif of the Plains.
A Ward of the Golden Gate.
A Sappho of Green Springs.
Col. Starbottle's Client.
Susy. | Sally Dows.
Bell-Ringer of Angel's.
Tales of Trail and Town.
A Protegee of Jack Hamlin's.
Clarence. [celsior.
Barker's Luck.
Devil's Ford.
The Crusade of the 'Ex-
Three Partners.
Gabriel Conroy.
New Condensed Novels

By OWEN HALL.
The Track of a Storm. | Jetsam.

By COSMO HAMILTON.
Glamour of Impossible. | Through a Keyhole.

By THOMAS HARDY.
Under the Greenwood Tree.

By JULIAN HAWTHORNE.
Garth. | Dust.
Ellice Quentin.
Sebastian Strome.
Fortune's Fool.
Beatrix Randolph.
David Poindexter's Disappearance.
Spectre of Camera.

By Sir A. HELPS.—Ivan de Biron.
By I. HENDERSON.—Agatha Page.

By G. A. HENTY.
Dorothy's Double. | The Queen's Cup.
Rujub, the Juggler.

HEADON HILL.—Zambra the Detective.

By JOHN HILL.—The Common Ancestor.

By TIGHE HOPKINS.
Twixt Love and Duty. | Nugents of Carriconna.
The Incomplete Adventurer. | Nell Haffenden.

VICTOR HUGO.—The Outlaw of Iceland.

By FERGUS HUME.
Lady from Nowhere. | The Millionaire Mystery

By Mrs. HUNGERFORD.
Marvel.
Unsatisfactory Lover.
In Durance Vile.
A Modern Circe.
Lady Patty.
A Mental Struggle.
Lady Verner's Flight.
The Red-House Mystery
The Three Graces.
Professor's Experiment
A Point of Conscience.
A Maiden all Forlorn.
The Coming of Chloe.
Nora Creina.
An Anxious Moment.
April's Lady.
Peter's Wife.
Lovice.

By Mrs. ALFRED HUNT.
The Leaden Casket. | Self-Condemned.
That Other Person. | Mrs. Juliet.

By R. ASHE KING.—A Drawn Game.

By GEORGE LAMBERT.
The President of Boravia.

By EDMOND LEPELLETIER.
Madame Sans-Gene.

By ADAM LILBURN. A Tragedy in Marble

By HARRY LINDSAY.
Rhoda Roberts. | The Jacobite.

By HENRY W. LUCY.—Gideon Fleyce.

By E. LYNN LINTON.
Patricia Kemball.
Under which Lord?
'My Love!' | Ione.
Paston Carew.
Sowing the Wind.
With a Silken Thread.
The World Well Lost.
The Atonement of Leam Dundas.
The One Too Many.
Dulcie Everton.
Rebel of the Family.
An Octave of Friends.

By JUSTIN McCARTHY.
A Fair Saxon.
Linley Rochford.
Dear Lady Disdain.
Camiola. | Mononia.
Waterdale Neighbours.
My Enemy's Daughter.
Miss Misanthrope.
Donna Quixote.
Maid of Athens.
The Comet of a Season.
The Dictator.
Red Diamonds.
The Riddle Ring.
The Three Disgraces.

By JUSTIN H. McCARTHY.
A London Legend.

By GEORGE MACDONALD.
Heather and Snow. | Phantastes.

W. H. MALLOCK.—The New Republic.
P. & V. MARGUERITTE.—The Disaster.

By L. T. MEADE.
A Soldier of Fortune.
In an Iron Grip.
Dr. Rumsey's Patient.
The Voice of the Charmer
An Adventuress.
On Brink of a Chasm.
The Siren.
The Way of a Woman.
A Son of Ishmael.
The Blue Diamond.
A Stumble by the Way.

By LEONARD MERRICK.
This Stage of Fools. | Cynthia.

By EDMUND MITCHELL.
The Lone Star Rush.

By BERTRAM MITFORD.
The Gun-Runner. | The King's Assegai.
Luck of Gerard Ridgeley. | Rensh. Fanning's Quest.
The Triumph of Hilary Blachland.

By Mrs. MOLESWORTH.
Hathercourt Rectory.

By J. E. MUDDOCK.
Maid Marian and Robin Hood. | Golden Idol.
Basile the Jester. | Young Lochinvar.

By D. CHRISTIE MURRAY.
A Life's Atonement.
Joseph's Coat.
Coals of Fire.
Old Blazer's Hero.
Val Strange. | Hearts.
A Model Father.
By the Gate of the Sea.
A Bit of Human Nature.
First Person Singular.
Cynic Fortune.
The Way of the World.
BobMartin's Little Girl
Time's Revenges.
A Wasted Crime.
In Direst Peril.
Mount Despair.
A Capful o' Nails.
Tales in Prose & Verse
A Race for Millions.
This Little World.
His Own Ghost.
Church of Humanity.
V.C.: Castle Barfield and the Crimea

By MURRAY and HERMAN.
The Bishops' Bible. | Paul Jones's Alias.
One Traveller Returns.

By HUME NISBET.—' Bail Up !'

By W. E. NORRIS.
Saint Ann's. | Billy Bellew.
Miss Wentworth's Idea.

By G. OHNET.—A Weird Gift.
Love's Depths. | The Woman of Mystery.

By Mrs. OLIPHANT.
Whiteladies. | The Sorceress.

By OUIDA.
Held in Bondage.
Strathmore. | Chandos.
Under Two Flags.
Idalia. | Gage.
Cecil Castlemaine's
Tricotrin. | Puck.
Folle Farine.
A Dog of Flanders.
Pascarel. | Signa.
Princess Napraxine.
Two Wooden Shoes.
In a Winter City.
Friendship.
Moths. | Ruffino.
Pipistrello. | Ariadne.
A Village Commune.
Bimbi. | Wanda.
Frescoes. | Othmar.
In Maremma.
Syrlin. | Guilderoy.
Santa Barbara.
Two Offenders.
The Waters of Edera.

By G. SIDNEY PATERNOSTER.
The Motor Pirate.

By MARGARET A. PAUL.
Gentle and Simple.

By JAMES PAYN.
Lost Sir Massingberd.
The Family Scapegrace
A County Family.
Less Black than We're Painted.
A Confidential Agent.
A Grape from a Thorn.
In Peril and Privation.
Mystery of Mirbridge.
High Spirits. By Proxy.
The Talk of the Town.
Holiday Tasks.
For Cash Only.
The Burnt Million.
Sunny Stories.
A Trying Patient.
A Modern Dick Whittington.

By WILL PAYNE.—Jerry the Dreamer.

By Mrs. CAMPBELL PRAED.
Outlaw and Lawmaker. | Mrs. Tregaskiss.
Christina Chard. | Nulma. | Madame Izan.
'As a Watch in the Night.'

By E. C. PRICE.—Valentina.
By RICHARD PRYCE.
Miss Maxwell's Affections.

By Mrs. J. H. RIDDELL.
Weird Stories. | A Rich Man's Daughter.

CHATTO & WINDUS, Publishers, 111 St. Martin's Lane, London, W.C. 29

THE PICCADILLY (3/6) NOVELS—continued.
By CHARLES READE.
Peg Woffington; and Griffith Gaunt.
Christie Johnstone. Love Little, Love Long.
Hard Cash. The Double Marriage.
Cloister & the Hearth. Foul Play.
Never Too Late to Mend Put Y'rself in His Place
The Course of True A Terrible Temptation.
Love; and Single- A Simpleton.
heart & Doubleface. A Woman-Hater.
Autobiography of a The Jilt, & otherStories:
Thief; Jack of all & Good Stories of Man.
Trades: A Hero and A Perilous Secret.
a Martyr; and The Readiana; and Bible
Wandering Heir. Characters.
By FRANK RICHARDSON.
The Man who Lost His Past.
The Bayswater Mystery.
By AMELIE RIVES.
Barbara Dering. | Meriel.
By F. W. ROBINSON.
The Hands of Justice. | Woman in the Dark.
By ALBERT ROSS.—A Sugar Princess.
J. RUNCIMAN.—Skippers and Shellbacks.
By W. CLARK RUSSELL.
Round the Galley Fire. My Shipmate Louise.
In the Middle Watch. Alone on Wide Wide Sea.
On the Fo'k'sle Head The Phantom Death.
A Voyage to the Cape. Is He the Man?
Book for the Hammock. Good Ship 'Mohock.'
Mystery of 'Ocean Star' The Convict Ship.
Jenny Harlowe. Heart of Oak.
An Ocean Tragedy. The Tale of the Ten.
A Tale of Two Tunnels. The Last Entry.
The Death Ship.
By DORA RUSSELL.—Drift of Fate.
By HERBERT RUSSELL. True Blue.
BAYLE ST. JOHN.—A Levantine Family.
By ADELINE SERGEANT.
Dr. Endicott's Experiment.
Under False Pretences.
By M. P. SHIEL.—The Purple Cloud.
By GEORGE R. SIMS.
Dagonet Abroad. In London's Heart.
Once Upon a Christmas Mary Jane's Memoirs.
Time. Mary Jane Married.
Without the Limelight. The Small-part Lady.
Rogues and Vagabonds. A Blind Marriage.
Biographs of Babylon.
By UPTON SINCLAIR.—Prince Hagen.
By HAWLEY SMART.
Without Love or Licence. The Outsider.
The Master of Rathkelly. Beatrice & Benedick.
Long Odds. A Racing Rubber.
By J. MOYR SMITH.
The Prince of Argolis.
By T. W. SPEIGHT.
The Grey Monk. Secret Wyvern Towers.
The Master of Trenance The Doom of Siva.
The Web of Fate As it was Written.
A Minion of the Moon. Her Ladyship.
The Strange Experiences of Mr. Verschoyle.
By ALAN ST. AUBYN.
A Fellow of Trinity. The Tremlett Diamonds.
The Junior Dean. The Wooing of May
Master of St. Benedict's. A Tragic Honeymoon.
To his Own Master. A Proctor's Wooing.
Gallantry Bower. Fortune's Gate.
In Face of the World. Bonnie Maggie Lauder.
Orchard Damerel. Mary Unwin.
Mrs. Dunbar's Secret.
By JOHN STAFFORD.—Doris and I.
By R. STEPHENS.—The Cruciform Mark.
By R. NEILSON STEPHENS.
Philip Winwood.

R. A. STERNDALE.—The Afghan Knife.
R. L. STEVENSON.—The Suicide Club.
By FRANK STOCKTON.
The Young Master of Hyson Hall.
By SUNDOWNER. Told by the Taffrail.
By ANNIE THOMAS.—The Siren's Web.
By BERTHA THOMAS.
The Violin-Player. | In a Cathedral City.
By FRANCES E. TROLLOPE
Like Ships upon Sea. | Mabel's Progress.
Anne Furness.
By ANTHONY TROLLOPE.
The Way we Live Now. | Scarborough's Family.
Frau Frohmann. The Land-Leaguers.
Marion Fay.
By MARK TWAIN.
Choice Works. Pudd'nhead Wilson.
Library of Humour. The Gilded Age.
The Innocents Abroad. Prince and the Pauper.
Roughing It; and The Life on the Mississippi.
Innocents at Home. The Adventures of
A Tramp Abroad. Huckleberry Finn.
The American Claimant. A Yankee at the Court
AdventuresTomSawyer of King Arthur.
Tom Sawyer Abroad. Stolen White Elephant.
Tom Sawyer, Detective £1,000,000 Bank-note.
A Double-barrelled Detective Story.
C. C. F.-TYTLER.—Mistress Judith.
By SARAH TYTLER.
What She Came Through Mrs. Carmichael's God-
Buried Diamonds. desses.
The Blackhall Ghosts' Rachel Langton.
The Macdonald Lass. A Honeymoon's Eclipse.
Witch-Wife. | Sapphira A Young Dragon.
By ALLEN UPWARD.
The Queen against Owen.
By ALBERT D. VANDAM.
A Court Tragedy.
By E. A. VIZETELLY.
The Scorpion. | The Lover's Progress.
By FLORENCE WARDEN.
Joan, the Curate. | A Fight to a Finish.
By CY WARMAN.—Express Messenger,
By A. WERNER.
Chapenga's White Man.
By WILLIAM WESTALL.
For Honour and Life. The Old Factory.
A Woman Tempted Him Red Ryvington.
Her Two Millions. Ralph Norbreck's Trust
Two Pinches of Snuff. Trust-money.
Nigel Fortescue. Sons of Belial.
Birch Dene. Roy of Roy's Court.
The Phantom City. With the Red Eagle.
A Queer Race. A Red Bridal.
Ben Clough. Strange Crimes.
Her Ladyship's Secret.
By ATHA WESTBURY.
The Shadow of Hilton Fernbrook.
By FRED WHISHAW.
A Forbidden Name. | Many Ways of Love.
By C. J. WILLS.—An Easy-going Fellow.
By JOHN STRANGE WINTER.
Cavalry Life; and Regimental Legends.
By E. ZOLA.
The Joy of Life. | His Masterpiece.
The Fortune of the Rougons.
Abbe Mouret's Transgression.
The Conquest of Plassans. | Germinal.
The Honour of the Army.
The Downfall. His Excellency.
The Dream. Money. The Dram-Shop.
Dr. Pascal. Lourdes Rome | Paris. | Work
The Fat and the Thin Fruitfulness. | Truth.
By 'ZZ.'—A Nineteenth Century Miracle

CHEAP EDITIONS OF POPULAR NOVELS.
Post 8vo, Illustrated boards, 2s. each.

By ARTEMUS WARD.
Artemus Ward Complete.

By E. LESTER ARNOLD.
Phra the Phœnician.

CHATTO & WINDUS, Publishers, 111 St. Martin's Lane, London, W.C.

TWO-SHILLING NOVELS—*continued*.

By Mrs. ALEXANDER.
Maid, Wife, or Widow? | A Life Interest.
Blind Fate. | Mona's Choice.
Valerie's Fate. | By Woman's Wit.

By GRANT ALLEN.
Philistia. | Babylon. | Dumaresq's Daughter.
Strange Stories. | Duchess of Powysland.
For Maimie's Sake. | Blood Royal. [piece.
In all Shades. | Ivan Greet's Master-
The Beckoning Hand. | The Scallywag.
The Devil's Die. | This Mortal Coil.
The Tents of Shem | At Market Value.
The Great Taboo. | Under Sealed Orders.

BY FRANK BARRETT.
Fettered for Life. | Found Guilty.
Little Lady Linton. | A Recoiling Vengeance.
Between Life & Death. | For Love and Honour.
Sin of Olga Zassoulich. | John Ford, &c.
Folly Morrison. | Woman of Iron Brace'ts
Lieut. Barnabas. | The Harding Scandal.
Honest Davie. | A Missing Witness.
A Prodigal's Progress.

By Sir W. BESANT and J. RICE.
Ready-Money Mortiboy | By Celia's Arbour.
My Little Girl. | Chaplain of the Fleet.
With Harp and Crown. | The Seamy Side.
This Son of Vulcan. | The Case of Mr. Lucraft.
The Golden Butterfly. | In Trafalgar's Bay.
The Monks of Thelema. | The Ten Years' Tenant.

By Sir WALTER BESANT.
All Sorts and Condi- | The Bell of St. Paul's.
tions of Men. | The Holy Rose.
The Captains' Room. | Armorel of Lyonesse.
All in a Garden Fair. | S.Katherine's by Tower
Dorothy Forster. | Verbena Camellia Ste-
Uncle Jack. | phanotis.
The World Went Very | The Ivory Gate.
Well Then. | The Rebel Queen.
Children of Gibeon. | Beyond the Dreams of
Herr Paulus. | Avarice.
For Faith and Freedom. | The Revolt of Man.
To Call Her Mine. | In Deacon's Orders.
The Master Craftsman. | The City of Refuge.

By AMBROSE BIERCE.
In the Midst of Life.

By FREDERICK BOYLE.
Camp Notes. | Chronicles of No-man's
Savage Life. | Land.

BY BRET HARTE.
Californian Stories. | Flip. | Maruja.
Gabriel Conroy. | A Phyllis of the Sierras.
Luck of Roaring Camp. | A Waif of the Plains.
An Heiress of Red Dog. | Ward of Golden Gate.

By ROBERT BUCHANAN.
Shadow of the Sword. | The Martyrdom of Ma-
A Child of Nature. | deline.
God and the Man. | The New Abelard.
Love Me for Ever. | The Heir of Linne.
Foxglove Manor. | Woman and the Man.
The Master of the Mine. | Rachel Dene. | Matt.
Annan Water. | Lady Kilpatrick.

By BUCHANAN and MURRAY.
The Charlatan.

By HALL CAINE.
The Shadow of a Crime. | The Deemster.
A Son of Hagar.

By Commander CAMERON.
The Cruise of the 'Black Prince.'

By HAYDEN CARRUTH.
The Adventures of Jones.

By AUSTIN CLARE.
For the Love of a Lass.

By Mrs. ARCHER CLIVE.
Paul Ferroll.
Why Paul Ferroll Killed his Wife.

By MACLAREN COBBAN.
The Cure of Souls. | The Red Sultan.

By M. J. COLQUHOUN.
Every Inch a Soldier.

By C. ALLSTON COLLINS.
The Bar Sinister.

By MORT. & FRANCES COLLINS
Sweet Anne Page. | Sweet and Twenty.
Transmigration. | The Village Comedy.
From Midnight to Mid- | You Play me False.
night. | Blacksmith and Scholar
A Fight with Fortune. | Frances.

By WILKIE COLLINS.
Armadale. | AfterDark. | My Miscellanies.
No Name. | The Woman in White.
Antonina. | The Moonstone.
Basil. | Man and Wife.
Hide and Seek. | Poor Miss Finch.
The Dead Secret. | The Fallen Leaves.
Queen of Hearts. | Jezebel's Daughter.
Miss or Mrs.? | The Black Robe.
The New Magdalen. | Heart and Science.
The Frozen Deep. | 'I Say No!'
The Law and the Lady | The Evil Genius.
The Two Destinies. | Little Novels.
The Haunted Hotel. | Legacy of Cain.
A Rogue's Life. | Blind Love.

By C. EGBERT CRADDOCK.
The Prophet of the Great Smoky Mountains.

By MATT CRIM.
The Adventures of a Fair Rebel.

By H. N. CRELLIN.—Tales of the Caliph.

By B. M. CROKER.
Pretty Miss Neville. | Village Tales and Jungle
Diana Barrington. | Tragedies.
'To Let.' | Two Masters.
A Bird of Passage. | Mr. Jervis.
Proper Pride. | The Real Lady Hilda.
A Family Likeness. | Married or Single?
A Third Person. | Interference.

By ALPHONSE DAUDET.
The Evangelist; or, Port Salvation.

By JAMES DE MILLE.
A Strange Manuscript.

By DICK DONOVAN.
The Man-Hunter. | In the Grip of the Law.
Tracked and Taken. | From Information Re-
Caught at Last! | ceived.
Wanted! | Tracked to Doom.
Who Poisoned Hetty | Link by Link
Duncan? | Suspicion Aroused.
Man from Manchester. | Riddles Read.
A Detective's Triumphs
The Mystery of Jamaica Terrace.
The Chronicles of Michael Danevitch.

By Mrs. ANNIE EDWARDES.
A Point of Honour. | Archie Lovell.

By EDWARD EGGLESTON.—Roxy.

By G. MANVILLE FENN.
The New Mistress. | The Tiger Lily.
Witness to the Dead. | The White Virgin.

By PERCY FITZGERALD.
Bella Donna. | Second Mrs. Tillotson.
Never Forgotten. | Seventy-five Brooke
Polly. | Street.
Fatal Zero. | The Lady of Brantome

By P. FITZGERALD and others.
Strange Secrets.

By R. E. FRANCILLON.
Olympia. | King or Knave?
One by One. | Romances of the Law.
A Real Queen. | Ropes of Sand.
Queen Cophetua. | A Dog and his Shadow

By HAROLD FREDERIC.
Seth's Brother's Wife. | The Lawton Girl.

Prefaced by Sir BARTLE FRERE.
Pandurang Hari.

By CHARLES GIBBON.
Robin Gray. | In Honour Bound.
Fancy Free. | Flower of the Forest.
For Lack of Gold. | The Braes of Yarrow.
What will World Say? | The Golden Shaft.
In Love and War. | Of High Degree.
For the King. | By Mead and Stream.
In Pastures Green. | Loving a Dream.
Queen of the Meadow. | A Hard Knot.
A Heart's Problem. | Heart's Delight.
The Dead Heart. | Blood Money.

TWO-SHILLING NOVELS—continued.
By WILLIAM GILBERT.
James Duke.
By ERNEST GLANVILLE
The Lost Heiress. | The Fossicker.
A Fair Colonist.
By Rev. S. BARING GOULD
Red Spider. | Eve.
By ANDREW HALLIDAY.
Every-day Papers.
By THOMAS HARDY.
Under the Greenwood Tree.
By JULIAN HAWTHORNE.
Garth. | Love—or a Name.
Ellice Quentin. | David Poindexter's Dis-
Fortune's Fool. | appearance.
Miss Cadogna. | The Spectre of the
Dust. | Camera.
Beatrix Randolph.
By Sir ARTHUR HELPS.
Ivan de Biron.
By G. A. HENTY.
Rujub the Juggler.
By HEADON HILL.
Zambra the Detective.
By JOHN HILL.—Treason Felony.
By Mrs. CASHEL HOEY.
The Lover's Creed.
By Mrs. GEORGE HOOPER.
The House of Raby.
By Mrs. HUNGERFORD.
A Maiden all Forlorn. | Lady Verner's Flight.
In Durance Vile. | The Red-House Mystery
Marvel. | The Three Graces.
A Mental Struggle. | Unsatisfactory Lover.
A Modern Circe. | Lady Patty.
April's Lady. | Nora Creina.
Peter's Wife. | Professor's Experiment.
By Mrs. ALFRED HUNT.
That Other Person. | The Leaden Casket.
Self-Condemned.
By MARK KERSHAW.
Colonial Facts and Fictions.
By R. ASHE KING.
A Drawn Game. | Passion's Slave.
'The Wearing of the | Bell Barry.
  Green.'
By EDMOND LEPELLETIER
Madame Sans-Gene.
By JOHN LEYS.—The Lindsays.
By E. LYNN LINTON.
Patricia Kemball. | The Atonement of Leam
The World Well Lost. | Dundas.
Under which Lord? | Rebel of the Family.
Paston Carew. | Sowing the Wind.
'My Love!' | The One Too Many.
Ione. | Dulcie Everton.
With a Silken Thread.
By HENRY W. LUCY.
Gideon Fleyce.
By JUSTIN McCARTHY.
Dear Lady Disdain. | Donna Quixote.
Waterdale Neighbours. | Maid of Athens.
My Enemy's Daughter | The Comet of a Season.
A Fair Saxon. | The Dictator.
Linley Rochford. | Red Diamonds.
Miss Misanthrope. | The Riddle Ring.
Camiola.
By HUGH MACCOLL.
Mr. Stranger's Sealed Packet.
By GEORGE MACDONALD.
Heather and Snow.
By AGNES MACDONELL.
Quaker Cousins.
By W. H. MALLOCK.
The New Republic.
By BRANDER MATTHEWS
A Secret of the Sea.
By L. T. MEADE.
A Soldier of Fortune.

By LEONARD MERRICK.
The Man who was Good.
By Mrs. MOLESWORTH.
Hathercourt Rectory.
By J. E. MUDDOCK
Stories Weird and Won- | From the Bosom of the
  derful. | Deep.
The Dead Man's Secret.
By D. CHRISTIE MURRAY.
A Model Father. | A Bit of Human Nature.
Joseph's Coat. | First Person Singular.
Coals of Fire. | Bob Martin's Little Girl
Val Strange. | Hearts. | Time's Revenges.
Old Blazer's Hero. | A Wasted Crime.
The Way of the World | In Direst Peril.
Cynic Fortune. | Mount Despair.
A Life's Atonement. | A Capful o' Nails
By the Gate of the Sea.
By MURRAY and HERMAN.
One Traveller Returns. | The Bishops' Bible.
Paul Jones's Alias.
By HUME NISBET.
'Bail Up!' | Dr. Bernard St. Vincent
By W. E. NORRIS.
Saint Ann's. | Billy Bellew.
By GEORGES OHNET.
Dr. Rameau. | A Weird Gift.
A Last Love.
By Mrs. OLIPHANT.
Whiteladies. | The Greatest Heiress in
The Primrose Path. | England.
By OUIDA.
Held in Bondage. | Two Lit. Wooden Shoes
Strathmore. | Moths.
Chandos. | Bimbi.
Idalia. | Pipistrello.
Under Two Flags. | A Village Commune.
Cecil Castlemaine's Gage | Wanda
Tricotrin. | Othmar
Puck. | Frescoes.
Folle Farine. | In Maremma.
A Dog of Flanders. | Guilderoy.
Pascarel. | Ruffino.
Signa. | Syrlin.
Princess Napraxine. | Santa Barbara.
In a Winter City. | Two Offenders.
Ariadne. | Ouida's Wisdom, Wit,
Friendship. | and Pathos.
By MARGARET AGNES PAUL.
Gentle and Simple.
By Mrs. CAMPBELL PRAED.
The Romance of a Station.
The Soul of Countess Adrian.
Outlaw and Lawmaker. | Mrs. Tregaskiss'
Christina Chard. |
By JAMES PAYN.
Bentinck's Tutor. | The Talk of the Town.
Murphy's Master. | Holiday Tasks.
A County Family. | A Perfect Treasure.
At Her Mercy. | What He Cost Her.
Cecil's Tryst. | A Confidential Agent.
The Clyffards of Clyffe. | Glow-worm Tales.
The Foster Brothers. | The Burnt Million.
Found Dead. | Sunny Stories.
The Best of Husbands. | Lost Sir Massingberd.
Walter's Word. | A Woman's Vengeance.
Halves. | The Family Scapegrace.
Fallen Fortunes. | Gwendoline's Harvest.
Humorous Stories. | Like Father, Like Son.
£200 Reward. | Married Beneath Him.
A Marine Residence. | Not Wooed, but Won.
Mirk Abbey | Less Black than We're
By Proxy. | Painted.
Under One Roof. | Some Private Views
High Spirits. | A Grape from a Thorn.
Carlyon's Year. | The Mystery of Mir-
From Exile. | bridge.
For Cash Only. | The Word and the Will.
Kit. | A Prince of the Blood.
The Canon's Ward. | A Trying Patient.
By RICHARD PRYCE.
Miss Maxwell's Affections.

CHATTO & WINDUS, Publishers, 111 St. Martin's Lane, London, W.C.

TWO-SHILLING NOVELS—*continued*.

By CHARLES READE.
It is Never Too Late to Mend.
Christie Johnstone.
The Double Marriage.
Put Y'self In His Place.
Love Little, Love Long.
Cloister and the Hearth.
Course of True Love.
The Jilt.
Autobiog. of a Thief.
A Terrible Temptation.
Foul Play.
The Wandering Heir.
Hard Cash.
Singleheart, Doubleface
Good Stories of Man, &c.
Peg Woffington.
Griffith Gaunt.
A Perilous Secret.
A Simpleton.
Readiana.
A Woman-Hater.

By Mrs. J. H. RIDDELL.
Weird Stories.
Fairy Water.
Her Mother's Darling.
The Prince of Wales's Garden Party.
The Uninhabited House.
The Mystery in Palace Gardens.
The Nun's Curse.
Idle Tales.

By F. W. ROBINSON.
Women are Strange. | The Woman in the Dark
The Hands of Justice.

By W. CLARK RUSSELL.
Round the Galley Fire.
On the Fo'k'sle Head.
In the Middle Watch.
A Voyage to the Cape.
A Book for the Hammock.
The Mystery of the 'Ocean Star.'
The Romance of Jenny Harlowe.
An Ocean Tragedy.
My Shipmate Louise.
Alone on Wide Wide Sea.
Good Ship 'Mohock.'
The Phantom Death.
Is He the Man?
Heart of Oak.
The Convict Ship.
The Tale of the Ten.
The Last Entry.

DORA RUSSELL.—A Country Sweetheart.
By GEORGE AUGUSTUS SALA.
Gaslight and Daylight.

By GEORGE R. SIMS.
The Ring o' Bells.
Mary Jane's Memoirs.
Mary Jane Married.
Tales of To-day.
Dramas of Life.
Tinkletop's Crime.
My Two Wives.
Zeph.
Memoirs of a Landlady.
Scenes from the Show.
The 10 Commandments.
Dagonet Abroad.
Rogues and Vagabonds.

By HAWLEY SMART.
Without Love or Licence. | The Plunger
Beatrice and Benedick. | Long Odds.
The Master of Rathkelly.

By ARTHUR SKETCHLEY.
A Match in the Dark.

By R. A. STERNDALE.
The Afghan Knife.

By T. W. SPEIGHT.
The Mysteries of Heron Dyke.
The Golden Hoop.
Hoodwinked.
By Devious Ways.
Back to Life.
The Loudwater Tragedy
Burgo's Romance.
Quittance in Full.
A Husband from the Sea

By ALAN ST. AUBYN.
A Fellow of Trinity.
The Junior Dean.
Master of St. Benedict's
To His Own Master.
Orchard Damerel
In the Face of the World.
The Tremlett Diamonds.

By R. LOUIS STEVENSON.
New Arabian Nights.

By ROBERT SURTEES.
Handley Cross.

By WALTER THORNBURY.
Tales for the Marines.

By T. ADOLPHUS TROLLOPE.
Diamond Cut Diamond.

By F. ELEANOR TROLLOPE.
Like Ships upon the Sea.
Anne Furness.
Mabel's Progress.

By ANTHONY TROLLOPE.
Frau Frohmann.
Marion Fay.
Kept in the Dark.
The Way We Live Now.
The Land-Leaguers.
The American Senator.
Scarborough's Family.
Golden Lion of Granpere

By MARK TWAIN.
A Pleasure Trip on the Continent.
The Gilded Age.
Huckleberry Finn.
Tom Sawyer.
A Tramp Abroad.
Stolen White Elephant.
Life on the Mississippi.
Prince and Pauper.
A Yankee at the Court of King Arthur.
£1,000,000 Bank-Note.

By C. C. FRASER-TYTLER.
Mistress Judith.

By SARAH TYTLER.
Bride's Pass | Lady Bell
Buried Diamonds.
St. Mungo's City.
Noblesse Oblige.
Disappeared.
The Huguenot Family
The Blackhall Ghosts
What She Came Through
Beauty and the Beast.

ALLEN UPWARD.—Queen against Owen.
By WM. WESTALL.—Trust-Money.
By Mrs. WILLIAMSON.—A Child Widow.
By J. S. WINTER.
Cavalry Life. | Regimental Legends.
By H. F. WOOD.
The Passenger from Scotland Yard.
The Englishman of the Rue Cain.
By MARG. WYNMAN.—My Flirtations.

NEW SERIES OF TWO-SHILLING NOVELS.
Bound in picture cloth, flat backs.

By EDWIN LESTER ARNOLD.
The Constable of St. Nicholas.

By Sir WALTER BESANT
St. Katherine's by Tower. | The Rebel Queen.

By H. BINDLOSS.—Ainslie's Ju Ju.

By McD. BODKIN, K.C.
Dora Myrl, the Lady Detective

By DICK DONOVAN.
Vincent Trill, Detective. | Wanted
Dark Deeds. | The Man from Manchester.

By G. M. FENN. A Crimson Crime.

By PAUL GAULOT.—The Red Shirts.

By OWEN HALL.—Track of a Storm.

By BRET HARTE.
The Luck of Roaring Camp; and Sensation Novels.
In a Hollow of the Hills | Sappho of Green Springs
Colonel Starbottle's Client.
A Protegee of Jack Hamlin's.
By HEADON HILL.—Zambra, the Detective.
FERGUS HUME.—The Lady from Nowhere.

By EDMUND MITCHELL.
Plotters of Paris. | The Temple of Death.
Towards the Eternal Snows.

By BERTRAM MITFORD.
The Luck of Gerard Ridgeley. | The King's Assegai

By J. E. MUDDOCK.
Maid Marian and Robin Hood.

By CHRISTIE MURRAY.—His Own Ghost.

By OUIDA.
Syrlin. | The Waters of Edera.

By J. PAYN.—A Modern Dick Whittington.

By DORA RUSSELL.
A Country Sweetheart. | The Drift of Fate.

By G. R. SIMS.
In London's Heart. | Rogues and Vagabonds.

By FRANK STOCKTON.
The Young Master of Hyson Hall.

By SUNDOWNER.—Tale of the Serpent.
SARAH TYTLER.—Citoyenne Jacqueline.
ALLEN UPWARD.—Queen against Owen.
By F. WARDEN.—Joan, the Curate.
BYRON WEBBER.—Sport and Spangles.

By JOHN STRANGE WINTER.
Cavalry Life; and Regimental Legends.
By LOUIS ZANGWILL.
A Nineteenth Century Miracle.

UNWIN BROTHERS, LTD., Printers, 27, Pilgrim Street, London, E.C.

www.ingramcontent.com/pod-product-compliance
Lightning Source LLC
Chambersburg PA
CBHW031956300426
44117CB00008B/790